P9-DIG-245

You Mean I'm Not Lazy, Stupid or Crazy?!

A Self-Help Book for Adults with Attention Deficit Disorder

KATE KELLY
AND
PEGGY RAMUNDO

Foreword by Larry B. Silver, M.D.

A Fireside Book
Published by Simon & Schuster
New York London Toronto Sydney Tokyo Singapore

FIRESIDE
Rockefeller Center
1230 Avenue of the Americas
New York, NY 10020

First Fireside Edition 1996

FIRESIDE and colophon are registered trademarks of Simon & Schuster Inc.

Designed by Tony Magliano

Manufactured in the United States of America

5 7 9 10 8 6

Library of Congress Cataloging-in-Publication Data
Kelly, Kate.
You mean I'm not lazy, stupid or crazy?!: a self-help book for adults with attention deficit disorder/Kate Kelly and Peggy Ramundo.
p. cm.
Includes bibliographical references and index.
1. Attention-deficit disorder in adults—Popular works.
I. Ramundo, Peggy. II. Title.
RC394.A85K45 1995 94-40538
CIP
616.85'89—dc20

ISBN 0-684-80116-7
ISBN 0-684-81531-1 (Pbk)

This book is dedicated to the memory of Fred Chaison, my dear friend and sometimes surrogate parent. With his unfailing compassion and sense of humor, Fred enriched the lives of all who knew him. He will be missed, but never forgotten.

Kate Kelly

This book is dedicated to my family:

To Rob—for keeping everything together so I could write it

To Alison—for filling my life with your boundless love and joy

To Jeremy—for struggling so courageously with your ADD and teaching me so much about mine

Peggy Ramundo

Table Of Contents

Acknowledgements

Kate Kelly: I find myself approaching this section with some trepidation. I wonder if my erratic ADD memory will do its job adequately. If I fail to mention someone who has contributed to this project, please chalk it up to faulty memory rather than a lack of appreciation.

First, I wish to thank the members of the Cincinnati ADD Adult Support Group for sharing invaluable information about their personal experiences with ADD. They have also functioned as cheerleaders, readers and resource people.

Special thanks are in order to the ADD Council of Greater Cincinnati which has organized a superb network of ADD parents, ADD adults and interested professionals. This community network has made my job easier.

George Schober has earned a heartfelt thanks for helping facilitate the support group, providing editorial assistance and being a good friend even as he struggled with a personal tragedy. George is an ADD adult who has become my role model for gracefully balancing the various parts of one's life.

I am eternally grateful to Dr. Bonnie Green who contributed to the process of writing this book in several ways. She did a superb job of supporting my husband through the difficult task of writing his doctoral dissertation. As his committee chair, she went above and beyond the call of duty, giving the extra encouragement I would have provided if I hadn't been so preoccupied with my own project. She has also been an enthusiastic supporter of this book from concept to completion.

I also wish to thank Rob Allard both for filling in as support group facilitator and providing feedback on the rough drafts of this manuscript. Billy Stockton, Marjorie Busching and Marta Donahoe also took time out of busy schedules to read and comment on the book. Thanks also to Angela Field who provided child care and the use of her computer when mine was unavailable. Suzanne Behle, my daughter's teacher for the past three years, has been a listening ear and support person whenever I needed it.

I wish to thank my co-author, Peggy Ramundo and her husband Rob Ramundo for their contributions to a great writing/publishing team. I have been part of many work groups in my life but none has functioned as well as this one. I hope we will continue to collaborate on projects for many years to come.

Last, but certainly not least, a round of applause goes to my family. To my parents, Barbara and Charles Kelly, who did a great job of raising a very difficult child. To my daughter Tyrell whose many love notes, drawings and hugs kept me going when the going got rough. Thanks, Tyrell, for being such a great kid and for being so patient with me. To my husband Doug who has believed in me from the beginning. He was there with his support when this book was only a half-baked idea. He didn't hesitate when we took the plunge together, committing most of our personal and financial resources to publishing it. Thanks Doug, for helping me make my dream a reality.

Peggy Ramundo: Words are inadequate to express my appreciation for my parents who supported me in countless ways during the process of writing this book. They reminded me to eat and sleep, took over many chauffeuring duties for my children and provided numerous child-free weekends. They didn't always approve of the intensity with which I approached this project, but they never failed to support my efforts.

To my husband, Rob—what can I say? You've kept me in clean, ironed clothes, my cabinets stocked with groceries, my car filled with gas, my computer stocked with paper and my children embraced with your love. You've fed the dog you never wanted and protected me when my old cat died. You've assumed all the roles I've given up the past two years—I couldn't have done it without you.

My children Alison and Jeremy have both shown incredible maturity and understanding at being semi-motherless. Thank you for getting your own breakfasts, entertaining yourselves, leaving love notes on my computer and working so hard to understand why mommy couldn't go away with you and your daddy for the weekend. I love you both so much!

I'd like to thank my friend, Bunny Hensley, for her emotional support. Thanks for your friendship, Bunny, and for encouraging me to take some time off once and a while.

Liz Wymer, my son's teacher for three years, has provided ongoing support and encouragement. Thanks, Liz, for taking such good care of Jeremy, providing the structure for him to manage on his own and putting up with all the times I've gotten him to school late!

My thanks to all the ADD adults and parents of ADD children who have shared their lives with me. Your insights, experiences and struggles have contributed in invaluable ways to this book.

From Both of Us: Mary Jane Johnson, founder of the ADDult Network has been an enthusiastic supporter of our efforts. She has reviewed the book at various stages and has shared both information and contacts. Her single-handed efforts at organizing ADD adults across the United States has produced impressive results. Thanks to Mary Jane, we have been able to gather information from ADD adults throughout the country.

Dr. Joseph Schroeder, a neuropsychologist who specializes in the diagnosis and treatment of ADD adults and adolescents, generously donated his time and expertise as a consultant. Dr. Wayne Harrison has contributed by passing on professional literature and offering his ongoing moral support.

Our thanks to Rita R. Stull for taking this manuscript on business trips and spending her free time helping us dot the i's and cross the t's. Thanks, Rita, not only for your command of the English language but also for your insights and experiences that have added to the quality of this book.

And last, but certainly not least, we'd like to thank David Stull for his contribution to naming this book. The title changed inumerable times during the process of writing it. Our pages of possibilities went in the trash after Dave's excited phone call one day. His creative brainstorming culminated in our creating the present title that we feel truly captures the reality of ADD.

Foreword

It is now clear that at least 50% percent of children with Attention Deficit Hyperactivity Disorder (ADHD) continue to have the disorder as adolescents. Recent studies confirm that at least 30% of these children continue to have ADHD as adults. The behaviors persist and cause as much difficulty as they did when the person was a child or adolescent.

Some adults first learn of their ADHD when their child is diagnosed. Suddenly they say, "That's me. I have the same problems." Other adults first learn of their problem when they read an article in a magazine or see a special on television. Unfortunately, too many adults never learn of their disability.

Adults with ADHD continue to be hyperactive, distractible, and/or impulsive. They can have difficulty with organization. In addition, many develop secondary emotional, social or family problems. Often there are career planning or job related problems. Further, many of these adults also have learning disabilities which, like the ADHD, might have been undiagnosed and untreated.

Thus, adults with ADHD need information about their disability and its impact on themselves, their families, their work and their social lives. Kate Kelly's and Peggy Ramundo's book, *You Mean I'm Not Lazy, Stupid or Crazy?!*, does an excellent job of providing this information in an accurate, clear and easy to read way. Of equal importance, these authors go beyond providing information by offering specific suggestions and programs to address each problem area.

It is critical for each adult to understand his or her past and how ADHD might have affected personal and family life as well as school performance and peer relationships. This understanding can result in a better understanding of past difficulties and can be the start of rethinking one's self-image. The authors help the reader do this. The adult is then helped to explore each area of his or her life, identifying problem areas. Possible problems with self, with communication, with meaningful others and with work are explored. Whenever a problem area is discussed, practical suggestions for addressing it are presented with many examples.

Men and women who first discover their disability in adulthood have much to learn and much to do. I thank Kate Kelly and Peggy Ramundo for writing such an informative and very helpful book. All adults with ADHD and all families of adults with ADHD will benefit from reading and studying this book.

Larry B. Silver, M.D.
Clinical Professor of Psychiatry;
Director of Training in Child and
Adolescent Psychiatry
Georgetown University
School of Medicine

Dr. Silver is a national leader in the field of Learning Disabilities and Attention Deficit-Hyperactivity Disorder. For over twenty years his primary research, clinical and teaching interests have focused on the psychological and social impact of subtle, often invisible neurological disabilities. His extensive writing includes over one hundred thirty publications. These include his popular book, *The Misunderstood Child* and two recent additions, *Attention Deficit Hyperactivity Disorder: A Clinical Guide to Diagnosis and Treatment*, for clinicians and *Dr. Larry Silver's Advice to Parents on Attention Deficit Hyperactivity Disorder*.

ADD Isn't Just for Kids Anymore!

If you're reading this book, you probably fit into one of the following categories:

1. You are well informed about Attention Deficit Disorder and are reading this book to see if it contains any new information.
2. You have been diagnosed with the disorder and are wondering, "What do I do now?"
3. You have a growing suspicion, perhaps fueled by your experiences with a child, grandchild or sibling who has attention deficits, that you may have the disorder yourself.

This book is for all of you. It isn't a scholarly text but a practical guide for understanding and managing the dynamics of ADD in adulthood. There is a lot of available literature about ADD in children. Books are filled with strategies for managing the symptoms of ADD at home and at school. But available information for managing ADD in adulthood is in short supply.

What do you do if you have ADD and aren't a kid anymore? How do you manage your own disorder? This book has been written to offer some answers to these questions.

This book is written for ADDers by ADDers. We both have extensive experience dealing with our own disorders and those of our children. We have also dealt with ADD issues in our individual professions of mental health and education. We have drawn on our professional experiences in writing this book. But at the heart of the book are our personal perspectives and experiences and those of many other ADD adults.

ADD is About Abilities and Disabilities
and
ADD Adults are Capable of Helping Themselves

These are the underlying principles of this book. Having ADD means that each of us must deal with an assortment of disabilities. But if you take off the "dis", you can discover a multitude of abilities as well! We are committed to the belief that each of us can use our unique abilities to manage our unique disabilities.

Our goal in writing this book is to educate and enlighten, and to encourage each reader to assume an active role in coping effectively with his or her disorder. We hope that each of you will use it not only as an examination of disabilities but as a celebration of differences:

ADD: A Disorder
OR
An ADDed Dimension?

CHAPTER 1

From the Porch to the Printed Page: A Reader's Guide to Understanding This Book

Dear Reader:

Please don't skip this section! Although it's really a preface, we've written it as a separate chapter. We thought that many of our readers might approach a new book the way we do—by skipping the miscellaneous pages and jumping right into the good stuff! But the information in this brief section is too important to gloss over. It will help answer some of the questions you may have as you go along.

Over two years ago, we sat on a porch swing and shared our vision for this book. Our original ideas took the form of a three page outline which became our framework throughout the writing process. Many long days and countless revisions later, our original *Porch Swing Planning* session evolved into the book you are about to read.

During the writing process, our vision changed little from our original outline. The chapter you are reading now is the only addition. We chose to add this section to share with our readers the underlying philosophy that guided our writing and the decisions we made regarding the book's format.

In the Introduction, we explained our goal of writing a book an ADD adult could use to understand and manage her disorder. We wanted this book to be practical and easy to read for anyone with specific reading and language deficits. To that end, we chose an informal writing style and worked hard to minimize the complexity of some rather complicated scientific concepts. We also included numerous cartoons to make the text more understandable.

We would like to comment on the organization of this book before you begin reading the three chapters that follow and question what we just said about ease of reading! During the editing process, we agonized over these early chapters that aren't as easy to read as the rest of the book. They are densely packed with rather technical information that is difficult to simplify. We didn't want to lose readers who might react in one or more of the following ways: 1. "Have I been tricked? Is this a text book? I thought it was going to be a practical, self-help book!" 2. "I've already read this information in several other books." 3. "How is this book going to help me if I can't understand the first chapter?"

We considered a variety of options from eliminating some of the information to reorganizing the format. We concluded that none of the options would solve the problem. We knew that our readers would have varying levels of knowledge about ADD and that some would need an in-depth introduction to the disorder. We were also keenly aware of the curiosity of ADDers who don't often accept suggestions without first asking, "But why?" We decided that without this background information, the anecdotes and practical suggestions that followed wouldn't make much sense. So we chose to leave the format alone and to offer the following guidelines.

If you've already done extensive reading in ADD, you might want to just browse these chapters. If you're new to ADD, just hang in there with the early chapters, taking them at your own pace and allowing time to digest the material. If you get really bored or befuddled, take a break! We promise the going will get easier and later chapters will take a look at the lighter, more practical side of ADD.

We also want to explain how we deal with the issue of sexist language in this book. The seeming erratic use of "he" and "she" isn't an editing error! We chose to alternate the use of male and female pronouns by chapters. As you will discover as you read this book, ADD isn't just a problem for boys and men. The assumption that the majority of ADDers are male has been challenged as knowledge about ADD has grown. Since this book is for all of you, men and women alike, we wanted to make the language as inclusive as possible. So, the odd numbered chapters use female pronoun references and the even chapters, male. By the way, there is no significance, other than a flip of a coin, for beginning with *she* instead of *he!* Paralleling this issue of sexist language, we have also tried to avoid stereotypes, including examples of both men and women in non-traditional roles. This seems appropriate, particularly since ADDers tend to be rather non-traditional folk.

Finally, we want to include a word of caution. In reviewing the book, a nationally known ADD expert raised an important issue. He voiced his concern that every adult who read it could identify with the described ADD behaviors and make a self-diagnosis of ADD. This concern is valid. In our work with classroom teachers, many report that the manifestations of ADD characterize every child in their classrooms!

We want to emphasize that ADD is a complicated syndrome with diverse symptoms of varying degrees of severity. It isn't surprising that educators observe ADD behaviors in many of their students because the symptoms of ADD are an exaggeration of behaviors and experiences that fall within the normal human range. Anyone can sometimes have lapses in memory, act impulsively or have difficulty concentrating. The problem with ADD is one of degree and persistence of the symptoms over time and across varying situations. ADDers have symptoms that begin in childhood and cause significant problems in school, work and relationships.

Another part of the diagnostic dilemma is that various mental health problems have symptoms that overlap those of ADD. For example, people with schizophrenia or depression have information processing problems similar to ADD adults but often to a greater degree. Virtually all mental health problems interfere with organization and information processing. So, it's not hard to imagine ADD becoming the new bandwagon everyone wants to jump on. We can picture the consternation of mental health professionals confronted with offices filled with people demanding treatment for the ADD they've self-diagnosed.

We can't emphasize enough that a diagnosis is not a *do-it-yourself* enterprise. A person with schizophrenia, for example, might have attention deficits but her treatment would be radically different from that of an ADDer. Using stimulant medication in her treatment would likely have the effect of dramatically worsening her condition. The point is, an accurate diagnosis is an essential component of treatment.

This book isn't a scholarly, diagnostic manual. Several excellent books of that kind are available and are listed in the appendix. If you're reading this book because you suspect you have ADD, follow the guidelines in Chapter 6. Develop a relationship with a professional who can provide a formal evaluation and diagnosis.

We don't believe, however, that an official ADD diagnosis is a prerequisite for reading this book. Individuals with other mental health problems and those without symptoms sufficiently severe to be considered ADD, can benefit from some of this material. Many of the self-help strategies are useful with or without a specific diagnosis. For example, a reader doesn't have to know why she is disorganized to benefit from some of our suggestions in Chapter 13. In addition, we hope that spouses, friends and colleagues of ADDers and other adults who struggle with related problems will read this book and develop greater sensitivity to individuals with special needs. We can all benefit from understanding how glitches in brain processes can wreak havoc in the daily lives of many people.

Finally, we hope that you'll find this book enjoyable and informative. If our readers have half as much fun reading it as we have had writing it, we will have accomplished our mission. We welcome your comments, personal experiences or anything else you would like to share with us.

Sincerely,
Kate Kelly and Peggy Ramundo

CHAPTER 2

Understanding The Disorder That Makes Us Feel Lazy, Stupid Or Crazy

It's difficult to grow up with the hidden handicap of ADD. Many of us feel that we've spent our lives disappointing everyone — parents, siblings, teachers, friends and ourselves. When we were children, our teachers repeatedly told us we could do our work but chose not to. Our report cards were continual reminders that we weren't very bright. Those C's, D's and F's didn't lie. They defined our self-perceptions as kids who were lazy. Sometimes we felt smart. We came up with wonderful inventions and imaginative play. We often amazed ourselves, our teachers and our parents with our wealth of knowledge and creative ideas.

We didn't want to cause trouble. We didn't start our days with a plan to drive everyone crazy. We didn't leave our rooms in total chaos to make our parents wring their hands in frustration. We didn't count the thumb tacks on the bulletin board because we enjoyed watching the veins pop out of a teacher's neck when he yelled at us to get to work. We didn't yawn and stretch and sprawl across our desktops, totally exhausted, just to make the other kids laugh. We didn't beg for more toys, bigger bikes or better birthday parties because we wanted our moms and dads to feel terrible for depriving us of these things.

We did these things because we had ADD. But unfortunately, most of us didn't know that. Most of our parents, siblings, teachers and friends didn't know that either. So most of us grew up with negative feelings that developed around behaviors everyone misunderstood.

Pay attention.
Stop fooling around.

If you would just try, you could do it.
You're lazy.
Settle down.
You can do it when you want to.
Why are you acting this way?
You're too smart to get such terrible grades.
Why do you always make things so hard for yourself?
Your room is always a mess.
You just have to buckle down.
Stop bothering other children.
Are you trying to drive me crazy?
Why can't you act like your brother...sister?
Why are you so irresponsible?
You aren't grateful for anything.

Have you ever heard any of these comments? If you're a parent, have you ever said any of them? Our bet is that your answer to both questions is a resounding, "Yes!"

It's unlikely that anyone would tell a child in a wheelchair that he could get up and walk if he tried harder. His handicap is obvious and everyone understands his limitations. Unfortunately, not many people understand the hidden handicap of an ADD child.

PR: "I have sometimes wished that my son had a physical handicap instead of ADD. Of course, I don't really wish he had a physical disability. If he did, though, it would be easier to explain his limitations to people who don't understand. It would be easier for me to understand his limitations."

For most of us the misunderstandings and faulty assumptions continued into our adolescent years. Since we were old enough to know better, our behaviors were tolerated even less. By the time we become adults, many of us are convinced that we indeed were—and still are—lazy, stupid or crazy.

Understanding Through Education

As we move through this book, we'll offer many suggestions and strategies for dealing with ADD. But the first and most important one is to repeat at least one hundred times:

"I am not lazy, stupid or crazy!"

If you aren't convinced yet, we hope you will be by the end of this book. We hope you'll be able to formulate a new, positive self-perception to replace the old one. Reframing your self-perceptions is your first job. To accomplish this, you'll need an in-depth understanding of ADD.

The ADD Council of Greater Cincinnati offers a variety of services related to ADD issues and has a mission to "Foster Understanding Through Education". This is also the mission statement of this book. To understand your symptoms and take appropriate steps to gain control over them, you have to learn as much as you can about your disorder.

Even if you've already done your homework in ADD, we encourage you to read the following section. You may not discover new information per se but you may discover a new framework for understanding specific issues of ADD in adults. We will use this framework as we examine the dynamics of ADD in your relationships, your workplace and your home.

About Definitions, Descriptions and Diagnostic Dilemmas: Is It ADD or ADHD?

ADD (or ADHD) is a disorder of the central nervous system (CNS) characterized by disturbances in the areas of attention, impulsiveness and hyperactivity.

Recent media focus gives the impression that ADD is a new problem. Some subscribe to the theory that ADD might not be new but is being used by increasing numbers of parents to excuse their children's misbehavior. A few years ago, one local principal concluded that ADD was the *Yuppie Disorder of the '80's!*

This observation would come as a surprise to Dr. G.F. Still[1], a turn-of-the-century researcher who worked with children in a psychiatric hospital. We doubt there were many yuppies in 1902 when Still worked with his hyperactive, impulsive and inattentive patients. Although he used the label, "A Defect in Moral Control", he theorized that an organic problem rather than a behavioral one caused the symptoms of his patients. This was a rather revolutionary theory at a time when most people believed that bad manners and improper upbringing caused misbehavior.

In the first half of the twentieth century, other researchers supported Dr. Still's theory. They noted that various kinds of brain damage caused patients to display symptoms of hyperactivity, impulsivity and inattention. World War I soldiers with brain injuries and children with damage from a brain virus both had similar symptoms to children who apparently had been born with them.

Over the years, many labels[2] have been given to the disorder. The labels have reflected the state of research at the time:

Post-Encephalitic Disorder
Hyperkinesis
Minimal Brain Damage

Minimal Brain Dysfunction
Hyperkinetic Reaction of Childhood
Attention Deficit Disorder with and without Hyperactivity

The focus on structural problems in the brain—holes perhaps, or other abnormalities detected through neurological testing, persisted until the '60's. Then research began to focus primarily on the symptom of hyperactivity in childhood. In 1968, the American Psychiatric Association (APA) responded to this research by revising its diagnostic manual (DSM-II)[3]. The revision included the new label: "Hyperkinetic Disorder of Childhood".

During the '70's, research broadened its focus beyond hyperactivity and concluded that subtle cognitive disabilities of memory and attention problems were the cores of the disorder. These conclusions, coupled with the discovery that attention problems could exist without hyperactivity and continue beyond childhood, required a second revision of the diagnostic manual.

In 1980, the APA's revised manual, the DSM-III[4] created new labels: "ADDH, Attention Deficit Disorder with Hyperactivity"; "Attention Deficit Disorder without Hyperactivity" and "Residual Type" (for those whose symptoms continued into adulthood).

If your son was diagnosed in 1985 with ADDH, why was your daughter diagnosed in 1988 with ADHD? Are you confused yet? Well, you guessed it. The labels changed again in 1987.

A number of experts believed that hyperactivity had to be present for an ADD diagnosis. They theorized that the other related symptoms were part of a separate disorder. Revised in 1987, the current version of the diagnostic manual, the DSM-III-R[5], reflects this theory with yet other labels: "ADHD, Attention Deficit Hyperactivity Disorder" or "Undifferentiated ADD" (for those without hyperactivity). And, just to keep you abreast of research developments, be advised that work is in progress on the DSM IV!

Is there any reason to remember the DSM label revisions? We suppose you could drop terms like the Diagnostic and Statistical Manual of the

American Psychiatric Association to impress friends at your next party! The information would be useful if you happen to be studying psychology and need the information for an upcoming exam. Otherwise, the only reason to know about the changing labels is that they reflect an ever-changing understanding of ADD.

The debate will continue about ADD issues—what is it exactly and who should be included in the diagnostic criteria? To provide guidelines for diagnosticians, the APA's manual attempts to label and describe various clusters of symptoms, assigning different groups into distinct categories of disorders.

The problem is that human beings don't cooperate with this attempt to categorize behavior. Behaviors just won't fit into tidy little boxes. If you have ever agonized over naming your business report or the song you just composed, you know the limitations of a title. It's difficult to capture the essence of something in a few words.

In practical terms, this means that relatively few people fit the classic DSM diagnoses. There is also much symptom overlap **between** different disorders so an individual may have symptoms of multiple disorders. The significance for an ADDer is that he shouldn't expect his symptoms to be exactly like his child's, friend's or spouse's.

For our purposes, we've made the decision to use the generic label of ADD in this book. First, it's easier to type than ADHD! Second and more important, the ADD label avoids the hyperactivity/no hyperactivity issue.

Specific Symptoms of ADD

As we review specific symptoms, you'll become aware of the imprecision of definitions and descriptions, particularly as they apply to ADD in adults. One reason for this imprecision is the complex nature of the brain and central nervous system. This complexity creates a billion-piece jigsaw puzzle of possible causes and symptoms. Each of us is a puzzle with an assortment of puzzle pieces uniquely different from another ADDer. Adding to the diagnostic dilemma are the rapid behavioral changes that make a precise description of the disorder, difficult.

Definitions and descriptions of adult ADD are also imprecise because adults don't have ADD, right? This was the prevailing theory until fairly recently. The focus on hyperactivity that frequently decreases by adolescence caused researchers to miss many of the more subtle problems that persist in adulthood.

Despite the diagnostic dilemma, you need to understand the impact ADD symptoms have on your life. You don't have to be a *Walking Encyclopedia of ADD*, but you do need sufficient knowledge to capitalize on your strengths and bypass your weaknesses. In the following section, we'll examine the three major symptoms of ADD. In Chapter 4, we'll take a broader look at an ADDer's differences that don't quite fit into the diagnostic criteria.

Inattention

Attention span is a concept that has recently captured the public imagination. There is even a tongue-in-cheek TV show, *The Short Attention Span Theater*, purportedly designed for the easily bored.

Most people characterize an attention deficit disorder as a problem of a short attention span. They think of ADDers as mental butterflies, flitting from one task or thought to another but never alighting on anything. In reality, attending is more than simply paying attention. And a problem with attending is more than simply not paying attention long enough.

It's more accurate to describe attentional problems as components of the process of attention. This process includes *choosing* the right stimulus to focus on, *sustaining* the focus over time, *dividing* focus between relevant stimuli and *shifting* focus to another stimulus. Impaired functioning can occur in any or all of these areas of attention. The result is a failure to pay attention.

Workaholism, single-mindedness, procrastination, boredom—these are common, and somewhat surprising manifestations of attentional problems. It might seem paradoxical that a workaholic could have attentional problems. It might seem paradoxical that a high-energy adult could have trouble getting started on his work.

These manifestations are baffling only if ADD is viewed as a short attention span or worse, an excuse. When **ALL** the dimensions of attention are considered, it becomes easier to understand the diversity of the manifestations of ADD.

The Workaholic might have little difficulty selecting focus or sustaining it but have great difficulty shifting his focus. Unable to shift attention between activities, he can become engrossed in his job to the exclusion of everything else in his life.

Similar behavior can be seen in the person who has trouble sustaining attention. He struggles so intently to shut out the world's distractions that he gets locked in to behavior that continues long after it should stop. It's as if he wears blinders that prevent him from seeing anything but the task at hand. The house might burn down and the kids might run wild but he'll banish that last dust ball from the living room!

The Procrastinator has the opposite problem. He can't selectively focus his attention and might endure frequent accusations about his laziness. In truth, he's so distracted by stimuli that he can't figure out where or how to get started. Sounds, smells, sights and the random wanderings of his thoughts continually vie for his attention.

Unable to select the most important stimulus, he approaches most

tasks in a disorganized fashion and has trouble finishing or sometimes even starting, anything. If the task is uninteresting, it's even harder for him to sustain focus.

Heightened interest and a belief in one's ultimate success improves the quality of attending. With an inability to maintain focus, many ADDers require intensely stimulating situations to maintain alertness and attentiveness. Without this stimulation, attention wanders and many of us are told we're unmotivated.

We're not unmotivated! Our problems with selective attention compromise our abilities to stay focused and productive. So it looks as if we don't care and won't try! In reality, we have to exert many times the effort of non-ADDers to maintain adequate levels of motivation.

Impulsivity

Impulsivity is a failure to stop and think. Being impulsive means that many of us act and react with astonishing speed and with little thought about the consequences. Our brains don't control behavior the way they should, so we say and do things rashly.

When we were children, we might have violated classroom rules, insulted our parents or run into the street without looking. As adults, we might blurt out confidential information or share intimate details with relative strangers. We might pull out from our driveways without checking the rear view mirror or leave work two hours early to enjoy a beautiful spring day. Controlling impulses is tough for many ADD adults!

Impulsivity plays out in other, less obvious ways. It can affect the quality of work on the job. The ADDer often rushes through tasks with little preplanning and many careless errors. He might get into debt with impulse buying, discard an important document or ruin a new piece of equipment because it takes too long to read the instructions.

> *"He knows the rules, but breaks them anyway."*
> *"His work is careless because he won't try."*
> *"He's wasting his ability."*

These comments reflect a misunderstanding of the impulsive words and actions of ADDers. Most of us do *know* the rules. We *know* our

work is neater when we work slowly. We *know* we are capable of more accurate work. Knowing these things, however, doesn't mean that we can easily control the impulsive behaviors. People who make faulty assumptions about us don't understand the enormous effort we expend keeping our impulses in check.

Hyperactivity

Hyperactivity is probably the first symptom people think of when they talk about ADD. They might immediately conjure up an image of an overactive child *bouncing off the walls* and *hanging from the light fixtures!* Without question, this random, excessive activity can be a primary symptom of ADD. But it describes only one part of a larger activity dysregulation that includes a wide range of behaviors.

Rather than moving too much, some ADDers talk too much! Barely pausing for breath, they talk so much and so fast that no one else has a chance to say anything. The speech has a driven quality to it as if the words have been bottled up for centuries and are desperate to get out!

PR: "At a recent conference, I congratulated myself for sticking to my schedule. Just in time for our break, I shared some information about my own symptoms. I commented that, unlike my son, I wasn't particularly hyperactive.

A member of my audience stopped me at the coffee pot and shared her observations of my presentation style. She said, 'You might not be hyperactive, but do you know how fast you talk? I have attended lots of workshops, but have **never** learned the quantity of information I just learned! And one more thing. Do you know how many times you took the top of your pen off and put it back on again?' At the end of the workshop, she thanked me profusely for the wealth of material I had shared so I guess I didn't overwhelm her too much with my non-hyperactivity!"

This anecdote has two messages. First, we can never stop learning about our behavior even when we think we have a good handle on it. Second, it points out that hyperactivity can manifest itself in more subtle ways than physical over-activity.

These subtle behaviors reflect the generalized restlessness and impatience many of us experience. We might have learned to stop bouncing off the walls and on the furniture but we might still feel uncomfortable when we have to sit still. So we fidget, tap our fingers or twirl our hair. Relaxing can be impossible so we might take on numerous hobbies, work second jobs or run in marathons on the weekend.

There is a final thing we should mention. Hyperactivity can be either a deficit or an asset, depending on the quality of the behavior. If the activity is purposeful, hyperactivity can help us get more accomplished.

Some researchers have studied hyperactive individuals who don't have any of the other symptoms of ADD. These folk are extremely active but don't seem to have problems with attention, mood swings or any of the other roadblocks that interfere with productivity. The issue for hyperactive ADD adults is that much of their activity is dysregulated, random and unproductive.

But. . .Why??

ADDers are curious folk. They are rarely able to let anything go by without asking, "But, why?" You may be asking this question about your symptoms. "I am inattentive, impulsive and hyperactive—**but why** do I have this baffling disorder?" If we could give you a tidy answer to your question, researchers would herald our discovery. Since no one knows for sure what causes ADD, the best we can do is examine possibilities.

To get started, you'll need a crash course in the *Neurology of the Brain and the Central Nervous System*. Don't close the book yet! We promise to make this as painless as possible. But it's difficult to understand ADD without knowing some of the "whys" of the disorder. Why is your ADD different from each of ours? Why do your symptoms seem to change so much? Why do your symptoms sometimes cause little or no problem? Without some basic knowledge, it's easy to assume that this disorder is your fault. So, here goes.

Research Tools

As knowledge about ADD has grown, research has increasingly focused on the possibility that the ADD brain and central nervous system are somehow *wired* differently. Testing some of the theories is tricky because researchers can't open up an ADDer's skull to study his brain! Even if they could, it would be nearly impossible to isolate and examine a particular chemical or a specific portion of the brain. The human brain is simply too complex and has many interrelated parts.

Instead, scientists are using sophisticated imaging devices to scan the brain. *Brain Imaging* is one promising technique that may provide information about the causes and treatment of ADD. You are undoubtedly familiar with the X-ray and CAT scan that provide pictures of structures inside the human body. Another imaging technique is nuclear magnetic resonance, (NMR), also known as magnetic resonance imaging (MRI).These techniques use magnetic fields to obtain clearer pictures than those of a CAT scan. All these methods, however, have limitations. They show the structure or shape of the brain but don't tell us much about *how* the brain works.

Scientists also use drug responses to indirectly study brain activity. They know that certain drugs increase the quantity of neurotransmitters in the brain. A positive drug response suggests an insufficiency of the neurochemical affected by the particular drug.

How does this fit into the theories about the possible causes of ADD? Let's take that crash course in Neurology to get a better understanding of the "why's" of your disorder.

The Basics of Neurology

The brain and other parts of the central nervous system (CNS) function as a wonderful and intricate *Command Center*. This command center coordinates all systems of the human body through a messenger system. It sends messages and receives those sent from various parts of the body and from the outside world. It also regulates and controls behavior.

The messenger system of the CNS consists of millions of nerve cells. These are cell bodies with long, thin projections called *axons* and *dendrites*. Impulses are carried along the length of a nerve cell and jump from one cell to another in much the same way electricity travels through a wire.

"The Brain's Postal System"

Messages are first received by receptors in the nerve cell's dendrite. The message in the form of an electrical impulse, travels from the dendrite through the cell body and the axon. At the end of the axon is a synapse, a gap between the nerve cells. The electrical impulse, or message is conducted across the synapse by chemical messengers called *neurotransmitters*. These chemicals carry the message across the gap from one cell's axon to another's dendrite.

You might be familiar with some of these neurotransmitters. *Endorphins* are the pain relieving neurotransmitters that act as the body's own morphine. An outpouring of endorphins during vigorous exercise causes the marathon runner's "high". This increase protects his body from feeling the pain of stressed muscles and joints—an athlete is often unaware of an injury until he rests. *Epinephrine*, better known as adrenalin, is the neurotransmitter that mobilizes the reaction to danger. This activates the *fight or flight* response. The heart beats rapidly and the breathing passages become wider so one can either run or fight an enemy.

That wasn't too bad, was it? Now let's use this information as we consider some theories that have emerged from research.

Current Theories About the Key Players in ADD

Since the Command Center is so complex, it isn't surprising that there are conflicting theories about the causes of ADD. Although there isn't consensus, many researchers agree that this interrelated system is dysregulated in some fashion. The following discussion examines some of the theories about this dysregulation as well as an assortment of other proposed theories.

Neurotransmitters

Some researchers have used indirect drug response research to conclude that an insufficient quantity of the neurotransmitter *dopamine* may play a role in ADD. Since stimulant drugs used in the treatment of ADD increase dopamine levels, an insufficient level of this chemical might be a part of ADD.

Frontal Lobes

Researchers[6] have found reduced blood flow in the frontal lobe area of the brains of ADD adults (See drawing). They have been able to observe the brain in action through a combination of scanning devices

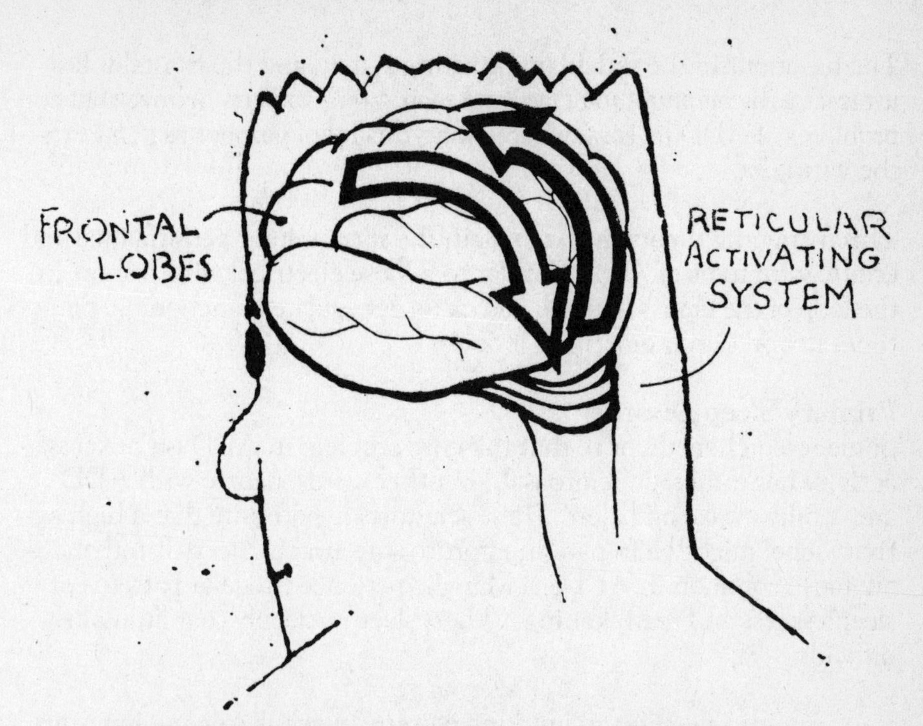

"The Communication Feedback Loop: The Reticular Activating System and the Frontal Lobes"

and radioactive tracers. Areas with high levels of the radioactive substance have the greatest blood flow. Since blood flow is an indicator of brain activity or work, a reduced flow in the frontal lobes suggests lowered activity in this area.

The frontal lobes are critical to many of the brain's executive functions. These functions include planning, initiative and the ability to regulate behavior. It makes sense that they might, therefore, play a significant role in ADD. Actual frontal lobe brain damage causes impulsivity, mood swings disinhibited behavior and sometimes hyperactivity. These symptoms resemble those of ADD but are more severe.

Reticular Activating System

The reticular activating system is in the brain stem. It's the seat of arousal in the human brain and regulates the state of alertness from deep sleep to full, waking consciousness. Since alertness is a big problem for an ADDer—he has trouble staying awake and paying attention—an impairment in this system might cause some symptoms of the disorder.

The functions of the reticular activating system and the frontal lobes interact as a *communication feedback loop*. Some experts believe that the problems of ADD lie somewhere along this loop, perhaps as a *short* in the wiring.[7]

This intriguing theory might explain the inconsistent performance and erratic symptoms of ADD. Similar to a loose electrical wire, a short in the loop of the brain's wiring could cause dysregulated functioning. Sometimes it works and sometimes it doesn't.

Primary Sleep Disorder

Some researchers theorize that the core problem in ADD isn't excess activity but rather, underarousal.[8] In other words, people with ADD aren't fully awake and alert. These scientists hypothesize that a high activity level might be in part an effort to stay awake. Sleep disturbances are fairly common in ADDers. Many experience irregular patterns of sleeplessness and reawakening. Others sleep so deeply that arousal is difficult.

Research into sleeping and waking patterns suggests to some investigators that the disorder arises from a primary sleep disorder. In other words, the person with ADD sleeps poorly and as a result, has arousal problems during the day. Other recent research indicates that deep dream states are necessary to anchor learning in memory. This suggests to us that some ADD adult may demonstrate associated learning problems because their sleep irregularities interfere with this deep dream state.

Parenting or Heredity?

There are many unanswered questions about ADD but we know that in many, if not most cases, it's an inherited trait. Children with ADD are likely to have ADD parents or close relatives. This might not come as a surprise if you are the ADD parent of an ADD child.

Not all family traits result from genetic inheritance. Parents *pass on* characteristics to their children through their behaviors and their child-rearing styles—children imitate their parents and tend to adopt their values. When your son talks to his playmates and sounds like a taped recording of your voice with precisely duplicated words, inflections and pauses, you know the power of modeled behavior.

The question of nature versus nurture has always been tricky. Do we inherit our behavioral characteristics or do we learn them?

PR: "When I was in college in the late '60's, the theme of respecting individual differences was an integral part of my "methods" courses. I was taught that behavior and learning problems resulted in large part from emotional and environmental factors. Was there a new baby in the home, a death in the family or a divorce?

The underlying philosophy of my training was that nurture, or environment was the primary determiner of behavior. During my four years of education courses, I don't ever remember hearing that nature, or inborn genetics played any role at all in learning problems."

Theory of Blame

This theory holds that the only reasonable explanation for misbehavior or learning problems is that someone, usually a parent, is doing something wrong. If you are a parent, you're probably well acquainted with *child-rearing experts* who believe in this theory. These folk are the friends, family and teachers who eagerly offer unwanted comments and advice about the correct method for raising your children:

> *"He would never behave like that in my house."*
> *"You are too tough on him."*
> *"You aren't tough enough on him."*
> *"All he needs is grandma's spatula on his bottom."*

Many of us do our own share of blaming, especially before we learn about our disorder. Unaware of the underlying ADD, we often grow up blaming our problems on our upbringing and believing that everything wrong in our lives is caused by our dysfunctional families. Our analysis focuses on the impact of environment, minimizing or excluding consideration of a neurological make-up.

This rather limited view of human behavior may be fostered by the value Western culture places on self-determination. We prefer to feel that we have control over events and can shape destiny by our actions. It's unnerving to think that our children *come as they are* and that we have somewhat limited influence on their behavior.

Although the jury may be out forever on this issue, adoption studies[9] indicate that heredity has a stronger influence on ADD than environment. For reasons that are unclear, a high percentage of adopted children have ADD even though their adoptive parents have a low incidence of the disorder. When research has studied the birth parents and families of these adopted ADD children, it has found a high incidence of ADD. These findings point to a genetic basis for the syndrome.

Many other studies support the theory of a strong heredity component. A University of Minnesota study published in 1988 examined the effect of genes on personality. The subjects were identical twins who had been separated at birth and reared apart. The study found that the twins shared characteristics such as a preference for cold coffee and wearing three rings on one hand and four on the other.[10] The research findings raised critical questions about environment as the primary influence on personality development.

Related research has focused on inborn personality characteristics, or temperament. The New York Longitudinal Study[11] followed a large group of children from birth until late adolescence. Three groups of different temperamental styles emerged from the research:

Easy Children	**Slow-to-Warm-up Children**	**Difficult Children**
adapt well to routines	adjust with difficulty to new situations	have irregular eating and sleeping patterns
adjust fairly quickly to change	withdraw from new experiences	display poor adaptability
show mild to moderate levels of intensity	withdraw quietly from change	respond with high intensity
cry only for specific needs: hunger, wet diaper, etc.	adjust well eventually	overreact to sensory stimulation
display positive moods and reactions		have generally negative moods
		have high activity levels

As infants and young children, ADDers often fall into the category of difficult children. In one group of young children later diagnosed with ADD,[12] as many as 70% had demonstrated symptoms of their disorder by age two or earlier.

Although not all difficult children have ADD, their irregular patterns of reacting, eating, and sleeping resemble the symptoms of ADD. Some experts consider ADD an extreme in the range of normal temperamental differences.

This research emphasizes that a child is born with a temperamental style that remains remarkably stable over time. Although a parent can influence the development of his child, he can't *cause* a difficult disposition.

Pregnancy and Childbirth Complications

No one is sure about the relationship between birth complications, prenatal factors and ADD. In a small percentage of cases, there is evidence that *pre* and *post* birth problems increase the infant's risk of developing symptoms of ADD. The risk factors include poor maternal health, maternal age of twenty or less, long labor, fetal distress or post-maturity.

Most people with ADD don't have a history of these risk factors. Conversely, most children with histories of prenatal and childbirth complications don't develop ADD. It does appear, however, that early damage to the CNS is a factor in a small percentage of ADDers.

Environmental Toxins

There is ongoing debate about an increase in the numbers of children newly diagnosed with ADD. Since definitions of ADD have changed over time, particularly regarding hyperactivity, it's difficult to analyze this increase. Some argue that the incidence hasn't increased but that improved diagnostic methods have identified children with more subtle forms of the disorder.

Others speculate that environmental toxins play a role. It is undoubtedly true that environmental hazards are threatening our health. One third of children with lead poisoning have symptoms of ADD. The role of other pollutants in causing or exacerbating ADD is a big question mark. It's reasonable to suspect that they might play a part as other substances do, in various patterns of neurological damage.

Food Dyes, Additives and Sugar

Have you seen the cartoon illustrating a mother in the grocery store with her hyperactive child? While he runs up and down the aisles, she reads the label on a box that promises: "This cereal will take the hyperactivity right out of them!" If only it were true.

For years, a number of parents and professionals have sworn by the *Theory of Food Dyes, Additives and Sugar* as the cause of ADD. Dr. Benjamin Feingold,[13] a pediatrician and allergist, developed a special diet to eliminate food additives and salicylates. The diet does seem to relieve the symptoms in about 5% of ADD children. Dr. Lendon Smith[14] holds that the primary culprit in ADD is the consumption of a large quantity of refined sugar.

These theories have been repeatedly tested with little corroboration of their proponents' findings. Some parents are convinced that sugar in particular, makes their children hyperactive. Scientific studies aside, if a particular food or additive seems to contribute to symptoms, it makes sense to eliminate it from the diet. There may be a subgroup of ADDers who are sensitive to some food substances.

Information Explosion

Some believe that "psychological hazards" of our increasingly complex society contribute to the higher incidence of ADD. In his book *Future Shock*, Alan Toffler[15] predicted that dire psychological consequences would result from the rapid changes in modern society.

The Theory of Information Explosion has validity. Many people regarded as entirely *normal* in a simpler society, could become overwhelmed by the demands of a fast-paced, complex one. This doesn't mean that the psychological hazards cause ADD. It does seem logical, however, that they could make the symptoms more noticeable and disabling.

Just a Bad Apple

We doubt that anyone is doing research on this popular, unscientific theory! It goes like this: *The erratic behavior of ADD children and adults is intentional, maliciously planned misbehavior.*

This variation on the theme of the *Theory of Blame* is based on the assumption that an ADDer can control his behavior but **chooses** not to. Of course, these theorists don't have ADD and don't have a clue what it's like to live with the disorder.

As an ADD adult, you didn't ask to be born this way but you do need to work hard to shoot holes in this theory. Using your disorder as an excuse for irresponsible behavior doesn't help your personal growth and gives the *Bad Apple* theorists ammunition. All of us need to develop strategies to manage our symptoms—but we need to do it with self-acceptance and forgiveness. Every person with a disability has to make the best of the cards he's been dealt.

How Common is ADD?

How many of us are there? Is ADD common? We have to say, somewhat apologetically, that we don't have the answer to these questions! But here are some *guesstimates*.

The prevalence figures reported in professional literature vary widely from 1% to 20% of the population. Studies that include individuals without hyperactivity cite a 20% prevalence figure. The estimate accepted many professionals is a conservative (in our opinion) 3-5%. Your question, "But why?" may be on the tip of your tongue. Why is there so little consensus?

First, there is a lack of agreement about symptoms. Some research studies include individuals without hyperactivity and some don't. Second, most research has focused on children and hasn't included adolescent and adult subjects. The lack of consensus about diagnostic criteria and a somewhat limited number of studies with ADD adults has resulted in statistics that vary from study to study.

Am I Still ADD After All These Years?

While the experts examine definitions, statistics and the existence of ADD in adults, many of us are too busy dealing with our disorder to debate these issues. We know, or at least strongly suspect, that we are *Still ADD After All These Years*. And we're struggling daily with the reality of this disorder in our lives. We've been trying to tell everybody with our words and behaviors that we haven't matured out of this "childhood disorder". Until fairly recently, no one was listening.

The nature of our hidden handicap and our ability to manage our symptoms have fooled scientists into thinking ADD is just for kids. As children we may have *worn our ADD on our sleeves* as we bounced off walls and destroyed everything in sight. By the time we become adults, however, most of us have learned to channel some of the energy into more socially accepted activities. Neurological changes might also contribute to some of these adaptive behaviors. The result is adults who still have ADD but who have learned to hide or redirect their more obvious symptoms.

KK: "My experience has heightened my awareness about the prevalence of ADD in adults. Three years ago I began teaching in a small liberal arts college. A year into my teaching, I discovered that I had ADD and began educating myself about the disorder in adults.

With this new understanding, I became acutely aware of students in my classes who were like me. The first thing I noticed was the fidgetiness. These students were not classically hyperactive but continually jiggled their feet, tapped their pencils or doodled. After the first of two lecture hours, they would begin to sigh impatiently.

I made the startling observation that I could identify problems of attention and organization in students solely on the basis of their activity levels. These students, often the brightest in my classes, continually interrupted to ask what I had just said or registered blank looks of confusion. Some had difficulty with written work, their brains going so fast they skipped over transitional ideas or left out important details. They also tended to blurt out irrelevant comments. Many had learned to compensate quite well but became disorganized in novel and stressful situations such as the start of new nursing clinical rotations.

Young readers who are just beginning adult life should take heart from my experiences. Many of my students were excellent learners and workers with positive qualities of extra energy and fresh, creative approaches. They are representative of many adults who cope successfully with ADD. I have little doubt that several of them will have distinguished careers.

My experience with nursing students brings me to another point. With one exception, the women I identified with probable attention deficits hadn't been diagnosed as children. This is common for many adults, particularly women. Little girls with ADD tend to be less physically hyperactive and aggressive than ADD boys. They may receive less punishment and disapproval than their male counterparts but often become lost in the shuffle. Their symptoms are so subtle that no one identifies their problems."

ADD is a Childhood Disorder that Occurs Primarily in Boys

We hate to break this news to the *old-school of thought* experts, but authors Kelly and Ramundo are ADDers who are neither boys nor children! The assumption that many more boys than girls have ADD, is being challenged as increasing numbers of adult women are newly diagnosed.

Historically, six times more boys than girls have been diagnosed with the disorder. The ratio is closer to one:one if ADD without hyperactivity is included.[16] These statistics suggest that the learning and adjustment problems of many ADD girls are too subtle to be identified. This apparent under-identification of girls and non-hyperactive boys is a serious problem. These children—and adults—have special needs that are too often overlooked.

We have considered several questions that don't have easy answers. Although most of us are uncomfortable with ambiguity, we need to focus our attention on other issues that do have answers.

> *"How has this disorder had an impact on my life?"*
> *"How do my differences play out in my daily life?"*
> *"How can I help myself?"*

In the next three chapters, we'll look at the impact ADD has at various stages of life and at the ways each of us is uniquely different from our non-ADD peers. We'll devote the remainder of the book to the third question and share lots of suggestions for managing symptoms and discovering your ADDed Dimension.

CHAPTER 3

The Impact of Growing Up with ADD

Remember the Theory of Blame? Blame often fuels a deadly cycle of disapproval. Consider the following scene.

You are in the grocery store trying to shop with your child who is tossing oranges across the produce aisle and pulling things off the shelves. You are keenly aware of the disapproving glares of other shoppers and hear several muttered, "I would never allow my child to act like that!" In response to the disapproval and your growing frustration, you angrily grab your child and tell her she is an embarrassment and you've just about had it with her obnoxious behavior. She responds either by throwing an orange at you or writhing in a temper tantrum on the floor.

Many of us have countless childhood memories of similar scenes. We were reacting predictably to the ADD wiring in our brains while our parents were trying to do the best they could in a tough situation.

These negative cycles of interactions and reactions result from blame. Teachers of an underachieving student blame the parents for not properly supporting the child's learning. The parents blame the teachers for their incompetence. And everyone blames the child. These negative interpersonal cycles begin early in an ADD child's life and impact in a variety of ways on her subsequent development.

ADD adults have to cope not only with individual symptoms but also with the negative reactions of others. It has been said that personality develops around the ADD handicap—the way each of us deals with our abilities and disabilities is affected by our life experiences.

To examine ADD's impact at different ages and stages of life, we'll borrow psychologist Dr. Eric Erikson's[17] framework of psychosocial development. The backdrop will be the Cycle of Blame and Disapproval that makes growing up with ADD so difficult.

Developmental Ages and Stages and the Cycle of Disapproval

Infancy–Trust vs. Mistrust

This first stage lasts roughly through the first year of life. The infant's world is filled primarily with sensory experiences. Especially in the early months, she has little control over her world and relies on caregivers for her safety and security. For many babies and their families, the stage of infancy means frequent diapering, soothing, dressing, 3:00 a.m. feedings and fatigue. But parent and baby develop a happy coexistence.

The ADD Infant: This stage can play out quite differently in the household of an ADD baby. Many of our own mothers might still talk twenty or thirty years later about how difficult we were before we were born! Even in utero, some ADD babies continually kick their mothers, allowing them little sleep. Some mothers of ADDers speak ruefully of the pregnancy as a training period for the lifetime to come!

Sleepless nights and harried days become a way of life as the parent copes with irregular eating and sleeping patterns. Her infant tends to be over active, cranky, easily stimulated and loud! Her attempts to calm and comfort her baby are frequently unsuccessful. In fact, holding her screaming daughter seems to make things worse. It isn't uncommon for this mother to say later that her baby "just didn't like her".

Difficult infants are uncomfortable and *unhappy*. Their parents feel a mixture of anger, disappointment and self-blame at their own apparent incompetence. During these early months, the dynamics of ADD already begin to have a negative impact on family relationships.

Toddler Years–Autonomy vs. Shame and Doubt

From about 12 months to 3 1/2- years old, the toddler develops ways of acting on and reacting to her world. This is a time for gaining self-control and a sense of pride as she begins to make choices.

During this time, she develops language skills and struggles for separation from her caretakers. She masters the word "NO!" and acquires the behaviors she'll need for admission into the elite *Terrible 2's* club. She's no longer totally dependent on others and begins to jockey for power in the family unit.

This *first adolescence* and the power struggles that ensue are remarkably similar to the one that follows about ten or twelve years later! Parents cling with desperate hope to the folk wisdom about the Terrible 2's not lasting forever. For many, this is a difficult period. It requires enormous patience as they attempt to guide their children's efforts towards independence without being over-controlling or protective.

<u>The ADD Toddler:</u> The battle of wills between the ADD child and her family really heats up during this stage. Tempers flare as the child's negative persistence and poor adaptability clashes with parental attempts to contain the out-of-control behaviors. Even the most consistent, conscientious parent can become disheartened at her child's seeming unwillingness to follow rules.

Once mobile, the ADD toddler may be somewhat less fussy as she discovers the excitement of new worlds to conquer. This is often a mixed blessing for her parents who are led on a merry chase! "My child never walked, she always ran," is a common refrain. The ADD toddler also rolls, climbs, jumps and swings herself into situations that strike terror in her parent's heart. Hyperactive, impulsive toddlers and preschoolers are more likely to have accidents and accidental poisonings than non-ADDers.

PR: "I have a vague memory from when I was 18 months old, of a room with yellow tile and a red lollipop in the corner of my mouth. That's all I remember about that early emergency room visit that ended with five stitches in my tongue.

But I vividly recall an accident several years later that was but one in a long string of injuries. As I crashed through my neighbor's white picket fence, I clearly remember yelling, "Oh, no, not more stitches!" And I also remember my mother looking at my bloody eye and saying, "Not again!"

KK: "One of my more memorable emergency room visits resulted from plugging a barbecue fork into an electrical outlet. The experience made a lasting impression. To this day, I have a fear of plugging in **anything** electrical!

I have been told that when my mother was feeling particularly desperate, she would tie me to a tree in the yard so I wouldn't hurt myself or

someone else. When I first heard this story, I was horrified! After I became a parent myself, I could empathize with the frustration my mother must have felt. And I only have one child—I can hardly imagine how my pregnant mother managed at all, with her 1 year old daughter and very hyperactive 2 year old!"

Some ADDers are rather calm and placid as infants and toddlers only to wake up later as preschoolers. The homes of these toddlers might not be battle zones but can bear a striking resemblance to *designated disaster areas* after a major storm! Debris from toys and belongings are often strewn all over the house by the distractible toddler as she flits from one activity to another.

The ADD child's lack of control gets in the way of her establishing a healthy sense of independence and creates serious feelings of inadequacy in her parents. Misunderstandings frequently erupt between the parents of this child, particularly if one parent isn't working outside the home.

The working parent usually spends just a few hours with the child in the early evening. This parent can be unsympathetic to the complaints of the exhausted spouse who spent all day with the difficult toddler. One stay-at-home mother reported that the best thing that ever happened was her husband's losing his job. After about three weeks at home with his ADD toddler, he profusely apologized for his earlier, unfair assessment of his wife's parenting skills!

Preschool–Initiative vs. Guilt

The preschool child learns to make increasingly purposeful decisions and behavioral choices during this stage in her development. She has mastered her autonomy, has a clear sense of herself as separate from others and begins to develop feelings of empathy. Through daily trial and error, she gains an awareness of her position in the scheme of things and assumes some responsibility for her behavior.

The ADD Preschooler: By this point in an ADD child's life, the parent knows that the folk wisdom isn't true. The Terrible 2's should be over by now but her child is as willful and difficult as ever. The power struggles that have been raging for a while, escalate. The parent often feels that she is fighting a losing battle against her child's inability to plan and accept limits. She worries that while other children are coloring, building with blocks and developing friendships, her daughter is wandering around aimlessly.

Some preschoolers continue to have irregular eating and sleeping patterns and resist all attempts at toilet training. Motor clumsiness can also become more apparent as the older preschooler undertakes the complex tasks of dressing and tying shoes, cutting, coloring and writing.

The preschool teacher is usually the first person to describe the ADD child as immature. It's a word that her parents will probably hear for years to come! In a preschool setting, the age-inappropriateness of the child's behavior is particularly noticeable. Tantrums that were normal during the Terrible 2's are an embarrassment at 3 or 4 years old.

Interestingly, many immature ADD children who often have difficulty with change, don't seem to suffer from the separation anxiety characteristic of their age-mates. The early, fierce independence seems to smooth the transition from home to preschool.

PR: "I counted the days until my young son would start nursery school. While my friends shared their anxieties about leaving their children, I could hardly contain my joy at the prospect!

With my son in tow, I hurried past several tearful mothers as upset as their children were about the impending separation. I must admit that I wasn't prepared for my feelings when Jeremy ran into his new classroom, never even turning around at the door to say goodbye! I wondered why he wasn't just a little sad about leaving me.

I didn't feel any better when I returned to pick him up. After dodging preschoolers leaping joyfully into their mothers' arms, I greeted my son who looked at me and said, "I don't want to leave."

Many parents begin their search for answers to the riddle of their ADD child during the preschool years. On the advice of the preschool teacher, a parent decides to find out why her daughter doesn't listen and follow directions. The fact-finding mission to the audiologist is usually unproductive. The evaluation rarely yields any information about a specific hearing loss.

This trip to the audiologist often overlaps multiple visits to the pediatrician for recurring bouts of otitis media (middle ear infections). The temporary hearing loss that accompanies these ear infections contributes to the ADD child's difficulties in listening and following directions in preschool. Developmental lags in speech or language can also occur if the infections become chronic. The parent might find herself visiting the audiologist again for her child's language therapy and ear tubes to prevent additional infections.

Not only is there a strong correlation between ADD and middle ear infections, there is also a high incidence of allergies, asthma and other respiratory problems.The families of ADD preschoolers often spend hours in physicians' waiting rooms!

The preschool years aren't necessarily easy ones for ADD children but are in general, less problematic than the school years that follow. The demands placed on young children take into account the wide differences between individual children of the same age. Preschool teachers expect children to be at different stages of social, emotional and academic development. Freedom of choice is built in to the structure of early childhood education.

Expectations change dramatically as these children move into elementary school. As an ADD child makes the transition to the next stage, she encounters increasing pressure to compete and perform socially and academically.

Elementary School–Industry vs. Inferiority

The elementary school years are critical ones as the developing child begins the process of acquiring the skills she needs to take her place in society. Children who are for whatever reason, unable to master the required skills, often develop a sense of inferiority. This is when the proverbial *you know what* hits the fan for many children with attention deficits.

<u>The School-Aged ADD Child:</u> The philosophy of early education is to teach children general skills through exposure to varied experiences. Within the preschool environment, the ADD preschooler's deficits may be relatively hidden or ascribed to immaturity.

In elementary school, however, the rules change. Suddenly, the curious preschooler becomes a *student*. She is expected to learn *specific* skills and *demonstrate* her knowledge in measurable ways, ie. tests. The grades marked on her papers and report cards reflect how she measures up to classmates. These measurements include specific subjects as well as effort and conduct. As demands for performance and comparisons to peers increase, she becomes at risk for failure and subsequent loss of self esteem.

Many ADD children have trouble learning in traditional classrooms where teachers talk and student listen. The overuse of written tests and one word answers as measures of learning adds to their problems. They often find it difficult to *measure up*.

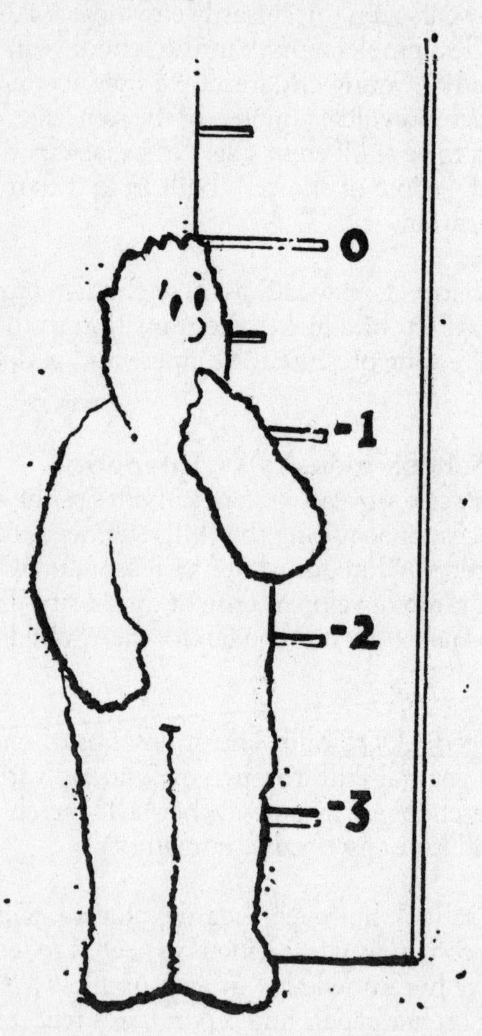

Strong verbal skills can help an ADD student fill in the gaps of the information she misses. On the other hand, she might suffer precisely because she can get by. As she moves up through the grade levels, she may begin to fail. The complexity of details and demands for instant memory recall tax her fragile skills. "Help" often comes in the form of lectures about her lack of effort. As the quantity of required written work exceeds her ability to produce, she is accused of carelessness, poor motivation and irresponsibility.

This litany is a constant theme in the lives of ADD schoolchildren whose quality of work varies from day to day. Information that seems clear on Monday is suddenly incomprehensible on Tuesday. Teachers often misunderstand the confusion these children feel and comment that they are too smart to be acting so dumb. This often leads to the label of "underachiever".

A child with less ability often escapes the criticism that plagues the underachiever but she may be written off and miss the opportunity to reach her potential. Faulty assumptions relegate this ADD child to the lowest reading and math groups where she is never expected to accomplish very much.

An impulsive ADD child often spends as much time in the hall or principal's office as she does in her classroom! The frustrated teacher sometimes suggests that the disruptive student be evaluated by the school psychologist. The testing rarely uncovers the attention deficits. More often than not, the child receives a placement in a special class for the emotionally or behaviorally disturbed.

In social situations, impulsive and hyperactive children are characterized as bullies and the non-hyperactive, reserved children as weird, flaky or nerdy. Although many ADD children experience social problems, the "bullies" seem to have somewhat less trouble than their "weird" counterparts. Peers often admire or at least tolerate rowdiness more than they do eccentricity. The impaired social skills of non-hyperactive ADD children (who are often girls) results in lonely isolation. Ostracized by classmates, they may spend their recess times playing alone. Parents often say their greatest concern is their daughter's lack of friends.

The drive to be competent in the school years includes a keen interest in excelling at extra-curricular activities. Even if an ADD child fails academically, her physical prowess on the soccer or baseball field can provide an opportunity for success and acceptance. On the other hand, if an ADD child makes humiliating mistakes in kickball **and** on the math test, she faces a double-whammy of failure. Her peers may ridicule her in class and reject her every time they choose players for their teams—and choose her last.

Relationships on the home front can also be shaky. Often the ADD child falls apart when she comes home from school. After hours of working hard just to tread water, her tired brain gives out. With anticipation of her arrival, her parent or babysitter might start searching for inner strength. The chances are good that the child will walk through the door with a display of her worst behavior.

The behavior seems to reflect a feeling of: *I can't keep it up any more... now that I'm safe at home, I just have to be me*. The ensuing battles over chores and homework undermine parent-child relationships. Mornings can be just as difficult as the ADD child anticipates the stresses of the coming day. The dawdling and procrastination drive her harried, late-for-work-parents, crazy!

The elementary school years can be very difficult. There are endless opportunities for humiliation at home, school and in the neighborhood. The *I don't care* attitude perfected by adolescence, often gets its start in childhood. The young ADD child starts constructing a shield to protect herself from embarrassment.

The picture isn't totally gloomy, however. Although the teacher might not appreciate the ADD child's improbable tales or detailed drawings of monsters, classmates often do. They know that a great imagination comes in handy at recess. Her creativity and imagination can be valuable assets. If she develops adequate social skills, she can become a leader when the group discovers that her ideas are interesting and fun.

Thankfully, there are many creative, outstanding teachers who appreciate and respect the ADD student's unique talents and gifts. Author Ramundo's son has worked with several. At the end of his primary cycle, his teacher said, "I thoroughly enjoyed having Jeremy in my class. The things I taught him don't compare to the things **he taught me** about children with learning differences."

Adolescence–Identity vs. Confusion
This is a period of searching for an identity and experimenting with different ways of behaving. During this time, the adolescent struggles to feel successful and competent. She measures her self-worth primarily by her success in academics, social relationships and extra-curricular activities. Although these are important issues for the school-age child, they have enormous significance for the adolescent.

The ADD Adolescent: Research has shown that adolescents with ADD are at greater risk for lowered school achievement, suspension from school, anti-social activity and poor peer relationships.[18] Although hyperactivity may have decreased, difficulties with attention, concentration and impulsivity generally persist. As the ADD adolescent measures her success in the three important areas, she often concludes that she has failed. The baggage of negative feelings she carries from childhood adds to ever increasing feelings of inadequacy. School often becomes a nightmare of unattainable goals even for ADD teens who managed to survive in elementary school.

The physical environments of large junior and high school buildings can be impossibly distracting—hundreds of students move about, lockers slam and bells ring. Due to the sheer numbers of students, education at this level resembles an assembly line:

Students file in to the classroom, listen, take notes, read the textbook, prepare research papers, and take pop quizzes and written exams. After 50 minutes, conveyor belts rapidly move the students and their hastily gathered materials to another work station in the assembly plant. At the next station, another teacher pushes the learning button of the next subject, and the process begins again.

We hope that our metaphor doesn't offend readers who are junior or senior high school teachers. But this is how it feels for the ADD adolescent who keeps falling off the conveyor belt—she simply can't regroup fast enough to keep up.

The heavy demands on fragile memory, writing and organization skills can overwhelm the ADD student who previously survived or perhaps even excelled, academically. Teachers and parents rarely consider the possibility of ADD. Instead, they assume peer pressure is causing the new academic failure:

> *"You know how a teenager is! She cares more about her friends than her school work. If she would just buckle down and spend less time socializing..."*

Without question, the peer group is of primary importance to adolescents who expend great energy trying to fit in. Unfortunately, many ADD adolescents don't do any better socially than they do academically. At this point in their lives, some may decide to give up on the idea of peer acceptance and quietly retreat from interpersonal relationships. Others develop an attitude—at least that's how parents and teachers sometimes characterize these ADD teens.

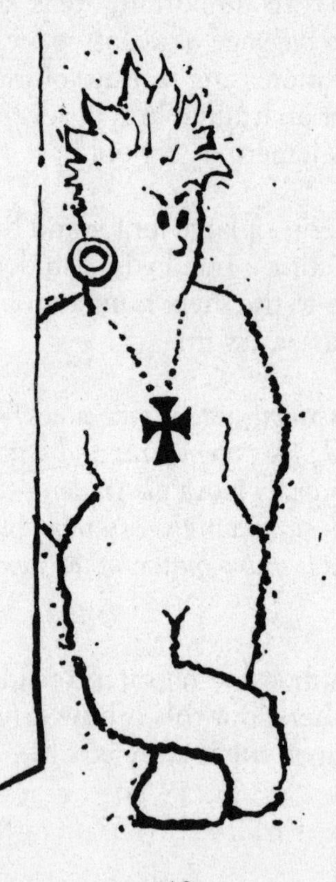

Failing at home, school and with peers, they work at perfecting the "I don't care" attitude they began fostering in childhood. This bravado of *being bad* often emerges to cover up social and performance deficits. There is usually a high school peer group who shares this attitude toward school and adult authority. Believing she has no other viable options, the ADD adolescent may gravitate to this group. She hopes to finally find a measure of peer acceptance.

Normal adolescence is a time for experimentation as teenagers struggle to define their identities and separate themselves from their parents. The impulsive ADD adolescent who experiences failure in every area of her life might take this experimentation to an extreme. The potential for serious trouble is real if she experiments with drugs, sex or other risky behaviors. When an ADD child becomes an adolescent, her parents take a deep breath and hope their growing child can successfully negotiate the hazards.

The transition to adulthood is generally a challenge even for a well-adjusted adolescent. Balancing the need to break away from parents with a continued need to be cared for, is tricky. This paradox is especially confusing for an ADD adolescent.

Although she may balk at rules and authority, she secretly fears that she won't be able to make it on her own. She is painfully aware of her shortcomings and knows that she needs to depend on her parents for so many things. She is overwhelmed at the prospect of taking responsibility for the details in her life. How can she manage her life when she can't even manage her homework assignments?

Emancipation from parents is generally stormy as she battles her parents and her fears of failure. The marked irritability of earlier childhood often develops into intense adolescent rebelliousness and argumentativeness. The normal moodiness of this stage is magnified in an ADD teenager and contributes to the tense atmosphere within her family.

The picture isn't totally gloomy, however. For some ADDers, adolescence can be a time of discovering special talents and abilities. A gift for writing, math, art, physical prowess or mechanics can rescue her—she might gain status within her peer group and useful skills for adulthood. Some socially skilled ADD adolescents become quite popular with peers who admire their energy and sparkle.

An early diagnosis and long-term supportive treatment can help the adolescent ADDer successfully weather this difficult stage. Without these factors, the journey is much more difficult, but not impossible! In spite of long-standing difficulties, most ADD adolescents are able to uncover their abilities. They grow up and join the majority of ADD adults who are self-supporting.

Adulthood

Escalating demands continue as the ADD adolescent enters adulthood. She still struggles with many symptoms of her disorder. And of course, she carries the excess baggage of failure and low self-esteem with her. These don't magically disappear when she finishes her school career.

The ADD adult might still find herself *alone on the playground,* eating at her desk while her colleagues go out to lunch together. She remains aloof because she can't trust her social skills. Her erratic attention, faulty memory and inability to read social cues impair her ability to participate in the give and take of conversations.

The grown-up ADDer often has trouble working steadily on the job, especially if the work is boring or repetitious. She mentally drifts off, distracted by the same things that have always derailed her. Inconsistency can affect the quality of her work. When she was a student, she turned in late projects. Now she misses deadlines and business appointments.

Although she doesn't run around her office, she might fidget a lot and make numerous trips to the water cooler. Her coworkers might complain that she doesn't do her share of the work because it seems she's always doing something other than working.

Arguments with spouses and coworkers and yelling matches with children can become a way of life for some ADDers. The short fuse that caused temper tantrums in childhood can now create problems of intensified, negative interpersonal relationships.

The adult with ADD experiences the world differently than others and externalizes her experiences, frequently blaming everything on factors outside herself. She is so distractible that she isn't *with her feelings long enough to deal with her emotions*. Unable to process emotions very well and blaming the world for her problems, she might experience explosive outbursts or depressive episodes. During these periods she can barely function at all.

Impulsive buying can create growing debt and financial hardship. A pattern of living for the moment with little attention to the future, makes household budgeting and long-term planning, difficult. Savings accounts might be non-existent. Credit cards might exceed their limits. Financial planning and guardianship for the children might be left to fate, with no consideration of a will. Impulsivity and a need for intense experiences often result in risky, thrill-seeking behavior. This might be a factor in the high incidence of auto accidents in the ADD population.

ADD adults are also at somewhat greater risk for substance abuse. Impulsivity, social isolation and an inability to handle emotions can make the escape of alcohol or drugs particularly tempting. There might also be a biological predisposition for substance abuse, but this question hasn't been adequately researched.

Adulthood is a mixed-bag. ADD does seem to improve with age but in many cases doesn't go away entirely. Research suggests that about half of ADD adults are sufficiently well adjusted that their symptoms cause little or no trouble.[19] It isn't clear whether the symptoms actually diminish or if the ADD adult has learned to manage them better. Marital instability, frequent job changes, substance abuse and an increased number of auto accidents are common characteristics of ADD adults who continue to struggle with severe symptoms.

There are some variables that seem to have an impact on adult outcome. They include: intelligence, social skills, socioeconomic status, family mental health and aggression. In general, intelligent children with good social skills and a mentally healthy family of higher socioeconomic status have the best prognosis. The variable of aggression seems to be a predictor of a poorer outcome in adulthood. Successful adjustment in adulthood is seriously compromised[20] for ADDers who display aggressive behaviors in childhood.

Adulthood is challenging for ADDers. We are *functional dysfunctionals*, struggling with roller coaster lives we rarely understand. We are high stakes' folk with the potential for both disaster and hitting the jackpot!

The picture isn't totally gloomy, however. Many ADD adults lead productive lives by using their particular strengths. Deficits can become assets. Hyperactivity can translate into incredible productivity and impulsivity into a strong need for closure—getting the job finished by the deadline. The risk-taking behavior that gives a parent a heart attack can become a source of pride when the child grows up. She takes the big risk that puts her on the map or makes her a millionaire!

Excitability can become sparkle, a decided advantage in social situations and the workplace. Persuasiveness and animation are assets in public relations, sales and advertising. Adults with ADD often shine in these fields. High strung, creative ADDers can be exciting presenters and welcome changes from calm, placid speakers who bore their audiences to death.

The ADD child who spent her school years in a fantasy land can learn to use her mental free flight in the creative process. This ability to see the big picture is valuable in jobs requiring vision and creativity. Many of us use this ability to assume positions of influence. If we learn to make our wandering minds obey us, they can become powerful tools.

The restless, novelty seeking adult can avoid sedentary jobs that make her symptoms so difficult to manage. A friend loves his job as a long distance trucker. He does have to sit for a long time but doesn't have to worry about bothering anyone with his singing, tapping and wiggling. And he likes the sensation of movement. Another acquaintance has turned her excess energy into a lucrative sideline, renovating old houses in her free time.

Without a correct diagnosis, many of us may blame our behaviors on depression, anxiety, traumatic life events or lack of character. Understanding that these behaviors are symptoms of a central nervous system disorder can have a powerful impact on these faulty assumptions. This knowledge can radically change our self-perceptions so we can learn to blend in with the rest of humanity. We can learn not only to ***survive*** but to ***excel!***

"Some forms of the disorder are more disorderly than others."

An ADD adult recently made this interesting observation. It really captures the essence of the complexity of ADD. If ADD were a matter of symptoms slotted into the three broad diagnostic categories, it would be far easier to understand.

Figuring out how ADD adults *tick*, however, isn't nearly this straightforward. The disorder is severely disabling for some ADDers and much less so for others. To understand how ADD plays out in individual lives, we need to explore the behavioral differences of the disorder.

In the next chapter we'll use these unique differences to understand why we ADDers behave as we do. This will provide the starting place for identifying your particular strengths and weaknesses and beginning your process of recovery.

CHAPTER 4

How Are We Different?

How Are We Different?

How Are We Different?

If you have ADD, your disorder makes you different. There's no doubt about it. You come into the world with differences that are part of the wiring of your brain. Not only are you different from others who don't have ADD, you are also different from others who do.

Different Doesn't Mean Defective

Yes, each of us is different but different doesn't equal defective. It's foolish to ignore our differences or pretend they don't exist. It's equally foolish to focus exclusively on the debit side of those differences. Although our lives would probably be easier without ADD, they wouldn't be more valuable.

In the first chapter we examined the three broad categories of ADD symptoms. Now we'll enlarge the discussion to consider the impact these symptoms have in your daily life. You'll learn about your disabilities. You'll also learn about your abilities—abilities that are sometimes hidden by the problems your symptoms cause.

So How Do the Differences Affect ADD Adults?

Although we talk of ADD as a distinct disorder, it makes more sense to think of it as a syndrome: a group of symptoms that tend to occur together. The concept of a syndrome seems an appropriate way of thinking about a central nervous system that doesn't work quite right.

Researchers disagree about the specific origins of ADD but most agree that the regulatory function of the CNS is somehow erratic and inefficient. With an impaired regulatory system, an ADDer may have wildly fluctuating behaviors from day to day or even minute to minute. He may also have learning problems caused by erratic attention and information processing.

The Wandering Mind Syndrome

Most of us have minds that wander hither and yon. We daydream and drift among loosely and tenuously connected thoughts. As our own thoughts intrude, we change the subject and interrupt with irrelevant comments.

Regardless of the "why" of distractibility, the behaviors associated with it are often mistaken for rudeness or eccentricity. *The Wandering Mind Syndrome*, like all ADD differences, has its pluses and minuses.

On the minus side, an ADDer might engage in mental free-flight when he should be working. Bosses regard his partially finished reports and unreturned phone calls as evidence of incompetence or a poor attitude. In conversations he may listen with one ear but continue on some level to follow his own train of thought. It's obvious to his boss or friend that he isn't *all there*. His seeming disinterest doesn't win friends or influence people!

On the plus side, he can use his wandering mind to notice things others miss and make new and interesting connections between ideas. His creative mind can roam beyond convention into imagination and possibilities.

If an ADDer can learn to control his wandering thoughts and capitalize on their richness, he can discover a valuable asset. Think about the stereotype of the absent-minded professor or the talented artist who has incredible gifts but stumbles along trying to manage the practical details of life. We don't believe this stereotype is merely a myth. If we were to survey individuals in creative professions, we feel sure we would find a disproportionate number of ADD adults.

One Channel Operational System

Most of us are *Equal Opportunity Attenders*. We give everything and anything the opportunity to grab our attention! An ineffective filtering system makes us vulnerable to distracting stimuli in the environment and in our minds and bodies.

It's hard to get things done when you keep thinking about and responding to so many different things. The quality of the work you do manage to accomplish is often marginal because your focus is interrupted so much. Although some ADDers are able to juggle several things at once, many find this difficult, if not impossible.

To accomplish anything, many of us have to operate on only one channel. Let's use the metaphor of channels on a radio to understand the dynamics of *One Channel Operation*.

During a drive through the mountains, you may have to simultaneously listen to several stations as they fade in and out. You may spend a lot of time hitting the scan button that is supposed to bring in the strongest channel. No sooner do you happily start singing along with your favorite song than it fades out as a stronger signal takes over your radio.

The normal brain doesn't seem to have trouble with channel selection. When a non-ADDer prepares dinner, he selects the *food* channel. He can attend to this strong signal and cook the food without burning it. At the same time, his brain scans and locates other strong signals that bring in important information. He monitors the *children* channel and switches to it when a sibling argument ensues.

An ability to tune in several channels simultaneously is useful and essential. The radio in the ADD brain, however, seems to have a malfunctioning scan button that won't let him switch channels efficiently. Rather than pulling in the strong signal, it pulls in every channel within a thousand mile radius! He keeps losing track of the channel he's listening to.

For many of us, the solution is to turn off the scan button. It's the only way to prevent the weak channels from interfering with our attention to the one we're trying to listen to. So we stay tuned in to only one channel. If we dare switch to the children channel, the pork chops become dried out, hardened objects, permanently attached to the pan we cooked them in!

We think the one channel phenomenon has implications for kitchen designers. They really should take a crash course in ADD. If they were aware of this phenomenon, they would never design kitchens with large, open spaces for preparing dinner and chatting with guests at the same time. It may be a great concept for non-ADDers. For one channel folk, however, this kitchen design results in lousy food or lousy conversation. Handling both at the same time is virtually "mission impossible"!

This difference causes undesirable behaviors in a one channel ADDer. Demands to switch channels are cruel intrusions. He snaps at the interrupting party, snarls at the person on the phone or loses track of what he's doing. He may tune out the interruption, not even noting it or reacting v-e-r-y slowly to it as he undertakes the arduous task of switching gears.

KK: "When I worked on a psychiatric unit, I shared the responsibility for answering the telephone. I had trouble switching gears fast enough to pick up the phone after a few rings. Often, I never heard it ring at all. Other staff members resented my failure to do my share of this job. They mistakenly assumed I thought I was "too good" to do this mundane task."

An ADDer can be at a disadvantage in the workplace when he has to tune in to many channels. The *phone, boss* and *coworker* channels all compete for his attention. Many workers complain that numerous interruptions force them to bring most of their work home in a briefcase. They can't get anything done at the office.

The Locking In and Blocking Out Phenomena

An interesting correlate to the one channel phenomenon is overpersistence. When an ADDer becomes locked in to a task, he can't stop. His overpersistence can make switching gears very difficult. It can also cause a friend, colleague or spouse to leap to erroneous conclusions. **1.** "It's obvious he can pay attention when he wants to." **2.** "He's so rude! He completely ignores me."

Erratic focus and the general dysregulation that cause problems with concentration and stick-to-itiveness seem incompatible with overpersistence. Aren't unfinished tasks and short attention spans characteristic of ADDers? Well, the paradoxical answer is yes. . .and no!

Much of ADD behavior is paradoxical. Overpersistence could be just another difference that is at odds with a "short attention span". But we submit that it's more than that. An ADDer expends great energy and effort to shut out the distractions of other channels. With an unfiltered sensory world rushing in to his brain, he has to develop some rather powerful defenses to survive. Overpersistence may be one of them.

We believe that an ADD adult may deliberately use this locking-in ability to shut out the rest of the world. It can insulate him from the wear and tear of handling the flood of incoming information. A one channel ADDer may use his overpersistence as a compensatory strategy in a society that values the ability to bounce many balls at one time.

Overpersistence is definitely a double edged sword. Spouses and friends marvel at the ability to sit at a computer and write for hours, oblivious to everything else. Envy of this self-absorption turns to annoyance, however, when rain pours unnoticed through open windows or the tornado siren evokes not even a blink!

The good news is that this disability/ability difference can be used to good advantage. The bad news is that locking-in can be inappropriate, counterproductive or downright dangerous in certain situations. Remember the tornado siren—locking-in to the computer instead of racing for the basement could have disastrous consequences!

The "I Hate Details" Dynamic

Many of us have an aversion to details. An inability to scan and switch channels plays into this aversion. To scan for details, we have to attend to numerous pieces of data. We find that our brains are uncooperative when we try to absorb many details simultaneously. We may forget much of what we see or hear. When we try to remember sequential details, we can lose the first step before we can assimilate the second. Our preference for the gestalt (the big picture) over miscellaneous details, may in part result from this difficulty with data processing.

The "Don't Do Today What You Can Put Off Till Tomorrow" Dynamic

Many people live by this creed. Filing several extensions on a federal income tax filing can put off this onerous task as long as possible. But we're not talking about a conscious decision to procrastinate. We're talking about the frustration many of us feel every time we try to get started on anything.

What appears to be stalling or an apparent unwillingness to do something is often a sign of the superhuman effort required to begin concentrating on a new task. Refocusing is painful. It takes a lot of blood, sweat and tears. Although an ADDer may do great after he gets going, he has to work hard to shut out the rest of the world and turn off the other channels. It's possible to become more efficient at self-starting but it takes time and self-discipline to learn this skill.

A Defective Filter

Another brain function that goes awry in ADD is the filtering mechanism. A brain that is working at peak efficiency can select what it needs to concentrate on and filter out extraneous distractions. It works much like the oil filter in a car. It filters out the dirty, useless particles so the engine can operate efficiently with clean oil. Coffee filters perform a similar function, preventing the bitter grounds from getting mixed in with the liquid.

A *Defective Filter* permits the "grounds to get mixed up with the coffee." An ADDer experiences the world as a barrage to his senses—noises, sights and smells rush in without barriers or protection. Normal noise levels can interfere with his ability to hear conversations or maintain a train of thought.

Even in a relatively quiet restaurant, background noises compete for his attention and interfere with his ability to listen to the server. During a telephone call, he may snap at a spouse who makes the slightest noise in the room. Unfiltered visual distractions can make shopping a nightmare. The process of scanning the contents of a large department store can be agonizing. The quantity of choices is overwhelming and often creates feelings of intense anxiety and irritation.

Touchy Touchability
An ADDer can be very touchy about being touched! His sense of touch is vulnerable to overstimulation as the rest of his sensory channels are. An intolerance of touch or close physical proximity is a fairly common difference noted by ADD adults. The term *Tactile Defensiveness* found in occupational therapy literature, captures the essence of this difference. Similar to most ADD symptoms, it waxes and wanes. At times the need for physical space is acute and an ADDer simply can't tolerate being around other people.

It's ironic that with his poor sense of physical boundaries, he may bump into someone else's physical space while he fiercely protects his own. One ADDer ruefully observed: "People like me—other ADDers—can drive me crazy. I hate to be touched and they keep bumping into me." Others say they don't like living with animals because pets don't have respect for physical boundaries!

Roller Coaster Emotions

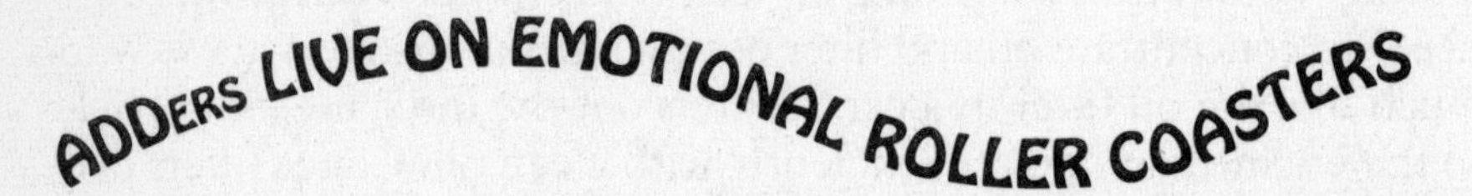

We're not exactly sure what causes the problems with mood and emotion in ADD. We do know that ADDers often say they live on emotional roller coasters. Feeling states fluctuate, with extreme alterations in the highs and lows over hours or even minutes.

Maintaining emotions on an even keel is an intricate process involving fine adjustments by different parts of the brain and nervous system. For an ADDer, this process seems to be dysregulated. He walks precariously on his high wire never knowing how he'll feel at a given moment. The people in his life may tiptoe around him, fearing his next bad mood.

Intense INTENSITY
People often describe ADD adults as *intense*. Feelings are amplified and blasted out with little restraint. When an ADDer is angry, he might yell or throw things. When he's happy, he often captivates people with dazzling displays of positive energy.

Low moods feel like the end of the world. Many of us have passionate natures, *artistic temperaments* that react quickly and to an extreme. Our tendency to boast and exaggerate may result from experiencing the world so intensely. If we always see the world in vivid living color, we'll describe it that way to others. It isn't a planned exaggeration but a valid reflection of our perceptions.

A Short Fuse

When something pushes an ADD adult's temperamental buttons, impulsivity often kicks in. It may take little to set off his explosive temper or turn him into an irritable grouch. The outburst that results can be as baffling to him as it is frightening to the people around him. After the explosion that seems to come from nowhere, he often feels ashamed. He can't understand why he made such a big deal out of nothing.

His anger usually disappears as quickly as it appeared but the anger he elicits in other people doesn't go away quite as fast. They shake their heads at his childish reaction to a burned piece of toast. He could just get another piece. Instead, he fusses and fumes. Since setbacks throw him off balance so easily, he starts complaining when he should be trying to solve the problem.

The IDP Dynamic—Irritability, Dissatisfaction or Pessimism

The moodiness in ADD can be expressed as generalized irritability. There may not be dramatic explosions of temper but rather, a continual *grumpiness*. Unfortunately, the irritable ADDer misses out on the highs, instead experiencing chronic dissatisfaction. He seldom expresses positive thoughts or feelings and travels through life exuding an aura of pessimism. Through no fault of his own, he views his world through gray-colored glasses.

Another manifestation of this generalized irritability has less to do with pessimism than with a feeling of being constantly annoyed by other people and events. The ADDer may be sarcastic, rude or abrupt with others.

Depression?

The symptoms of depression and those of ADD can be remarkably similar. Mental health professionals sometimes have difficulty distinguishing one disorder from the other. When in doubt, many choose an antidepressant as the medical treatment since it can help symptoms of both disorders.

Sometimes Clinical Depression and ADD occur together in the same individual. Dysregulated emotions can also appear to be symptoms of depression when they're not. The symptoms can mask underlying attentional problems. It isn't uncommon for a mental health professional to make a diagnosis of depression and totally miss the ADD.

The depression-like symptoms of ADD adults might be part of the neurological dysregulation that causes the disorder. They might be part of an emotional response to repeated failure. Likely, the moodiness of many ADDers is a little of both. Differentiating ADD from Clinical Depression can be difficult but it's vitally important. The emotional piece of ADD is often just the tip of the iceberg of other problems that must be addressed.

Bottomless Pit of Needs and Desires

"I want...I need...I must have"

On any given day, parents everywhere hear these immortal words! In the grocery store checkout, the begging can be for a pack of gum or candy and at the toy store, for the latest, greatest water pistol. Although it isn't easy for children to learn that they can't have everything, they usually grudgingly learn to accept the deprivation. For many ADDers, the intense feelings of need continue forever. It's part of the dysregulation of ADD.

An insatiable ADD adult experiences ongoing problems with his appetite for many things—sex, alcohol, excitement, etc. He is a bottomless pit of needs, always looking ahead and never feeling satisfied. The simpler pleasures of life are too mild. Intense experiences must match his voracious appetite.

This insatiability can manifest itself in varied ways. Inside, it feels like an overwhelming craving. The craving is often non-specific—

it's for *something* but not for anything in particular. An ADDer might use food, sex, liquor or shopping sprees to appease the greedy *Needs Monster.* Unfortunately, feeding the monster makes him grow larger and more insistent so the ADDer sets a vicious cycle in motion. He can exhaust friends and lovers with demands for attention and affection because ***no amount is ever enough.***

Some ADDers develop patterns of behavior that include habitual overeating or binge drinking. It's conceivable that a significant percentage of the members in the "Anonymous" groups—alcoholism, codependency, and sex and love addictions, could have ADD.

With hard work, an insatiable ADD adult can learn to say "No" to the non-stop "I want, I need, I must have" message of his Needs Monster. He might quiet his restless cravings by dabbling in sports car racing or bungee jumping. He might assuage his need to *shop till you drop* through a strategy an acquaintance of ours has designed.

She goes on periodic shopping binges, frantically charging hundreds of dollars of merchandise. Having happily fed her Needs Monster with all her packages, she heads home. But wait a minute. Doesn't that make him grow even larger? In her case, it doesn't because there's a second part of her strategy. The key is that she has taught herself to bring the packages home and **never open them.** She has learned that within a few hours or days, the cravings for her purchases will have subsided. Then she goes on another shopping trip to return everything she bought!

Activity Levels in Flux

Some ADDers are hyperactive, though not all the time.
Some ADDers are hypoactive.
Most ADDers are hyperactive and hypoactive.

Literature frequently refers to ADDers as *hyperactives*—a reference to excessive activity levels. This reflects a viewpoint that is both controversial and somewhat outdated. Although some professionals still focus on high activity levels in diagnosing ADD, we prefer to consider the issue of hyperactivity as one piece of a more generalized *dysregulated activity level*. This dysregulation can include *too much* action (hyperactivity) *too little* action (hypoactivity) and *fluctuations* between the two extremes.

Some ADDers know something that many professionals don't understand: hypoactivity can be a troubling part of ADD. A hypoactive ADDer moves in slow motion and hears many "*Get moving's*." If only he could. It would take a bonfire beneath him to cause any movement at all! He may envy his hyperactive counterpart.

A hyperactive ADDer's differences are most noticeable when he has to sit still. That's when he starts swinging his leg or gnawing on his pencil. If his job permits physical activity, the hyperactive adult can be indistinguishable from his non-ADD colleagues.

Traveling salespeople cope with restlessness by staying on the road and on the move. Nurses joke about needing roller skates to get from one end of the shift to the other. Likewise, the construction worker has a job that lets him expend physical energy. The level of activity required in these jobs can provide a needed outlet for hyperactivity.

Many ADDers are both hyperactive and hypoactive. It seems that activity levels fluctuate between extremes, much like the other dysregulated symptoms of ADD. Sometimes the ADDer moves and talks at mega-speed only to flip to a state of inactivity that makes him appear nearly comatose.

Some ADDers report that on a given day, their activity levels seem to build from morning to evening. They are slow moving and thinking in the morning, functioning well only if they can carry out routines without interruption. Early morning conversations with family members can consist of grunts and one word answers. These ADD adults describe themselves as operating on "autopilot", capable of little more than routine, automatic functions.

Nothing helps to speed up this process. These folk begin to gain alertness by midmorning which is a problem when they work standard daytime hours. By noon, they're going full tilt, using their energy to talk nonstop to coworkers over lunch. With energy reserves drained by mid-afternoon, the big slump often hits with a fight to stay awake. The cycle often continues with a late afternoon shot of newly found energy when they start revving up again. For many, the evening hours are the most productive—late afternoon or evening shifts enable them to work at peak efficiency.

This pattern is certainly not unique to ADDers. After eating in particular, many people suffer from a slow-down as their bodies mobilize for food digestion. The practice of the *siesta* in many countries may be related to this normal physiological cycle.

An ADDer's cycles, however, seem to have more intense peaks and slumps. As a group, ADD adults tend to be night owls. Many have trouble getting started in the morning and display irregular patterns of hyperactivity and lethargy throughout the day.

Although many experts regard hyperactivity as a primary symptom of ADD, others hypothesize that it's an attempt to compensate for underarousal. Likely, both theories hold parcels of truth. At times, the ADDer seems to be frantically trying to keep himself going by being physically active. Instead of taking Ritalin to maintain focus and regulation, he might use strenuous exercise to boost his flagging energy and attention level. At other times, he seems frantically driven by his hyperactivity, a force over which he has limited control.

People with high energy levels can accomplish many things in a short time. While others complain that a twenty-four hour day isn't long enough to get everything done, an ADDer might search for extra things to fill up the unused hours. Hyperactivity can be helpful. Unfortunately, many ADD adults energetically spin their wheels, go in circles and get nowhere. The goal of treatment or self-help can't be just to *slow the ADDer down*, but to help him learn to use and direct his energy more efficiently.

Thrill Seeking

Lack of restraint can cause an ADDer to risk life and limb in pursuit of excitement. As a group, we tend to be thrill seekers, minimizing inherent risk and danger. As children we fell out of trees and dove from great heights. We may have made frequent trips to the emergency room to have our bruised and battered bodies patched up. As adults we're on our own without anyone to remind us of the dangers. We may still be making emergency room visits for far more serious injuries. Instead of climbing trees, we may be climbing mountains or skydiving.

An ADDer isn't the only adult who enjoys activities with a high element of risk. But he may approach these activities without sufficient planning. His behavior can be more risky because he engages in thrill seeking without recognizing the inherent risks involved. He fails to pay sufficient attention to register them. Since he doesn't register or process the information about risks, he doesn't really believe in them. Fuzziness about the external world may make him feel invincible and may give him a false sense of safety.

The Intractable Time Tyrant

Time is an elusive entity to many of us. Sometimes we feel we've have entered a time warp—a twilight zone where we tread water, get nowhere and accomplish nothing. Our sense of time is elastic and we characteristically underestimate the time it will take to do anything.

As children, we're late for school, stay out beyond our curfews and miss homework deadlines. As adults, we might be late for work and have trouble completing projects on time. Teachers, bosses and co-workers often misinterpret the tardiness as laziness or an indifference to their needs. In reality, our behaviors can result from an altered time sense and an inability to plan.

An unscientific diagnostic tool could be to count the items on a person's "To Do" list for a given day. In Chapter 13, we'll offer a "test" we've developed to diagnosis ADD as a measure of disorganization! The daily list of an ADDer usually includes far more than any human could accomplish in three or four days. A professor friend planned to write three articles, a book and two grants over the summer months. His unrealistic goals were quite typical for an ADDer!

Perhaps there is a brain function called "Time" that doesn't operate efficiently in an ADDer's brain. More likely, his *Time Troubles* are caused by various deficits and his failure to factor in their impacts on his life. He figures that it shouldn't take more than two hours to prepare a small dinner for friends. So, he decides to add a few extra things to his afternoon plans. Regrettably, he fails to plan for the inevitable distractions that will derail him. Preparing the meal always takes much longer than he thinks it will.

Time Troubles play out in other ways as well, with time passing both more quickly and more slowly than it should. When an ADDer is lost in his own compelling thoughts, the hours fly by in an instant while routine work hours inch along at an excruciatingly slow pace.

Sometimes, even unpleasant tasks can grab the ADD adult. Most people don't think of housework as their favorite activity. Then why does an ADDer who hates housework spend hours "spit-shining" his house while other chores remain unfinished? The answer lies in overpersistence. It's not uncommon for him to become locked-in, obsessively attacking tiny specks of dirt. The day evaporates as he scrubs a small portion of a room into antiseptic perfection. This would be okay if he had the time or inclination to spend his life pursuing the elusive dream of a spotless home. Of course, his time is limited and must be divided among a variety of chores.

The time he never accounted for is eaten up by lists that are too long: Another day is gone...It's 3 o'clock in the morning...The alarm will go off in three hours...Doesn't the Time Monster ever sleep???

Space Struggles

An ADD adult can also have a distorted sense of space and problems of directionality. As an adult, he might still rely on the visual clue of his wristwatch to identify right and left. He might have difficulty following a road map or understanding the compass settings of North, South, East and West.

He can also have a distorted sense of how his body moves in space in relationship to other objects. As a consequence, he bumps into other people or furniture. He might be unable to gauge the speed and direction of a ball in tennis or baseball games. Sports that demand finely tuned spatial abilities can be particularly difficult for him.

Similar to a distorted sense of time, an altered sense of space might be related to excessive speed and deficient planning. It can also result from the impaired information processing of a specific learning disability.

Spatial problems aren't limited to sports activities and directionality. They also have an impact on organization. An ADD adult often lives with a daunting amount of clutter and disorganization. Even when he slows down to take the time to tidy up, he faces a nightmarish task of figuring out what to do with his chaotic surroundings. He may dream of having enough money to hire the right person to organize all the *stuff* in his life so he can get on with the business of living.

The ADD brain seems to have trouble *sorting and filing*. We ADDers tend to focus on all the exceptions to the orderly rules of the world. We play a perpetual game of "But what about...?" It's difficult to organize either space or a filing system without an ability to decide which things belong together.

Memory also plays a role in an ADDer's Space Troubles. Before he can organize his belongings, he has to remember where they are. After he finds them he still has to figure out what to do with them!

Some of us dismiss the effect of clutter on our lives, assuring ourselves that tidiness is simply a waste of time. Others become obsessed with putting things in order and have time for little else. Although neither course of action is particularly helpful, problems with spatial organization are common for many of us with ADD.

The ADDer's environment is a confusing one over which he constantly struggles to gain a semblance of control. A certain degree of order is important for emotional well-being. Preventing the overwhelming feelings of confusion that result from untamed piles of junk is an important goal.

Information Processing

Some of the differences of ADDers can be understood within the context of information processing. How do we think about and act on the information we receive from the environment? Do we have unique ADD thinking and acting styles? To answer these questions and examine other differences in ADD adults, we'll use the *Theory of Systems* as a working model of the brain's functions.

Systems consist of assorted parts organized into a whole to serve a function or reach a goal. Every system uses energy and resources from the environment as its input. It transforms, or *processes* the input into an alternative form called *output* and sends it back to the environment.

A computer system takes input from humans by way of the keyboard. It processes it and produces new information as output on a printout. Similarly, the human brain receives input from the outside world through the senses, processes it and produces output in the form of words or actions.

If a computer malfunctions, we look at the three parts of the system to find out what's wrong. Human error can interfere with input if information is keyed incorrectly. A problem in the information processing of the computer itself may also exist. Finally, the output function can be flawed if there is a mechanical problem with the printer.

Breaking down the workings of the brain in to these three components can help us better understand what's happening when things go wrong. A significant problem for many of us with ADD is mismatched input, information processing and output capacities.

In general, an ADDer processes internal information rapidly but has a less efficient capacity for the input and output functions. Problems with selective attention and filtering compromise the quality of input—getting information into his brain. Difficulties with impulsivity, activity levels, memory retrieval, motor control and rambling speech compromise the quality of output—effectively communicating or acting on the processed information. Let's take a look at how input/output weaknesses and internal processing strengths create some unique ADD differences.

Action and Inaction Imbalance

We know that as ADD adults, we have problems with attention. That's why our disorder is called an Attention Deficit Disorder. We have trouble with *selective attention*—focusing on one part of the vast array of information that bombards our senses. This is just the first step in processing information, however.

We also have trouble with the second step, *selective intention*—selecting one response from a variety of possible action choices. Levine[21] examines the interplay of selective intention and selective attention in his book on developmental variation. He makes the point that it's rare to find a person who has difficulty with attention without also having difficulty with intention, or action.

When your teacher complained that you weren't paying attention, was he observing the neurological process in your brain? Of course not! He was observing behavior. Your action—looking out the window rather than at your math book—resulted from listening to the blue jay instead of your teacher.

The action part of attention depends on balancing the forces of action, *facilitation* and inaction, *inhibition*. The brain needs to facilitate, or support helpful actions while it inhibits, or blocks the harmful ones. Many of the differences unique to an ADDer result from an imbalance in this area. When he should be in his inaction mode, he blurts out a hasty, sloppy response he should have inhibited. When he should be in his action mode, he fails to answer a question he should have facilitated.

In tennis, facilitation helps him react quickly to return a shot and inhibition prevents him from reacting too quickly and moving when he should be waiting. A bad game of tennis is one thing but social errors are something else.

Disinhibition causes many of the social problems an ADDer experiences. He says things he shouldn't say, interrupts conversations and intrudes on a friend's personal space. Because he has trouble slowing down enough to stop and think, he may not even realize his mistake. Sometimes he may realize it but is too embarrassed to apologize.

Failure to restrain or inhibit can cause problems far more serious than a social faux pas. An ADDer tends to react quickly and intensely to his impulses. He may strike out at his children or let loose a stream of verbal abuse. Arguments with his spouse can quickly get out of hand as he says things in the heat of the moment only to regret them later.

He doesn't mean to lash out and is ashamed of his behavior. The hasty words or actions were neither planned nor intended.

> *If behavior is judged by intentions, we ADDers are blameless—we didn't mean it!*

While it's true that we're not calculating criminals, we need to look beyond good intentions. These impulsive words or actions can destroy relationships and psyches. We have to consider the impact of our behavior on other people, especially our loved ones.

A failure to inhibit one's words isn't always a negative quality—an ability to say just about anything can come in handy. Talking about personal experiences and problems can open doors for others to share confidences. Most people are enormously relieved to discover that others share their fears and insecurities. The mushrooming number of support groups is evidence of this need to share and be intimate. Many people seem to be starved for connections to others.

People laugh when the truth is exaggerated, twisted, or expanded to the level of absurdity. An ADDer who doesn't inhibit the flow of his thoughts can dream up outrageously funny things to say—things that others wouldn't dare to utter! If he can learn to monitor himself sufficiently to keep from stepping over the line into offensiveness, he can contribute a sparkling sense of humor.

The Supersonic Brain

Stated simply, the ADD brain goes fast! Although we've listed it separately, the *Supersonic Brain* is closely related to the action/inaction balance.

An ADDer's *altered cognitive tempo* can translate into unmonitored rapid-fire speech. Without pausing for breath, he may prevent anyone else from getting a word in edgewise. Handwriting and other aspects of task performance can also suffer as he fails to slow down enough to balance his internal processing and physical capabilities (output). As a result, he makes careless errors and has trouble with motor tasks. The authors, for instance, have had a long-standing love/hate relationship with tennis that has resulted in part from the Supersonic Brain phenomenon.

PR: "Kate and I should have our names listed on a plaque of notable accomplishments, a kind of *Guinness Book of Records*. We merit inclusion on the basis of our record setting number of years in beginner and advanced beginner tennis lessons! Regardless of how hard we worked at our game, we never seemed to make much progress. After we both started taking Ritalin, we experienced a startling improvement in our skills on the tennis court.

Lest struggling athletes read this and race to their pharmacies for their physical skill pills, I need to emphasize that the improvement we experienced was one of *mental* skill. We were playing better because we were thinking better, or at least more slowly and with better planning.

Taming our runaway thinking tempos gave us a more accurate sense of time. Our abilities to strategize and s-l-o-w d-o-w-n improved our game. With relief and a sense of accomplishment, we finally graduated from our beginner lessons."

Applying the brakes to our Supersonic Brains often gets easier by the time we become adults. Many of us manage to achieve some degree of balance and an ability to stop and think—at least more often than we did as children. Unfortunately, as soon as we start feeling complacent, something invariably goes wrong.

KK: "I'm certainly no whiz at higher mathematics but I can accurately add long columns of figures. I prefer doing my addition without a calculator so I don't have to worry about pushing the wrong buttons.

Several years ago, however, I made the mistake of rapidly calculating our household budget to ascertain whether my husband and I could afford a major renovation. I didn't recheck my figures before assuring my husband that the project was financially do-able. I swept away his natural caution with my enthusiasm and energy and implied that he was a stick-in-the-mud for raising questions and objections. After we had committed to the project and were up to our ears in plaster dust, I found a glaring omission in my figures. I had neglected to add the mortgage payment to our monthly budget!

My sainted grandmother bailed us out. If she hadn't given me a portion of an inheritance, we might still be in debtors' prison—assuming such places still exist! We could have lost our house and still feel the pinch of my mistake. Frankly, it scared the devil out of me!"

This anecdote is illustrative of an important balancing act for many of us with ADD. We have to put the brakes on our racing thoughts gradually enough that we don't come to screeching halts, paralyzed by fears of making impulsive mistakes. Alternately, we don't always apply the brakes when we should, especially when we're working on something easy or familiar. When we're feeling overconfident we may "put the pedal to the metal" and send our racing thoughts careening out of control!

Paralysis of the Will

The balance can also tip in the other direction, with a failure to act at all—something like a paralysis of the will. The output function totally stops working. When this happens, the ADDer may find himself in a frozen state, unable to take appropriate action. He may watch the softball whiz by as if he were a spectator instead of the player responsible for intercepting it. When it's time to answer someone's question, he may stand back feeling stupid, because he can't think of a response. Input problems probably also play a part in this paralysis of the will. If he hasn't input the information he needs to properly respond, the quality of his output will be impaired.

Reaction Time Irregularity

Our discussion of the fast-thinking brain may seem puzzling. You may be thinking, "That's crazy! My brain moves with the speed of a glacier and it makes me feel pretty stupid." This is another of the ADD paradoxes. Your brain moves both very slowly and very rapidly—depending on the task.

If an ADDer is free to direct his own thoughts and actions, the rapid freewheeling aspect of his brain takes over. When he has to fit into someone else's agenda either with words or actions, he finds it more difficult to function well. In other words, *it's easier to act than react*. Reacting depends on the problematic input and output functions of an ADD brain. If you can rely on your ability to process information internally, you can often take swift and decisive action.

Fluent self-expression is independent of an ability to respond to questions. A person with the gift of gab who ignores you when you ask direct questions, might not be rude or disinterested. He might have trouble retrieving things from memory in a demand situation.

PR: "I have a particular gift for speaking and conduct workshops without missing a beat. When I get ready to share information with an audience, I become energized and focused. I thoroughly enjoy this work and am never at a loss for words. But informal gatherings are a totally different matter. Even in a group of friends, I often find myself groping for things to say in response to questions.

This baffling behavior confused me until I understood my ADD. Now it makes perfect sense. I am in charge of my thoughts and the direction of my work during my conferences. I rely on the wealth of my knowledge and my excellent long-term memory to orchestrate these sessions. The question and answer period isn't a problem either because the focus is something I know well. But at the social gathering, I have to react and respond to conversation generated by other people. My brain often doesn't work fast enough to find what I need to say. On the way home from these gatherings, I usually think of many things I could have said."

Clearly, most people function best when the task or subject is something they know well. You don't have to have ADD to be at a loss for words. But ADDers seem to regularly experience this phenomenon. It results from a significant imbalance in action and reaction capabilities.

Connections to the world are generally slow and inefficient while internal connections work with lightning rapidity. Output can be difficult because the ADDer has to synchronize his mental speed with his slower output. An inability to respond quickly to requests seems to be stubborn or non-compliant behavior. In reality, these behaviors can be manifestations of irregular reaction capabilities. His mouth, brain and body just don't cooperate very well in demand situations.

As many of us struggle with mismatched input/output capabilities, we feel out of control. We live in a world of paradoxes, a world that seems to toss us about by inexplicable forces. Our need for control doesn't come from a desire to be one up on others. It is often a desperate attempt to manage a situation so we can function with a degree of competence. Otherwise, it's so easy to look and feel stupid.

ADD children may not work well in the group setting of a classroom but perform well with a tutor. An ADD adult can have difficulty working as a committee member yet perform admirably as the chairperson. He may stand around the kitchen of a friend preparing a dinner party, unable to figure out how to assist. But he may successfully orchestrate a social activity of his own design.

These behaviors can make you feel lazy and bad about ourself. It's important to remember that this is another piece of ADD. These contradictory behaviors can reflect your genuine inability to react quickly and efficiently to situations.

The Minuscule Mental Fuel Tank

Unless you happen to be in excellent aerobic health, a frenzied hour long chase through the park after your escaping Great Dane would probably do you in for the afternoon. If a nap wasn't warranted, a *kick back, put your feet up and read a book* break probably would be. You are exhausted!

This scenario is similar to the daily experiences of an ADDer. Though his body might not dash madly around a park, his thoughts can race around his head. He is mentally tired. A rapidly working brain expends much energy and quickly uses up its daily allotment.

ADDers tend to process information at a mind boggling pace and burn out just as quickly. An eight hour workday can be torturous for someone

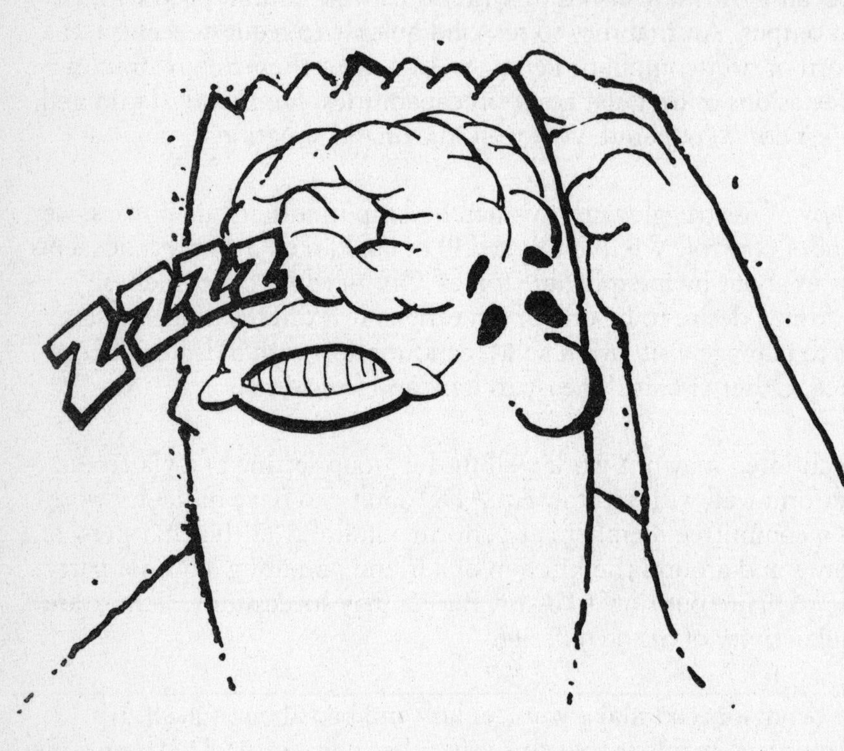

whose mental energy and productive times simply don't last long enough. Some have sufficient energy to get through the day but run out of steam when they get home. Families can't believe that the slug in front of the TV could ever be of any use on the job. For years, they have never seen him move off his couch!

Many of us think faster and fatigue more quickly than our non-ADD peers. Each of us needs to be aware of the impact of cognitive fatigue on our work tempo. Some adults conserve their resources by coasting at work, particularly if their jobs aren't too demanding. This strategy can backfire. Without a high level of motivation, the ADDer's job performance can really suffer. Conversely, the mental fatigue caused by a demanding job can overload his brain's capacity to function well. The challenge is to conserve his mental energy by working at his own pace and rhythm.

Shut Down Susceptibility

What happens when the brain's capacity to process information is exceeded? ***It shuts down.*** Many of us live in terror that we'll shut down at a critical moment and become useless in a crisis. We may freeze in response to loud noises or unexpected events and feel that we're in slow motion.

An ADDer's overloaded system can make him so tired he can barely move, talk or think. It is as if he is in a temporary coma. He experiences attempts of communication as assaults on his very being. He either ignores the assault or snaps an irritable reply—taking any action is an impossibility.

An overloaded brain is similar to an overloaded computer system. If you load up the working memory of a computer with excessive data, it might crash, losing data or the functions of the software. Your program will be temporarily useless. On a mainframe computer, overload can shut down the entire system. With excessive sensory information, the brain can also suffer from overload.

Even the most efficient, resilient person can become disorganized under certain conditions. Recent discoveries in the brains of individuals suffering from *Post-Traumatic Stress Disorder* are good examples. Research of this condition has grown from an interest in the mental health problems of Vietnam era veterans.

Post-Traumatic Stress Disorder follows a psychological trauma to events of war, sexual abuse or natural disaster outside the usual range of human experience. The symptoms include nightmares, flashbacks, substance abuse and an exaggerated startle response. Previously well adjusted people aren't immune to the disorder—the symptoms can occur in anyone who has experienced severe trauma.

The symptoms often persist years after the traumatic event. Recently, psychobiological researchers have discovered actual biochemical changes in the brains of individuals with post-traumatic stress.[22] It appears that the massive overload experienced in extreme situations can alter the brain, perhaps permanently.

Although no one can explain the biochemistry that causes *Shut Down*, we know from experience that it's troubling for many ADDers. Of course, we aren't the only people who shut down under demanding situations. The difference is in degree. It takes a fairly low level of stress for the ADD brain to yell "uncle". And when it happens, it's definitely not fun!

This baffling coma of Shut Down is troubling but essential for our continued well-being. It is as if our brains must stop the onslaught so we can heal ourselves and renew our depleted reserves of mental energy. Rather than fighting it, we need to give in to it and accept the self-imposed rest time. Our brains must recharge. Each of us has to find the best way to facilitate this renewal.

Undependable Memory and Learning Systems
If you look at a picture of the brain, you won't find an area labelled *The Memory*. Memory is a process rather than an identifiable part of the brain. The function of memory is a system with multiple parts scattered throughout the brain. Some of the differences ADDers experience are related to problems with memory. In the following section, we will examine the impact of ADD symptoms on the memory process.

The First Step of Memory: Acquisition—The first step in the process, acquisition, is closely related to selective attention. Besides paying attention to incoming information, it involves a preliminary decision to accept and store it.

As ADDers, many of us feel embarrassed by how much we don't know. Our selective attention deficits make it difficult to acquire information that never even finds its way into our memories! The positive side is that an ability to notice things others miss, results in a fascinating and eclectic storehouse of interesting knowledge!

The Second Step of Memory: Registration—We have to register information before it can become part of memory. In this second step of the memory process, we consciously make an effort to secure the information in our memories for subsequent recall. If we superficially register the data, we'll have difficulty retrieving it later. Problems of arousal or alertness often impair adequate registration. We may only partially understand conversations, phone messages or directions and jump the gun on new tasks.

Coding and *rehearsal* are two important parts of registration. Every time you use a file cabinet, you are using a system of coding. You decide whether to file the piece of paper by subject, writer's name or type of required action. If you recall from the discussion of spatial organization, this is no small task for some ADDers.

Registering information involves essentially the same kind of sorting and filing. We decide to code, or file incoming information as a visual image, a word or a sound. For example, we can code the name "*Tom Thumb*" in several ways. The code can be a "picture" of Tom the midget with an enormous thumb (visual), a word, "finger" (verbal) or a sound, "Tom Thumb is a bum" (auditory).

Rehearsal is what children used to do in their one-room schoolhouses—memorizing by reciting their lessons aloud. We use rehearsal to practice and repeat information until we anchor it in our memories. To be effective, rehearsal must be more than rote memorization. It must include *elaboration* of information. If you have ever memorized a word list by singing a silly song you created from the words, you have used rehearsal elaboration.

Rehearsal is another problem for an ADDer because it's tedious and requires patience. These are usually not his best qualities! He is creative, though, and can be quite inventive with the sometimes off-the-wall coding methods he designs.

The Third Step of Memory: Storage—The third step involves storage of the processed information. There are four storage systems: *instant recall, active working memory, short-term memory* and *long-term memory*. These storage systems aren't characterized by their size but by their duration or how *long* information is stored in each.

Instant recall has the shortest duration. *Seeing* the flash of lightening in your mind's eye is an example of instant recall. Touch-typing also uses this kind of memory. The typist holds the key's location in his mind only long enough to press on it.

Active working memory functions much like the working memory of a computer. While you work, the words on the screen are held in the computer's temporary storage. If the power goes out, you lose your work forever unless you have saved it to permanent disc storage.

RAM memory capacity varies from one computer to another. If you try to run memory intensive software, your computer might respond to the overload with a shutdown and loss of data. If you're lucky, it might give you a a chance to close files or change software by alerting you to its low memory.

Similar to RAM memory, your active working memory can shut down if you try to overload it. It's too bad your brain doesn't give clearer messages of impending shut-down—maybe something like, "This is you brain. I am preparing to self-destruct!" Complexity of detail seems to shrink the storage capacity. An ADDer often has a remarkably unreliable temporary memory that regularly loses power and data. He begins the first step in solving a complex problem only to lose it as he undertakes the second step. The jigsaw pieces keep falling off the table before he can put the whole puzzle together.

Short Term Memory also functions as temporary storage. Its capacity is quite limited with a maximum of five seconds or seven items (plus or minus two). Its unique limitations make it vulnerable to a variety of interferences. Distractibility wreaks havoc with short term memory. It doesn't take more than a brief mind trip for a person to lose data that he wasn't mentally present to register.

An imaginative thinking style can also interfere with short term memory storage. Elaboration and association of old and new data is a great anchor for long term storage. But it can compromise the quality of short term storage that requires focus on specific details.

Long Term Memory is the permanent, seemingly unlimited storehouse of facts, experiences, values, routines, and general knowledge. You can think of it as a huge bank vault that contains numerous safe-deposit boxes. Memories you need to store forever are in a separate box deep inside the cavernous vault. The ones you need to remember while you complete your errands are in your safety deposit box right inside the vault's steel door.

The data in this bank vault is *consolidated,* or translated into a permanent code. The code determines which box will store the information. When you identify a Honda, Buick and Ford as automobiles, you are using consolidation. From experience and learning, you form associations by elaborating on the characteristics of each car and cross referencing them to other vehicles.

A rich imagination enhances these associations and is an asset for long term memory storage. Since an ADDer tends to be a conceptualizer rather than a rote learner, his consolidation skills can be superb. He may possess a wealth of information in his bank vault but routinely forget where he put his car keys!

Fourth Step of Memory: Access—Access is the process of recalling stored information through recognition or retrieval memory. Recognition relies on *familiarity* to refresh the memories of superficially learned data. For example, you use recognition memory to take a multiple choice test or find your way to a location by noting landmarks along the way.

On the other hand, *retrieval* requires precise, accurate recall on demand. When you take an essay exam, you have to retrieve information as an accurate whole. Finding a specific word in your memory banks is another retrieval task.

Retrieval relies on data you have firmly fixed in memory. To anchor data in memory, you have to use specific strategies. Precise recall is only as good as the strategies you used to store the information. That's why rote recitation is a less effective strategy than memorizing by principle. Rote learning results in isolated details rather than general ideas and abstractions.

An ADDer's unique abilities and disabilities cause great variability in his ability to access information. Accurate retrieval is a combination of attention to the details of what he needs to memorize, planned strategies for storage and fast information processing.

With an aversion to details, an ADDer tends to approach memory chores in a rapid, superficial and haphazard manner. This compromises his ability to develop strategies for registration. His limited reserves of mental energy impair his ability to maintain sufficient effort to memorize something. As he quickly burns out, he often rushes to get the memory chore finished.

His divergent retrieval is usually much faster and more accurate than his convergent retrieval. Remember the dynamics of reaction time?

An ADD adult functions better when he *acts* (divergent retrieval) on his own ideas than when he *reacts* (convergent retrieval) to a direct question. He often impresses his friends and himself (!) with the fluency of thoughts structured around his knowledge base. Everything is great until someone interrupts with a question or even worse, changes the subject. He suddenly feels anxious and annoyed that he has to switch to his faulty convergent retrieval.

Fifth Step of Memory: Transfer—Transfer is a complex process of rearranging individual pieces of data to form new knowledge. It can include combining fragmented pieces into a larger whole. It can include applying data from one application to another. It can also include generalizations of the common threads between seemingly unrelated ideas or events.

A precise memory for facts is invaluable in answering questions about a specific subject. It is less valuable in information transfer that depends on associations. For instance, children and adults with mental retardation can't transfer skills from one setting to another. They have to learn skills in each of the settings they will use them.

Transfer of knowledge depends on the creative and flexible use of a knowledge base. If data is stored in separately labeled boxes, transfer of knowledge is impossible. Mixing the contents of the boxes or combining them in new ways is unthinkable!

An ADDer tends to be a creative, divergent thinker with an ability to put knowledge and ideas together. He resists putting things in boxes with neat labels. Although this can be a disadvantage when he needs precise memory, it is a decided advantage for transferring knowledge. He can wander through his safe-deposit boxes, finding information to use in new and interesting ways. He can apply knowledge and solve problems in ways undreamed of by more orderly thinkers.

ADD adults don't have bad memories but their unique symptoms create gaps in the memory process. Although each of us has a unique memory profile, we share some fairly consistent patterns. Recognition memory is usually good. That's why many of us performed well in classroom discussions about the historic implications of world events but failed miserably on tests that required one-word answers.

It makes sense that your memory would be good for a specific subject or task that comes easily to you. But what about that tough physics class in high school? Why did you do so well in a difficult subject that required *on demand* memory retrieval? Your teacher might have wondered the same thing. He might have pointedly used this as evidence of your ability to do it *when you wanted to*.

Your teacher was partially correct in his assessment. Your ability to excel was related to motivation but not in the way he thought—your lack of motivation wasn't the result of your poor attitude. It was the result of an ADDer's need for intensely compelling motivation to grab the dysregulated selective attention. It also had a lot to do with individual teaching styles.

Everyone has his own unique learning style. The visual learner learns by seeing, the auditory learner by hearing and the kinesthetic learner by doing/experiencing. If you are a visual learner and the course in question was taught with many charts, diagrams and other visual aids, your brain received the optimal kind of stimuli. Your memory was given just what it needed to function efficiently.

Recognizing individual learning styles can be very helpful in bypassing weak areas and focusing on strengths. The memory of an ADDer can compromise his attempts to learn, converse and carry out instructions. Understanding the process goes a long way toward helping him readjust his self-assessments.

We ADDer's aren't stupid or oppositional. We just need to learn and to demonstrate what we've learned, differently than others do. We'll examine these differences in greater depth later in the book.

Impaired Social Skills' Control Center

ADD has a profound impact on all areas of life, including social adjustment. Symptoms of the disorder can affect interpersonal relationships in a variety of ways.

Some people seem to be born with social gifts and skills of intuition that they use to "read" other people. Perhaps they have highly developed "Social Skills' Control Centers" in their brains! With little effort, they seem to interact admirably in social situations. Many of us with ADD, however, really have to work hard at learning and using social skills.

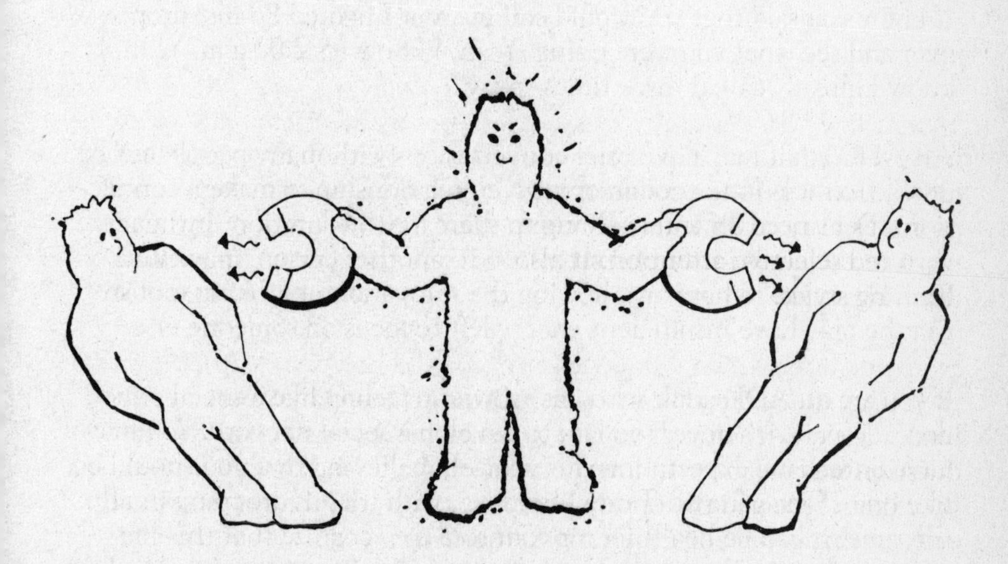

We learn manners and other forms of social rules in childhood—but successful relationships require more than memorized rules. The rules are somewhat flexible and can change from situation to situation. The development of social skills is more an art than a science because we must learn to read the ever-changing reactions of others. If deficient selective attention gets in the way, an ADDer's perceptions may be flawed by inaccurate or incomplete information.

If we are unsure of the rules in a given situation, we watch other people for clues and gauge their reactions to our behaviors. An inability to process information efficiently can result in a failure to assimilate the new rules quickly enough. Combined with impulsivity, this deficit can lead to numerous social mistakes.

Developing friendships can be difficult for an ADDer whose restlessness interferes with the process. Building lasting friendships requires slow, careful planning and nurturing. Many of us simply can't wait around long enough for this process to take its course. So, we try to speed it up and come on like gangbusters, pushing ourselves into other's lives.

"I know you said that you would call me, but I figured I'd just drop over and see what you were doing. Yeah, I know it's 2:00 a.m. Yeah, I know I already called three times today."

An ADD adult may have brief conversations with many people but be unable to focus long enough on a given relationship to make a connection. It's just too difficult to hang in there for the duration. Intimacy, with its demands for careful attention to another person, may elude him. He works so hard at following the rules and not looking foolish that he may have insufficient energy left to focus on someone else.

If you are an ADD adult who has grown up feeling like a social reject, don't despair! It's never too late to develop a social network. You may have unrealistic expectations for yourself, believing that you should be like one of the gang on *Thirty something*, with friends dropping in all the time. It can be healthier for your soul to recognize that this lifestyle may be unnecessary and undesirable. Using your energy to develop one or two positive relationships can be a much better way to go.

Some of the eccentric traits that caused an ADDer's childhood peers to label him "weird" often become admirable traits in adulthood. Weird becomes unique, special or interesting. Creativity, a special talent, a sense of humor or an enthusiastic zest can be a social magnet, drawing other people to him.

By this point in your reading, we hope you have a better understanding about what ADD is and the impact it has had on your life. We hope you have begun to forgive yourself for the failures and shortcomings you may have blamed on your lack of character. We hope you know that your ADD isn't your fault.

In the next chapter, we'll look at some additional dynamics of ADD. Our focus will be the unproductive ways many of us have learned to cope with our disorder. Growing up different affects the way each of us interacts with our individual worlds and the people in them.

By understanding your disorder you've already begun the process of dismantling your self-defeating assumptions. To continue this important process, you need to consider both the adaptive and maladaptive coping strategies you've been using to cope with being different. With this knowledge, you can make decisions about your behaviors and modify those that are getting in the way of your recovery.

CHAPTER 5

The Not So Fine Art of Coping

"I won't think about that today...I'll think about it tomorrow."

Scarlett O'Hara used this classic line several times in the movie, *Gone with the Wind*. She had mastered the art of dealing with the problems in her life by avoiding them—she put them out of her mind. Scarlett may have been a fictional character, but she did what **all** human beings do. She developed coping strategies, *defense mechanisms*, to defend herself against psychological and emotional harm.

Defense mechanisms are the survival techniques we learn through our life experiences. Scarlett learned to protect herself against feeling guilty for her less than admirable behaviors with her, "I'll put it out my mind" defense. Defense mechanisms become armors that shield Scarlett and all of us, from hurts and disappointments.

Because of our differences, we ADDers endure more than our fair share of disappointments, rejection and feelings of inadequacy. By the time we reach adulthood, many of us have erected elaborate defense systems to hide our differences or distract others from seeing them. **We don't want to be different** and will jump through hoops to fit in and gain acceptance. So, we build shields to defend ourselves against emotional harm.

Defense mechanisms can be psychologically beneficial. They can be adaptive, positive coping mechanisms. They can also be psychologically harmful, maladaptive coping mechanisms that undermine growth. Scarlet sometimes used her *Denial* defense—"If I don't think about the problem, it doesn't exist" as an adaptive coping mechanism. When she killed a man in self-defense, her refusal to think about the devastating circumstances enabled her to survive its horror.

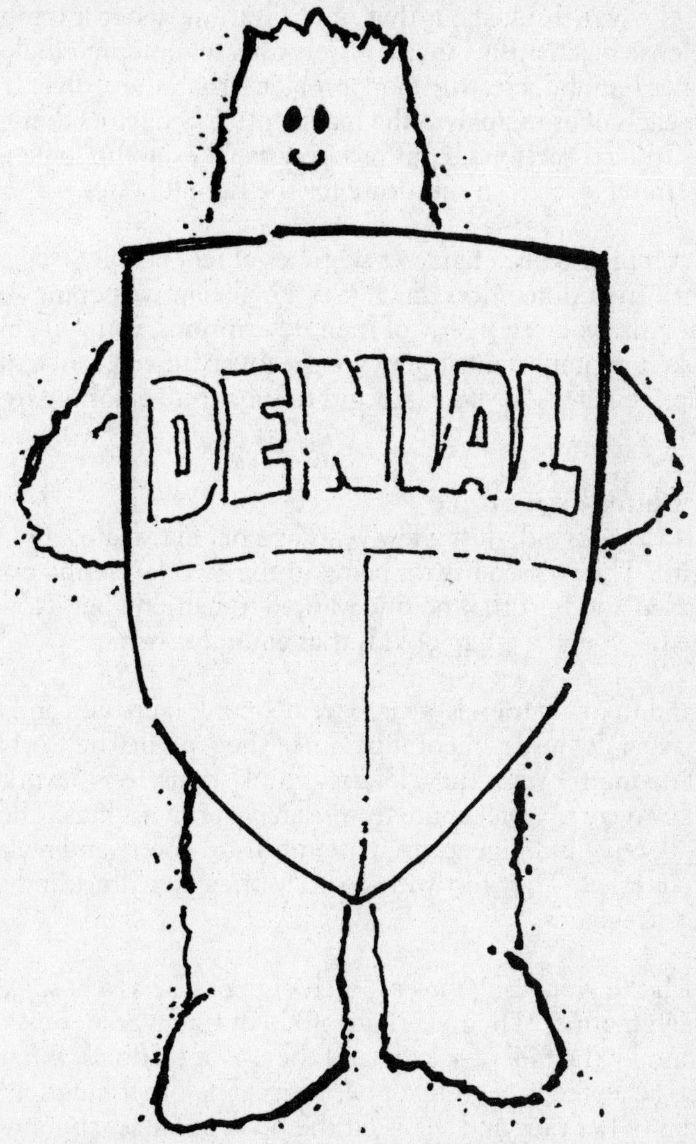

Unfortunately, Scarlett overused the defense. She used it not only to survive emotional harm but also to insulate herself from ever thinking about the possible consequences of her actions. Because she didn't allow herself to consider the impact of her behavior, she realized too late that she was destroying her marriage. Even in the final scene when Rhett Butler leaves with his declaration that their relationship is over, Scarlet refuses to confront reality. Again she invokes her standard refrain, "I won't think about that now, I'll think about it tomorrow." The defense mechanisms that ADDers use are sometimes helpful and sometimes harmful, creating more problems than they solve. It's important for each of us to analyze the maladaptive behaviors that get us in trouble. In later sections about recovery, we'll examine some adaptive coping strategies we can substitute for the harmful ones.

We've compiled some character sketches of real people struggling to cope with their differences. Each uses a maladaptive coping strategy. If you recognize yourself in any of their descriptions, you will already have taken an important step in your recovery. If you can analyze your maladaptive defenses, you can begin to substitute emotionally healthier ones.

Bad is Better than Stupid

Susan is 15 years old. Just a few years ago her classmates thought she was weird. They teased her for being in the "ozone" during class. She was puzzled and hurt that no one wanted to befriend her. Now at long last, she has found a group of kids that embraces her.

Susan and her new friends wear extreme, punk hairstyles and clothing. They have a doomsday mentality. Since they're sure the world is going to Hell no matter what they do, they think it's useless to work hard at school or to try to excel at anything. They are smart kids. They use their collective intelligence to write nihilistic poetry and make darkly humorous jokes. They flirt with death as they take drugs and have sex without safeguards.

Although the group isn't violent, each of the kids has a hostile, sarcastic and tough manner. Their peers are afraid of them. Sometimes Susan is scared too by the talk of suicide and the use of IV drugs. But at least she feels accepted by a group of her peers. The other kids don't dare make fun of her now and she is off the hook as far as school work goes.

Elementary school was always difficult for Susan, but junior high and high school have been nightmares. Many ADDers can empathize with her. She has always felt incompetent, stupid and rejected. Slow and awkward in learning new sports and mastering the art of conversation, she hasn't fared any better in physical prowess or in her social life.

She has learned one thing very well—adolescents admire kids who are cool and in control. Driven by the adolescent's intense need to fit in, Susan has learned that rebellious behavior is more acceptable than the uncertain fumblings of someone struggling with disabilities. She has decided that *Being Bad* is better than *Being Stupid*.

Faced with reality as she experiences it, Susan chooses inclusion in the gang over humiliation and alienation. She has a third choice. She can learn new ways of dealing with her differences. She doesn't consider this option because she is driven to save face. She's always in trouble with her parents and teachers but is willing to pay this high price for acceptance.

The defense mechanism Susan has learned is common in adolescence. A defiant and *smart* reply to a teacher's questions can get a few laughs and perhaps some admiration from other kids. It's a way to avoid answering a question without looking stupid. The stint in detention hall that follows can be a reasonable price to pay for maintaining one's image. And anyway, getting plenty of detentions is cool.

TOUGHNESS creates a smoke screen to mask VULNERABILITY.

If you separate Susan and her friends from their group and manage to dig beneath the tough shells, you find troubled, uncertain kids. Many vulnerable ADD adolescents continue to wear their shields of toughness into adulthood. They usually manage to keep themselves and their tough facades within the bounds of society's rules and don't become major league criminals or radicals. A hostile attitude, however, intimidates other people and prevents anyone from getting too close. This defense mechanism does double duty as a cover for problems and an insulator from other people. Unfortunately, Susan and her counterparts may pay a high price, indeed.

The Perfectionist

Unlike Susan who protects herself by rebelling against society's rules, Debra has taken the opposite tack. She has decided that being the best, regardless of the cost, is the only way to hide her deficits. Debra is a *Perfectionist*.

She has ADD but those who know her would never believe it. Although her poor conduct grades reflected her restlessness, her behavior wasn't disruptive enough to cause serious discipline problems in school. In general, she followed the rules and did what was asked of her. Before she graduated —in the top 3% of her high school class of one thousand— she took part in many extracurricular activities. Everyone counted on her to volunteer for any task that needed to be done.

You might be asking how someone with ADD could function so well. Well, Debra wasn't really functioning very well despite her carefully constructed facade. She rarely slept more than four or five hours each night. This had nothing to do with insomnia. She didn't sleep much because she didn't have time—she had to study twice as long as everybody else to learn the material. She regularly "pulled all-nighters" and never had time to relax or hang out.

Sometimes she desperately longed to get off her treadmill but didn't dare risk disclosure. If she failed to do everything, her secret would be out. Everyone would know she wasn't normal. The hitch was that Debra didn't have a clue about what "normal" was. She had kept her secret so long that she had inflated ideas about what other people could accomplish. She thought that if she said "No" to anything, she would be found-out.

Her inability to say "No" got her into serious trouble in all areas of life. Beginning in seventh grade, she had sex with any boy who asked and pushed the bad feelings about herself to the back of her mind. Even a pregnancy and an abortion didn't change her sexual behavior. Her impaired sense of self, distorted by differences she didn't understand, caused her to do anything that would bring acceptance.

Now 32 years old, Debra is married and has a set of twins and a successful business. She still works herself to death, compelled to *do it all*. It's becoming increasingly more difficult to do it all with so many conflicting demands on her time. Children, husband, volunteer work and clients all vie for her attention. Lately she feels that she's losing control and that at any moment something horrible is going to happen.

She can't keep all the pieces together anymore.

While Debra may look good to outsiders, she feels terrible inside. She has to spend all her energy running and hiding behind her facade of perfection. Knowing that she has just about pushed herself beyond her limits, she wonders when she'll totally self-destruct.

There are many Debra's around. It's interesting to speculate the numbers of *super* men and women who struggle with disability beneath their *in control* exteriors. Readers who are familiar with codependency may recognize similar traits in Debra. She's trying to gain control of her life by taking care of everything and everybody. Recovering codependents could tell her that it doesn't work.

The Blamer
Steve never admits he's made a mistake. When he can't find important papers in the *black hole* that constitutes his office, he accuses his secretary of losing them. He terrorizes his wife, kids and employees by flying off the handle and accusing them when anything goes wrong.

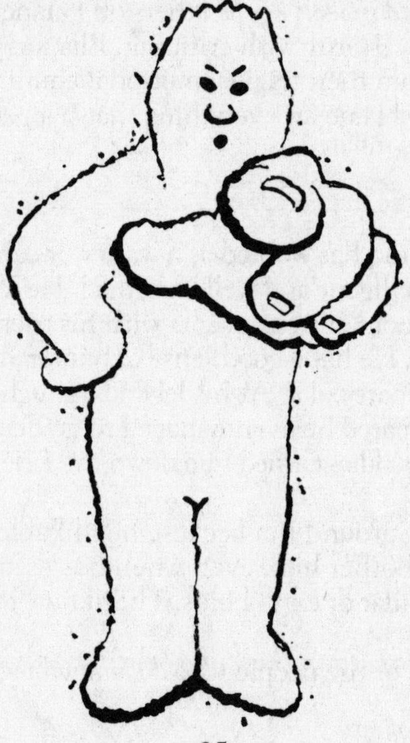

At 28 years old, Steve is a chronic *Blamer*. If food falls out when he jerks the refrigerator door open, he yells at his wife for putting the groceries away incorrectly. If his kids don't understand his instructions, he blames it on their stupidity or inattention. It's an impossibility that his instructions were unclear. Enduring his daily accusations and anger, his family begins to believe they are at fault.

Most people who know Steve characterize him as an arrogant SOB. What they don't realize is that beneath his blustery, aggressive exterior is a scared, rejected kid. Steve is shielding himself against feelings of inadequacy by shifting the blame to others. This keeps everyone from looking too closely at his performance. He's terrified that he'll be exposed for the bumbling idiot he really is. Although he's a successful businessman, he still feels like the kid who was regularly ridiculed and punished. Tapes from the past keep playing in his head, "How could you be so stupid! You'll never be worth anything!"

The defense mechanism of *Blaming* is similar to *Being Bad* except that the blamer fends off people by actively accusing them of stupidity or wrongdoing. The *bad* person keeps others off balance with anger and hostility but not necessarily with criticism. Blamers can never let anything go. To maintain their fragile emotional equilibrium, they must have a scapegoat to blame for everything that happens. For the blamer, accidents don't exist.

"Who Cares?"

Jim is 30 years old and has worked as a waiter or cab driver most of his adult life. He is intelligent and well-informed. He loves to engage in lively discussions about current events with his friends and anyone else who will listen. He has a good sense of humor about things in general and himself in particular. At his legendary high school graduation (his friends were amazed he ever managed to graduate), he joined in the laughter as his buddies carried him down the aisle on their shoulders.

People enjoy being around Jim because he's likable and easy going. Nothing seems to bother him, even when bosses and coworkers ask him to work unpopular or extra hours. They know he won't complain.

Jim makes excuses for the people who *do him wrong* or maintains that the things they do don't bother him. He professes to be content with his life the way it is. Secretly he feels bad that he didn't go to college as his brothers and sisters did. He isn't at peace with himself and has many physical symptoms to prove it: tension headaches, high blood pressure and an ulcer that regularly flairs up.

Jim feels that he's a failure and masks his feelings of inadequacy with his *Who Cares* persona. His wide circle of friends and broad knowledge base don't make up for his academic shortcomings. The defense mechanism he uses to protect himself is similar to Susan's. Borrowing from the fox in the sour grapes' fable, both pretend that things out of reach aren't worthwhile, anyway. Susan's arrogance and Jim's indifference are shields of armor to prevent anyone from seeing their disabilites.

Jane presents a slightly different version of the *Who Cares* defense. Jane, a 42 year old mother of two, is intelligent and creative and has impressive artistic talents. Despite her gifts, Jane's ADD made school a monumental struggle. It took twice the customary time for her to complete college. Before choosing to stay home with her children, she had always held jobs well below her educational level.

Jane is outspoken about the excessive competition and materialism in today's society. She is proud of her skill at budgeting money and has learned to live without the many consumer goods others consider necessities. She doesn't own a VCR or clothes' dryer.

Jane's wise use of resources enables her to devote time to her family and have enough left over to pursue her own interests. Her choice of saying "No" to the rat race to live by her own values, is admirable. The problem is, Jane isn't entirely comfortable with her decision. She "Doth protest too much" when she scoffs at academic and career achievement. There is a distinctively angry, defensive edge to her voice when she rationalizes her life choices. She spends much time explaining herself.

Jim's indifference is passive and Jane's is assertive, but both are carefully designed masks. Jane doesn't feel successful. She uses so much energy on defense that she can't accept herself or honestly evaluate her choices. Perhaps beneath the bristly *Who Cares* defense is a real desire to accomplish some of the things she rejects. Perhaps the choices she has made are right for her. Regrettably, she works so hard at protecting her fragile ego that she has little energy left for living the life she has chosen.

Jim, on the other hand, can't realistically assess himself because he works so hard at pretending nothing bothers him. His "what me worry" attitude masks his real feelings that probably include anger. He is angry at himself for his shortcomings and at the people who take advantage of him. His armor protects him but also prevents him from grappling with ambitions he's never been able to admit. If he's ever able to let his guard down, he'll need to confront his anger. If he can learn to deal with his feelings up front, he may even find that his physical health improves.

Manipulation

Todd is 47 years old and is restless, attractive and charming. He frequently changes relationships, living arrangements and jobs. He uses his disarming, boyish manner as a powerful lure to hook others into willingly taking care of him. He never pulls his weight at work, relying instead on his mastery of manipulation to get others to do the work for him.

Faced with a tedious or difficult task, Todd flatters and cajoles others into bailing him out. Sometimes he acts helpless, getting coworkers to do his job under the guise of teaching him. He says something like, "I never was any good at that. I really admire people who can do it." Sometimes he tells a tale of woe about his boss piling work on him or about emergencies in his life. His manipulative behavior usually works and someone steps in to bail him out. As soon as he feels restless or coworkers *get on to him*, he simply changes jobs.

Todd usually makes decent money but regularly ends up flat broke because he's careless and impulsive with his spending. To deal with his financial difficulties, he relies on the women in his life to support him. His women do more than simply contribute to his financial support. They are also charged with keeping him out of trouble. They keep track of his checkbook and his household and social responsibilities. Todd manipulates them by using guilt, charm, sex appeal—whatever maneuver will work in a given situation.

Often he manipulates his current woman into keeping him together enough to hold down his job. She gets him up in the morning, monitors his performance and smooths things over with the boss when Todd messes up. More often than not, he ends the relationship when he feels too constrained by the "mothering". His behavior sounds a lot like an alcoholic's but he doesn't drink. He has just learned to manipulate like someone who does.

Todd might seem like a ruthless, unfeeling user who will stop at nothing to ensure that his needs are met. He isn't pure villain, however. He's an ADD adult who has learned to use *Manipulation* as a cover for his underlying problems.

He lives in a constant state of emergency, running scared all the time. He knows he regularly makes mistakes but feels helpless to prevent them. So he survives by using other people to cover for him. It's the only way he knows to survive although he's aware that it's unacceptable for a grown man to be cared for this way.

Todd simply hasn't figured out an alternative method for satisfying his needs. His manipulations are neither conscious nor premeditated. He doesn't connect his actions with their impact on others. His impulsivity and lack of attention to detail make him unaware of much of his behavior and its consequences.

Webster defines manipulating as "controlling or playing on others using unfair means". Manipulation may be a dirty word but everyone uses it on occasion. Although we may not like being manipulated as puppets on a string, we may need to occasionally use this defense as a matter of survival.

ADD adults in particular can become masters of the art of manipulation. It's a tough, competitive world out there with dire consequences for those who sink to the bottom of the heap. Many of the newly homeless are hardworking folk who slid over the line into poverty following a setback such as unemployment or illness. If someone starts out in life with a physical handicap, learning disability or ADD, the stakes are higher and riskier. There is a great temptation to use any available means to improve one's odds of survival.

This isn't to say that the majority of people with disabilities become manipulative. Most are rather heroic in their striving to achieve. They generally cope by learning to work harder than non-disabled people. ADD adults, however, have additional risk factors that increase the odds of their becoming masters of manipulation.

Withdrawal

Barb is both unattached and detached. Twenty-five years old, she lives with her parents and works as a file clerk. She has rarely dated, has no close friends and spends most of her free time watching TV. Occasionally she goes out to dinner with a coworker but that's the extent of her social life. She spends her vacations tagging along with her parents. Although Barb has an above average IQ, she is a marginal worker on the job. She makes many mistakes and has trouble keeping up with her colleagues.

Barb is different from most of the ADDers you've met in this chapter. She isn't anxious about her performance and doesn't worry about her less than glowing appraisals. After a childhood of academic and social failures, she has decided that giving up is the safest thing she can do. She has chosen to accept her mediocrity. The price she pays is a life of boredom, loneliness and depression. Barb is free from the risks she would face if she decided to live her life fully. But is it worth it?

Similar to many ADD adults, Barb's handicap has never been identified. She is neither hyperactive nor impulsive. Everyone has always told her that she is lethargic and spacey. Barb believes this characterization. She has chosen survival through *Withdrawal*.

This defense is a cousin to the *Who Cares* stance but operates slightly differently. Barb has given up completely and has carefully buried her feelings and doubts. She never gives any thought to the possibility that her life could be different. Jim, on the other hand, maintains nagging doubts about his abilities and lack of achievement. On some level, he continues to think about these issues that trouble him.

Insulated from pain by suppressing feelings of inadequacy, Barb can't make a thoughtful decision about her life. The Barb's of this world haven't made peace with themselves—it's as if they're buried alive.

Chip on the Shoulder
While Barb quietly withdraws, Paula aggressively poises for full-scale battle every moment of her life. She's only 19, but has developed an especially prickly suit of armor. When her husband asks if she has taken out the trash, she reacts defensively. She offers a long-winded explanation of why she hasn't been able to get around to the chore yet. As she becomes increasingly angry and indignant, she switches to the offensive, attacking her husband for overworking her with his demands.

Paula's husband asked about the trash only because he was going outside and wanted to take it with him if it was still in the house. He wearily retreats from the house, wondering how his good intentions ended up in this ugly scene. Paula retreats to nurse her anger at a world that is always dissatisfied with her efforts.

Paula is a selfish shrew, making her saintly husband's life miserable. She has a colossal *Chip on the Shoulder*, responding to innocent comments with a barrage of defensive excuses and explanations. At least this is the way she acts. But appearances aren't always what they seem.

Paula is an ADD adult who spent much of her childhood rebuked for things she forgot to do or didn't finish. Her soul is raw from all the times she worked her heart out only to be chastised for the one thing she didn't do. Her life has been filled with false accusations of thoughtlessness and laziness that no one knew were symptoms of her subtle disability. She ruminates about the injustices in her life and the unfairness of it all.

Paula's *Chip on The Shoulder* is a protective suit of armor designed to shore up her sense of self. She continually defends herself as a matter of reflex even when she isn't being attacked. The intensity of her defensive stance may be out of proportion to the imagined slight but her life experiences have taught her to expect criticism. She can never let down her defenses. She has to be ready for the next assault on her being.

Paula's defense serves another purpose. It inoculates her against requests for her time or energy. With deficits that interfere with an organized lifestyle, she frantically tries to keep up with demands that are sometimes overwhelming. Her prickly shell fends off at least some of the extra demands as it makes people think twice about approaching her with questions or requests for her involvement.

There isn't anything inherently bad about emotional self-defense in the face of real injustice. In Paula's case, however, her knee-jerk defensiveness is the maladaptive suit she wears every moment of her life. She has suffered so many wounds that she can't differentiate between real and imagined assaults. She focuses exclusively on protection, never allowing herself to find the strengths that would lead to positive growth.

Take Me or Leave Me

You probably know highly effective people whose self-confidence you admire. They are self-assured and comfortable with themselves. They assume a healthy attitude of "What you see is what you get—I'm okay and have nothing to hide." They use this posture in a positive way. They are unlikely, for example, to waste time on relationships that probably wouldn't work anyway.

Pete is a *Take Me or Leave Me* man in his mid-'30's. He is attractive and affable, drawing people to him with his sense of humor and gift of gab. He comes across as honest, straightforward and comfortable with his limitations. He sincerely apologizes when he misses an important deadline at work or forgets to attend his daughter's school play. Pete disarms most people by being the first to admit his weaknesses. He frequently makes himself the butt of his own jokes.

"What you see is what you get" Pete, has chosen a positive coping mechanism. . .Or has he? What makes Pete different from the self-confident people we described? The difference is that Pete's Take Me Or Leave Me attitude is a carefully fabricated facade behind which he hides.

He is a grown-up class clown who "keeps' em laughing" so no one will notice the things he can't do. He uses his excellent sense of humor to create a smoke screen to hide difficulties and deflect criticism. Would-be critics find the wind taken out of their sails when Pete beats them to the punch by making a joke about his failings. He leaves them with nothing to say.

It's healthy to take ourselves less seriously. Pete, however, does it to excess. Though he readily admits his weaknesses, he never does anything about them! He retreats behind his self-deprecating facade instead of honestly studying his behavior.

He's busy hiding and is unaware of the increasing frustration and anger of his friends. They continue to forgive his failings but are beginning to have nagging feelings that *something is rotten in Denmark*. Pete's basically a "good guy", but he's totally undependable. He isn't doing anything to improve himself. His mistakes are getting less funny and his refusal to take anything seriously is causing increasing resentment.

Pete's coping mechanism does protect him, but it's maladaptive. It prevents the introspection he needs to make positive changes in his life.

It Ain't So

Donna's family of five lurches from crisis to crisis. She always attributes her family's problems to external events and people. *Everything will be fine when the excitement of Christmas is over or when one of the kids gets a new teacher.* She spends much of her time waiting for things to return to normal, but they never do.

Donna is 34 years old and has given up a professional career to stay home with her three children who are all hyperactive and disobedient. Donna is gentle and spacey, rarely raising her voice to her children or asserting herself with other adults. She works hard at a difficult parenting job but her children continue to be unruly, and her household remains noisy and disordered. When a crisis erupts, she consults with professionals but promptly disregards their advice. She denies that a real problem exists.

Several years ago Donna was diagnosed with ADD. Her physician prescribed Ritalin and she took it for a short while. She explains that she stopped taking the medicine because it interfered with her sleep but she never bothered telling her doctor about the side effect.

It's obvious to anyone who knows Donna that her ADD has a big impact on the problems she experiences. The chaos created by her unruly children overwhelms her. Her deficits make it nearly impossible to provide the firm discipline and structure her children need so desperately. She continues to delude herself into thinking she can manage everything by herself.

Donna avoids her problems the way Scarlett O'Hara avoided hers. She chooses to deny they exist. Denial is an integral part of grief when a loved one dies. It provides time for mobilizing strength to cope with the realization of the loss. Denial is a healthy, essential step that leads to ultimate acceptance.

The end of a relationship or a job, the loss of a body part or an alteration in self-image can also set the grief process in motion. Donna is grieving the loss of *a perfect, healthy self*, replaced with the label of ADD. She has always known that something was wrong but hasn't found comfort in her diagnosis. Similar to a widow who keeps her long deceased spouse's belongings as if he were still alive, Donna is stuck in denial. Because she can't acknowledge her limitations she can't move beyond them toward a stage of acceptance.

Donna uses her *It Ain't So* defense to run frantically in circles, trying to avoid facing herself. Unable to *own* her ADD, she continues to attribute her problems to something or somebody else. She refuses to take needed medication or avail herself of professional help. She expends considerable energy trying to keep everything together. Her misguided efforts, however, don't yield results. If she can ever face her situation realistically, she'll be able to use her creative mind to find solutions.

Learned Helplessness

Tracy is a modern day Prissy, the flaky servant girl in the movie *Gone With the Wind* who didn't "know nothin' 'bout birthin' babies". Played by Butterfly McQueen, Prissy affected a simple-minded air that helped her avoid responsibilities.

In the era of slavery this defense was both clever and appropriate. "Stupid like a fox" Prissy used her helplessness as a mechanism for control without risking the severe consequences of outright rebellion. Tracy has learned that helplessness works as effectively for her as it did for Prissy. Approaching her fiftieth birthday, she has spent years learning to play the role to the hilt.

Tracy never worries about failure. Similar to the manipulator, she avoids her responsibilities at work and in her social life by getting others to do everything for her. She smiles charmingly as she appeals to others for help. Her method differs from Todd's. She openly uses helplessness as her ploy. She flatters and boosts the egos of her rescuers, contrasting her poor, *dumb little me* act with their competence.

Women have been frequently characterized as incompetent and helpless. We aren't trying to perpetuate an unfortunate stereotype by casting Tracy in her maladaptive feminine role. Her helplessness is a coping strategy used by many members of oppressed groups such as minorities and women. If you are otherwise powerless as Prissy was, you can use helplessness to survive and exercise some control. Few men use this coping strategy because playing helpless isn't an acceptable male role in our society. Men can't get away with it!

Although Tracy is bright and personable, her ADD has always made her feel unable to cope with the realities of her life. *Learned Helplessness* makes her life easier to handle. She manages to remain unstressed, but also unchallenged. Tracy needs help in affirming her abilities so she can feel comfortable enough to risk failure and find success.

Controlling

You probably know Jack or someone similar. At 56 years old, he lives by the adage, "He who has the gold, rules". He establishes himself as the undisputed ruler of his kingdoms at home and at work. He has used his intelligence, creativity and high energy level to rise to a high powered position in a large corporation. Jack has aggressively and relentlessly climbed high on the ladder of success. He seems to have used the symptoms of his ADD to his advantage and should be congratulated for his efforts. . .Or should he?

Jack measures his success against external rewards of financial gain. Unfortunately, he has orchestrated his success through his domination of the people in his life. He monopolizes conversations and insists on having the last word. He makes all decisions at home and on the job. He regards his beautiful wife as an earned bonus and treats her as a *subject* in his kingdom. At work he always sets the agenda at meetings even when it isn't his responsibility. If someone else chairs a meeting, he subtly undermines the agenda, steering it in a direction that suits his needs.

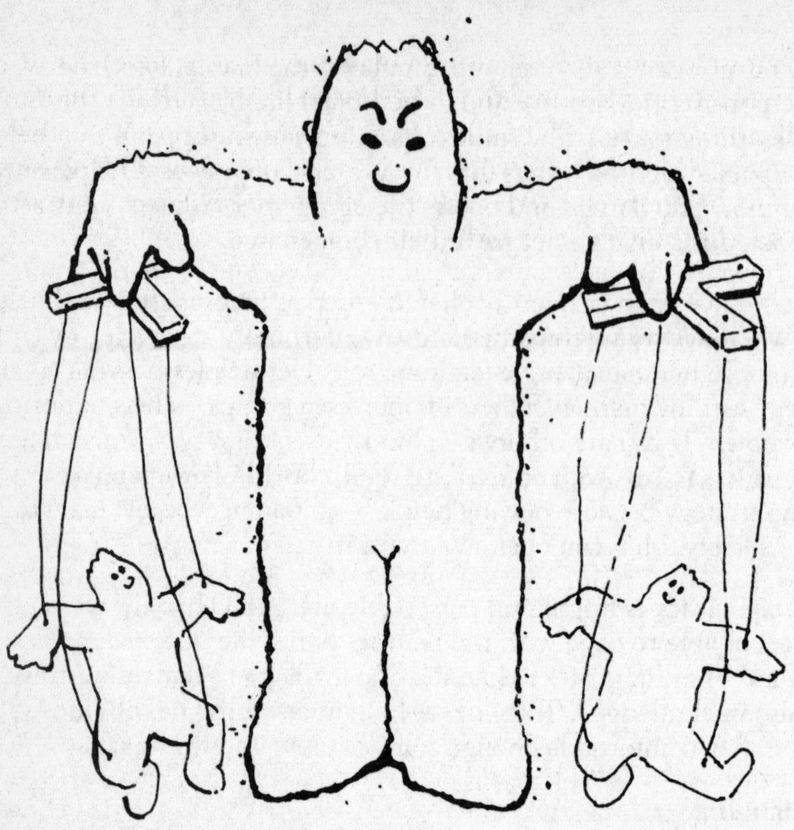

He makes unilateral decisions, often incurring the wrath of his peers for his failure to consult with them. His resentful colleagues and employees are ready to lynch him. His wife is fed up and is thinking about leaving him. He has made an impressive array of enemies who would like nothing more than to *overthrow the king*.

Just as Tracy seems the stereotyped helpless woman, Jack represents the stereotyped domineering, aggressive and controlling man. Certainly there are women who operate in similar fashion to Jack. Usually they are toppled more quickly. In general, controlling behavior in females isn't accepted any more than helplessness is in men.

One could argue that "The way Jack is, is the way he is; he's just a controlling kind of guy." It's true that men and women with ADD may be aggressive and bossy by temperament. Controlling behavior like Jack's, however, can be more than an expression of one's nature. It can be a learned defense mechanism that becomes a hiding place from deficits.

While it isn't readily apparent from his behavior, *King Jack* lives in perpetual terror of looking stupid. At home, he controls his family's agenda to avoid the risk that his wife will choose an activity that will expose his weaknesses. At work, he *commands* all discussions because he knows he's only effective when he follows his own train of thought. By not letting anyone else contribute, he avoids the confusion and embarrassment he feels when questions and comments derail him.

Jack's *Controlling* defense mechanism may backfire. One false move and he may maneuver himself out of a job and a family.

Character Sketches of Folk You May Know

The ADDers you've met use acquired defense mechanisms to protect themselves from public exposure of their deficits. We've examined the rationale for their choices and the ways in which their coping strategies are maladaptive.

Human behavior is too complex to explain within the context of defense mechanisms alone. Beneath the defenses are the individual characteristics we are born with. Maladaptive ADD behaviors are a combination of various learned defensive maneuvers and specific deficits.

In the next section, we'll look more closely at behavioral manifestations of specific deficits. These vignettes aren't condemnations of ADDers—we get plenty of them! Rather, we have designed them to illustrate what can happen if ADD symptoms flourish without control or intervention.

The Peter Pan Syndrome: 48 Going on 12

You may be familiar with the *Peter Pan Syndrome*, popularized in a book on the subject.[23] People in our society normally experience some regret at leaving childhood and taking on adult responsibilities. Most of us, however, manage to bite the bullet and make the transition into adulthood. Chris is a *Peter Pan* who has decided that growing up is simply not worth it.

As Chris approaches his forty-ninth birthday, he continues to live in a state of perpetual childhood. He has a personality that attracts people. Energetic optimism, a wacky sense of humor and a warm acceptance of others make the people around him feel good.

He always has more invitations than he can accept. The ease with which he connects with people promises an intimacy that never materializes. After an initial period of an intense connection, would-be lovers and close friends find him an elusive man, impossible to pin down. He refuses to make plans, preferring to live from moment to moment. The notion of commitment to goals or a relationship is incomprehensible to Chris. He just wants to have fun and is mystified when other people feel betrayed by his broken promises.

He disappoints bosses and coworkers as well as friends. His high energy level and intelligence generate expectations for superior job performance. After an initial burst of energy, Chris typically becomes bored with a project and loses motivation. His work becomes sloppy and careless. When a job becomes boring or a boss begins pressuring him to *get serious*, Chris switches to another one.

Lovers get similar treatment. When they begin to make demands for a more committed relationship, they find that Chris has moved on. The women hurt by his "love 'em and leave 'em" lifestyle feel used and abused. Chris believes, however, that he's just operating under a different set of rules. He lives according to the pleasure principle and its primary goal of maximizing pleasure and minimizing pain.

All of us operate on the pleasure principle to a certain extent. When we're born, we're virtual bundles of wants and needs without any sense of people outside ourselves. As we grow and are socialized by family and society, we gain awareness of our responsibilities to others. The psychologically healthy adult learns to strike a balance between her needs and the needs of the people in her world.

Chris is an adult by virtue of his chronological age but he hasn't developed psychologically or emotionally beyond a child of 12. Similar to Peter Pan, he just *don't wanna grow up*.

People with ADD often have many childlike qualities. A lifelong sense of playfulness and an ability to take risks are delightful qualities. But if we allow our essential nature to have free rein, we can begin to resemble Chris. We can drift mindlessly through life, heedless of our responsibilities and our impact on other people.

The Space Cadet

It isn't uncommon for ADD adults to say they are spacey. When the mental fog descends, they can become disoriented and forgetful. Some of us, however, settle too comfortably into waking dream states, becoming lifers in the *Academy for Space Cadets!*

Sean is 37 years old and has joined the academy. He is a gentle soul with a fanciful imagination and a gift for poetry. He spends his days daydreaming, writing, and having long philosophical conversations with his cronies. Sean takes little notice of practicalities. He earns meager wages as a writer but doesn't worry because material things are of no consequence to him.

He does his own thing, oblivious to the world around him. When he was single, his lifestyle wasn't a problem. But now he's married and has four children. Sean's wife is exhausted and at her wit's end trying to cope single-handedly with the large family. Sean is always pleasant and soft spoken with his spouse and children. He tries to do whatever they ask of him—that is, when they manage to capture his attention!

Sadly, Sean makes little effort to tune in to the world around him. Unless someone demands his attention, he's content to spend time drifting on his own mental clouds. He never set out to dump all the responsibility in his wife's lap but that's effectively what has happened. He plays with the kids when he wakes up long enough to notice them but his wife rarely leaves him alone with them. She's terrified that the toddler would poison herself right under her daddy's less than watchful eye. Sean isn't callously allowing his wife to work like a dog while he sits and daydreams. *He doesn't even notice*. The varied duties and details of family life totally escape him.

Sean may not be a manipulative user but he certainly isn't off the hook. It's okay to retreat to a dream world when you have only yourself to consider. It's a different story entirely when you're responsible for a family and the welfare of young children. Even though Sean's ADD can't be cured, he could work harder to shoulder his responsibilities. Right now he's too comfortable in the fog that obscures things he should worry about.

The Party Animal

The *Party Animal* lives for the weekend, enduring the work week that pays for her fun. She reluctantly controls her impulsive and hedonistic tendencies enough to earn a living, but lets them run amok after hours. Some adults with ADD don't even try to curb their impulsivity. They cut loose whenever they can, short of getting into big trouble.

You may know Ginny. She is an ADD adult in her late '20's who works full time at a secretarial job she absolutely hates. She doesn't do anything about changing her work situation, however, because she thinks all jobs are probably equally boring. At work she spends as much time as she can get away with, chatting on the phone with friends, doing her nails and dreaming about winning the lottery.

She wears a bored expression and frequently yawns when people talk to her. She bides her time, counting off the days until the glorious **TGIF!** On Fridays, as the hands on the clock point to 5:00 p.m., Ginny turns into someone you wouldn't even recognize.

Her routine follows the same pattern every week. First, she hits several *Happy Hours* with a group of partying friends. She gets more than a little smashed as she flirts her way around the room, making only brief contacts with individual men. After the happy hour, Ginny and her friends go out dancing and usually close the place down.

She spends a good chunk of her paycheck on clothes and most of her free time on shopping and scoping out the latest dances and fads. Despite her talent for tracking current fashions, she hasn't apparently heard about safe sex or the joys of sobriety.

Ginny has never had trouble finding other *Party Animals*. She has a great sense of fun and enough energy to get any party off the ground. Her weekend is an endless round of sex, drugs, dancing and anything else that seems to be fun. Lately, however, Ginny has been feeling a little uneasy about her lifestyle—one of her friends recently tested positive for the HIV virus. Her partying crowd seems to be getting younger and younger. Friends her own age are settling down to career goals and families.

Nonstop partying is a lifestyle that begins to look pathetic as the years go by and the expected settling down never happens. It isn't only empty but downright dangerous in this age of deadly diseases and rampant drug problems.

Ginny may be singing "The Party's Over", sooner than she thinks…

Emotional Incontinence
This behavior doesn't have anything to do with bodily functions! Rather, it is rampant, uncontrolled emotional output. As ADDers, we have a hard time modulating our erratic moods. Staying reasonably calm can be a full time job! Unless we want other people to write us off as immature or crazy, we have to expend the effort.

At 27 years old, Jeff has a serious case of *Emotional Incontinence*. He doesn't make any effort to control his extreme ups and downs. The atmosphere in his house is always thick with the fallout from his latest mood. His family rides the roller coaster along with him, cowering from his rages, sinking into gloom or becoming infected with unreasonable giddiness. The members of his household feel exhausted and tense. They deplete their energy reserves as they try to cope with his moodiness. He has lost more than one job because of his temper and is close to losing his second wife, as well.

Sadly, in social situations beyond his home, Jeff doesn't have any impact at all. Other people size him up quickly and decide not to take him seriously. They view his rages as the pathetic tantrums of a young child. They ignore his great ideas because he always expresses them in an embarrassing outpouring of enthusiasm. They treat him as a child who lacks restraint. Acquaintances pat him on the head as they quickly dismiss him.

In Jeff's case, **more is definitely less.** Emotional expression has greater impact as it becomes more intense—but only to a point! Drama can quickly deteriorate into melodrama, evoking laughter rather than empathy. People like Jeff who don't control their emotional output run the risk of becoming caricatures of themselves.

The Blabber

Mary is Jeff's close relative. She also has a bad case of incontinence but hers is *Verbal Incontinence*. Although her official title is "Manager of Order Processing", her colleagues have dubbed her *Typhoid Mary, Rumor Distribution Manager.* They can count on hearing the latest office dirt from Mary who has assumed responsibility for broadcasting everyone's confidential information.

With her warmth, good listening skills and grandmotherly manner, 60 year old Mary easily made friends with coworkers. Her new friends, however, quickly learned to keep their distance when they discovered that Mary talked as much as she listened! Now, everyone fears the effects of her loose tongue.

She isn't a vicious back-stabber. She truly cares about her colleagues and wants to lend a listening ear when they have problems. But she fails to reflect on the confidentiality of shared information and indiscriminately and inappropriately *distributes rumors*.

The angry reactions that greet her news continually surprise her. Since she has no qualms about sharing her own deepest secrets with total strangers, she can't understand why others are upset when she shares their secrets. To Mary, the human race is just one big happy family and families don't keep secrets from each other, do they?

The Bulldozer

A bulldozer is a well-designed piece of machinery. In short order, it can transform an acre of tree-covered land to a flattened, barren landscape. In similar fashion, some ADDers *bulldoze* their way through their lives, leaving little untouched or unharmed. This is Richard's style and it has left him with an empty life.

Richard's mother says he was born with a will of iron and a voice that could shatter glass with a whisper. From his earliest days, he made everyone in the household dance to the tune of his angry cries. Throughout childhood, he went directly for anything he wanted and shoved anybody aside who got in his way. Now that he's a 43 year old adult, he seems ruthless and cold as he continues to bulldoze his way over other people's feelings. He is successful in business but lives in a lonely world. He doesn't understand why people seem to avoid him.

Richard really doesn't get it at all. He's oblivious to the impact of his forceful nature and is honestly puzzled when others keep him at arm's length. As he pushes his way through life, he's aware only of his goals and takes little notice of the people he shoves aside to reach them.

Please remember that the negatives of ADD comprise only one dimension of the disorder. ADDers come in an assortment of packages. There are differences in specific symptoms and in the ways each of us manages these differences. Many of us do an amazingly wonderful job of coping with symptoms of the ADD we never even knew we had!

Lacking an understanding of their deficits, many ADDers feel compelled to spend inordinate time and energy trying to *pass* as normal.

This is a term we've borrowed from Afro-American history. With a long history of discrimination in this country, it isn't surprising that some lighter skinned Blacks managed their lives by pretending they were white.

In similar fashion, many of us with ADD can pass as normal (whatever normal means). We work hard at hiding our differences. We can identify with the adults in this chapter who have been somewhat successful in their efforts but who have paid dearly for fitting in.

We spend our lives in fear,
feeling like impostors who will be found out at any moment.

A recurring theme throughout the vignettes is the importance of squarely facing one's behaviors and honestly evaluating them. Many of us, along with the people in our lives, have spent lifetimes wondering why we do the things we do. We have never considered our behaviors as symptoms and haven't analyzed our coping strategies as defense mechanisms developed to hide inadequacy. Lacking knowledge about the role ADD plays in our lives, we resign ourselves to the "truth" of the assumptions made about us—we are indeed lazy, stupid or crazy!

If a parent or teacher suspected a problem, she usually attributed it to poor motivation or a dysfunctional family. Even when a diagnosis of hyperactivity was made in childhood, the prescription was for Ritalin and patience. "Take this pill twice a day, Monday through Friday during the school year, and wait until you outgrow your hyperactivity in adolescence." Some of us have been waiting a very long time for this miraculous change to occur!

The fact is, many of our readers have never been evaluated at all. Although there isn't anything magical about a diagnosis, it is a vital, initial step in changing faulty self-perceptions. Even if you feel fairly certain that you have ADD, you owe it to yourself to have a complete evaluation.

In the next chapter we'll look at the process of a diagnostic evaluation and share information that can help you make some decisions about accessing this help. As you may guess, the diagnostic evaluation of

ADD adults is less well defined than that of children. So, you'll need to proceed with caution in finding the professional you'll work with in this important part of your recovery.

CHAPTER 6

I KNOW...I THINK...I HAVE ADD WHAT DO I DO NOW?

The diagnosis and treatment of a garden variety illness is fairly straightforward. A throat culture uncovers a strep infection and the patient takes a round of antibiotics and goes on his way. A few days later he feels great. He has come to expect that powerful antibiotics will quickly and easily fix his illness. He views his medical care as a relatively simple process:

Symptoms—medical tests—diagnosis—treatment—CURE!

The process of uncovering ADD is considerably more complicated. Often, the process never even begins because the symptoms are behavioral, not physical. Many people view behavior as the **cause,** not the **symptom** of disorder. It usually goes something like this:

Behaviors—faulty assumptions—blame—punishment—
POOR PROGNOSIS!

For many, if not most of us, the initial discovery of ADD doesn't come from a professional. It comes from reading an ADDer's life story that could be our autobiography. It comes from talking with a friend whose description of his ADD sounds remarkably similar to our own behaviors. It comes when our children, who are "chips off the old block", are diagnosed with ADD.

Adults in support groups talk of learning about their ADD in all these ways. Most of these adults say they waited a while before seeking professional help to confirm their self-diagnoses. They used this time to read about ADD and to examine their lives to see if the information fit their experiences. Unable to find much information about ADD in adults, many resorted to reading the predominantly child oriented literature.

Your Job as a Mental Health Consumer

If you are beginning a similar process of self-discovery, your first responsibility is to thoroughly educate yourself about this disorder. Part of your self-education should include learning about the professional resources in your community. When you're ready to proceed with an evaluation, you shouldn't *let your fingers do the walking* through the yellow pages of the phone book to find the services you'll need!

We recommend that you contact the nearest chapter of an ADD support group. The group can give you a list of ADD informed professionals in your area. Make sure that you ask for names of professionals who are competent in diagnosing and treating adults. Also ask your local organization to put you in touch with other ADD adults who can tell you about their experiences with professionals on the referral list. You may be fortunate to locate an ADD adult support group that can be an invaluable, informal referral network. For help in locating a group in your area, refer to the resource list in the appendix.

Remember that you are the customer and a consumer of mental health services. To be an informed consumer, you need to do your homework before you make your first appointment. You need to proceed carefully because many good therapists have little knowledge about ADD.

When you first meet with the mental health professional you have chosen, ask as many questions as you want. If you aren't comfortable with him after your initial meeting, don't hesitate to go on to the next professional on your list. Your mental health is too important to entrust to someone you don't think understands your issues.

After the evaluation is completed, be sure to request a follow-up appointment to discuss the results of your testing. If you don't specifically ask, the professional may just send a highly technical report to you or your psychiatrist.

Psychologist or Psychiatrist: What's the Difference?

If you have had limited experience with the mental health profession, you may find a confusing array of titles:

Ph.D., Psy.D., Ed.D., M.D.
Clinical Psychologist, Neuropsychologist, Psychologist, Educational Psychologist, Cognitive Psychologist, Neurologist, Psychiatrist

It really isn't quite as confusing as it appears! But a brief clarification of the role of these various professionals may be in order. The specialties fall into two broad categories: psychologists and physicians. Although some physicians (psychiatrists) have expertise in testing, the diagnostic evaluation is usually done by a psychologist. This professional will be from the field of Clinical Psychology, Neuropsychology, Educational or Cognitive Psychology. A neurologist who is a medical doctor, sometimes does the evaluation. A neurological evaluation, however, is usually unnecessary except in cases of a seizure disorder or other specific neurological problems.

After the diagnosis, your mental health professional will make recommendations about treatment options and may refer you to someone else. You can choose any ADD informed professional for subsequent non-medical treatment but you must consult with a psychiatrist (MD) for drug treatment. The psychiatrist will prescribe and monitor medication in concert with your psychologist or as part of his own overall treatment plan for you.

The Diagnostic Evaluation

Parents sometimes ask how they should prepare their children for the medical tests that will be part of the diagnostic process—the blood tests and brain scans. This is a reasonable question since these testing procedures are often part of a medical diagnosis. Although blood tests aren't included, extensive neurological work-ups are sometimes used with ADD children. In general, this won't be included in the diagnostic evaluation of a suspected attention deficit disorder in an adult.

If you haven't gone through the evaluation process yet, you may also be wondering what to expect during the testing. After all, the very thought of tests may strike terror in your heart!

Tests—aren't those the things we always failed??

Well, you may "fail" some of these too, but that's okay. The tests will be used for the right reasons—for knowledge and discovery of your strengths and weaknesses. You won't have to cram for these tests and we can't even tell you exactly which ones to expect. Each psychologist uses a slightly different battery of tests from a number of available choices. Your psychologist will evaluate the results of these tests to confirm what he has learned from the history of your problems and his observations of your behavior.

The psychologist uses the test results in much the same way your physician uses a chest X-ray to confirm his diagnosis of your pneumonia. Although your physical examination and reported complaints may strongly suggest pneumonia, your doctor reduces his margin of error by confirming his diagnosis with the X-ray.

Since there are no lab tests available to confirm the ADD diagnosis, mental health professionals often rely on educational and psychological testing. They provide a more unbiased, objective method of diagnosis than observation and history alone.

Understanding Your Diagnosis

Your follow-up appointment should be a detailed, fact-finding mission. You should ask questions about why certain tests were used, what they measured and how you compared with the normal range for a particular test. When your psychologist explains your results, ask for clarification if he uses terms you don't understand.

No two ADD people are alike. You should use your follow-up meeting to learn as much as you can about your unique neuropsychological profile. If you leave this meeting armed only with your checklist of deficits, you'll have only half the information you need. You must also have a clear understanding of your unique strengths and the positive compensatory strategies you already use.

You can't expect to leave this meeting with all the tools you'll need to manage your ADD. You can expect to leave with specific information about your individual strengths and weaknesses and a framework of treatment options.

After the Diagnosis—Your Role in Treatment

The homework you did in locating your mental health professional will pay dividends as you begin treatment. You must become an active participant in your treatment, working with your physician or psychologist to problem-solve. Since information about adult ADD is limited, a flexible, experimental approach to treatment is usually necessary.

If you're going to use medicine in your treatment, it's essential that you establish a partnership with your physician. Finding the right medication and dosage is generally a trial and error process. There isn't any magic formula the physician can use to determine in advance the medicine that will work best for you.

If your mental health professional becomes defensive or pats you on the head when you ask questions or offer ideas, find a new one! We've been contacted by adults who can't find informed professionals in their areas. Should you find yourself in a similar situation, you may have to seek out someone who is willing to learn!

The Practical Side of Evaluation and Treatment—
What's it Going to Cost?
This discussion wouldn't be complete without a word about cost. The testing process is time consuming and can rapidly run up a large bill—the fee for psychological testing can range from $400 to $1500. Before committing to testing or treatment, ask about approximate costs and ways to cut corners if you are uninsured or on a tight budget. You may be able to work out a payment schedule in advance if the bill for testing is too large to pay at one time.

Carefully scrutinize your insurance policy. Some don't cover or only partially cover psychological services. Some specifically exclude ADD from coverage. We don't want to discourage you from seeking a diagnosis and treatment. **You are worth the price** even if it means skipping your summer vacation this year. We just want you to be prepared so you can plan and avoid rude financial shocks.

In a later section we'll talk specifically about various treatment options for ADD adults. Although professional help will likely be an important part of your treatment, we want to focus primarily on self-help which is the guiding principle of this book. We firmly believe that you are capable of helping yourself and we want to help you learn how to do it.

Getting Down To Work

Okay, so you know, or feel fairly certain that an Attention Deficit Disorder is at the root of your problems. You know you were born with the deficits and grew up with them. You know you're different from someone without ADD. You know you've learned various *not so great* ways of coping with them. SO WHAT DO YOU DO NOW?

What you do now is take a deep breath, find some time for yourself and look squarely at your ADD. It is inseparable from who you are. What you do now is decide that **you are worth all the work it will take to recover.**

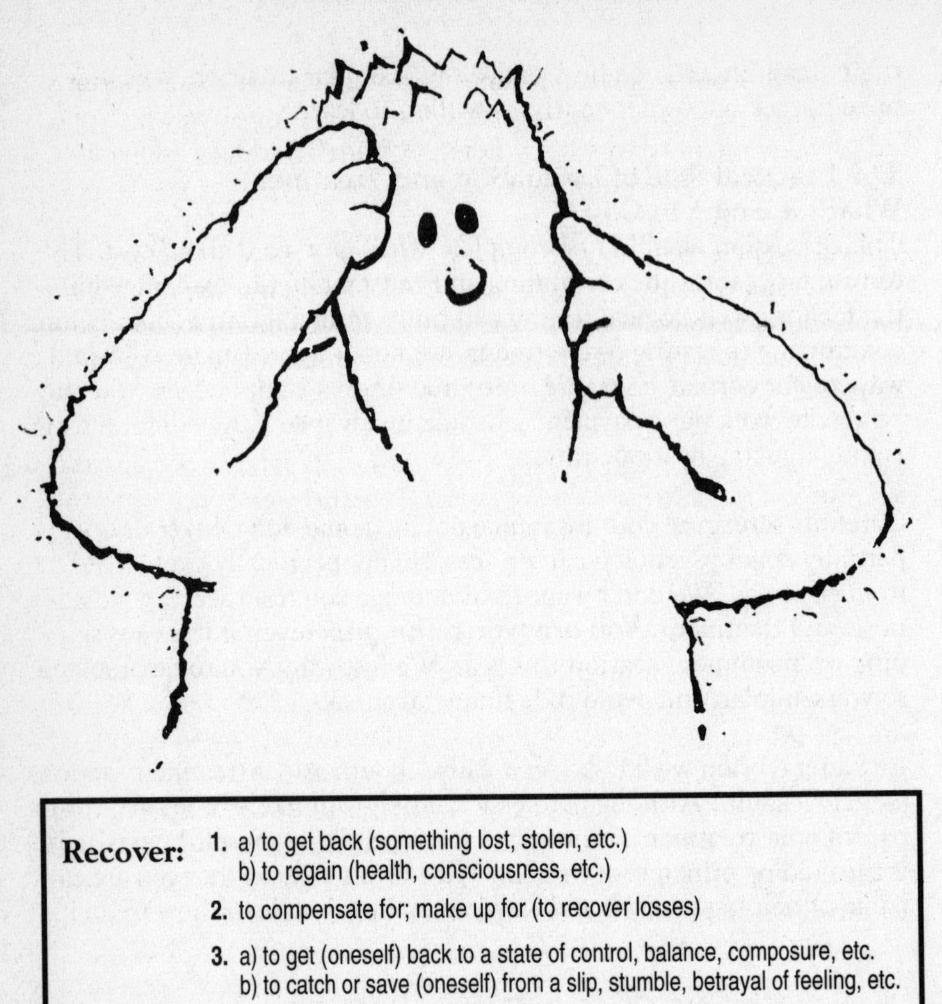

Recover:

1. a) to get back (something lost, stolen, etc.)
   b) to regain (health, consciousness, etc.)
2. to compensate for; make up for (to recover losses)
3. a) to get (oneself) back to a state of control, balance, composure, etc.
   b) to catch or save (oneself) from a slip, stumble, betrayal of feeling, etc.

New World Dictionary of the American Language, Simon and Shuster, 1980

To regain, compensate, get back control and balance, save oneself—this is what you do now. The remainder of this book is about this process of recovery. We'll move from the theoretical to the practical and offer specific guidelines and suggestions that can make recovery possible.

We can't emphasize enough that recovery is a process that requires a lot of work. It isn't something that will magically happen after you read this book. You must commit yourself to believing that you are worth all the work it will take to recover.

If you're still reading, we can assume that you've made this important commitment to yourself. You won't be sorry. You have so much to offer and so many talents to discover! Let's get started and take a look at some important issues you'll need to consider.

ADD is inseparable from who you are. We made this observation at the outset but what does it really mean? ADD is an acronym for Attention Deficit Disorder. *Deficit...? Disorder...?* If ADD is inseparable from who you are, does this mean that disability is your only dimension? Absolutely not!

Your differences are only one part of you. If society has learned anything from the efforts of the physically disabled to gain equal access, it's that we are all people first. If more time and energy were spent developing the unique abilities of all people, we would have a more productive society.

As you learn to help yourself, you must never focus more on your disabilities than the total person you are. It's a mistake, however, to totally ignore your differences. The tricky thing for ADD adults is that many of us grew up never knowing we had a disability. ADD is inseparable from who we are because we forged our senses of self around it, never knowing it was there. Most of us haven't grown up with the benefit of knowing we had a handicap. We grew up thinking we just weren't as smart, competent or valuable as other people.

Now that you know you have ADD, it should be easy to make a recipe to turn out a great person, right? Well, it doesn't quite work that way. You may know intellectually that you have ADD. Grappling with that knowledge on an emotional level, however, is a very different and difficult proposition:

It is a task of truly accepting that you aren't perfect.

You must say good-bye to your old self-image, whatever that may have been and admit that your problems won't go away by changing your job, your friends or your spouse. The vague feeling you've always had that something was wrong has been confirmed and given a name. What a scary place to be—in adulthood, trying to figure out who you'll be when you grow up.

Your newly acquired self-knowledge may be scary but it's also liberating. It offers a wonderful opportunity to take control of your life by looking squarely at your limits and growing beyond them. This requires courage and time. It requires working through a process of self-acceptance that begins with grieving.

When a loved one dies we can't move on with our lives until we have grieved and moved through the stages of shock, anger, denial, bargaining and depression. Similarly, when we lose a part of our psychological selves including an alteration in our self-concept, we must grieve the lost sense of self before we can work on building a new one. You may not have thought of your ADD in this way, but:

Grieving has to be the beginning of your self-discovery.

Let's take a look at how the process works. You may already have moved through some of the stages. It never hurts, however, to regroup and rethink your progress since recovery is an ongoing process.

Grief—The Shock of Recognition

The diagnosis is often both a punch in the stomach and a vindication of years of struggle and feelings of inadequacy. We knew something was wrong and now we have the test results to prove it. We don't have to feel like impostors anymore, living in fear of being found out. What a relief!

KK: "When I went through psychotherapy in my '20's, my constant theme was that I felt different. I always struggled with comparing myself to other people, unable to figure out how they could so easily manage the things I sweated over. I wondered if they had some secret to which I wasn't privy or if they managed to accomplish a lot at the expense of their families.

Since I couldn't go to college and do much of anything else at the same time, I assumed that being a student meant giving up everything outside school. I didn't know that it was just easier for other people. I assumed that I was too self-indulgent to accept the challenges.

When I was diagnosed with ADD, the relief was enormous—I was finally able to make sense of my struggles. Having ADD meant that I wasn't bad, lazy, unmotivated or stubborn. It meant that I could look at my life through different colored lenses. I could stop filtering my accomplishments through the expectations I based on comparisons to others. I began to marvel at all I had managed to do in spite of a significant disability.

The mid-life crisis I had been working on resolved itself when I shed a positive light on the life I had lived up to that point. Although I had gained positive self-esteem as a result of psychotherapy, it was nothing compared to the boost of my changing view of myself as a heroically struggling adult.

I began to feel less apologetic for my shortcomings and more deserving of help and understanding. Accompanying the relief was the hope that I could be fixed now that I finally understood the basis for my problems."

PR: "I always struggled silently with my deficits. Neither my grades in school nor any of my relationships ever suffered outwardly. The only person who knew I was a failure was me. It was an incredible burden.

The people in my life didn't destroy me. I destroyed myself with intense feelings of inadequacy. Perhaps the worst period in my life was when my little brother died. I was 14 years old and into driving my parents crazy with my adolescent stuff. Roger hit a tree when he was sledding and died the next morning. He was only 10 years old and indisputably the perfect child in my family. He was so perfect. I was so imperfect. And he had to die! I knew that it should have been me.

No one ever knew how I felt. To this day, my parents don't know how I agonized over screwing this one up by not being the one who died. Learning at 39 that I had ADD didn't miraculously free me from my impaired sense of self, but it offered a peace I had never known before. It was a relief to know, at least in my intellectual self, that my feelings had a basis. My struggles came from deficits over which I had no control. The diagnosis alone didn't undo years of silent pain but gave me a reality I could use to work on readjusting my self-image.

I wish my brother hadn't died but I've been able to alter my perspectives of his life and mine. Neither of us had more value than the other. His death just happened and I finally believe that it's okay that it wasn't me instead."

Grief: Anger—"Why Me?"

The initial stage of relief and euphoria often gives way to a period of anger. The diagnosis that frees us from faulty assumptions begins to feel like an unbearable burden. Facts don't lie. We are imperfect and it just isn't fair!

> *"Why me? Why did I have to be born this way?"*
>
> *"Why did everyone—parents, teachers, therapists—blame my difficulties on depression, lack of motivation or poor character?"*
>
> *"Why didn't somebody believe in me?"*
>
> *"Why did everybody assume the worst—that I just wasn't trying hard enough?"*
>
> *"Why was I misunderstood and reprimanded when I was trying my heart out?"*
>
> *"Why did all those mental health professionals pretend to know more than they really did?"*

We may feel furious at the people in our lives who failed to recognize our deficits. We understand that no one knew much about ADD ten or twenty years ago. But somehow, we still feel that if only our parents had loved and respected us enough, they would have figured it out. They should have known our problems were real. We often begin to feel helpless and victimized.

Grief: Denial—Not Me!

Remember Donna? She struggles with her inability to move beyond the *intellectual* knowledge of her ADD to the *emotional* knowledge. It's not that she rejects the reality of her disorder. She simply denies its impact on her life.

Denial can take several forms. After an initial sense of anger, we might decide to reject the diagnosis, wondering why we ever wasted our money on the evaluation. We might, as Donna does, announce to friends that we have ADD but then not seek treatment. We might pick up our prescription for Ritalin but never use it. We might take the medication with the mistaken belief that we have found the cure for our problems. We move into this new phase of our lives with rosy fantasies of how with the help of our local pharmacy, we can conquer the world.

Regardless of the brand of denial we choose during this stage, we aren't dealing yet with the reality of our ADD. We need time to process our new knowledge and confront ourselves with our weaknesses. At this early stage in the process of recovery, we don't recognize the face reflecting back to us in the mirror:

*"That isn't the person I used to be,
and I'm not ready to figure out who it really is."*

Bargaining—It Can All Be Fixed

As we begin to make sense of everything, we bargain with God or fate to forestall facing the inescapable fact of our disorder. The deal goes something like this: "If I'm really good, you'll give me back what I've lost."

For many ADD adults the bargaining is around medication that often brings at least initially dramatic, positive changes. A whole world opens up as the medication helps us emerge from lifelong fogs. Sights and sounds that had previously drifted by our conscious awareness are noticed for the first time. We are better organized and focused. We feel energized with a new sense of purpose and feel calmer and happier. This new tool is a great bargaining chip.

We promise ourselves to work diligently at pursuing the right dose of medication. When we find it, we know that our symptoms will go away. We'll be able to take responsibility for our behaviors and be like everybody else.

This strategy works for a while until awareness grows that maybe this isn't the answer to our problems. Our improved ability to pay attention makes us increasingly aware of our mistakes. We grudgingly acknowledge that our medicine hasn't cured them. It doesn't make us normal even though we promised to do everything right if only the Ritalin would fix us. We begin to notice the drug's uneven symptom control over the course of the day and our decreased functioning when the drug is at a low level.

Our diagnosis vindicates us from the invalid assumptions people have made about us. We've spent our anger railing about the injustice and have taken a step towards dealing with our symptoms. But we aren't fixed. Our bargaining doesn't work but we're still not ready to own our disorder. **We still aren't ready to accept that we'll struggle with ADD for the rest of our lives.**

Reality Sinks In—Depression

Our diagnosis is supposed to free, not imprison us. But that's often what happens at some point in our grief process. As adults, we resent having to relive the identity crisis of adolescence. We may not have been doing great before but at least we thought we knew who we were. At this point depression often sets in. For some ADD adults it returns periodically, threatening to undermine progress.

KK: "When depression set in, it was compounded by the growing certainty that my daughter also had ADD. I mixed us up in my mind during that time. Tyrell was my bright hope for the future. I put a lot of energy into carefully nurturing her self-esteem so she wouldn't have to go through what I did as a child. When I realized that ADD was at the root of many of my problems, I was frightened for my daughter.

In my state of gloom, I began to think that she was doomed as I was. If this problem was inherited and biological, there was no escape. I agonized over Tyrell's fate and my own. I ruminated about all the things I couldn't do and all the times I had failed. I relived each painful and humiliating experience from my past. My positive attributes and accomplishments ceased to exist. There was the triple whammy of feeling helpless as a parent, generally incompetent and without hope for the future. I said good-bye to many of my dreams, both the realistic and the unrealistic ones.

This stage was marked by extreme fragility. I constantly burst into tears and innocent remarks set me off. I laugh at it now but just hearing the word "memory" would bring tears to my eyes because it reminded me of my deficits. I sat in church every Sunday trying to hide the tears streaming down my face."

PR: "The relief I felt after my diagnosis was short-lived. In the months that followed, it was replaced with an assortment of conflicting feelings. Depression was one of them. It was a place I had frequently visited during my life. This time, however, there was no vagueness about my feelings of gloom.

I had often lived under a cloud of helplessness and hopelessness. The discovery of my ADD, however, brought my negative feelings crashing down around me. I had previously been able to pull myself out of my black fogs by reasoning that things really weren't **that** bad. My diagnosis brought this reasoning to a crashing halt. **Things really were that bad!** I would never be okay.

I already knew that my then 8 year old son would never be okay. I vividly recall the moment two years earlier when my fantasies about R. Jeremy abruptly ended. I sat in the psychologist's office, mentally checking off all the things he would never be able to do. Four months pregnant with a baby girl conceived after several years of infertility treatments, I felt gut-wrenching terror for both my children.

Remember my brother Roger? Well, I had given my son his name and I had an intense, frightening feeling of déja vu. What awful curse had I visited on my son? Would he also come to some terrible end?

Depression set in with a vengeance. I had previously resolved my issues around Jeremy's deficits and had accepted his imperfections. But here it was again—that damned ADD. This time it was mine. My feelings and fears about both my son and myself converged into some pretty self-destructive thoughts. Just when I was getting a handle on his problems, I was faced with the reality of my own.

It wasn't easy to move beyond my depression. It didn't happen overnight. But I did it. With persistence and a sense of humor, I climbed out of my deep, black hole again. I decided I didn't like it in there—it was too dark and I'm into bright, open spaces! I figured that with my family of four, I was *2 down, with 2 to go*. I did it twice and if I had to, I could do it again."

Out of the Depths—ACCEPTANCE!

If you keep working on the grief process, you will come to a new and better place in your life. The stages you will go through are often difficult and painful but **they're essential.** When the going gets rough, don't get discouraged. Visualize where you're going—to a place where you will discover and learn to use your valuable gifts.

PR: "One day last summer a terrible thunderstorm rocked our house and terrified my 4 year old daughter. When it finally ended there was an incredibly beautiful double rainbow stretching across the sky. Alison was dumbstruck because she had never seen a rainbow. After watching it a while, she announced that she hoped we'd have another bad storm soon so she could see another rainbow. Her fear disappeared, replaced with her child's optimism.

I've thought often about that storm since Alison comforted herself with the wonder of the resultant rainbows. It may be a cliché but my journey through my own personal storm has taught me to believe in the gold at the end of rainbow. It's there. It's real. It's within my grasp.

I know that I'll probably always have more storms than rainbows but that goes with the territory. I know that my journey will be an uphill struggle but the rewards are worth my efforts. I accept my son and myself as we are. We're all we've got, so we'd better make the most of our lives. Those complex and beautiful rainbows symbolized limitless possibilities. And so do we, my son and I."

KK: "I don't remember exactly when the depression began to lift. I know one sign of my emergence from gloom and doom was regaining the ability to laugh at myself. I joked about starting a new kind of AA group for people like me. I would call it *Airheads Anonymous*.

Understanding that I wasn't to blame for the way I was, relieved me of the guilt I had lived with for so long. I was a valuable person with a disability. I had deficits but they no longer defined who I was. They took their rightful place as one dimension of a multi-dimensional person. I began to feel more confident about my parenting skills and became less anxious about my daughter's future. I reasoned that if I could make it without any help during my childhood, Tyrell could do even better with support.

Coming to terms with my ADD meant spending far less time and energy hiding my deficits. I concentrated on understanding them without being consumed by them. I was finally free to take charge of my life and realistically assess it.

The months that followed were exciting and productive as I evaluated various career options. It became clear that I had a gift for writing and an ability to understand and connect with people. I was already using my people skills in my teaching and nursing but realized that many of the routine details of my work were painfully difficult for me. I decided to use my risk-taking ability to embark on a new venture, although it wasn't readily apparent what it would be!

I had been intensely interested in ADD since my diagnosis and wanted to specialize in it in some way. I just didn't know what direction to take. I liked the flexibility of teaching and enjoyed mentoring students but sensed that perhaps this wasn't quite the right niche. I wrestled with the issue of security vs. optimally using my interests and talents. With my newfound sense of inner strength, I was sure that I would eventually find what I was looking for.

When the answer came, everything fell in to place. I decided to write this book and asked Peggy to join me in this venture. The project had my name on it! I knew there were millions of people struggling with ADD and that there was limited help available for them. This book would be the perfect work choice for me.

I had impeccable credentials—who could know ADD better than someone who lived with it? I could use my experiences, varied background in education and mental health and my people and writing skills to work at something in which I was intensely interested. What a perfect job!

Life still has its ups and downs but I feel that I'm living it more fully now than I ever could have before this journey. Instead of hiding my weaknesses or working at things that are wrong for me, I can now celebrate my gifts."

In the remaining chapters of this book, we will offer a framework you can use to maximize your abilities and minimize your disabilities. The focus will be on what you **can** do rather than what you **can't** do. We want to help you discover your hidden strengths and talents and celebrate the person you are.

We don't presume to have all the answers. We can, however, help you formulate the questions you need to ask as you take responsibility for your recovery. We share your pain and your hope because we are struggling alongside you.

As you continue on your personal journey of recovery, consider the following quote by Cathy Better of Reistertown, Maryland. It appeared in the *Community Times* newspaper and is an empowering affirmation of the possibilities available to you with hard work and a deep commitment to yourself.

Each day that we awake is a new start, another chance.
Why waste it on self-pity, sloth and selfishness?
Roll that day around on your tongue, relish the taste of its freedom.
Breathe deeply of the morning air, savor the fragrance of opportunity.
Run your hands along the spine of those precious 24 hours
and feel the strength in the sinew and bone.
Life is raw material. We are artisans.
We can sculpt our existence into something beautiful,
or debase it into ugliness.
It's in our hands.

CHAPTER 7

About Balance, Toyotas,® Porsches,® Circus High Wires, and the Twelve Steps of Alcoholics Anonymous

Did we get your attention? Are you wondering about the connection between balance, cars, high wire acts, AA, ADD and recovery? Well, there is a connection and it's an important place to start learning how to effectively manage your ADD.

Balance may be something you only think about at the end of the month when your bank statement comes. One of life's little joys is a balanced checkbook. This doesn't happen nearly often enough. How many times do you decide that it isn't worth trying to figure out the discrepancy—that it's easier to accept the balance your bank says you have?

"The ADDer's Precarious High Wire Act"

As ADDers, achieving balance in our lives is critical and considerably more difficult to achieve than balance in our checkbooks. What is balance? It's a general concept, similar to freedom or success, that each of us defines individually. Let's find out how balance issues have an impact on the lives of ADD adults.

Warning—It's Very Easy for an ADDer to Lose Her Balance!
ADD folk have nervous systems that are erratic and poorly regulated. Rapid thoughts and an excitable nature are at odds with a central nervous system that can't handle too much input. The paradox is of an enthusiastic, creative and impulsive ADD adult who is often driven to get involved in more than she can handle. Since having ADD means that her basic nature is at war with itself, her life can indeed be a *High Wire Act!*

Achievement and Less Tangible Goals: There are many ways for an ADDer to lose the balance in her life. The delicate balance between achievement and other, less tangible goals is a critical balancing act. These days it seems that many people feel they live on fast-moving treadmills that lack off switches. Careers eat up family time and escalating demands create pressure cooker environments.

Unlike people who react to this pressure with mild stress symptoms, ADDers can fall apart completely. Of course this is often a first, essential step toward recovery. Falling apart can be the equivalent of an alcoholic hitting "rock bottom". For some alcoholics, rock bottom is getting a DUI citation. For others, it is a string of DUI's, a divorce, unemployment and hitting skid row. As awful as rock bottom may seem at the time for an alcoholic or an ADDer, it's often the starting point for a new and better life. It begins the recovery process because its awfulness forces the person to make some changes.

Structure and Freedom: To keep ourselves from falling off our high wire, many of us also need a proper balance of structure and freedom. We ADDers often balk at the structure we desperately need. A tendency to become easily over-stimulated means that chaotic lifestyles can get us into trouble. On the other hand, lives routinized into dullness by too much regimentation don't provide sufficient challenge.

We know that an ADD child needs externally imposed structure to thrive. When she becomes an adult, she continues to need limits but has to provide them for herself. Adults are expected to manage their own lives. The challenge is to establish a balance that offers order without stifling creativity, one of many ADD adults' best attributes.

Ways of Thinking, Activity Levels, Emotions and Needs: ADD brains and nervous systems are often out of balance with behavior swinging rapidly from one extreme to the other. An ADDer tends to excesses, alternating between bouts of workaholism and sluggish inactivity. Her moods swing up and down and her performance is erratic. The following list outlines some of these balance issues that can cause you to lose your footing on the high wire:

Work vs. Play
Do you tend to get over-involved in one or the other and have trouble shifting gears?

Your Needs vs. Others'
Are you oblivious to the feelings and points of view of others or do you always put yourself dead last?

Over vs. Understimulation
What is your optimal level of stress, noise, work and challenges?

Hyperactivity vs. Hypoactivity
Are you so active that you drive others crazy or do you vegetate most of the time? This includes sleep and rest patterns as well as daily activity levels.

Detailed vs. Global Thinking
Do you get caught up in too much detail unable to see the forest for the trees, or do you tend to focus on the gestalt or whole picture? If you focus on big pictures, do you have trouble keeping track of details?

Depression vs. Euphoria
Are your moods out of balance with too much sadness or excessive happiness? Do you swing between these two extremes?

The Value of Examining Balance Issues

It's easy for your balance in each of these areas to become skewed in either direction at different times. Alternately, you may find yourself regularly swinging erratically from one extreme to the other. The point of examining each of these areas is that imbalance in any of them can cause problems for your mental health or family life.

What's the connection we mentioned between balance, Toyotas and Porsches? In some respects, the ADD adult is designed like a Porsche. She is spirited, dynamic, powerful, exciting and ready to go with the rapid acceleration of an expensive sports car. Her non-ADD peers are more like the family Toyota. Equally well engineered, this Toyota has a more "even temperament." It is designed for comfort, reliability and fuel efficiency. If the ADD adult is to maintain and maximize the high performance of her Porsche, she has to take especially good care of herself.

One of the best ways you can do this is to work on achieving balance in your life. Having a well-balanced lifestyle is akin to taking good care of your car. It subjects the system to less wear and tear. To use the metaphor again, working on balance is similar to continually tinkering with and tuning up your car. If you want to keep your whole system in working order, you'll have to make on-going adjustments.

With limitations they can't ignore, ADDers who recover may well lead the rest of society to a saner way of life. Competence and levels of achievement have become the societal standard that measures a person's worth and success in life. Those who are "unproductive" due to age, health, or disability have been devalued because they don't "measure up". Society no longer values children or the aged as it previously did. A shocking number of children sink into poverty while stressed caregivers abuse many senior citizens.

This philosophizing isn't just the wandering of creative minds but relates directly to achieving balanced lives. You have a unique opportunity to redesign your success model and get off the crazy treadmill everyone else is on.

If you pay attention to the messages of your body and soul, you'll realize that you can't be all or do it all. If you work at your recovery, you can use your new self-knowledge to design a life that really works for you. You can be at peace with yourself and your environment while the rest of the world skyrockets out of control.

We've already talked about the connection between balance, cars and high wire acts. Now let's consider the last part of this chapter's title—Alcoholics Anonymous—as we move from general concepts to practical applications for achieving balance in your life.

How-To's of Achieving Balance

To help you get started, we're going to borrow the invaluable framework of the *Twelve Steps of Alcoholics Anonymous*. Although this program specifically refers to alcohol and alcoholics, it's possible to substitute virtually any chronic problem or disability. A variety of support groups have adopted this framework which is a sound program for creating a balanced life.

Briefly, the program is a systematic plan for acknowledging limitations to oneself and others, making amends to others whenever possible and coming to a greater self-acceptance. *Working the program* means making a commitment to follow the steps in daily life.

The Twelve Steps of A.A.[24]

1. We admitted we were powerless over alcohol—that our lives had become unmanageable.
2. Came to believe that a Power greater than ourselves could restore us to sanity.
3. Made a decision to turn our will and our lives over to the care of God as we understood Him.
4. Made a searching and fearless moral inventory of ourselves.
5. Admitted to God, to ourselves, and to other human beings the exact nature of our wrongs.
6. Were entirely ready to have God remove all these defects of character.
7. Humbly asked Him to remove our shortcomings.

8. Made a list of all persons we had harmed, and became willing to make amends to them all.
9. Made direct amends to such people wherever possible, except when to do so would injure them or others.
10. Continued to take personal inventory and when we were wrong, promptly admitted it.
11. Sought through prayer and meditation to improve our conscious contact with God as we understood Him, praying only for knowledge of His will for us and the power to carry that out.
12. Having had a spiritual awakening as the result of these Steps, we tried to carry this message to alcoholics, and to practice these principles in all our affairs.

Using The Twelve Steps for Your Personal Recovery from ADD

The steps are framed around a central concept of spiritual awareness that has relevance for ADDers. It's the glue that holds all the steps of the program together so that peace and self-acceptance can be achieved.

Spiritual awareness isn't specific to organized religion. The *Twelve Steps* carefully talk about *"God as we understand him"*, leaving the specifics to the individual. The word "God" can be replaced with a more generalized "higher power" that has meaning for each individual. The higher power could be the fellowship of other alcoholics (or in our case, other ADDers) or the whole of mankind. The idea is to focus on something greater than ourselves and realize that *we can't go it totally alone*. The Serenity Prayer sums up this philosophy:

GOD GRANT ME THE SERENITY
TO ACCEPT THE THINGS I CANNOT CHANGE,
TO CHANGE THE THINGS I CAN,
AND THE WISDOM TO KNOW THE DIFFERENCE.

Closely related to spiritual awareness and integral to the program is the issue of morality and wrongdoing. For the alcoholic, this issue is a critical part of her recovery. Typically the alcoholism has caused havoc in the lives of her friends and family and she must assume responsibility for her actions. This includes making amends to each of the people she has directly hurt.

These issues aren't relevant to your recovery from ADD except as they relate to those aspects of self you can change. For instance, if you've learned to use some maladaptive coping mechanisms that have hurt other people, you should take responsibility for your behaviors and make appropriate amends.

The issue of *powerlessness* detailed in the first three steps, however, has a direct implication for you as an adult with ADD. It means that you are powerless over your ADD in that it isn't anyone's fault and can't be cured.

Applying these steps in your own life means that you need to stop blaming your parents, spouse, children and yourself for the problems caused by your ADD. This doesn't mean that you absolve yourself from all responsibility for your behavior. It means that you acknowledge the reality of your imperfect self. Confronting your powerlessness includes an admission that you can't do it all—you are human and have unique limitations. If you have begun your process of grief, you may already be confronting and working at accepting your limitations.

The fourth principle also has significance for you as an ADD adult. This step instructs the individual to take a *moral* inventory. This should be similar to the one you develop for your homeowner's or renter's insurance. Rather than noting the condition and value of possessions, you should examine and list your assets, or abilities and your liabilities, or disabilities.

Your inventory is central to your recovery. Since your ADD can't be cured, your goal shouldn't be to **eliminate** your deficits. Instead it should be to **identify**, **accept** and **manage** them. A failure to confront your limitations can result in damaged emotional and spiritual health and a diminished sense of self. Later in this discussion, we'll offer some suggestions about how to compile this important inventory.

Evaluating Balance Issues in Your Life

We talked earlier in this chapter about general balance issues that can be important for you as an ADD adult. Now it's time for you to think about the balance in your own life. The following is a list of questions you can use to get started. You may never have really thought about some of them and may not be able to answer all of them right now. But keep them in mind throughout the discussion in this chapter. If you try some of the things we suggest, you may be able to answer them later.

1. What is your daily/weekly work capacity?
2. How much sleep and rest do you need, including "down time" when there are no demands placed on you?
3. What is your financial bottom line—how much income do you require to maintain an acceptable standard of living?
4. How much time should you devote to family and friends?
5. What must you do to renew yourself spiritually, not just in the sense of religion but regarding anything that gives your life meaning?
6. How much and what kind of recreational activities are critical for your well-being?
7. How long can you work efficiently without a break?
8. What obligations must you fulfill?
9. What things are cluttering your life and should be eliminated?
10. How much time do you spend daily on self-maintenance: grooming, dressing or health care?

Is Your Life in Balance?

You probably know that "all work and no play makes Johnny a dull boy." A balanced life must include time for work, relationships, spiritual renewal, recreation and rest. In today's fast track, dual career society, the pressures are such that even calm, well-organized folk become frazzled as they attempt to find time for everything.

The juggling act is daunting for you as an ADD adult. If you just go with the flow, you're likely to find yourself drifting in directions that aren't particularly helpful. You can get immersed in work and forget that you have a family or allow your socializing at work to interfere with the quality of your performance. Since you're distractible and have an elastic sense of time, you can't expect to let balance take care of itself. You have to carefully design it.

Conduct Your Own One Rat Study

To answer the questions we posed about the balance in your life, you'll need to conduct your own research experiment. It should include a daily log that tracks your activities for several weeks. Write down everything you do and how much time it takes. Also keep track of the difficulty of each task or event.

Rate the difficulty on a scale of one to ten. If you have trouble deciding how to rate something, pay attention to stress indicators. What happens when you face too many demands? Some people react to stress with muscle tension or headaches. Others become irritable or start tuning out. What is your pattern of stress indicators?

When your diary is complete, examine it for observable patterns. Did your stress indicators increase after a certain length of time on a task? If so, you have discovered how long you can work without a break or a shift to another activity. In similar fashion, you can begin to estimate your overall daily and weekly work capacity.

By keeping track of stress symptoms and altering the number of hours you work, you can determine how long you can work efficiently. Don't neglect the other areas of your life when you analyze your diary. Does exercise seem to lower your stress level and improve the quality of your work? What about the time you spend with your family?

Make a Personal Schedule

It's time to develop a tentative weekly schedule that includes an estimate of the time it takes to do each activity. As you pencil in time estimates on your schedule, be very careful. Refer to your diary to find out how long it took to complete various tasks and factor in extra time. Doubling your estimate for everything except sleep will give you a cushion for unexpected events and the distractions that inevitably derail ADDers.

We can almost guarantee that after the first week, you'll decide that your schedule is unworkable! You will probably find that everything you needed to do didn't fit into your time frames. We bet that if you did manage to stay on schedule, you were frazzled by the end of the week.

Your life is out of balance because you're trying to fit too much into it! This includes not just the quantity of activities but an accumulation of demands on your capacity for work and stress. After you've recovered from the shock of recognizing the impossibility of doing it all, you'll need to review your schedule with the goals of slicing and dicing it!

The demands on your life need to match your capacity and abilities and also fit into the time you have available. How do you get started figuring out what to cut out? In the next section, we'll get back to the moral inventory we talked about earlier. This will be the place for you to start.

Analyzing Personal Strengths and Weaknesses

Although we wouldn't presume to minimize the enormous task of recovering from alcoholism, in some respects it might be easier than recovering from ADD. As an ADD adult, your flaws are less apparent than those of the alcoholic's and may therefore be somewhat easier to deny and ignore. You have the power to take control of your life by looking squarely at your limits.

Acknowledging your limits offers an opportunity for you to grow far beyond them. By limiting the activities that stress your fragile skills, you will free up energy and time for those you do well. It's time for you get busy on your moral inventory to help you better understand your strengths and weaknesses. Use the following questions as an outline for this important job.

What Can I Do Well?

This first question may be the hardest to answer! Members of our local adult support group were initially stumped when they tried to describe some of their strong points. Several expressed that they couldn't think of anything positive because they were so accustomed to focusing on their mistakes. Over time, it became apparent that there was indeed a wealth of talent among us. After several months, group members gradually became less tentative about their strengths.

If you have a similar problem, we suggest that you work first on enlarging your thinking about what constitutes an asset. For instance, as some of our group shared particular talents in their jobs, one participant (we'll call her Sarah) was initially apologetic about not working outside the home.

As the sharing continued in subsequent meetings, it became apparent that Sarah was a virtual genius at living a balanced life. She had conducted her own elaborate "one rat study" to determine her work capacity. She added up all the mental and physical tasks performed in a typical week to arrive at a total number of working hours. Her calculations were very precise. Sarah determined that travel time to her son's school conference constituted work and time spent at the support group was leisure. She informed the group that she didn't count the time it took her to get dressed in the morning—but if she had to change into her grass cutting clothes during the day, she counted it as work!

Sarah spent several weeks tracking her signs of stress as she manipulated the numbers of hours she worked in a given week. At the end of her study, she concluded that she could work no more than fifty hours a week without exceeding acceptable levels of stress. Since she already had two children, motherhood wasn't an optional role but she knew that she could make decisions about her other roles.

She realized that she could only manage a part time job outside the home but didn't waste energy fretting about the lowered family income. Instead, she turned her creative talents to devising strategies for living well on less money. She grows much of the family's food in a backyard garden, swims in a small pool dug with family labor and barters with friends for other goods and services. She carefully considers the impact of labor and money decisions on the family system not only as financial expenses, but also as the cost and value of energy and time.

The result is a family that is truly in balance. Sarah, whose particular gifts aren't easy to measure or define by societal standards, is extremely successful. She could be a valuable consultant to many harried, stressed families.

When you make your list of things you do well, go beyond the obvious. Many of us with ADD measure personal worth by the yardstick of people with more orderly or ordinary lives and minds. We consider ourselves successful if we play tennis or golf well, have careers with a steady upward climb and perform tasks efficiently. Remember, our abilities are often more offbeat!

KK: "My younger brother has ADD and is a mechanical genius. When he was a kid, he got in mega-trouble because he always took things apart and neglected to put them back together. He did, however, have a talent that was very useful. He could figure out how to open any kind of lock. We always called on him when family members had locked their keys in the car.

He was a lifesaver when my dad who worked for Colt firearms accidentally locked my Aunt Mary in a pair of police handcuffs one Friday night. Unfortunately, the key was in Dad's office that was closed until Monday morning. Aunt Mary would have spent a very uncomfortable weekend had my brother not come to her rescue!

My brother would have made a great burglar but he might also have turned his unusual talent into something both income-producing and legal! I don't know. Maybe he could have designed security systems. Actually, he became a chef who happens to have many other untapped talents.

When I was 23 years old and doing my own self-assessment, I was initially hard-pressed to figure out what I did well. A string of failures had left me wondering if I had any abilities at all. I sidestepped the question of my abilities by taking a look at what I liked to do. Identifying my talents followed logically from this starting point.

The first item on my list was that I liked to spend time talking with my friends. I realized that not only did I like it, I was also good at it. People often called on me for help when they were in trouble or feeling unhappy. Bingo! I realized that I was an effective, albeit untrained, therapist.

I added my love of reading to my list. I realized that besides books, I loved reading *people* and trying to understand them. My list grew to include attributes such as my tolerance and acceptance of others' faults and my problem-solving skills."

When you begin working on your own list, try starting with the things you like to do. Since we often prefer activities that come easiest to us, you may find yourself focusing on your talents without even realizing it. Include as many things as you can. Don't limit yourself to standard or marketable skills such as being a computer whiz or a good dancer. If you can tie a knot in a cherry stem with your tongue, include it on your list. If your talent is playing the Star-Spangled Banner on your teeth, don't hesitate to write it down. These abilities might not have any apparent value. But some creative thinking can lead to some surprising uses for seemingly useless and strange talents!

What Can I Do Adequately?

Your downhill skiing talents may not exactly qualify for an Olympic gold medal. If you can manage, however, to get down the hill in one piece, add this item to your inventory. What about the costumes you sewed for your daughter's school play? Maybe some of the seams ripped apart and had to be pinned together for the performance but you did manage to get the twenty-five costumes sewed together.

The point is, you should include each thing you can do *reasonably* well. These activities may not be your favorite things to do and they may not be a showcase of your talent, but at least you can get by with them. If you are a mediocre tennis player, include it as long as you don't play so poorly that you face humiliation each time you step on the court. If your cooking is fairly routine and unexciting but edible, it belongs in this category.

What Can't (or Shouldn't) I Do?

This final section of your inventory is extremely important because it will help you make decisions about the things you should simply stop doing. Do you remember Debra who tries to hide her deficits by doing everything? Not only does she try to do everything, she tries to do everything brilliantly! Of course, she continually feels stressed and inadequate due to her unrealistic expectations.

Even if you aren't trying to do it all, you are probably trying to do things you shouldn't do. You may be a whiz in mathematics but that doesn't necessarily mean that you should do your income tax preparation. Do you really have time to fit this in to your schedule or should you pay an accountant to do it? What about those things that really aren't your forté? If you are experiencing failure when your efforts don't accomplish what you want them to, perhaps your only failure is in trying to do some of these things at all. No one can be wonderful at everything.

Many ADDers try so hard to be *normal* that they are unrealistic about their capabilities. If playing softball always results in an agonizingly embarrassing experience, don't do it—even if your three closest friends pressure you into joining them for this great pastime. Bland, rather tasteless meals are acceptable but if you repeatedly burn down major sections of your kitchen, it's time to reevaluate your cooking.

These activities should be added to your *Can't/Shouldn't Do* list. As you examine your assets and liabilities, be honest about your weaknesses. We certainly don't encourage you to focus exclusively on your deficits. But through the process of examining and identifying them, you can move on to the abilities they mask.

Balancing Acts Aren't Just for Circus Performers: Climb on the High Wire But Make Sure There's a Safety Net Underneath!

Not all high wire circus performers use safety nets, but many do. We think they are an absolute necessity for most of us with ADD. Each of us needs a custom designed net to break the fall from a life that is out of balance.

You'll use your moral inventory as a blueprint for organizing and simplifying your life and building your safety net. The wise folk who brought us the Twelve Steps were acutely aware that balance is a critical component of recovery. In AA, a repeated phrase is, "Keep it simple". Balance can only be achieved by uncluttering your life.

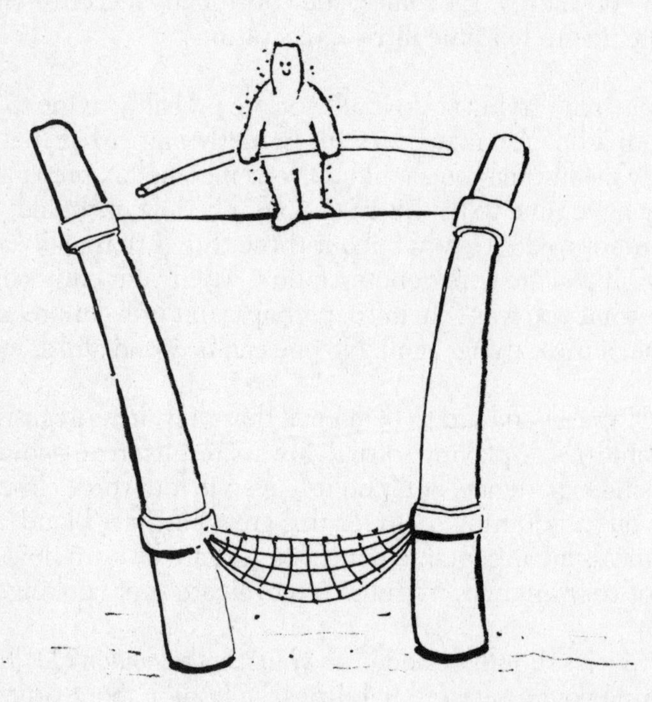

"An ADDer's High Wire Act with a Safety Net Underneath"

If you support your rather unbalanced nervous system with a carefully planned lifestyle, the external structure will provide some degree of internal order. You need to figure out how you can do more of the things you do well and less of those that cause repeated failure. Be ruthless about eliminating the unnecessary from your life to avoid the overload that causes stress.

We bet you're thinking, "Come on, be realistic. I can't do what I want and get away with it." Of course you can't do exactly what you want all the time. But there are many things you can control and alter to suit your individuality. Let's look at a framework you can use for cleaning house.

Evaluating the "Should-Do's" and "Must-Do's" in Your Life

Refer back to the questions we posed about the balance issues in your life. Reconsider them as they fit with your assets/liabilities list and take another look at your schedule. Are the numbers of things you're trying to accomplish exceeding your capacity? To get them all finished, are you using the time you should be sleeping? Too little sleep can impair the quality of your concentration and performance. Is there little time left for doing things you enjoy, either by yourself or with your family?

Can you make some realistic adjustments to your list of activities and responsibilities? Consider the things you've listed as obligations. How obligatory are they? Can you work on being more assertive when other people make demands or requests? There are unlimited numbers of things we all *should* do in the sense that they are important and worthwhile. Somebody needs to work on the church committee, organize the Parent-Teacher Association or coach the soccer team. The question is, does it have to be *you?*

Many of us with ADD have worked so hard all our lives to stay afloat that we're unrealistic about our limitations. We're so afraid of not measuring up to expectations that we drive ourselves to do anything and everything. Many times we're doing more than our fair shares but don't know what a fair share is. Even if we aren't doing as much as our peers, we may be working to the limits of our capacities.

We can't answer any of these questions for you. Only you can make a determination about the should-do's and must-do's in your life. But we want to share some of our thoughts about a couple of them. As you think about the ideas that follow, carefully consider the to-do's that are an accepted part of your lifestyle. Reflect on them within the context of your inventory and schedule—are you absolutely sure that they should be part of your life or do they throw the balance off?

Analyze Your Financial Equation

As you review your diary, take a hard look at your standard of living. Is there a way to make changes in this area? Obviously if you're just meeting basic needs for food, shelter and health care, there isn't anything to cut out. Many of us do, however, have the flexibility to get by on less money. If you're stressed by exceeding your work capacity, you probably need to look at ways to reduce the demands. This may mean a reduction in income. Prioritize your commitments with these questions in mind:

What is essential for survival?
What is important?
What can I do without?

As you try to figure this one out, think of it as an equation. On one side of the equation are your needs and desires for a certain standard of living. On the other side is the toll it takes to earn that living. Only you can decide the best way to balance this equation! You may decide to reduce your work load by shortening your hours or by taking a less demanding job. Use your creative ADD brain to come up with ideas for living well on less money.

You may want to read Doris Janzen Longacre's excellent book, *Living More With Less*.[25] The book is based on the worldwide experiences of the Mennonites whose religion and culture is built around living the simple life. We aren't suggesting that you join the Mennonites or make other radical changes in your life! But you might benefit from the moral support the book provides for living with less emphasis on material goods. Besides philosophical considerations, the book has many suggestions about how to live well on less money.

Analyze Your Simplicity/Complexity Equation

The key to simplifying our ADD lives is maintaining a proper equilibrium between too much or too little of each balancing act. Although we've been stressing the value of *keeping it simple*, it's possible to make it **TOO** simple. If you've been coping with your ADD by severely limiting yourself, you can tip the balance in the opposite direction. Without sufficient challenge, ADDers don't function well, either.

If you often feel bored, lethargic or depressed, you may be understimulated. You may need to push yourself a little more—just enough to function at an optimal level. Your task will be to figure out how to inject more challenge into your life without taking on too much. Ask yourself the questions again to determine if your problem is overstimulation or understimulation.

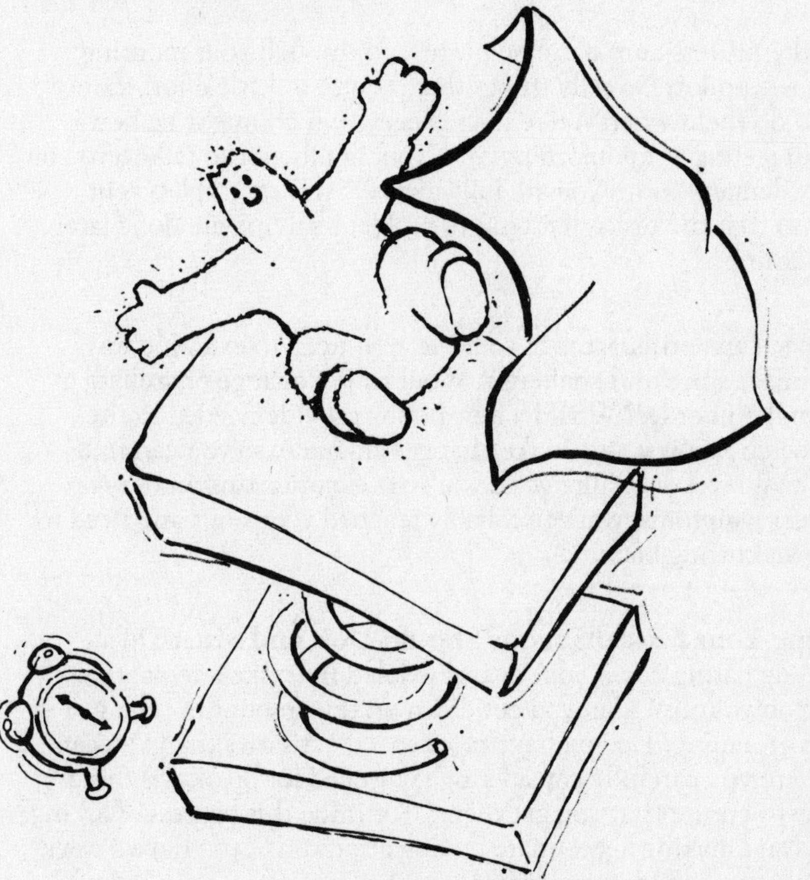

The Revolutionary Bed Ejector–A New Invention That Gets You Up And Moving In The Morning!

Are you getting too much rest or sleep? Experiment by cutting back on the number of hours you sleep each night. Do you feel better with less sleep than you have been routinely getting? If so, set your alarm clock every night, even on weekends, and make yourself get out of bed no matter what. Or buy a *Revolutionary Bed Ejector!*

Train yourself to hop out of bed at the first sound of the alarm even though your natural tendency is to shut it off and go back to sleep. Getting yourself going in the morning isn't easy and if you think too much about it, you'll get cold feet! Once it becomes a habit, you may feel better and more productive during the day.

Making the process automatic helps. Just go through your morning ritual on auto-pilot. Do only things that require so little effort that you could do them when you're half-asleep—which might be how you're still feeling at midmorning! Ask your family not to talk to you or make any demands until you are fully awake. Also try to plan your workday so that the tasks that require problem-solving are done later in the morning.

In looking at the other areas of your life, you need to examine ways you can inject spice and challenge. Would a job change or seeking a promotion be in order? Would a new hobby provide needed excitement? The choice is yours. Make changes gradually so you can find your optimal level of challenge. If you start experiencing anxiety or other stress symptoms, you've probably reached your limit and need to think about cutting back.

Analyzing Your Miscellaneous Should-Do's and Must-Do's

To continue paring down your overscheduled life, take a look at all the areas on your list. Can you cut down on the amount of time you spend on grooming? Do you have more social activities than you can handle? Are you carefully considering your need for breaks? Is there some way to ensure that you get them? Continue this process of asking questions and making appropriate modifications until you have a weekly schedule that's more manageable.

How-To's of Slicing and Dicing

We hope this discussion of balance issues can help you take a studied look at your lifestyle. The decisions you make about them will be the basis for constructing your safety net to reduce undue burdens. Only you can decide what a balanced life means for you and what methods will work in achieving it. But how can you make the changes you've decided will simplify your life?

Of course, we can't tell you exactly how you should proceed with your slicing and dicing. But some of the ideas that follow may give you some things to think about. We don't recommend that you impulsively start acting on them all! We do recommend that you try some of them and modify or toss out the ones that won't work.

Slicing and Dicing Techniques

Can You Make a Budget to Determine How You Spend Your Money?
This is a long process of reviewing your checkbook, bank receipts and bills for an entire year. If you can push yourself through it, you will gain invaluable information. Most people are surprised at the money they fritter a way. If you can afford it, hire a financial planner to help you with the overwhelming details of making a budget.

Can You Cut Down on Impulsive Purchases?
Since one of the hallmarks of ADD is impulsivity, you may buy first and think later. Simply being aware of your tendencies may help. Train yourself to stop and think before you buy anything—"Do I really need this? Can I afford it?" Make a rule not to make any major purchase until you have discussed it with your spouse or family. If impulse buying is a problem, you may have to stay out of stores, cut up your credit cards or plan your shopping trips with an empty wallet!

Can You Resist the Pressure to Keep Up With the Joneses?
Many of us have lifelong habits of measuring ourselves against others. We worry so much about our inability to keep up with other people that it's easy to buy into the equation that "Competence equals Material Success". We rashly jump on the endless treadmill

of consumerism, afraid we'll be left behind. Each of us can reduce stress by rethinking our values.

Can You Change Your Job Responsibilities or Change Jobs for a Better Fit?
What can you save in emotional wear and tear by working fewer hours or making a job change? Perhaps a different job would actually lower your commuting, child care or wardrobe expenses.

Should You Get a Job Outside the Home if Fulltime Parenting Isn't Your Forté?
Not everyone is cut out for staying at home with her family. You may not want a full-time career but maybe you need the stimulation of a part-time job. The rewards of a little extra money and connections to other people might make your life more interesting. You might find yourself in a better emotional state of mind to deal with family issues when you have some time away from them.

Can You Barter for Goods and Services?
Do you have a skill or talent that would benefit someone else? Exchange it for something you need. Bartering is a time-honored system for exchanging duties to save money and aggravation and to maximize your talents.

Can You Get Some Outside Help?
Baby-sitters, cleaning people, gardeners—anyone or anything you can afford or can barter for—can help you make your life more manageable. You don't have to do everything yourself.

Are You Asking for Help When You Need It?
Don't let pride stand in the way when you're overloaded. You can return the favor later. You probably have friends or family who would be willing to do some things for you. Why can't your sister pick up the milk you need when she's at the store? You don't have to attend every one of your daughter's soccer games. Ask another soccer parent to take her sometimes and cheer her on.

Are You Firm About Meeting Your Essential Needs?
If you need a half hour of quiet at the end of your work day, take it

without guilt or apology! If you are the ADD parent of an ADD child, you probably have your hands full managing the details of both your lives. Do you have to donate the little time left over to volunteering on the local library committee? Practice saying "No" to requests for commitments of your time. State politely, firmly and without apology that you are already doing as much as you can handle. If the request is made more insistently, repeat your refusal without anger or defensiveness and promptly end the conversation. If you want to help in some way, discuss possibilities with a clear statement of how much you are willing to do.

Can You Lower Your Standards?
Is a super clean house really necessary or can you subscribe to the *Dim Light Bulb Theory of Housekeeping*? You may not be crazy about your spouse's ironing capabilities, but if he's willing to assume the chore, can you learn to live with the wrinkles in your blouses?

Are You Keeping the Sabbath?
If you used to attend religious services but have cut them from your busy schedule, rethink your decision. If this is an important part of your life, you need to make time for it for your emotional well-being. Even if you are a dyed in the wool atheist, there is wisdom in having a sanctioned day of rest. Your day of rest could be a trip to the museum or to your fitness center. Just be sure to schedule some rest time. Make a deal with a friend to alternate childcare so both of you can have some time off.

Balance Maintenance

As time goes by, you'll become more skilled at achieving balance in your life. You'll need to continually update your plan to reflect new challenges and life changes. Each time you add a new responsibility or make changes in your life plan, reevaluate the equation and check the balance. Is your capacity for work and stress still roughly equal to the demands placed on it? If your life is out of kilter, you need to return to your drawing board for further adjustments. If you neglect to do this, your life can start to unravel.

Finding the right balance is a complicated process. If you decide to fulfill a lifelong dream to learn Chinese, keep in mind that it will be a slow process! It takes a good supply of mental energy to learn something new. After you've mastered the new skill, you can think about using your energy to take on a new challenge. The trick is to continue cautiously and not pile on too many changes at the same time. If you *up the ante* in measured steps, you can maintain your optimal level of stimulation, accumulate an impressive number of new skills and still keep your life in balance. You may also discover new opportunities and choices that were previously unattainable.

As ADD adults, we need to apply the metaphor of the high wire performer to our lives. Every day we face extraordinary risks and challenges as we attempt to balance ourselves above the crowd. One slip and we'll find ourselves plunging to the ground. We can't eliminate our missteps but we can build safety nets to catch us when we fall.

This book is about building personalized safety nets. We've already examined several steps in the construction process: educating yourself, dismantling unhealthy defenses, grieving and balancing your life. Education is probably the easiest step. We hope that you're using your new knowledge to erase faulty assumptions and to make some decisions about your life. The other steps require greater effort.

If you're still struggling with excessive sadness or anger about your ADD, you might need to reread this book later when you're emotionally ready to begin making some changes. Until you can work through the grief process and achieve a degree of self-acceptance, it will be difficult to make a realistic assessment of your capabilities. Grieving is important work that takes a lot of energy. Don't add impossible burdens by making too many major life changes at the same time.

If you're feeling a bit overwhelmed, slow down, take a deep breath and remember that recovery is a slow, ongoing process. If you're squarely facing your ADD and your coping mechanisms and are taking a studied look at the balance issues in your life, you're ready to move on to some other steps in your recovery. So let's turn to Chapter 8 to begin exploring the dynamics of ADD in interpersonal relationships.

Interfacing In Action: In Groups and Friendships

This chapter marks a change in direction from the first part of this book. In educational jargon, the information in the first seven chapters was *Readiness*. We were providing information that will be the basis for everything that follows. Since we want to be effective teachers, we need to remind you to periodically review some of the old material as you continue your reading. We will use the moral inventory again so if you haven't completed it, we hope that you have at least been thinking about it.We hope that at a minimum, you've added it to your To Do list!

In preceding chapters we talked about the impact of ADD on other people within the context of specific symptoms, differences and defense mechanisms. Now we're going to examine the impact of ADD specifically within the context of relationships.

We've borrowed from computer terminology in naming chapters eight through ten. The term "interfacing" is used to describe communication between computers. We think the term captures the essence of the issues of "getting along".

Although much of the focus of these three chapters is interfacing and communication, we'll also consider related issues. In Chapter 9, for instance, we'll examine various factors that have an impact on an ADDer's ability to "relate" to his job responsibilities. Now that you know where you're heading in your reading, let's get busy examining interfacing in action.

We all interact daily with other people. When we talk on the phone, participate in a meeting or share dinner with a friend, we're relating with other people. The success of these interactions, whether brief, one-time encounters or long-lasting relationships, depends largely on adequate communication skills.

Virtually everything we do as members of the human race is a form of communication. Volumes have been written about the art of *effective communication*. Family and marriage therapists focus on its importance and attempt to help people keep the *lines of communication open*. College courses teach *positive communication* skills. Based on all the attention given to issues of communication, one can assume that it must be considerably more complex and difficult than simply talking!

Of course you already knew that. Relationships would be a breeze if this were the case. In reality, even the briefest of interactions can fall apart through a misunderstanding. So let's take a brief look at the dynamics of communication as a starting place for our discussion of interactions and relationships.

We interact with each other by transmitting our thoughts, feelings, and desires through the medium of language. In its simplest form, language involves speaking and listening: I talk and you listen and you talk and I listen. Sounds simple, doesn't it? To understand how language is anything but simple, we'll consider communication in the world of computers.

Communication in the Computer World

With the exploding technology of the past thirty years, many different kinds of computers have become available and are almost indispensable for personal and business use. With the arrival of modems and networking, computers rapidly send mail electronically. We don't have to wait for the US Postal Service to deliver a letter two days later. We can instantly send the report on our computer screen to someone else's through telephone cabling.

This capability has been limited by communication problems identical to the ones encountered by a German who tries to speak to an American. They can't communicate because they speak different languages.

In the world of computers, great strides have been made in developing software that bridges the capabilities of dissimilar programming languages. Macintoshes and IBMs, for example, use hardware and programmed languages unique to each of them. Both computers can use a word processing software package called Microsoft Word™, but their "brains" (hardware) can recognize the program only if it written in their own "language". Before the advent of special software programs that translate the unfamiliar language of one computer for the other, Macs and IBM's were unable to interface and communicate with each other.

Even when two computers have the same hardware, they may be unable to communicate with each other if they don't use the same software. For instance, a Macintosh that uses the word processing software MacWrite™, hasn't been able to read a letter formatted in Microsoft Word™ because the programming languages are different.

Similarly, people come in different models with individualized hardware and software packages. Each of our brains processes information differently and uses software that can't read the language of other people. If an IBM lacks the capability of talking to a Macintosh, it simply works by itself and does its own thing. When differences in programming make communication between people difficult, we still have to interface with each other because we share the world as human beings.

The Art and Science of Communication

Although Mom and Dad often frantically try to figure out exactly what the crying signifies, *their one second old* infant is already communicating. Long before the growing baby acquires real language, he uses squeals, gestures and facial expressions to "talk".

Unless we have a speech problem or a specific language disability, most of us learn to talk fairly early in our lives. We learn the *science of communication* rather effortlessly. We learn to pronounce words correctly and to use them to communicate our needs.

The *art of communication* is often considerably more difficult to learn. Successful interactions with the taxi driver or a spouse rely on a mastery of this art form. Similar to a painting, communication can be designed and interpreted in a variety of ways. It sends a message that includes multiple elements of form, color intensity and shading, subtlety, and detail. Unless you are an art aficionado, you may walk away from an abstract painting as confused as you are after some conversations.

An adult with ADD can have real problems with communication and relationships because the rules of the art form continually change. As he tunes in and out, his deficits interfere with his ability to truly understand the meaning of conversations. He may communicate messages he never intended and misinterpret the messages he receives.

The Rhythm of Language

Unlike a painting, communication isn't a static art form. It has rhythm and movement. We have to synchronize ourselves to its flow and to know where, when and how much to contribute to a conversation. Similar to a ballet, a conversation has many elements. It includes a proper time to make an entrance, an awareness of what others are doing, allocation of time for a solo and rules for executing a graceful finale and exit. Many of us could really use some dancing lessons!

Verbal and Nonverbal Communication

Communication is an interplay of words and body language. In general, people from one country use words incomprehensible to foreigners. People in the same country may speak different dialects depending on the ethnic group or area they come from. It has also been suggested that men and women speak different languages.

ADDers and non-ADDers alike differ in their ability to read the interplay of verbal and body language. For some of us, the additional clues of body language help rather than hinder our communication skills. We can use observable gestures and facial expressions to fill in the gaps of words we would otherwise misunderstand.

Others may grasp the precise meaning of spoken words but misunderstand the message of non-verbal language. During a visit to Australia, President George Bush held up his fingers in the "V" recognized by Americans as the classic symbol of victory. Much to his chagrin, he learned that an Australian uses the "V" to communicate the same thing as an American holding up his middle finger! President Bush really should have taken a crash course in the *Art of Nonverbal Communication* before he made his historic blooper!

Communication is fraught with the potential for misunderstanding. You may know the meaning of the words, "You should leave" but your response will vary according to your ability to use the art of communication. If you rely only on the words themselves, you might respond, "Yes, I probably should get going." But what about the accompanying body language?

You **should** leave:	The speaker is relaxed and smiling. He looks at his watch and realizes that it's time for your next class, so **you SHOULD leave.** He is enjoying the conversation but is concerned that you'll be late.
You should leave:	The speaker moves close to you and his face is expressionless. He looks at his watch and says angrily that **YOU should leave.** He isn't at all concerned about your punctuality. And at the moment, he doesn't care much about leaving for his class either. He wants *you* out. NOW!

You should **leave:** The speaker backs away from you and his eyes are little more than slits. His mouth is set and his lips barely move as he grabs at his watchband and hisses that **you should LEAVE.** The message is that you've done enough already—he doesn't want you to breathe, flinch or talk. He wants you to *leave* and never, ever think of coming back!

We think you get the message. Words, voice inflections, facial expressions, gestures, body posture and positioning all communicate subtle (or not so subtle!) messages. An ADDer can repeatedly face social slippery spots as he attempts to negotiate around the obstacles to successful communication. Let's examine just two particularly dangerous hazards before we move on to issues of various relationships in our lives.

Hazard–Social Slippery Spots!

Social Slippery Spot #1—Basic Manners: We would venture to say that most of us with ADD need to proceed very cautiously in this area. We're not saying that ADDers have cornered the market on bad manners. But societal conventions of politeness can be hazards because of our particular differences.

When people talk about good manners, they're usually talking about rule-governed speech and behavior. Grandparents brag about their well-mannered grandchild and teachers admonish their students to show better manners. Good manners require adequate communication skills that include an ability to monitor behavior and pay close attention to detail. Since these skills can be shaky in an ADDer, he may behave in an unmannerly fashion, making errors of both omission and commission:

Teacher: "I will thank you to keep those opinions to yourself!"
You: "Oh, you're welcome!"
Woman whose place in line you just took over: "Well, excuse me!"
You: "Oh, am I in your way?"

An ADDer may fail to say, "Excuse me" when he jostles someone (omission) and interrupt and monopolize conversations (commission). He probably knows the rules, but haphazardly applies them. Since these skills may not come naturally to him, he needs to make a conscious effort to learn and practice the behavior expected of adults in our society.

KK: "When I first lived away from home, I remember being shocked that the rest of the world didn't function the way my family did. Since most of my family was affected to some degree by ADD, we developed a style of interaction based on behavior that came naturally to us. Mealtimes were a free-for-all, with everyone talking at once and no one listening. Interrupting was normal behavior. It was a revelation to discover that most people take turns talking and listening to each other!"

PR: "The ADD Council's hot-line coordinator recently shared a humorous anecdote with me. He had a conversation with a repeat caller who usually spoke with one particular phone volunteer. When he suggested that the caller speak with the volunteer she had previously spoken to, she replied, "Oh, I don't have enough time to talk with "Melissa". She's been a great help but she'll talk so much and keep me on the phone so long that I'll forget the one question I needed to ask!"

I don't know who the phone volunteer was, but it could have been me! As ADDers sometimes do, if I'm not careful, I can get carried away with a one-sided conversation. I become so involved with sharing my advice and experiences that I forget the cardinal rule of effective communication: LISTENING!

I have gotten much better at this but sometimes fall into old habits. I sometimes have to put my hand over the mouth piece of my phone to cue myself to stop talking. Perhaps the Council's phone line coordinator should teach this trick to his talkative volunteer!"

Even if an ADDer avoids clearly rude actions and bad manners, his social life can be hampered by the general fogginess of ADD. He may be unable to clear the clouds sufficiently to really connect with other people. "Is anyone home?". . ."Earth to Mark!". . ."What a space cadet!". . . He may be so vague and dreamy that he doesn't seem to exist in the real world.

He may be ridiculed for being *out to lunch* or rebuked for caring only about himself. He doesn't mean to be rude or uncaring but his failure to respond can look like selfishness.

Social Slippery Spot #2—The Telephone: A great deal of daily communication is conducted by telephone. Telephones are a great invention but they sometimes do a terrible disservice to ADDers. It's not that we fail to appreciate the convenience, but we're not too crazy about the uncanny ability of a telephone to change our personalities!

Have you ever met someone for the first time after talking to him only by phone and been amazed by the difference? Can this bright, fascinating person really be the same character who seemed so dull on the telephone? What about the sparkling telephone conversationalist who becomes almost mute in face-to-face encounters?

The telephone can also cause a remarkable change in our dispositions. Perhaps you can identify with this phenomenon of *Telephone Transformation:*

PR: "I suffer from TTTS: **T**esty, **T**elephone **T**yrant **S**yndrome! A ringing telephone can transform me into a mean, confrontational person. If you are the unfortunate individual who walks into the room when I'm on the phone, you will endure scathing looks. If you make the mistake of making noise or talking to me, you'll endure far worse. Simply stated, I *get nasty!* My children watch in continual amazement as their relatively even-tempered mother transforms into a *screaming meanie!*

I have never understood the power this inanimate object wields. When the phone rings, I instantly go into a stance of defense or attack. I wait, hoping someone else will answer the incessant ringing. After the third or fourth ring, I reluctantly answer it, after announcing that "Nobody better interrupt me during this call." If my warning goes unheeded, my family is in for the assault of the telephone tyrant!"

KK: "Before either of us knew anything about ADD, my husband used to accuse me of having a disease he called *Phone-a-Phobia*. He claimed I inherited it from my mother who has similar symptoms."

A phobia is a fear out of proportion to the actual threat in a situation and people with phobias generally try to avoid the situations they fear. Some ADDers do avoid using the telephone. The avoidance, however, isn't a phobic reaction to inappropriate anxiety or fear—they have real problems with telephone communication.

The problem is sometimes an inability to process the meaning of words without the visual clues of body language. Telephone conversations may be peppered with silences, requests for the speaker to repeat himself and charming phrases such as "Uh" and "Um!" An ADDer may forget to identify himself, leave out important information or abruptly end the conversation.

An inability to filter out background noise also contributes to the difficulty with telephone conversations. An ADDer can become a telephone tyrant as he fights to shut out noises and interruptions. Listening and making sense of communication is hard enough work without having to contend with outside interferences.

Survival Tips for the Telephone

The telephone may never be your preferred mode of communication but there are some things you can do to make it more user-friendly. Here are a few telephone strategies that may reduce your Phone-a-Phobia and TTTS:

- Rehearse and write down what you're going to say before you make a call—your greeting, the major points you want to make and the way you'll politely end the conversation.
- Keep your notes in front of you during the call to jog your memory.
- Stick to your script to avoid the "wandering" conversation.
- Make your phone calls in a quiet, distraction-free place. One person we know had a phone jack installed in her bathroom so the white noise of the exhaust fan would block out distractions. If you try this, don't forget one ***very*** important detail. Telephones are electrical devices. Used in water, they can have far more serious consequences than Phone-a-Phobia and TTTS!
- If someone calls and catches you off guard, briefly excuse yourself, saying you'll have to switch phones, answer the door or return the call later. Then take a few minutes to compose yourself and gather any written information you might need for the conversation. If you have taken the call in a noisy area of your house, take the time to request quiet or switch to another phone.

With this general framework of communication and interactions in place, we'll turn our attention to interfacing in group and one-to-one encounters. As you consider these issues, your guiding principle should be the theme of this book—maximizing your strengths and minimizing your weaknesses. Don't attempt to become like folk with calm temperaments. You'll fail miserably and lose sight of the plus side of your moral inventory. Since we're advocates of the open book test, we encourage you to keep your inventory notes handy as you continue reading! We'll test you at the end of the book. Only kidding. . .

Relationships: A Play with Multiple Acts and a Cast of Many Characters

If the world were filled with fellow ADDers, many of us would probably do just fine in our relationships. With our personal experience with ADD, we would understand the "quirks" of the ADDers around us. Of course, the world is made up of many different kinds of people, many who can't figure us out at all! If we're going to fit in, we have to figure out how to communicate with and relate to others.

You may need to completely reprogram your mental computer to improve its interfacing capabilities. You may have unique strengths in this area and need only minor adjustments to your program. You may already be using your identified strengths to bypass any weaknesses in this area of functioning. You may have a keen sense of humor and vivid imagination that attracts people and repairs the damage of a social faux pas. You may be judiciously using your disinhibition—saying or doing things other people censor—to develop a frank and open communication style that disarms others and puts them at ease.

Act I: Interfacing in Groups

We live, work and play in groups—families, social clubs, meetings and committees. We can't avoid these interactions even if we wanted to. If you are like many bright, enterprising ADD adults, you may face group situations with about as much enthusiasm as you do a trip to the dentist! What can you do to prevent the social suicide you fear? To help you with this issue, let's observe some social situations in action.

Michael
Michael is standing in a cluster of four people who have been talking about a variety of topics. He hasn't added much to the conversation because he doesn't know anything about the latest software or the movement to protect endangered caterpillars. His brain is racing to think of *something* to say, before somebody asks him something he won't know how to answer.

He is preoccupied with planning his verbal entrance to the conversation and vaguely hears a comment about recent activity in the *Oval Office*. Since he's a builder with a specialty in custom renovation, he eagerly jumps in with his account of an interesting circular room he once built.

It suddenly occurs to him, halfway through his story, that something isn't quite right. He looks up to see four faces etched with question marks! He gradually realizes the enormity of his blunder and slinks away with a half-hearted chuckle: "Oval Office. . .White House. . .I knew that. I just wanted to see if you were paying attention."

Amanda
Between bursts of small talk with her two companions, Amanda twists around to watch her friend Michael humiliate himself. She asks of no one in particular, "Can you believe he just said that?" She quickly switches gears as she observes that her companion's tie looks just like the one her Uncle Joe used to wear. To her companion's comment about the benefits of using glass instead of paper products, Amanda asks, "Do funeral directors recycle the dearly departed loved one's clothing? The reason I'm asking is that your tie looks exactly like the one Uncle Joe wore at his funeral."

She laughingly assures both men that she's only kidding and wonders if they've noticed how many people have already left the party and if they have any suggestions about what she should say to Michael about acting so stupid.

Elizabeth
Elizabeth is standing with a large group near the buffet table. An animated conversation about the plight of the homeless is so engrossing that everyone ignores the delicious food. Elizabeth is the only person in the group who isn't saying anything. Her eyes look glazed and her face is expressionless. To the woman who asks her opinion about this serious topic, she replies with a yawn, "Oh, I don't really know." Someone else offers to drive her home in case she's been drinking too much and needs to sleep it off.

Notes: Act I

Mental Gymnastics: Do you remember the discussion about dividing attention and shifting gears? They are a kind of mental athletics. Successful group interfacing depends on an ability to shift gears rapidly. The exchange of a conversation is a challenging task for an ADDer who can't make quick mental adjustments. He has to follow the flow of talk as it bounces from person to person. He has to concentrate enough to understand what the speaker is saying. He also has to be sure he doesn't get locked in. Otherwise, he comes to a grinding halt while the general conversation goes on without him.

Some of us take mental time outs to process the conversation. Remember our slow reaction time? A break can give us time to deal with our less than trustworthy memories. We may be so intent on frantically rehearsing and remembering what we're going to say that we block out everything else. We do mental handsprings as fast as we can. Unfortunately, we often end up interjecting seemingly irrelevant comments. We're talking about spring soccer when the conversation moved on five minutes earlier to the winter Olympics.

Creative thinking also plays into the mental athletics. Rather than getting locked in and taking a time out, an ADDer's mind may move at breakneck speed, taking a detour at the end of the track! A comment during the conversation stimulates an idea that sends him on a wild, imaginative journey. Several laps later he ends his little detour and shares some tidbit. His comment is greeted with either raised eyebrows or replies of, "What the H- - - are you talking about?"

The comment that makes perfect sense to him is incomprehensible to the rest of the group. They didn't go on the mental journey with the ADDer and don't know where he's been. If he's among friends, they'll probably just shrug it off. If he's with strangers, they might wonder what planet he comes from!

Running Out of Gas: There are other reasons for an ADDer's difficulties with group interactions. The atmosphere of a group can be intensely stimulating. Impaired attention and a defective sensory filter can be pushed beyond their capabilities. Attention can jump from a companion's perfume to the crackling fire across the room. Where should he focus—on the speaker's words or on the body language of the person standing next to him? Bombarded with sights and sounds from many different directions, his senses rapidly reach an uncomfortable level of overload. Similar to a car climbing a long mountain road, he quickly uses up his reserves of fuel. *He may run out of mental gas*.

Have you ever been in a stimulating group situation, feeling as if you've just taken a sleeping pill or gone into a coma? We have. It's as if the body stays in the same spot while the brain goes off to a quiet corner somewhere to rest and regroup. That's just great for your brain, but what about you? You end up standing there with a blank look and a yawn. You may not exactly endear yourself to the speaker who is sharing fascinating information.

It's not that the conversation is boring—although it might be! It's that the overstimulation of a group situation causes mental fatigue. Simply put, an ADDer might either tune out or fall asleep. That's precisely what happened to Elizabeth who attributes her poor social skills to a lack of sleep.

Cruise Controls Set on Mega-Speed: Conversely, the mental cruise control may be flipped on and set way above the speed limit. The Porsche is revved and ready to go! Foot in mouth disease escalates out of control as the ADDer barrels around the track, heedless of anyone who might be in his way. With a poor sense of boundaries, he may careen, literally and figuratively, into other people. He fidgets too much, talks too fast and drives everyone crazy with his intensity. The people around him alternately view his behavior as amusing or annoying.

Impulsivity and disinhibition are sometimes attempts to fend off mental fatigue and maintain alertness. Of course, no one else knows that! Many of us often talk and act first and think later. As Amanda does, we may fill up physical and emotional space with our presence and chatter. Inappropriate, rude or silly remarks are out of our mouths before we know it! How many times have you said to yourself, "I can't believe I just said that."

Synopsis: Act I

It might seem that you process information too slowly when you're in a group conversation. Is it possible, however, that you process the information *in greater depth* than others do? Do you make connections that elude everyone else and have real value? It might seem that your mental detours are inappropriate but that doesn't mean they're worthless. Perhaps your tangents and wild leaps of imagination can lead the group to creative problem-solving.

And here's something interesting to think about. Are your problems in groups caused by your deficits or by *the rules for interaction that are ill suited to your style of thinking?*

KK: "With professional experience as a group leader, I mentally geared up for a difficult challenge when I agreed to start an ADD adult support group. I pictured a group of people talking non-stop, interrupting each other and jumping from topic to topic. I figured my main function as the facilitator would be to referee.

What has happened is vastly different from what I imagined. The flow of ideas does jump around a lot but this doesn't seem to be an obstacle to the group process. Generally, the group as a whole is able to follow the logic of the conversation and sometimes moves it off into wonderful, productive tangents. The tempo is much faster than I have encountered in other groups. But group members, often left behind in "normal" groups, are able to keep up with the speedy conversation."

Perhaps the logic of a non-ADD thinker is a different brand from an ADDer's. His logic, formulated by the generalizations and connections of his distractions, may in some ways be superior to the logic taught in school. It makes sense that if he could play by his own set of logical rules, his communication would flow more freely.

The dance of conversation in an ADD group seems to move to music entirely different from that of other groups. It seems to have its own unique rhythm, tempo and patterns. Perhaps we ADDers don't need dancing lessons after all. We may just need to dance to our own ADD beat!

If you have an ADD friend, get together and enjoy the dance you share. Of course, you can't always dance to your own beat just as you can't always do what your impulses drive you to do. Since you can't avoid being in groups of non-ADDers, you'll have to learn some of the conventional steps. Here are some survival tips that might help you on the dance floor.

Survival Tips for Act I

Be Prepared: Before you arrive at the social gathering, make sure you're prepared. Start taking notes as a newspaper reporter would. Find out who will be there and write down their names, occupations, interests, etc. If you're lucky, somebody else who loves radio controlled race cars as much as you do, will be in attendance. Ask about the dress "code" so you won't arrive in jeans if everyone else will be wearing suits and ties. Make sure you write down the date and time of the gathering! Arriving for a dinner party an hour late will definitely not win rave reviews from your host.

Do Your Homework: If your mind and mouth inexplicably shut down in group settings, rehearse ahead of time. Part of this rehearsal should be keeping up, at least superficially, with current events. This doesn't mean you have to sit down on a daily basis with the lengthy New York Times. It does mean that you should know that the changing *nuclear family* isn't a topic about folk glowing in the dark with radiation poisoning!

The value in having an awareness, however vague, of names, places and events in the news is that it provides a file of information on which you can draw. If the subject turns to the primaries, you won't interject a comment about your son's experiences in the primary grades of your local school. Instead, you might offer, "Campaign activity is really heating up, isn't it? I haven't seen the paper the past few days. Is there anything new going on?"

Practice: Rehearsing means just that. Write a script. Rehearse. Practice. When you arrive, what will you say to the host? How will you join a conversation? What words will you use? How will you introduce yourself? How will you respond to the inquiry, "What do you do for a living, Don?" Develop a standard script for these questions that come up in groups. Then practice it with a spouse or friend or in front of a mirror.

When you work on your script, consider ways you can respond to information shared by others. After you've answered the inquiry about what you do for a living, how do you respond when somebody tells you about his job?

Someone asks: "What do you do for a living, Don?"
You start your script: "I restore antique furniture. What's your job, Fred?"
Fred replies: "I am a media center specialist."
You comment: "Oh, really..."

The conversation stops dead in its tracks. What happens now? Rather than feeling uncomfortable and trying to fill the dead space with rambling, you can refer to your memorized script of canned responses. Questions are excellent because they keep the conversation going and draw attention away from you. Generic comments can bail you out if you have no idea what a media center specialist is. A rehearsed list of questions and comments can also help with any problems you have with monopolizing conversations. Try some of these scripts and add some of your own:

"How did you get interested in that area?"
"I don't know very much about that field. What exactly does your work entail?"
"Have you always done this work or did you start off in a different field?"
"That sounds like an interesting job. Can you tell me more about it?"

The focus of the conversation will probably come back to you after this question and answer period. By then you should have found some familiar territory and will be able to talk comfortably about a subject you know. You may get in a bind and exhaust the items in your script. If this happens, you can excuse yourself to make a phone call or to ask the host something. Include these *emergency exit* techniques during your rehearsal. Also include your spouse or friend in your practice sessions so you'll have someone to bail you out when you need help.

If you're a member of a support group, you can learn about your behavior by watching yourself. Arrange for a video or audio recording of your group's interactions. Although the camera might be somewhat distracting, you can learn a lot when you review the tape.

This is a valuable process not only for reviewing what you did wrong, but what you did right! If you're a member of an ongoing support group, you might be able to tape a series of sessions. You can use the tapes to monitor your progress as you practice new ways of behaving. Of course, this idea presupposes that you feel comfortable in the group and that none of the members objects to being taped.

Watch and Listen: When you're with an unfamiliar group of people, initially keep a low profile. Look and listen a lot and talk very little. Watch the others to see how they behave. Find out how much personal information people share with each other and try to figure out any unspoken rules. Most groups have informal codes of conduct that govern the behavior of members. The hidden code may tell you which subjects are taboo, where to sit or even how to dress.

We don't advocate blind conformity to rules or buying into the idea that you must fit in. It will be up to you to decide whether to continue your association with a particular group. You can, however, make a reasonable attempt to be cordial and respectful of the group's rules at least for one evening. If nothing else, use the evening to practice your conversational skills.

Watch Your Watch: Focus on the speaker. Force yourself to make eye contact. Play close attention to the dance of conversation and don't give a solo performance. Before you start talking, make sure that you aren't interrupting. Make it a practice to ask the speaker if he has finished before you jump in and cut off his next thought.

Wear a watch with a second hand and unobtrusively note how long each person speaks. When it's your turn, time yourself. Set a mental alarm clock to *turn yourself off* if you exceed your allotted time. *Watching your watch* can also help you maintain focus as it gives you something to do. In case somebody watches you watching your watch, you can always claim that the battery seems to be wearing out. It's better to wear out your battery than your audience!

Watch Your Wandering: Pay close attention to the number of tangential journeys you take so you won't start jumping all over, monopolizing the conversation. In a safe group of friends, ask someone to signal you when you're getting off track. If all else fails and you're off and running before you know it, acknowledge your rambling. Say something like, "Boy, my mind is really on a mental marathon, isn't it? Sorry about that. . ."

Work on Your Reading Skills: Remember that people communicate through verbal and non-verbal channels. You'll need to practice reading both kinds of language. The verbal channel uses the voice as the instrument to produce words while body language and facial expressions provide valuable clues about the impact of your behavior.

If you notice a look of horror, it's a good bet that your words sent an unintended message—unless of course, you wanted a particular reaction! Immediately apologize if you know your words were impulsive. If you hate to apologize, grit your teeth and do it anyway! Think of it as balancing your checkbook or doing pushups. It's not fun but it makes life easier in the long run.

If you don't know what caused the negative reaction, ask! You could say, "I noticed you frowned when I said such and such. Is there a problem?" An alternative is to make a joke about your impulsivity. You could say something like, "I have a bad case of foot in mouth disease today. Please let me know if I've said or done anything out of line." A lighthearted approach can make it easier for the other person to provide feedback about your behavior.

Welcome the Feedback: When you receive the feedback, **LISTEN TO IT!** The advice is three simple words. Responding appropriately to comments about your behavior, however, is anything but simple! Your tendency might be to put up your shield and go into *auto-defense and attack mode*. You really should try to leave your shield at home or in the trunk of your car. Remember, you can't do this all by yourself. You need help.

Think of this learning process as therapy. In physical therapy, for instance, the slogan used to inspire patients is, "No pain, No gain." And of course, comments don't have to be negative. Don't be afraid to ask for positive feedback as well and don't forget to thank the person for taking the time to help you.

Careful listening is hard, accepting criticism is harder and changing your behavior is the hardest of all. But these are essential parts of your recovery. Using feedback to change your behavior can have a powerful, positive impact on your social success.

Carefully Choose Your Social Activities: If you feel washed up and worn out after every social event, it might be time to reread the section on balance. Be honest with yourself. Do you attend these functions because you want to or because you feel compelled to? When an acquaintance shares his very full social calendar, do you feel somehow that you just don't measure up socially?

There may be some social events that you must attend. Prepare carefully for these and do the best you can, but *Just Say "No"* to the others. Be selective and base your decision on a realistic assessment of your abilities and disabilities. Small group gatherings may work better for you.

This doesn't mean you should give up on learning and practicing your interfacing skills. You will need them everywhere from PTA meetings to office planning sessions. Just remember that there isn't a rule requiring you to be a social butterfly.

Act II: Interfacing in One-to-One Encounters

Some of us prefer large group interactions that enable us to remain somewhat anonymous. We may feel far less comfortable in one-to-one relationships because it's impossible to hide. Our carefully constructed shields don't work well in close relationships that illuminate our shortcomings.

Even if your experiences in relationships have been unsuccessful, don't resign yourself to solitary confinement. If you've been working hard at your recovery, you have knowledge and skills you may have lacked before. Your newfound understanding about your balance sheet can support you as you risk the self-disclosure inherent in developing close relationships. You can be successful if you're aware of the potential pitfalls and design strategies to avoid them.

In Act II, we'll study some other relationships in action. These are the one-to-one encounters with friends and acquaintances. Let's see what we can learn from them.

Ken
Ken looks up to see Paul walking down the aisle. He runs over him, expressing surprise and delight to see him again so soon after their first meeting. He asks if Paul received the three messages he left for him on his answering machine yesterday. He invites Paul to dinner that evening and without waiting for an answer, begins asking what his new friend would like to eat. Ken begins telling his new friend all about the cooking classes he's taking and what he's learned about designing healthy menus.

Carolyn
Carolyn invites Jason, her new neighbor to join her for a cup of coffee. She talks briefly about the neighborhood and comments that she's sure he'll like it much better than where he used to live. Jason tells her that he'll miss the cookouts he used to have with his three neighbors. Carolyn responds by telling him not to worry about it. She tells him that in this neighborhood, fifteen families share a block party every summer! Carolyn refills her coffee but doesn't notice that Jason's is empty. She responds to his story about the tree house his son built in their old yard, by gazing out her back door. She advises, "Well, I bet with my son's help, your boy will be able to build a really great tree house in his new backyard."

Notes: Act II

Many of the rules for interactions are the same for both group and individual encounters. We must take turns listening and speaking, watch for non-verbal behavior and monitor verbal and non-verbal communication. Beyond these similarities, though, individual interactions require somewhat different skills.

Is your friendship mode similar to Carolyn's or Ken's? Don't worry if you identify with either of them because they have a lot going for them. With some refinements, they could develop good interaction skills.

Ken shows genuine affection for Paul and is willing to work hard at developing this new friendship. What he needs to do is work equally hard at not working so hard! He needs to learn to redirect his focus from his needs to his friend's needs.

Then there's Carolyn. Desperately wanting her new neighbor to like her and his new neighborhood, she overwhelms him with her intensity. She needs to think about her words and review the messages she sends. She needs to watch Jason's body language and note his attempts to add comments to her one-way conversation. By singing the praises of her neighborhood, she's trying to help him adjust to his new home. Jason's body language would give her a good clue that she's sending an unintended message of boasting and "one-upping".

Synopsis of Act II

There's both good news and bad news for an ADDer in one to one social interactions. The good news is that these encounters put fewer demands on the ability to switch gears—there are fewer details to track and fewer people to read. The bad news is that tuning out is more obvious—the focus is on him with no one to run interference! He can't afford to take mind detours because there's no one to pick up and carry the conversational ball.

If you haven't come to terms with your disorder, one-to-one communication can be particularly scary. You might talk yourself into failure.

"What if she doesn't like me?"
"I don't have anything interesting to say."
"He's a professor and I barely finished high school!"
"What if I forget her name?"
"What if I run out of things to say?"

Engaging in negative self-talk is destructive because you look at only one side of your equation. Never forget the other side of your balance sheet! Henry Ford said, "Whether you think you can or whether you think you can't, you're right." If you run from potential friendships, you're acting and believing *you can't*. On the other hand, if you affirm yourself as a capable person who happens to have some disabilities, you are acting and believing *you can*.

Many of us have excellent people skills. We can learn to be great listeners, locking in our focus to give a flattering level of attention to the other person. The rhythm of the exchange is slower and easier to follow in one-to-one encounters. We can focus intently, noticing things that others miss and offering sensitive and empathic support.

You may be fortunate to have a close friend. You may have several close friends. But if your friendships are rocky or shorter-lived than you'd like them to be, you may need to get to work. As you think about your own skills in one-to-one relationships, consider these tips. They may be useful and give you added confidence in these situations.

Survival Tips for Act II

Relax and Listen: Don't feel you have to fill every second with conversation. ADDers tend to go to extremes, talking a mile a minute or completely tuning out. Some silence is okay. If you check out altogether, your companion will think you're uninterested in what he has to say.

The key to maintaining a correct balance between the two extremes is active listening. Active listening enables you to interact without filling up the conversation with your words. Send a message that you are listening and interested in what your companion has to say by nodding your head, leaning forward and maintaining eye contact.

Watch his body language and pay attention to the message it sends. Interject comments that let your companion know that you are listening.

"Go on"... "Tell me more"... "Could you explain that a little more?"

If you find yourself talking excessively or feeling uncomfortable at a lull in the conversation, share your confusion:

"Am I talking too much?... I've run out of things to talk about. . . Do you have any ideas?"

Clarify the Message: Remember that communication is an art form. The clarity of the message has an impact on the listener's understanding. Moreover, each of us interprets language from an individual frame of reference. The intent of the message can be misinterpreted regardless of how clearly it is stated.

Statement:	*"Things are a mess in this house."*
Possible Interpretations:	*"He's accusing me of being a slob."* *"He's telling me to clean up the house."* *"He's just noticing and commenting on the state of the house."*

Although history may support the first statement, don't jump to conclusions. To avoid communication misunderstandings, clarify the way you interpreted the message—restate it in your own words.

Restated Interpretations:	*"Are you trying to say that I should do something about the mess in the house?"* *"When you said that, I thought you were criticizing me. Is that true?"*
Effective Clarification:	*"I thought you said..." or "Were you saying ..."*

Avoid "Fightin' Words": We talked about the importance of active listening. To ensure that your companion will interpret your message accurately, take great care with the words you use. One sure-fire method for shutting down the channels of communication is using the words "you always" or "you never". Strike them from your vocabulary unless you want a full scale battle to erupt! These words feel threatening and accusatory. They assign blame and create feelings of defensiveness. Even if your spouse rarely remembers your anniversary, he has been around for fifteen years and remembering dates may be difficult for him.

A better technique is to rephrase your words as *I-messages* to communicate your feelings about how something affects you. When you use

You-messages, you direct the focus to your listener and force him to argue his position. Here are some examples of the differences between these two kinds of messages:

I-message: *"When you didn't call yesterday, I wondered if you were mad at me."*

You-message: *"You never call when you say you will."*

I-message: *"When you start talking before I'm finished, I feel that what I have to say is unimportant"*

You-message: *"Why do you interrupt me all the time?"*

Watch your listener's body language. If he looks puzzled, stop talking. Ask him to clarify his understanding of what you said. He may be hearing something very different from what you're trying to say.

There are many other useful communication techniques but we hope you get the idea from these examples. It might be helpful to increase your learning experiences by taking part in a class or group that practices these skills. The communications department of a local university would be a good place to look for this kind of training.

Watch Your Intensity Level: ADD adults can be intense, passionate and single-minded about personal interests. If you're not careful, you can scare a calmer person to death!

Be cautious when you find yourself discussing one of your favorite subjects or pet peeves. If you find the other person mentally or physically backing off, lighten up! Tell a joke, ask a question or change the subject.

An ADDer can get carried away with a topic because of his intensity. It can also cause a more general problem that pervades the whole relationship. He often overwhelms other people with the ferocity of his friendship. He might shower a friend with sincere, but excessive flattery that leaves him feeling embarrassed or wondering if we're really teasing. As Ken does, he might get physically too close, oblivious to the other person's need for space.

Slow Down: Even if an ADD adult is adept at verbal and non-verbal communication, he can have difficulty maintaining a friendship over the long haul. He doesn't want to wait for the natural progression of phases in developing relationships. He may not be attuned to the pacing and gradual easing into involvement, trying to get too close, too fast.

If this is a problem for you, it may help to keep a diary or calendar that tracks your behavior in friendship-making. Don't just pick up the phone to call your new acquaintance until you check your journal. Pencil in when you make a contact and jot down notes about the encounter, paying particular attention to the other person's response. Indicate in your journal a date for your next contact and don't call or drop in before that date!

In the next chapter, we'll move on to relationships in the workplace. Although our focus will be on issues of interfacing and communication, we'll also do a brief task analysis. We'll look at some of your *jobs on the job* and offer some suggestions for improving your skills in some of them. We'll also look at your *relationship to your job* to help you analyze any failures you may be experiencing. This analysis will include an important question. Are you failing on your job or is your job failing you?

CHAPTER 9

Interfacing in Action: Getting Along on the Job

Careers can be made or destroyed according to how well we get along with other people on the job. Work relationships are an interesting variation on the theme of interfacing. There are elements of both one-to-one relationships and group interactions. The one-to-one relationships of employees aren't close friendships but require similar maintenance over time. Likewise, the group interactions of employees are different from social gatherings in that they are ongoing.

In the one-to-one relationships of friendships you can choose the people with whom you'll share your time and personal involvement. The same is true of the social gatherings you attend—you can choose to skip a party if you aren't crazy about the people who will be there. But you can't choose the employees with whom you'll interact and you can't choose the meetings you'll attend. You have to interact with your co-workers in a variety of settings.

The workplace is a social arena and arguably a political one as well. Success on the job requires good interpersonal relationships and an ability to understand the "politics" within the work setting. These dynamics create some unique problems for an ADDer with shaky communication skills. With her friends, she can count on a degree of understanding about her ADD. With her colleagues, she has to manage her deficits with great finesse.

As an adult with ADD, your success in the work world is also largely dependent on how well you get along with your job. Because of your particular deficits and differences, you have to carefully build a safety net for your job as you do for the other parts of your life. Are there some strategies you can use to improve the quality of your work? How can you make your job work for you? Is your job the best match for your particular abilities and disabilities? In this chapter, we'll expand interfacing to include these specific aspects of job management.

Act III: Getting Along on the Job

Diane

Diane found her niche in sales and quickly became a top saleswoman. Single-handedly, she increased the sales' volume of her department after being on the job only a few months. Her hard work and talents were rewarded with large commissions, bonuses and a promotion to the position of Sales Manager.

Three months later, Diane started taking aspirin on a daily basis and considered getting back into therapy. She recently found a crumpled piece of paper on the floor and is trying to figure out what to do about it. The paper is a caricature of her drawn by one of her salesmen. In the picture, she is towering over her sales force, clutching a huge megaphone in both hands. Words are shooting out of the megaphone and raining down like fireworks on her "subjects" below.

Notes: Act III

Diane is a hardworking, energetic and creative ADD woman. She's an excellent employee whose performance has been noted and rewarded by her superiors. So what is going wrong for her?

There are probably a number of explanations for the problems Diane is experiencing in her job. The most obvious is that her managerial skills aren't as good as her selling skills. Selling a product isn't the same as selling people on one's ideas for managing a sales force. Diane's social deficits may have caught up with her. Although she rose rapidly to an administrative position, she is learning that staying up there is tricky.

Diane's impulsivity may play a role in her problems. She is a can-do woman who is used to getting the job done—now! When her sales people don't solve problems as fast as she does, she grabs her megaphone and starts issuing directives. She greets a question about her policies as a hindrance to her sales' figures. She can't understand why some of her employees refuse to work the same fifty or sixty hours she does every week. She rants and raves that she has to do the work or it would never get done.

Synopsis: Act III

The work environment is a mini-society governed by rules formulated to protect the rights and establish the responsibilities of the people who work there. The relationships in a work environment are affected by the positions people hold, individual personalities and job responsibilities, and multiple interpersonal relationships. Although ADD adults may have some unique problems in this work setting, they are only one part of the equation.

Large, complex organizations have a great potential for breakdown. Many people are part of work relationships and some of them also have ADD or other disabilities. This makes for some very interest-ing interfacing! Consider, for example:

The boss who never seems to listen and who asks the impossible of you.

The coworker who doggedly sticks to her job description even when deadlines loom and colleagues are desperate for help.

The boss who continually makes his emergency, yours.

The coworker who adamantly refuses to take responsibility for a screw-up.

There isn't much you can do about the hidden agendas of fellow employees. If you remember that you're only one piece of the puzzle, you can view a situation from its proper perspective. When a work relationship unravels, you shouldn't assume that it's exclusively your fault—or your unreasonable colleague's. Perhaps she's struggling with deficits similar to yours. As an adult with ADD, you should be sensitive to the needs of colleagues who might also have hidden disabilities.

What does all this mean for you? It means you really have your work cut out for you! To be successful in the world of work, you'll need to review many of the things we've talked about in previous sections of this book. Review your inventory and pay close attention to your balance sheet. It will be an invaluable framework as you begin to develop your management strategies. If Diane paid attention to hers, she might decide to give up the higher pay and executive title to do what she does best—sell products. Let's take a look at some ideas for dealing with problems in the world of work.

Survival Tips: Act III

Rules, Procedures and Policies

Many ADDers hate to swallow these bitter pills—unfortunately there's no way to sweeten them! Unless you own your company, you have to play by someone else's rules. You have to follow company rules, procedures and policies because you don't work in isolation.

Much as you may hate your policy handbook, study it anyway. It outlines your company's system of government and chain of command—things such as who reports to whom and areas of individual responsibilities.You can't leave this homework undone! You must be very clear about where you fit within the overall structure to avoid overstepping your bounds or failing to carry out your responsibilities.

Make Sense of the Rules: Don't arbitrarily ignore the rules that don't make sense to you. Work at trying to understand their rationale. When you're away from work, talk with your spouse or a close friend about them. Make a list of all the policies you disagree with and analyze each of them. Do some have validity for the organization as a whole even though you personally disagree with them? If so, you'll have to learn to live with them.

Perhaps you can set up a reward system as a motivating tool. You may decide that not being allowed to listen to rock music in the office is totally unfair. You can't change the rule but you can reward yourself for following it by treating yourself to a favorite tape during your break.

Question the Rules Carefully: You've probably heard the adage, "Rules are made to be broken." We suggest you modify the words slightly: "Rules are made to be changed." If a rule doesn't seem to make sense for you individually or for the company as a whole, question it. Make sure your communication skills, particularly your listening skills, are solidly in place. Think through the rule you're disputing and approach the appropriate person with your question. And then **listen**.

If you receive the response,". . .because I'm your boss," you can forget about doing anything beyond swallowing your objections and toeing the line. On the other hand, if your superior offers information you had overlooked, thank her for entertaining your ideas. At least, you'll have a reading on her as someone who is willing to negotiate. The door will be open for future exchanges.

Sell Your Ideas: Although it's unwise to challenge authority at every turn, questioning policies and procedures can be a positive quality. Just don't move too fast. Keep your impulsivity in check and proceed s-l-o-w-l-y and tactfully. Don't start shaking things up after you've been on your new job exactly forty-five minutes!

No one in the company will buy your ideas if you are an unknown quantity. First, you should demonstrate your loyalty and dependability. Work on building positive relationships. Spend time keeping a low profile and doing what you're expected to do. Arrive at work on time, take one hour for lunch and not a minute more, and don't take advantage of your sick days. After you've earned the respect of your superiors and coworkers, you can start making suggestions for change.

If you have a great proposal, try it out on a trusted person in the informal office network to see if it's workable. She can help you evaluate its merits and confirm that you've included all the necessary facts before you formally present it.

Letting the boss think she came up with your idea is a time honored method to facilitate change. A carefully conceived proposal that focuses on the benefits for her as an individual and the company as a whole, can also work. Make sure you do your homework first. If you come up with a new system for order processing without bothering to find out that old one is your boss's "baby," you probably won't be in her good graces!

Unwritten Rules, Procedures and Policies

You won't find everything you need to know in the company's policy handbook. Much of the vital information is unwritten and is part of an informal network of office politics, rules, procedures and policies. This network is the office grapevine that reflects the complex dynamics of the people who work together. It holds the inside information about the real power structure in an organization. For instance, a secretary who isn't officially high on the chain of command, may wield enormous power. With detailed knowledge about the company and ready access to the boss, she may have great influence within the company. The real chain of command may operate through her, bypassing the vice-president who is simply a figure-head.

Get Inside the Inner Circle: If you have trouble figuring out the informal network, develop a relationship with someone who seems to know what's going on. Gradually draw her out to learn how the company operates. Take it easy, though. Usually the employees in "the know" are old-timers who have earned their status and play their roles to the hilt. If you try to make an instant friendship or start grilling someone over lunch, you may find her unwilling to divulge her knowledge. You'll need to earn her respect to enter the inner circle.

Follow the Unwritten Rules: If written policy dictates that memos should be sent to Mr. S and Ms. T, don't fail to send one to Mr. R. if the unwritten rules call for it. It won't sit well with your boss or employees if you fail to let them know what you're doing or forget to share vital information. They don't know or care about your memory problems and attention deficits. They'll view you as an arrogant employee who won't accept authority or consider the opinions or feelings of subordinates.

Make a list of these informal procedures. Use your checklist to be sure you're following proper formal and informal procedures. Better still, you may want to carry a small calendar or notebook where you keep these confidential materials, especially if employees in your work site don't lock their desks.

Technology and Communication

Since we've already talked about the dynamics of communication in various relationships, we won't repeat ourselves. Review the information about communication skills and continually practice and rehearse. Our discussion and suggestions here will be the dimensions of communication that are somewhat unique to work settings.

Communication is the transmission of messages from one person or group to another. We've focused on communication as spoken words and body language but in the workplace, it is frequently in the form of written expression. Businesses have always relied on written documentation and record-keeping. Now there's a high tech twist—the price sheet is faxed, the ad is scanned, the memo is E-mailed and the report is networked! This is another good news/bad news situation for ADDers.

For the Good News—High tech equipment, particularly the computer, may be the best thing that's ever happened to an ADDer. It won't put gas in your car before your business trip but it can remind you to do it! It will check the spelling and grammar of your letters and send the contents, already formatted, to the printer. You don't even have to wait impatiently at the door for the mail carrier. In a flash, your computer or fax machine with a little help from the telephone company, can send inquiries and receive responses.

For the Bad News—*Have you heard the joke about the employee who got his tie caught in the fax machine and ended up in New York?* Three things may have happened when you read this little tidbit:

1. Nothing:	You have no idea why this is funny because you have no idea what a fax machine is.
2. You laughed:	If fax machines had this capability, you can think of at least one person in your office who would routinely end up in another state.
3. You cried:	If fax machines had this capability, you know that the person routinely ending up in New York would be you.

Each of these responses illustrates the disadvantages of modern technology. E-mail, networking, scanning and faxing may mean absolutely nothing to you. This isn't a reflection of your IQ! It's mind-boggling how rapidly new methods for transmitting information have developed.

While this book isn't a training manual for high tech equipment, it wouldn't be complete without a discussion about technology's impact on communication. Even if you approach a TV remote control with fear and trepidation, you might have to use the fax machine and telephone that have more buttons than the front of your shirt!

Let's take a quick tour of the world of high tech computers and their relatives. What can and can't they do? How can you learn to use them so you don't fax yourself out of state or maneuver yourself out of a job—you know, when your cartoon of your boss Diane inadvertently ends up on her computer screen instead of your buddy's? And finally, how can you use them to your advantage?

Computer and ADD Compatibility: Computers are similar to people. They come in a variety of shapes, sizes and colors. Each has its own "personality" and communication style. If your office uses several different kinds of computers, you might have a choice about which kind to use. Matching your learning style to your computer is important.

Briefly, you communicate through a Macintosh computer with metaphors (visual channel) and an IBM with words (auditory channel). If you're starting out on either one and having a terrible time, don't jump to the conclusion that you are computer illiterate! You and your computer may simply have communication problems because of learning styles' incompatibility.

Written Expression—Memos, Letters and Reports: A computer can perform incredible feats if you are *computer comfortable*. You may find it very helpful in your job. It can relieve you of the tedium of details and become your personal secretary. Even if you use spell checkers and word processing programs, however, you might continue to have problems with written expression.

If the writing requirements of your job are primarily internal memos and business letters, consider buying an easy to use software package of templates. Templates are prepared generic letters for everything from order confirmations to congratulations for a colleague's job promotion. With the software, you choose a template that matches your need, change the names and dates, and presto—you have a polished business document. In the appendix of this book we've listed several available software packages. Check with your dealer or the adults in your support group for other suggestions.

If your responsibilities include writing reports and other more complex documents, you can still use various templates as your framework but will need to do the actual writing yourself. Remedial writing classes may help you work on shaky writing skills. Consider working with a tutor or checking out continuing education classes at your local university.

You should also remember to use some of the bypass strategies we talked about in previous chapters. If you have a secretary, dictate your letters. Otherwise try using a tape recorder to "write" your first drafts. Your ideas may flow more easily if you talk first and write later. Show your work to a sympathetic colleague for a critique before you send it out.

Don't forget to use bartering as a tool to bypass your weak writing skills. For example, you can collaborate with a coworker who writes clearly but has problems generating original ideas. Together you may be able to write reports that outshine any either of you could produce alone.

Office Equipment and Cheat Sheets: Many people have trouble using mechanical or technical equipment. This isn't exclusively a problem for folk with ADD. But some of the ADD differences do compound the problem.

You've seen how increasing complexity has an impact on your performance. This is true whether you're doing math problems, interacting with large groups of people or figuring out how to use a complicated telephone system.

Related to this is an impaired memory. How many times have you approached the duplicating machine to hand-feed a two-sided document and couldn't remember how to do it? Ten tries later, with the wastebasket overflowing with pages reversed and printed upside down, you finally get it right! Not only have you wasted an entire package of paper, you've also wasted valuable time.

You probably should make a cheat sheet for yourself. Make a list or chart of the procedures and tape it to the top of the duplicating machine. If you share the machine with others, you may need to keep your set of directions in your desk drawer. Do the same thing for the fax machine, telephone, etc. You might find that this memory by-pass system ultimately helps you to memorize the procedure because you use multi-sensory learning as an anchor. You <u>see</u> the directions as you <u>perform</u> them.

Work-Related Stress and ADD

An ADDer's boss may compliment her on the quality of her work but express concern about the quality of her relationships with coworkers. Superiors and subordinates alike might complain that working with her is difficult. They are probably commenting on her general irritability and moodiness which are, of course, symptomatic of her disorder.

These symptoms typically get worse as demands from the environment increase. Although the symptoms can't be eliminated, their severity can be minimized by managing stress levels in the work environment. The general strategies taught in stress management programs are useful but there are others more specific for the unique problems of ADDers.

Noise, Doors and Telephones: First, try to figure out the source of your stress. If the source is everything about your job, you might be in the wrong vocation! Our guess is that noise probably contributes a great deal to your stress. Intrusions of noise can be very distracting and irritating.

If you have an office with a door you can shut for periods of time, take advantage of it! There are important reasons for keeping your door open. An opened door sends the message that you are available as an active participant in the work environment. But you have to balance the need to maintain work relationships with your need for quiet to handle the details of your job.

Explain to your coworkers that you can't concentrate on detailed work when there is excessive noise. Then close your door. You don't have to tell them about your ADD. Many people are bothered by noise and will understand your need to work without interruption. Just make it clear that this is *your* problem. You haven't closed your door because you don't like your coworkers!

Your shouldn't retreat behind your closed door any longer than absolutely necessary. When the detailed concentration work is over, open your door, literally and figuratively. Don't allow yourself to get so involved with a task that you snarl at a colleague who comes in for a consultation.

You will win brownie points if you're only available during certain hours but are calm and welcoming when your door is open. Even if this means taking some of your work home, it may be worth it if you can minimize your stress during work hours.

The same principle applies to the telephone. Your work quality and telephone manners might improve if you schedule a designated time for handling telephone calls. You'll accomplish much more without the constant interruptions. Before your scheduled telephone time, you'll have time to gather everything you'll need to handle the calls in a friendly and efficient manner.

You may be thinking, "These ideas sound great, but I don't have any control over my schedule" or "I don't even have my own office". If you work in an open area where you can't close the door, is it possible for you to wear headphones when you need to concentrate? You could listen to music as you work or a tape of white noise if music is distracting.

Your boss might be more amenable to suggestions if you offer them as ways to improve your efficiency. Document your increased productivity to convince her that these strategies really work. Again, you don't have to share your diagnosis unless you're confident she'll act on your disclosure in a positive way.

If you feel that you have no control over your schedule, are you absolutely sure that's the case? A number of corporations have experimented with designated hours for employee phone calls. They have found that the decrease in interruptions throughout the day improves productivity. Approach your boss about this. Ask if your office or group could experiment with designated phone hours or even designated quiet time for work that requires heavy concentration.

Talk with coworkers to find out if noise and interruptions bother them. Chances are, they probably also have trouble with excessive distractions. Enlist their support. You may be able to make changes in your workplace that will make the environment more user-friendly for everyone. It may be surprising to you, but these strategies are taught in time-management courses. You may elicit support for these changes under the guise of wanting to manage your time more effectively.

If you try everything and still can't control the noise and interruptions, think seriously about looking for a new job or even a different line of work. The stress level from a highly distracting environment can be a threat to your mental health. Are you failing or is your work failing you?

Miscellaneous Strategies
For ease of reading we've tried to group the management strategies into categories. The ones that follow don't really fit anywhere else, so we've included them together in this section.

Take Your Medicine: This probably goes without saying, but if you need to take medicine to manage your symptoms, make sure you take it during your work hours. Your ability to handle details and interruptions will improve. Moreover, the condition of your finger nails and the anxiety of your office mate will probably also improve! As an ADD adult, you may not be in perpetual motion anymore but may have mastered the art of foot tapping, finger drumming and knuckle cracking.

This constant fidgeting can be extremely annoying to other people. These behaviors are definitely not conducive to improving interpersonal work relationships.

Manage Your Symptoms: Actively work on your problematic ADD behaviors to decrease them or make them less noticeable. Try substituting a behavior that is less distracting to other people. Can you move your hands or swing your leg under the desk so that no one sees you doing it? Tapping your fingers against each other is quieter than kicking your desk or drumming your fingers on the desktop. Can you gnaw on the top of your pencil so you look as if you are deeply engrossed in your work?

How about using your "closed door time" to spin happily on your desk chair? What about carefully spaced trips to the water fountain, file cabinet or duplicating machine? Volunteer to run needed errands. Find acceptable excuses to get up from your desk periodically.

Control Your Foot in Mouth Disease: Have you ever filed a medical insurance claim for *Foot in Mouth Disease?* It may not be on the list of covered medical conditions but if you have ADD, you probably have it! This condition causes an ADDer to spend most of her life with at least one foot in her mouth because she doesn't monitor what she says before she says it! It's no wonder she stumbles along in work relationships. Hopping on one foot while extricating the other from the mouth makes it difficult to manage the details of a job!

Of course we're talking about that troubling impulsivity of our ADD that keeps getting us in hot water. It got us poor grades in conduct on our school report cards and gets Diane an unsatisfactory grade as a manager. A thoughtless remark or a poorly worded memo can make enemies and even contribute to the loss of a job.

Our advice to you on this one is to **Be a S.T.A.R.** You have to work hard to stifle yourself at work. Monitor every word that comes out of your mouth and think twice before saying anything. Before you speak, act or approach someone, remind yourself to stop and think, look, and listen. When you take action, reflect on the results of your actions. If necessary, glue a large S.T.A.R. on your desktop as a memory teaser for **S**topping, **T**hinking, **A**cting, and **R**eflecting. It will take a lot of effort to pull this off. You may need to reward yourself by finding a like-minded individual you can trust. Together, you can let off steam at lunch or during breaks.

Review Chapter 8 Again: All the issues we discussed in group and one-to-one interfacing apply to the work setting. Refer to the strategies in the previous chapter for continued work on interpersonal relationships and communication.

The remainder of this chapter is a departure from the format we've been following. We'll use this discussion to explore the question we posed earlier: "Are you failing in your job, or is your job failing you?"

What Do You Want to Do When You Grow Up?

Have you ever poured over the want ads in the newspaper looking for a job that matches your qualifications? How many times have you closed the newspaper without responding to even one inquiry because you couldn't find a match? Let your ADD imagination roam for a moment and pretend you've just seen the following ad:

WANTED

Fast growing company looking for one special employee! The perfect candidate will be someone who has:

difficulty with rules and authority,
ineffective communication skills,
trouble switching between tasks,
an intolerance to noise,
an inability to handle interruptions,
an irritable, moody, unpredictable and impatient personality,
an intrusive, impulsive and hyperactive behavior style.

Now, there's a job designed for ADDers! But let's get back to reality. The chances are slim to none that you'll ever come across an ad like that. Don't just toss it aside, though, until you take a closer look. To do this, you'll need to refer to your inventory again. Use your creative thinking and growing awareness of your ADD advantages to hypothesize about ways to use both sides of the equation.

Negative OR	Positive Qualities?
difficulty with rules and authority	develops possibilities and solves problems
impaired communication skills	only with excessive complexity
trouble with switching gears	super focus+ability to get one job done well
intolerance to noise	super focus+ability to get one job done well—if it's quiet
inability to handle interruptions	super focus+ability to get one job done well—in small setting
irritability, impatience	shaking up complacency; getting things done
intrusive and impulsive	not so bad in a small setting; energizing
hyperactive	getting things done: stimulating

Whether you're twenty, forty or sixty years old, it's not too late to reassess some of your life choices. Your asset and liability sheet may help you evaluate the question about job failure. Perhaps the job you're in is dead wrong for you.

Vocational Planning: For our young ADD adult readers who are considering their future professions, pay careful attention to our want ad and list of positive and negative qualities. You may decide based on your interest and math aptitude, that accounting is an obvious choice for you. Before you spend substantial time and money on a college education, give plenty of thought to your balance sheet. You may love math but do you love details and paperwork? If not, the painstaking detail of accounting work may bore you to tears. If your real love is the creative, problem-solving aspect of mathematics, you might be happier in certain kinds of engineering or computer work.

To avoid costly mistakes, do your homework first. Check with your local support group about vocational counselors in your area. There isn't to our knowledge, vocational testing designed specifically for ADDers. But you may be able to latch on to a competent professional with experience in ADD issues. The information gained from vocational testing can supplement your balance sheet and help you make important decisions about additional training or higher education.

If you can get by without the earnings of a summer job, consider using your free time to do volunteer work in your field of interest. You'll learn a great deal more about a profession by experiencing it firsthand than reading about it in a book.

Talk to people in the profession you're considering. Ask them detailed questions about what they do every day. Find out what they like and dislike about their work and think about how this fits with your new self-knowledge. Are you cut out for spending much of your working day writing lectures, grading papers and going to endless committee meetings? If not, you may need to rethink your decision about using your love of literature to become a college professor. Perhaps becoming a freelance writer would be a more rewarding, though less lucrative, choice.

If you want to attend college but have only a vague idea of your future career interests, try to attend a university that offers a variety of degree programs. Talk with a college counselor about the course work in various programs. Credits often apply across degree programs. You can use credits you've already earned in a new program if you decide to switch your major. If you plan carefully, you can save wasted time, effort and money.

You're Grown Up and Still Asking: "What Do I Want to Do When I Grow Up?"

Even if you've invested tons of money and time in your career and current job, you don't necessarily have to throw it all away. Before you decide to jump ship, thoroughly examine your current situation. In many careers, there is latitude for change within the profession. Psychiatric and community health nursing, for example, require creative problem-solving and a gestalt approach. Unlike hospital nursing, they don't include extensive detail work. In teaching, possibilities exist for a change of grade level or subject matter. There are also options for supervisory or counseling positions.

Find Your Niche: Perhaps the job you need is the one you already have, with a twist. You might be able to find or negotiate a job description that fits your abilities and offers unique benefits to your company. You may be thinking about beginning a degree program in counseling because you feel that you're wasting your people skills. Before you act on your decision, consider possibilities within your current organization.

Many businesses offer training and consultation services to their employees. Can you become the in-house trainer or consultant? With your individual talents and some seminar training, you can offer your services at a fraction of the cost your company typically incurs in hiring outside consultants. Your company may even be willing to pay for the additional training you'll need.

Match Yourself With Your Job—Start Your Own Business: Maybe you're not a perfect candidate for someone's want ad and will need to design a job to fit your qualifications. Is the oversupply of rules and regulations coupled with the snail's pace of change in a large organization, unbearable? Perhaps you should explore ways of working by and for yourself. The difficulties you experience in someone else's business may disappear when the business is your own.

You may be able to use the niche you developed within your organization as a jumping-off place for other business opportunities. As you continue to collect a paycheck and gain invaluable experience, you can begin networking outside your company. You may at some point decide to go off on your own and contract with your previous employer and other related businesses to offer your services.

As a consultant, you have the advantage of being your own boss. It can be easier to ignore arbitrary rules and rigid people if you aren't a permanent employee. You don't have to get caught up in the office politics and can move on when policies and people start getting on your nerves. And it's usually easier to be on your best behavior when you're in a new situation only for a short time. You may also be able to retain some of the benefits of working for someone else—use of office equipment, secretarial support and the established network of business contacts.

If you choose to join the ranks of many ADD adults who start their own businesses, do it carefully. Take a hard look at your balance sheet and your list of perceived financial needs. Can you afford financially and emotionally to live with less while you work at developing your own business?

If you decide to take the calculated risk of working for yourself, use your list of assets to explore possibilities that offer the best match. Keep in mind that working on your own offers flexibility but requires long hours in the initial stages of establishing your business. It also requires great self-discipline.

With no time clock and policy handbook, you'll need to be very careful to establish a firm schedule and set of rules to keep yourself on track. After you've completed your self assessment, seek the assistance of a professional to help you develop a business plan for the first three to five years of your new endeavor. A business plan will provide the structure, schedules and task list an ADDer needs to stay on track.

Temporary Work: Rather than establishing your own business, you might try temporary work as a satisfactory compromise between self-employment and working for someone else. In temporary work, you "rent" your skills by the hour, day or longer but usually work for an agency that employs a number of temporary workers.

Temporary work offers several advantages. The ADDer can satisfy a restless nature by changing job settings frequently. Another advantage is the ability to control the hours of work. Many of us find a standard forty-hour, five-day work week incompatible with our unique capacities. Some of us find full time work too taxing. Others prefer working for long stretches and then taking large blocks of time off. Many ADDers are also night people, unable to function well until the afternoon. In temporary work, unusual working patterns can often be accommodated.

If you're fairly adaptable and can get along with people for short periods of time, temping may work well for you. Of course it doesn't offer carte blanche to do anything you please. If you're irresponsible about completing tasks or develop a reputation for being difficult, you'll stop getting assignments.

If you have had a history of employment failure, use your new self-knowledge to reassess the reasons for it. Your awareness of your balance sheet can help you realistically analyze your situation, sorting out the problems that result from your behavior and those that are related to the behaviors of others. You may be in a better position to figure out whether you have failed on your jobs or your jobs have failed you. Your new insights may even help you become more accepting of the quirks of your colleagues.

Your main goals should be to improve your work relationships and limit the time you spend in interactions that are difficult for you. You may decide that you can and should make some behavioral changes. You may decide that you should change your job or career. You may decide that you've already made the correct choices and are happy with them.

If you decide that some changes are in order, move slowly and thoughtfully. Although you need to base your decisions on your individual strengths and weaknesses, don't forget to include your family in the decision-making process.

Maintaining friendships, surviving in group encounters and interacting on the job aren't easy tasks. But developing intimate relationships can be even more difficult. In the next chapter, we'll turn to Interacting, Acts IV and V. We'll watch some scenes taking place in dating and family relationships. These higher risk relationships share some elements of the ones we've already examined. But they are unique in their depth and complexity and require special care and nurturing. We'll offer some specific ideas you can use to make them work successfully.

Chapter 10

Interfacing In Action: In the Dating Game and the Family

The "rules" of dating and family relationships are similar to those of group and one-to-one relationships. The level of complexity and emotional investment is very different, however. And the stakes are much higher if the relationships fail.

Act IV: The Dating Game

Sharon and Brad

Sharon returns from work to the four messages Brad left on her answering machine. She told him last week that she doesn't want to see him anymore but he is unwilling to accept her decision. He's sure that she doesn't really mean it.

He drives to her apartment complex late each night and leaves notes under her windshield wipers. He calls her at work several times a day and shows up at her door with flowers and gifts. Brad is heartbroken because he knows that Sharon is the only woman with whom he wants to spend the rest of his life. Sharon doesn't know it, but she is Brad's third "only woman I'll ever love" in the past year. Brad falls deeply in love—again and again.

Angela and Simon

Angela and Simon spend every waking hour together. They are truly in love and Simon is planning the perfect time and place to propose to her. He met Angela just a few weeks ago but wines and dines her almost every day.

As weeks turn into months, Angela begins to orchestrate some conflicts that prevent her from seeing Simon. When they are together they have a wonderful time, but Angela is beginning to feel a bit closed in. One afternoon, she asks Simon to stop by her house. When he arrives, another man answers the door. He tells Simon that Angela is busy and can't see him now.

Notes: Act IV

With the exception of Sharon, all the actors in the preceding scenes have ADD. We can only speculate about why Brad, Angela and Simon feel compelled to behave as they do.

Brad may approach his new relationship as he approaches projects at work—with intensity and impulsivity. He may be accustomed to making quick decisions and getting things done in a hurry. Unfortunately he doesn't understand that he can't control the women in his life the way he does the facts and figures on his sales' plans. He can't enjoy positive relationships and doesn't give himself time to consider his needs—he never evaluates the reality of his feelings of love.

Brad's problems with his relationships may also result from his battered sense of self. He may be one of the *walking wounded*, believing that he can be emotionally whole only when he has a "better half." Men and women alike can have unrealistic expectations about being saved by a relationship. But the powerful myth of Prince Charming seems to be an illusion with greater appeal to women.

Angela's behavior may reflect her insatiability. Although she genuinely enjoyed Simon's company during the first months of the relationship, she may have become bored. She has an ADDer's tendency to become absorbed quickly in relationships and to become bored by them just as quickly. As the initial, intense stimulation of her romance has dwindled, so has her interest in it. Although Angela probably doesn't chart her conquests, she may leave a trail of discarded partners, including Simon, as a reminder of her frequent, intense affairs.

Clearly, this behavior isn't unique to ADDers. Adults may behave this way for a variety of reasons. The specific symptoms and differences of an ADDer, however, can engender this less than admirable behavior.

Apart from the moral issue of hurting other people, this callous treatment is also self-destructive. The *Don Juan* (or *Donna Juan!*) lifestyle is initially exciting but gets old and lonely after a while. Over time even friends who previously enjoyed hearing about the escapades, stop asking about them. An ADDer's chance to form an intimate bond is undermined by the reputation that precedes him.

While Angela runs from a close relationship with Simon, he runs headlong towards it. In most relationships there's a subtle or not so subtle tension between the desire to be close and a fear of that closeness. Simon seems to desperately fight for closeness. Angela seems to desperately fight to protect her individuality which she thinks is threatened by the closeness.

Simon's impulsivity may also play into the demise of his relationship with Angela. He drives the relationship with his need for closeness. Angela's insatiability aside, she may be terrified that Simon will "swallow" her individuality. Given time, it's possible that her love for Simon would win out over her fears of closeness. But she never gets the chance because Simon's intense need for closeness tips the precarious balance of their relationship much too quickly. Angela would rather lose her love than her identity.

Synopsis: Act IV

It sounds pretty gloomy, doesn't it? Is it time to head out to a hermit's hut? Well, if you've been paying attention—sorry, we couldn't help it—you know how we feel about doom and gloom. It's fine for disaster movies on the big screen but it's counterproductive to your recovery.

Intimate relationships are a sensitive, delicate variation on the theme of communication and interfacing. They are dances choreographed with intricate steps and have great potential for disaster.

Dating relationships are vulnerable to an ADDer's intensity and impaired communication skills. His enthusiasm or sparkle can be a strong magnet that initially attracts his love interest. But over time, his level of intensity can suffocate his lover. She's left gasping for breath and backing away to get some space. The ADDer, comfortable with the

intense pace, may not recognize his lover's need for a gradual progression to closeness. Unless he is good at finding people who share his intensity, he must teach himself to control his impulses and slow down.

In a romantic or sexual relationship, an individual risks revealing himself big time! Everyone shares this risk which is the inherent nature of intimacy. The risk can be greater for the ADDer who has failed so many times and in so many different ways. His generalized feelings of inadequacy, borne of differences he's never understood, can explode when he bares his soul and body to a partner. When he dares to reveal himself to a lover who subsequently rejects him, he can suffer a serious blow to his fragile self-worth.

Some adults experience ongoing difficulties in intimate relationships because they regard them as safe ports from their feelings of inadequacy. Even with changing roles, many families still condition their daughters to believe that the roles of wife and mother will protect them. An ADD woman's life of negative experiences can reinforce this myth. She may believe that the only escape route from her demanding life is through a wedding ring and then a diaper bag. She comes to view a partner as a lifeline or safety net and may scare suitors away with the weight of her clinging dependency.

PR: "A close friend of mine has been married and divorced three times. Before the ink was dry on her divorce degree, she invariably fell in love again. After her second date with a new man, she would call me to describe her new love. This was the one! I often envied her ability to find so many suitable matches while I found myself hung up on one from which I couldn't extricate myself.

As she continued falling in and out of love, I sat waiting for my knight in shining armor. When he finally arrived, he came in the form of a newly divorced man involved in a new, intense long-distance relationship. Though we ADDers aren't known for our patience, I was very patient. I ignored his repeated warnings that he was in love with someone else and really wasn't interested in a long term relationship anyway. For four years, while my friend remarried and divorced, I hung around waiting for my reluctant love to fit me into his busy social calendar.

To say this was painful is putting it mildly. I truly believed that he was my lifeline—I knew with my whole being that I would drown without him. My sights were set on marrying him. I knew that my tortured self-esteem would be healed only when I had his name. I'm sure the only reason my dependency didn't totally overwhelm him was that he was so incredibly independent.

Eighteen years and two children later, my reality has changed considerably, not because *he and me* did ultimately become *we*, but in **spite of it!** Becoming Mrs. did save me but not in the way I had imagined. When my lifeline turned into a weighted anchor that dragged me under instead of securely holding me, I cut it loose.

No, I didn't divorce him. Incredibly we're still together and the *we* is still a big part of us. I changed the equation by adding a stronger, more self-reliant *me* into it. I also cut every picture of Prince Charming out of my daughter's story books. . ."

Some ADDers do just fine with intimate relationships—you may be involved in a positive, fulfilling one right now. Or, you may be taking some time to regroup after a relationship you've chosen to end. On the other hand, you may be struggling with repeated failures in your attempts to connect with a significant other. If you are, you'll need to analyze the reasons for your failures.

We didn't use our stories to illustrate what **will** go wrong in your relationships but what **might** go wrong. An ADD adult's differences can contribute to problems in maintaining intimate relationships. By understanding the dynamics of your disorder, you may be able to figure out what's going wrong. If you're aware of potential hazards, you can be prepared the next time you meet someone special, to stop and think before you act.

Having clarified our message—an important part of positive communication —we'll look at some ways to avoid the pitfalls and improve the quality of your relationships. Here are a few pointers on successfully playing the dating game.

Survival Tips: Act IV

Play Hard to Get: You should never utter the words, "I love you" after just a few dates! Watch your partner's signals for clues about the progress of the relationship. Use the dynamics of approach and withdrawal behaviors to your advantage. Even if you immediately set your sights on your new love interest—as we both did on our spouses—play hard to get for a while. This keeps the desire and fear of closeness in proper balance until the other person has time to catch up with your willingness to make a commitment!

This approach may sound somewhat manipulative but it doesn't have an evil intent. Let's face it, an ADD adult has to carefully plan many aspects of his life to make them work. Why should relationships be any different? After all, the hard to get approach is just a variation of learning to stop, think, act and reflect, right?

Monitor the Relationship: Spontaneity is a lovely thing but ADDers can get in trouble when freedom reigns. To a certain extent, you'll need to approach intimate relationships as you do everything else—with careful planning and ongoing monitoring. Keep your finger on the pulse of the relationship. If your partner seems skittish, back off and lighten up! When the intensity level is too high, be less available for a while.

Don't swing too far in the other direction either. You can chase a love interest away with your apparent indifference. Relationships require continual work and maintenance. The challenge for an ADDer is to sustain attention to the relationship over the long haul.

Work at your communication skills. Remind yourself to listen to your partner, ask questions to draw her out and pay attention to moods and non-verbal clues.

Don't Lose the "Me" in "We": Be sure to maintain your usual interests when you begin dating someone new. This will help you keep a reasonable distance from the relationship to prevent your total immersion in it. This will also help you maintain your own identity.

Watch Your Impulsivity: Impulsive behavior can create an assortment of problems in an ADD adult's life. In a sexual relationship, it can cause life threatening trouble! In this day of serious sexually transmitted diseases, more than emotional well-being is at stake. It's wise to wait a while before beginning any sexual relationship.

You may need to make some rules for yourself to prevent impulsive decisions. Talk to a trusted friend who seems to be in control of his life. Ask for his advice. How long does he think a person should wait before having sex, saying "I love you" or living with a new romantic interest? Ask how long he thinks a person should know a lover before marriage.

Use this information to make a vow to wait x-amount of time before taking any of these steps. Enlist your friend's help with your vow. In many support groups, a sponsor helps the individual stick to his *program*. Your friend could become the sponsor you call on when you're having trouble sticking with your program, ie. your rules for dating behavior.

Stop and Think: If you're feeling restless just thinking about such an unbearably slow pace of a relationship, use your imagination and consider this. Visualize a *whole lifetime of restlessness* with a spouse who bores you to death! Visualize a giant vise systematically tightening down and squeezing out all your hard work at recovery and rebuilding your sense of self. You are worth too much to throw away your progress by impulsively hooking up with someone who is wrong for you. The consequences of an impulsive marriage can be heavy, particularly if children are involved.

Debunk the Prince Charming Myth: This one is for women who grew up believing the myth. Don't look at every date as a stepping stone to marriage. Try to enjoy your evening of dinner and dancing without visualizing yourself at the altar!

Watch out for your yearnings for Prince Charming! We know we're repeating ourselves but the trap is so tempting that it can snare you before you realize it's happening. This comment isn't a condemnation of the weakness of women. It's a reality of a world that still teaches women to depend on men for their salvation.

When the going gets tough in school or in careers, it's easy to indulge in fantasies about marriage as an escape route. There is **nothing** wrong with wanting to be a wife or mother. Just make sure that you make the decision for the right reasons—out of choice. Don't do it because you feel you can't do anything else or want a way out of your current, unhappy situation.

KK: "When I was in my '20's, I made a rule that I wouldn't get married or have children until I had found a satisfying way to support myself. I didn't know about ADD then but did have a sense that my survival and self-esteem depended on my having a sense of competence.

As an older mother, I enjoyed the experience without losing my self-esteem. Motherhood was a joyful choice rather than a retreat from a world I couldn't handle. I kept a part time job as a psychiatric nurse, knowing I could go back to full-time work at any time. I didn't suffer from doubts about being *just a mother* as many of my peers did. I think this was because I had made a clear and conscious choice from a position of strength rather than weakness."

Act V, Scene 1: Interfacing in the Family

Now we'll examine the most complex kind of relationship. We'll introduce you to the Baker family to help us explore the unique issues of family interactions. The family includes Jan, Tom and their three biological children, Amy, Zachary and Jennifer. Each of the five members of the family has ADD although each has slightly different problems associated with it.

Tom

Tom, a successful real estate broker, is extremely restless, hyperactive and irritable. He earns a good living but the family experiences ongoing financial crises. Everyone in the family spends the money as quickly as he can earn it. Tom has a Jeckle and Hyde personality that changes at the drop of a hat. He flips back and forth from an enthusiastic, fun-loving man to an irritable, withdrawn grouch. Jan and the children are always a bit afraid of him.

Jan

Jan isn't particularly moody or hyperactive. She is more of a gentle space cadet. She has trouble organizing the household and disciplining the children. She is so overwhelmed by the demands of life that she just lets them wash over her. Having few reserves of energy to gain control of her life, she manages to do little more that survive each day.

Amy

The oldest daughter Amy, is an extremely bright, chronic underachiever. She has always been a maverick. She has problems following rules and fitting in with other children. She's continually in trouble at home and at school. Amy shares her dad's symptoms of moodiness, impulsivity and hyperactivity. At 13, she's becoming increasingly rebellious, refusing to take her Ritalin and hanging out with a group of kids who take drugs.

Amy and her dad have an explosive relationship since they both regularly fly off the handle. She and her mom don't argue a lot but they have a tenuous relationship. Amy treats Jan with contempt, not even attempting to hide her low opinion of her mother. She can't understand why Mom is so wishy-washy about everything.

Zachary

Ten year old Zachary is quiet and rather passive. He doesn't make waves. He struggles in school and receives only mediocre grades despite putting in long hours doing homework. He's anxious most of the time and has a number of health problems including asthma, severe allergies and frequent stomach aches. He's shy and has trouble making friends.

Zachary was evaluated and diagnosed with multiple learning disabilities and ADD. His psychologist recommended intensive tutoring but the family never has enough extra money to hire anyone. Jan has taken on the job but can't do it with any regularity because she's so overwhelmed by the details of her life. So Zachary struggles along without the educational help he needs.

Jennifer

Jennifer is the baby of the family and her parents treat her that way. They place few demands on her. At 8 years old, she's a delightful child with a sunny personality and an engaging sense of humor. She's fairly hyperactive but doesn't display the irritability and moodiness of her father or sister. She channels some of her excess energy into gymnastics, cartwheeling or dancing around the house much of the time.

At school she has become the class clown, entertaining her peers and keeping her teachers so busy laughing that they ignore her difficulties with school work. Her grades are even worse than her brother's, but no one gets on her case about it. Her teachers assume that she just isn't very bright. Her parents are busy arguing with each other and with Amy. They work so hard at just surviving that they don't have time to worry about their youngest child. They figure that at least they have one normal child even if she isn't any smarter than the rest of their kids.

Notes: Act V, Scene 1

Marriage and child rearing present all the challenges we've already discussed and then some! The intricacy of the dance of family relationships is dramatically more complex than that of groups, friendships or romantic interactions. In this regard, we would like you to consider these new math facts. Are you ready?

$$1 + 1 > 2$$
$$2 + 1 = 4$$
$$2 + 2 = 11 \textit{ plus}$$

We're not going to tell you quite yet what these equations mean, but the answers are correct. . .Sort of. . .It depends on the questions you're asking. We'll get back to this in a few paragraphs.

As soon as two individuals become a *legal we*, the rules change and the complexity and intensity of the relationship increase whether or not either has ADD. There are often unrealistic expectations that the spouse will fulfill the roles of Savior, Mother, Father, Best Friend, Expert Lover, Tower of Strength, Therapist, etc.

Further complicating the relationship of a couple, particularly as time goes on, is the history they have shared. Communications are colored with memories, both good and bad. An innocent remark can spark an argument about a past hurt or unresolved conflict that had an impact on the relationship. If we add a spouse with ADD to the picture, the relationship can change unpredictably.

Jan and Tom were delighted to find each other and had an exciting courtship. Jan loved the spontaneity of impulsive trips to the beach and phone calls at 3:00 a.m. Tom loved having Jan help him remember to put gas in the car and agree with his opinions.

When Amy was born in the first year of their marriage, they seemed to become totally different people. The transformation they experienced is certainly not unique to ADDers. Virtually all parents, even those who carefully plan their families, say it's impossible to imagine the magnitude of the changes that occur with the birth of a child.

This brings us back to the answers in our equations. They are correct if we ask the following questions:

What does one spouse plus one spouse equal?
What does one couple plus one child equal?
What does one couple plus two children equal?

Jan and Tom assumed that their problems resulted from baby Amy's constant crying. A difficult infant can definitely add stress to a relationship. Even if Amy had been a calm, placid baby, our couple would have experienced a transformation in their relationship.

With the addition of each child, the relationships between and among family members become increasingly complicated. The complications grow not arithmetically, but geometrically. This may be why parents often say a second child adds more than just double the work of an only child. The extra work doesn't have nearly as much to do with extra laundry or meal preparation as it does with an exploding number of relationships. Let's look at what happens to the number of relationships when you add children to a family:

The Couple = husband and wife (plus their individual + collective "baggage")

The Couple+One Child = husband and wife
husband and child
wife and child
husband, wife and child

The Couple+Two Children = husband and wife
husband and first child
husband and second child
wife and first child
wife and second child
first and second child
husband, wife and first child
husband, wife and second child
husband, first and second child
wife, first and second child
husband, wife, first and second child

Synopsis: Act V, Scene 1

If computer programmers think it's difficult to interface an IBM™ and a Macintosh,™ we wonder what they would think about interfacing a family unit. They would have to program individual personalities to interface with the multiple relationships among family members. The dyad of husband and wife alters the one:one relationship of pre-marriage days even before children add to the complexity of interpersonal relationships.

Since ADD tends to run in families, it dramatically alters the dimensions of the family unit and exponentially ups the ante as children are born. Raising ADD children is a challenging job that taxes the resources of non-ADD parents. Many adoptive parents can attest to this. In a family like the Bakers where several people have the disorder, the potential for discord and communication breakdown is enormous.

Does this mean that the equation of **ADD adult(s) + children = disaster?** Absolutely not! It only means that the stakes may be higher and the pitfalls deeper and more treacherous. You may be a wonderful parent! ADDers are lively people. Many can respond to the challenges of child rearing with incredible enthusiasm and avoid the pitfalls by leaping energetically over them!

A decision as important as whether to bring a new human being into this world—into your world—must be made *very carefully*! Planning this area of your life may be **THE** most important job you have. You **must** stop and think about your balance sheet of strengths and weaknesses.

What if you already had children before you knew anything about ADD? What if having a family is what you do because you never considered not having one? Well, you're certainly not alone! Many people have children because their religious or family script teaches them to. What if you would have loved to plan your family better but medical science failed and you ended up with an unplanned pregnancy?

Our goal isn't to establish ourselves as critics of your religious principles or contraceptive practices, but to help you think about some important issues. You will need to examine your ADD balance sheet and consider how it fits with parenting and the math of family relationships. If you already have children, we hope the discussion will help you clarify and better understand this dimension of your life.

The Job of Parenting: ADD adults have strengths and weaknesses when it comes to parenting. A typical balance sheet for an ADD parent may look something like this:

STRENGTHS	**WEAKNESSES**
active	impatient
creative	moody
open-minded	intolerant of noise and chaos
compassionate	careless with details
sense of wonder	shaky communication skills
curious	limited capacity for work + stress
enthusiastic	easily bored
passionate	impulsive
good sense of humor	disorganized

How does this balance sheet play out when you become a parent? It's hard to say with certainty. Your child's personality and the interrelated profiles of you, your spouse, and your offspring all have impacts. You might become a parent who yells a lot or is grouchy much of the time. The added noise and stress of having children may push buttons that weren't pushed before. You might look at your reflection in a mirror and wonder where the mean, angry person came from.

On the other hand, you might take advantage of the wonderful "immaturity" everyone used to criticize. With your children in tow, you can giggle, climb on the monkey bars and sing aloud in the grocery store without questionable looks from other people. You might effectively use your compassion and open-mindedness to roll with the inevitable punches of parenting.

Your effectiveness as a parent will be tested by the genetic probability that one or more of your children are likely to have ADD. Their high-strung temperaments will require special handling. In some respects your own ADD uniquely qualifies you as a provider of special handling. You have insight unavailable to your non-ADD peers. If you haven't yet achieved a workable balance in your life, however, you may still require too much nurturing for yourself. You may be unable to provide the careful guidance your ADD child needs.

Parenting has been compared to a scary, exciting, unpredictable roller coaster ride. We submit that when ADD is an issue, parenting becomes a more treacherous journey. It's like guiding an out of control rocket

ship at the speed of light towards an unknown destination! Is this necessarily so bad? Just think of all the teacher conferences and emergency room visits our parents would never have made if it hadn't been for us! What would they have done with all that extra time? Just think how boring the world would be without us.

Can we learn any lessons from this survey of the family dimension? We think the most important one is the need for planning. Your parents and teachers probably complained so often about your poor planning that the very word makes you uncomfortable. As much as you may dislike planning, it's probably the singularly most important thing you should do for yourself. Use the following considerations as a framework for your "Planned Parenting". The job of parenting is too important to leave to chance.

Survival Tips: Act V, Scene 1

Spacing of Children: Carefully consider the spacing of your children. This has nothing to do with the psychology of spacing as it affects a child's adjustment. Rather, careful spacing allows you to absorb the impact of each child on your capacity to handle the additional demands. If you have several children in the space of a few years, you may be pushed beyond your limits before you know it. Spacing buys you the time you need to make a wise decision.

Personal and Financial Resources: If you and your spouse want to continue full-time employment, can you both emotionally handle the second shift of parenting? If not, can you survive financially if one parent has only a part time job or stays at home? Of course if you're a single parent, you won't have an option in this regard.

Realistic Assessment of Effort and Money: Do your homework. Ask other parents, especially parents of ADD children, about the work and money it takes to raise children. Everyone knows that children are expensive. But when ADD is part of the financial picture, you'll need to think about the added expenses you may incur. Your child may need extra help. He may need among other services, tutoring, speech therapy, medicine or psychological counseling.

General Strategies: What resources are available to lighten the load? Are there relatives living nearby who are willing to help? Can you reduce your financial obligations? Can you organize the work load so each parent can have periodic breaks? When you add children to your life, you need to be even more ruthless about simplifying it to maintain balance.

Post This List and Reread it at Frequent Intervals: Each time you consider adding a child to your family, go back over this list. Make sure you are handling what's already on your plate before you dish up another serving. If you and your partner plan carefully, your family relationships can be satisfying ones that add to the quality of your life. You'll be able to pass on to your children your valuable, hard-earned knowledge about overcoming obstacles. Your children can become enterprising, productive adults.

Act V, Scene 2: Interfacing in the Family

In the following scenes we'll offer a glimpse of the Baker family's interactions. They are illustrative of the complexity of family relationships when ADD is added to the mix.

Jan, Tom and Zachary
Jan is tutoring Zachary at the dining room table. Tom walks in and starts to tell her some exciting news about work. When she doesn't respond, he becomes increasingly exasperated by her seeming disinterest. When his raised voice finally elicits Jan's request to "wait a minute", he leaves the room in a huff.

Tom, Jan and Jennifer
Tom sits bleary-eyed at the breakfast table, drinking his first cup of coffee and trying to read the newspaper. Jan who is a morning person, chats to him non-stop and reminds him that it's garbage day. Tom finally looks up from his paper and announces that the garbage needs to be taken out. Jan testily replies that if he'd been listening he would know that she's aware of that fact. Jennifer suddenly appears out of nowhere to give her startled parents bear hugs. She is reprimanded for being so rough and slinks out of the room wondering why her mom and dad rejected her affection.

Jennifer, Amy and Zachary
Jennifer rushes into her sister's room and pounces on the bed to give Amy a morning kiss. Amy who is just beginning to wake up, shoves her off the bed and feels only mildly remorseful when Jennifer scrapes her knee on the way down. Now fully awake, Amy heads down the hall for a shower and lets loose a string of epithets when Zachary walks in to brush his teeth.

Notes: Act V, Scene 2

The Baker family includes five people whose individual deficits collectively combine to create *Chaos on the Cul-de-Sac*. All families share some of their problems—balancing the rights of individual members with the needs of the larger family unit. The Baker family has an extra layer of shared ADD disabilities that makes this balancing act particularly difficult.

Families who live under the same roof share both physical and emotional spaces. If the family is to live peacefully together, each member has to have his fair share of both. Each of the Bakers has a poor sense of physical and emotional boundaries and impulsively invades each other's territory. Acting on autopilot most of the time, they bump, jostle and literally step on each other's toes as they repeatedly miss both obvious and subtle requests for space.

A closed door or a sign that says, **"Keep Out"** is a fairly clear statement of a desire for privacy. Most of us understand its obvious significance—but what about the subtle, non-verbal requests for privacy? Many of us with ADD misread these "signs".

These non-verbal signs are the invisible circles that people draw around their bodies for privacy and protection. The circles define the perimeter of personal space and convey the message: "Don't come any closer than the circle I have drawn around me."

These circles aren't fixed in time and space. The diameter of your own circle constantly changes according to your mood, circumstances and relationship to the other person. The circle narrows to encourage a lover or a beloved child to get close and widens to keep the stranger or someone you dislike, at a safe distance. If you're angry or depressed, the circle may become huge even for loved ones as you send out the message: **"Stay Away"**. For an ADDer, the circle sometimes inexplicably widens when he can't stand to be touched or to allow anyone in his immediate vicinity.

Synopsis: Act V, Scene 2

Awareness of and respect for these invisible circles requires good non-verbal communication skills. Lacking these skills, the Bakers impulsively trounce on each other's feelings and invade personal physical spaces. Since the whole family has ADD, each person has a unique need for space. Each person also has an inability to prevent his needs from colliding with the needs of everybody else. Privacy is as hard to come by in this family as peace and quiet are. The experience of living in this kind of family is feeling intruded upon and overwhelmed.

Most ADD families experience some degree of difficulty in their interactions. What can an ADD family such as the Baker's do to make its home more of a haven for the people who live there? The first order of business is to see a family therapist.

This family has been in trouble for a long time. They need an objective outsider to analyze and balance the needs of the family as a unit with the individual needs of family members. The therapist's job is to help the family system become healthier so it can better meet the needs of each member. Right now, the family is too stressed and chaotic to provide the necessary structure and nurturing.

We can't emphasize enough that treating a troubled family is not a do-it-yourself enterprise! A Band-Aid approach may temporarily slow down the bleeding but it won't stop the hemorrhage! **If your family is really in trouble, get professional help ASAP!**

If your family is basically okay and needs only minor adjustments, that's wonderful. There are several techniques you can use to support and build your family system. The following discussion includes specific suggestions for improving communication and managing boundary issues.

Survival Tips: Act V, Scene 2

Creating Living Space Large Enough for the People Who Share It
When we talk about living space, we're not suggesting that you increase the square footage of your house or apartment! We're talking about carefully designing sufficient *emotional* living space so that family members can coexist with relative harmony.

Teach Respect for Boundary Needs: Suggest that your family visualize a boundary as a hula hoop. We know we're showing our ages—many people under 35 have never even played with one! Anyway, if you have a hula hoop lying around, put it around you to demonstrate your personal circle. Ask each family member to picture himself surrounded by his own personal hoop.

The room suddenly starts to shrink in size as people and hula hoops begin to take up space. As everyone starts to move around in the space, the inevitable happens. There's a fair amount of confusion as hula hoops start bumping into each other.

Each family member should put this image in his memory bank for future reference. The next time he starts to intrude on someone else, he may be able to call up the hula hoop image in his mind. "Seeing" Dad in a hula hoop might just be enough to make junior Stop, Look, Listen. . .and Laugh!

Design Rest and Relaxation Zones: In many families, there are unwritten rules regarding private space. The den may "belong" to the parents—the children understand that this space is Mom and Dad's retreat. Similarly, the children often use their bedrooms as escapes from the demands of the family.

ADD families need to establish written rules regarding the boundaries of privacy. Each member of the family should have his own designated zone. In a small apartment, this space could be the balcony, the hall or half of a shared bedroom. Each family member has a right to privacy and needs a private retreat—a place that is off-limits to everyone else. "Out to Lunch" or "Temporary Shutdown" signs can indicate current occupation of a personal zone.

This provision for *down time* is essential to forestall the negative behaviors of frustration. Each person has a right to state his need for space. When he makes the request, other family members shouldn't talk to him or expect a response. The same rules apply about being touched. If someone doesn't want to be touched, his wishes must be respected.

Designated Quiet Zones: You should also designate specific quiet zones in your home as places for reading, studying or resting. The television and stereo should be in an area with a door that can be closed. This area should also be as far away as possible from the quiet zones. A sound proof room for noisy equipment would be ideal but most homes don't have this luxury. One option is to establish a rule that TV or stereo users must use earphones.

Rules for Communication and Respect for Boundaries: You can't take anything for granted in an ADD family! You need to design structured rules to protect the emotional and physical circles of family members. Some of these suggestions may be helpful:

•**Set Aside Specific Time Periods for Quiet** when the TV should be turned off and the answering machine turned on. Develop a family schedule with designated times for studying or other quiet pursuits as well as times to be together as a group.

•**Observe a Period of Silence** when the noise level is too high or emotions are getting out of control.

•**Require Each Family Member, Including Parents, to Ask Permission** before borrowing anything from someone else.

•**Impose a Stop—Look/listen—Speak Procedure** for all communication between family members. When a conversation is in progress, the person entering the room must wait until he's invited to join in. If someone is doing something that requires concentration, such as reading or paying bills, he shouldn't be interrupted except for an emergency.

•**Determine What Constitutes an Emergency.** An untied shoe string can be an emergency for an ADD child. You may need to discuss and make a list of real and perceived emergency situations. Insist that everyone refer to the list before interrupting a conversation in progress. If an interruption is necessary, everyone should abide by the following rules. Get the person's attention by gently tapping him on the shoulder, wait for a response and then excuse yourself before you begin to talk.

•**Prohibit All Long Distance Conversations** except for announcements that the house is burning down! Yelling up the stairs or shouting from another room to find someone is a no-no. There are two reasons for this. First, if family members have to strain to hear, they will frequently misinterpret the message. An ADDer can have enough trouble sending and receiving messages without the added burden of trying to talk to someone in another room. Second, it's rude! Yelling upstairs to get someone to come down is a lot like calling the dog—and it feels like it too.

•**Use Intercoms.** You might want to invest in some intercoms to communicate with people in other parts of the house. Be careful not to over-do it. A buzzing intercom every five minutes can be as annoying as a bellowing voice!

•**Prohibit All "On The Run" Conversations.** Talking to someone while you rush to finish a task, isn't conducive to effective communication. The intended recipient of this one-way conversation has to listen to a program that fades in and out or follow the speaker around on his travels. On the run conversations are rude and contribute to miscommunication.

•**Enforce a Rule to Prohibit Unwanted Teasing or Joking** about individual family members. ADDers often read the literal meaning of messages and miss the intended meaning. Since impulsive ADD family members often fail to notice the discomfort of others, their teasing can quickly escalate into perceived full-scale attacks. Teasing can feel like torture and must not be permitted. All requests to stop teasing must be respected. The butt of the joke shouldn't be labeled a party pooper or poor sport. If a joke hurts someone, it's not funny.

•**Set Up a Message Center** in a prominent place. The kitchen may be a good place for this as it's often the center of family activities. The best location is near a phone with an answering machine. Preferably, the space should have a counter or desk for a writing surface. The center should include a bulletin board, a method for filing mail and important papers, a large calendar and an ample supply of paper and pens.

The bulletin board needs to be sufficiently large to provide a specific section for each family member and one for the whole family. Keep extra colored paper tacked in each section or use color post-it pads. Each family member can have a personalized color that makes it easy to post and retrieve messages. A white board may be a good backdrop to the colored notes. Be sure that everyone, including small children, can reach the bulletin board.

The *General Messages* area is for anything the whole family needs to read. The rest of the board should be divided into sections for individual family members. Make a rule that every message must include the signature of the person who posted it, the date and the time. Whenever possible, telephone calls should be handled at or switched to, the message center phone.

Encourage family members to make a habit of checking the message center several times a day and every time they come home. As soon as someone reads a message, he should remove it from the board. This will reduce visual clutter and improve the odds that the family won't overlook posted messages. If someone adds a general message to the board, he should initial it at the bottom. As each person in turn reads the message, he should add his initials. The last reader will know that everyone else has seen the note and that he should remove it from the board.

Besides looking for posted messages, each person needs to check his mail slot and listen to the answering machine. Phone calls should be added to the board and the tape should be rewound. Before making any plans, everyone should check the message center's master calendar for important family dates.

We're not suggesting that families do all their communicating by way of the message center! Putting things in writing can a big help, however. Otherwise, an ADD child might forget to mention that Dad is stranded with a flat tire and Sister is in the emergency room with a broken arm! A disorganized ADD family can truly benefit from a structured system that tracks family messages and appointments.

•Continually Monitor Your Family's Emotional Temperature: Monitoring your personal stress level is important, but in your excitable, roller-coaster ADD family, the effect of workload or stress snowballs. It's similar to what happens to the number of relationships when you add new family members: 2+1 is greater than 3.

This is how it happens. One of the children comes home after a bad day at school and is bouncing off the walls. Mom arrives an hour later in a bad mood after a difficult day at work. In a matter of minutes, Mom and the hyperactive child are at each other's throats as the child's noise and activity irritate a mother who has no reserves of patience. The fight that erupts puts everyone in the family on edge and before long the house feels like a war zone.

Because the stress level of each person has such a profound effect on the family, it's important to monitor the demands on the family as a whole. If an individual family member is pushing himself too hard and feels irritable as a consequence, it isn't just an individual matter. If the family as a whole is trying to do too much, the stress makes relaxation and down-time, impossible.

Before we close this chapter, we want to at least mention the wider family circle—the extended family. Grandparents, in-laws, aunts, uncles, etc., will all have an impact on the dynamics of your family. Their support or lack of support can be a powerful influence on your efforts to be a successful ADD family. We can't examine this issue in depth because the subject is too complicated to address in a few sentences. These chapters just scratch the surface. We'd like to write another book that focuses exclusively on ADD family relationships.

But there are some other important family issues we're going to address in the next chapter. With family relationships as the backdrop, we'll revisit the Baker family to examine some management issues unique to the functioning of the family.

CHAPTER 11

From Mealtime Mania to Outing Ordeals: How-To's of Decreasing Discord

The family is a microcosm of society. It includes individual and group rights, responsibilities and rules. It's a system of multiple interpersonal relationships that must be carefully managed.

Hundreds of sociological studies have explored the entity of the family and how it functions. Since we are neither sociologists nor family therapists, we don't presume to be experts in these fields. We do, however, consider ourselves experts in two specific areas: **The ADD Families of Kelly/Pentz and Ramundo.** Our experiences could fill volumes as we're sure yours could too.

When we use the word expert, we use it humbly as a reflection of our lifetime experiences, not as a measure of our expertise. We can't give you all the answers about ADD families because we don't have them! We can share some of our observations and the collective experiences of other ADDers and their families. We'll rejoin the Baker family to help us do this.

Our previous visit with them provided a glimpse of a family living in the sitcom *Chaos on the Cul-de-Sac*. If you recognize your family in the description of the Bakers, do you have to resign yourself to being part of the neighborhood? Is there anything you can realistically do to make your family life more manageable? We're going to take take on the role of the Baker family's therapist to find some answers.

To begin unravelling the family's complex problems, we'll encourage each family member to communicate her own version of the *Baker Family Story*. This sharing will have to happen over time and within an atmosphere of mutual support.

Tom: "I feel helpless, angry and worthless most of the time. I know I lose my temper too much and it hurts people, but I just can't seem to help it. The angry words are out of my mouth before I know it. I feel lonely too. Jan doesn't seem to know I exist unless she's cringing because I got mad. She's always busy with something. She doesn't look me in the eye and never pays attention to me when I try to talk to her. I'm scared all the time. I worry that I can't keep pretending I'm in control. Work just takes it out of me. When I get home, I don't have any energy left for my family. I'm supposed to be strong—the man of the family—but sometimes I feel as though I'm just barely hanging on."

Jan: "I feel as if I'm under water all the time, fighting to swim to the surface but never getting there. No matter what I do, I never seem to get anything accomplished. I work hard to take care of the house and family but I never have anything to show for it. The place is always a mess and we never seem to have a moment of peace. Everyone is always fighting. I'm a failure. Tom and Amy are always yelling and putting me down. I probably deserve it. I'm pretty useless."

Amy: "Everybody thinks I'm just a rotten kid but they have no idea how I really feel. I'm scared that I'll never be able to make it as a grown-up. I know I'm a "smartass" but that's just a cover-up. I'm mean, have terrible moods and can't seem to get it together to do anything worthwhile. What am I going to do when I finish high school? With my grades, I probably won't make it to college and I'm not fast enough to do something like waitressing. Sometimes I wish I were more like Zachary. I make fun of him for being a wimp but he's a nicer person than I am. Sometimes I wish I were dead."

Zachary: "I hate the fighting at my house. Even when my family is laughing or joking, I'm always waiting for something terrible to happen—for Dad or Amy to start a big screaming match. I can't stand it when people yell because the noise hurts me. I don't know how to protect myself. I get so mad sometimes I just want to yell at them to shut up but I can't get the words out. It's hard enough to talk when I'm feeling calm. When I get upset, I get so confused I can't think straight. I feel like a dope. I work harder in school than anybody I know but I still get mostly C's. My dad gets impatient with me because I'm not good at sports and I won't stick up for myself. Mom seems to like me better but never has enough time to help me with school work. I hate to even ask her because she seems so busy and tired most of the time. I know I cause a lot of trouble because I hear mom and dad fighting all the time about my doctor bills. I wish it was more peaceful at my house."

Jennifer: "It's crazy at my house! I especially hate dinnertime because it takes too long. Everybody's always telling me, Sit down, Jennifer. . . Be quiet, Jennifer. . .Stop falling off your chair, Jennifer. I can't stand to sit there all that time. I'd rather be outside playing. I like it when my family tells jokes but a lot of times people yell and get in fights. I hate the yelling. Most of the time, I don't think my family even notices I'm there. My mom and dad don't even seem to care when I bring home D's on my papers. They do say that it's too bad I don't get grades for my talking because I sound so smart. I wish they would watch me dance and do gymnastics but they're too busy talking, doing other stuff or fighting. I don't like going to school either. My teachers make me be quiet and sit in my seat until I want to jump right out of my skin!"

It's obvious that nobody in this family is happy with the way things are going! There's one common thread that weaves through everyone's story in the Baker family: the noise and emotional levels are too intense. Tom and Amy don't directly complain about the noise but we can observe their sensitivities to it. Their hot tempers escalate in direct response to sensory intrusions. They also have some awareness of the impact of their yelling on other family members and don't feel very good about it.

Families who deal with the dynamics of ADD face numerous challenges every day. We can't discuss them all but we can examine two that are illustrative of several fairly common problems in an ADD family—*Mealtime Mania* and *Outing Ordeals*.

Mealtime Mania

It's Mealtime Mania at the Baker house. There are several poorly trained dogs who bark, jump up and beg for food throughout the meal. Amy and Tom who are both sensitive to noise and touch, constantly yell at the dogs and push them away but do little else to train them. Jennifer adds to the general discord and busyness of the family meal by jumping up and down to dance or turn cartwheels.

Three separate, one-way conversations go on as Amy, Tom and Jennifer talk non-stop to no one in particular. Zachary and Jan try to follow the conversation but quickly tune out as they become overwhelmed by the chaos.

Jan rarely sits down at the table. She spends dinnertime wandering absent-mindedly. She fetches the forgotten items of silverware, napkins or food that took longer to cook than the rest of the meal. Zachary quietly fades into the woodwork, trying to eat his dinner without getting a stomach ache and hoping that a big fight doesn't break out. He knows that his mother won't be much help in averting the battle that will inevitably ensue between his father and sister, Amy.

The anticipated knock-down, drag-out fight between Tom and Amy is a common occurrence at some point in the meal. Both have hair trigger tempers coupled with foot in mouth disease. This lethal combination means that each of them frequently makes careless remarks that touch off an explosion in the other. Both Tom and Amy tend to hear only half of what is said and to misinterpret the other half.

Sometimes the chaos is fun with lots of joking and fooling around. When Tom's in a good mood, he likes to become a kid again, telling silly jokes and instigating animal noise contests and food fights. Jan and Zachary don't participate very much but they laugh and enjoy the antics of the others during these happy times. They're always a little nervous though, knowing that when things get out of hand, the party atmosphere will rapidly and disastrously change. They know that Tom and Amy, the instigators of much of the rowdiness, are unpredictable and irritable. The mood of the gathering can change abruptly if either of them becomes annoyed with the noisiness or by someone stepping on their toes.

Easily enraged, their anger quickly generalizes to everyone else in the family. They frequently yell at Jan for burning part of the dinner, at Jennifer for leaping around like a frog and at Zachary for sitting like a bump on a log. Invariably, Amy stomps off before the meal is over since she has been grounded to her room "for the rest of her life".

Zachary feels sick to his stomach and can't eat and Jennifer dances around at a manic pace. Sometimes the atmosphere at dinner isn't as much chaotic as it is deadly silent and chilling with everyone brooding and poisoning the environment with silent misery.

Notes: Mealtime Mania

With their difficult temperaments, Amy and Tom seem to dominate the picture in the Baker family. But they're not singularly responsible for the impaired family interactions. Each of the family members has shaky communication skills and a limited capacity for stress and stimulation. Individually and collectively, these behaviors contribute to the family chaos and stress level.

If you plug the individual behaviors into a chart of family interactions, you can understand how things get so out of hand for the Bakers. As family tension escalates, Jan becomes increasingly more disorganized and disengages herself from the family. Tom gets more stressed out as the burden of discipline falls on him. With his short fused temper, he's ill-equipped to handle it. He feels increasingly angry at Jan's failure to take charge of the house and children. It's not that Tom is a sexist pig—he and Jan had agreed on the division of labor when she quit her job to stay home.

Tom gets burned out easily. After a day at work, he can do little but collapse. Amy desperately needs firm, calm, structured discipline but doesn't get it. Zachary doesn't actively bother anybody, but through no fault of his own, puts great demands on family financial and emotional resources. Jennifer contributes to the noise and chaos level with her clowning and hyperactivity. She must learn to take responsibility for her behavior. Unfortunately, there isn't anyone available to teach her how to do it.

The Baker family is a group of related individuals who have compelling needs for structure, support and understanding—but there doesn't seem to be enough to go around. Having fewer children probably would have helped, but it's too late for that option. It isn't too late, however, for the family to make some important changes to reduce the chaos and turn the volume down. If Mealtime Mania seems to be a way of life for your family, think about these ideas and consider trying them.

Survival Tips for Decreasing Discord

Reduce or Eliminate Unnecessary Distractions: During meals, the answering machine should be turned on or the phone should be taken off the hook. The television or radio should be turned off and the newspaper should be put in another room. The family dogs should be trained to stay away from the dinner table or should be kept in another room until the meal is over. To further minimize the extra distractions, the family might consider finding a new home for one of its dogs.

Establish a Family Signal: The signal cues everyone that the noise level is getting too high. Make a family rule that a moment of silence will be observed if anyone, including the youngest child, signals for less noise.

Make a "No Arguments at the Dinner Table" Rule: Conflict isn't all bad but mealtime battles aren't very good for the digestive system! Arguments should be shelved and resumed at a designated time and place for discussion.

Plan a Weekly "Work Detail" Ahead of Time: This should include a list of individual responsibilities for meal preparation and setting and clearing the table. Family members should rotate these jobs from week to week. Preplanning eliminates much last minute confusion. There is nothing more chaotic than an ADD family trying to work together without the direction of a plan! When other family members pitch in to help, the cook is free to join the family instead of aimlessly wandering around fetching things. The family should follow a rule that no one sits down to eat until the meal is on the table.

Maintain Order by Establishing Structure: Meals should have a carefully designed structure for dinner conversation. Structure, order—what is this, boot camp? What happened to the idea of home as the place you can let your hair down and be yourself? *Letting your hair down is fine as long as you don't drop it in someone else's food!* In families with ADDers, there is a good possibility that letting one's hair down will disintegrate into a family free-for-all.

Structure and order can take the form of a family ritual or tradition. The ritual signals the beginning of special, shared family time. It can help family members put aside the stresses of the day, concentrate on being with each other and become aware of the comfortable haven of home. When the family has gathered, say grace, recite a poem or sing a song. Try a "Show and Tell" time for sharing anecdotes or telling jokes. Begin your meal with word games, trivia or threaded stories that each person builds on in turn. The ritual can be **anything.** The idea is to impose structure so family members take turns and learn to listen to each other.

Change the Rules: If someone is having a difficult day or is particularly hyperactive, she should have permission to leave the table. Just be sure to have an established procedure for requests to miss family meals.

If All Else Fails, Eliminate Family Meals: They are a lovely convention and can help families connect. In an ADD family, however, the disadvantages of a family meal can outweigh the advantages. When temperamental characteristics come together in a small space, the mixture can be combustible!

PR: "Family meals are nothing more than a memory for my family. During our initial visit to our therapist, we decided that our nightly ritual frequently destroyed an otherwise reasonable day and had to be eliminated.

Our family meals resembled a hotly contested sporting event with angry opponents. My hyperactive son is particularly sensitive to smells and is an extraordinarily picky eater. Jeremy spent most of our tortuous dinner hour falling off his chair and using his gifted verbal skills to compare the smell of the meal to various decaying animals. My husband performed as head coach of the opposing team. He spent most of the mealtime describing the lack of food in his parents' mountain village in southern Italy. He used every means at his disposal to force Jeremy to eat. I donned my referee's cap, quoting scientific research to support my assertion that our son would not die of malnutrition—and I attempted to maintain order.

The compromise that Dr. Melowsky helped us reach reduced the stress and brought peace to our kitchen. We decided that we would invite Jeremy to dinner but he wouldn't have to join us. The dinner rule was that he could decline to eat with us but had to refrain from character assassination of his mother's cooking. When he finally got hungry, he would be responsible for fixing his own sandwich and cleaning up after himself.

I suppose one could argue that we gave in to our son by letting him skip the family meals. But the key is that we didn't eliminate our rules. We simply changed them to meet our family's needs. The family harmony has been well worth the skeptical and disapproving looks of outsiders who don't understand the dynamics of ADD."

We're going to leave the family dinner and join the Baker family in an Outing Ordeal. We invite you to join the scene already in progress.

Family Fun: An Evening at the Movies

The Baker family is getting ready to go out for a movie and Jan feels more anxious with each passing moment. As usual, she feels perplexed that she's always late for everything. Before the children were born, she had always managed to get to appointments on time. She doesn't stop long to ponder this because Jennifer interrupts, asking where her purse is and Amy engages her in combat over the outfit she won't be caught dead wearing.

As she begins to put on her make-up, Tom demands a consultation on his slacks and the color of his sweater. Amy's discovery that her blouse is wrinkled sends Jan running to the laundry room to iron it. Now immersed in distractions, she momentarily forgets the time deadline and decides to pick up the dirty laundry on her way downstairs. When she gets to the basement, she starts working on a stained pair of jeans and throws Amy's blouse in the washer instead of ironing it.

The timer she set as a warning for the family to finish their preparations, goes off. Jan realizes with a start that she has gotten off track again! She arrives back in her bedroom to Jennifer's bloodcurtling screams for protection against Amy who has threatened her with death if Jennifer doesn't stop hiding her shoes. As the time ticks away and the stress mounts, the yelling gets louder as everyone blames somebody else for the problems with getting ready on time.

Finally all the members of the Baker family are ready to leave—everyone except Jan. Zachary, the only person who took care of himself, attempts to come to his mother's aid as the rest of the family accuses her of making the family late, again!

Notes: Outing Ordeals

Many of us with ADD aren't well known for our punctuality. With our time sense, or lack thereof, we regularly set new records for travel time from point A to point B. Somehow, we manage to climb in our cars precisely at the moment we're supposed to be arriving at our meeting on the other side of town! We have trouble organizing, we get distracted and we routinely forget things.

Getting oneself organized to be somewhere at a certain time is difficult, but getting an entire family organized is infinitely more complicated! If your family is anything like either of ours, getting dressed and out the door for an outing is a major production. Jan can't figure out why she's always late but it really isn't hard to understand. If you multiply the difficulty by the number of people in a family, the extra time required grows exponentially as family relationships do when each new member arrives.

This scene is avoidable if the family designs an action plan. Without a specific plan, an ADD family's Outing Ordeals will continue. The following suggestions might be useful for your family's action plan.

Survival Tips for Outing Ordeals

Identify Individual Dynamics: The first step is for each family member to identify her unique contributions to the family's disorganization. It's easy to point the finger at someone else—each family member does contribute to the general disorganization and chaos. A more productive approach would be to help each family member decide what she needs to do to be ready on time. Then the whole family can come together and figure out an action plan.

For instance, Jan may require an uninterrupted half hour to get herself together and Tom may need help choosing his clothing since he's colorblind. If Tom and Jan discuss their needs in advance, they can strike a bargain. Tom can agree to give Jan the time she needs by running interference with the kids and saving his own requests until she's ready. Jan can agree to give Tom her undivided attention to help him choose an outfit after she's ready.

Establish Family Responsibilities: The family needs to think through the chores that must be done before anyone can leave. Who will feed the dog and put her in the basement? Who will have the responsibilities for turning on the porch lights and answering machine? The division of labor should be explained and assigned in advance to each of the family members.

The planning may even need to include things such as a bathroom schedule to avoid the problem of everyone trying to get in to one or two bathrooms at the same time. It would also help if everyone gets dressed and ready in separate areas so they don't distract one another. Clothing should be assembled and laid out well in advance, so there's time to do needed laundry or repairs.

Prepare a Work Detail for the Family: To reduce the number of "I forgot's" or "What am I supposed to do's", give everyone her own check-list of responsibilities.

Reduce Distractions: It never fails that the phone rings in the middle of preparations. Take it off the hook or turn the answering machine on. This isn't the time for reading the newspaper or watching TV, either. The "No Distractions" rule for mealtimes should apply as well. The television should be off-limits, the newspaper or other reading material set aside, and the stereo turned off. If someone operates more efficiently with background music, she should wear headphones to reduce the distractions for other family members.

Set a timer: Jan's use of a timer is a good idea but she should probably set it to sound a warning and then a final signal when it's time to leave. To allow for a margin of error, the departure time should should be set earlier than is really necessary. It's nice to have extra time to clean up the dirt from the flower pot Jennifer knocks over when she cartwheels into it!

If it's important to get to an event on time, a pre-warning signal should be set. This gives everyone plenty of time to get dressed and ready before the second warning rings. Family members can read, watch TV or play short games during the extra time.

If all this careful planning seems like too much work, weigh it against the stress and conflict your family experiences when it operates in the usual fashion. Try it both ways before you decide.

We have explored some techniques for creating the important balance of rights and responsibilities within the ADD family. But implementation can be tricky. **HOW CAN YOU ESTABLISH RULES WHEN EVERYONE IN YOUR FAMILY HATES RULES AND RESISTS FOLLOWING THEM?**

This dilemma will be our focus in the following chapter. We'll offer a framework for designing a system of family government that fosters co-operation and minimizes conflict.

CHAPTER 12

Principles of Government: Family Style

Successful families operate as democratic institutions. The parents have specific rights and responsibilities and so do the children. Collectively they learn how the process works through the experience of living in the family unit. It is understood that each member plays a different role and contributes differently to the effective functioning of the group. In ADD families, however, the interplay of *you* and *me* is less clearly understood.

Similar to a country under siege, the ADD family stands poised, ready for defensive maneuvers or attack. Since various family members may resist following rules or have trouble with the give and take essential to successful relationships, continual conflict may become a way of life.

It's difficult to eliminate these counterproductive power struggles. But it is possible to reduce their frequency and intensity. To help you accomplish this, we'd like you to think about the model of family government that follows. If you can make your family's system of government more democratic, you may find that things will go more smoothly.

In the mini-society of the family, the parent must assume the role of president. If you're a parent, the ultimate responsibility for a successful government is yours. But every president needs legislative and judicial bodies that provide a system of checks and balances and a method for ensuring compliance of rules.

Every president needs an advisory council. The key to establishing a workable system in your family is *sharing the authority*. A shared family government means that each person functions as a participant in the advisory council and the legislative and judicial bodies. If individual members are part of the decision-making process, they are more likely to assume their responsibilities as citizens of this mini-society.

The Family Meeting is an excellent way to establish a shared government. Within its structure, the family can develop a detailed policy handbook. The meeting helps the family monitor its operations through a democratic process. Before we offer specific "how-to's," we want to examine the goals and objectives of family meetings.

A Forum for Positive Communication, Conflict Resolution and Group Problem-Solving: The family meeting provides an organized structure for determining the needs of the family as a whole. It provides a non-threatening, positive environment for making decisions about chores and individual rights and responsibilities. Within the safety of a family meeting, individuals can learn to develop positive interpersonal relationships and practice new behaviors. This can strengthen the skills required for effective interfacing in the outside world.

A Sounding Board: The family meeting provides an appropriate outlet for feelings of injustice, anger, complaints and frustration. But it is more than a simple gripe session. It's also the place where family members can share positive feelings and provide mutual support and encouragement. A family operating in a war zone can be so preoccupied with problems and complaints that it loses sight of the positive qualities of its members.

An Assessment of Family Stress Levels: Within the structure of the family meeting, family members can make a plan of action to ascertain the ways in which individual stress impacts on the family unit. It's appropriate for family members to discuss how one person's reaction to stress is affecting everyone else. The entire family may be trying to do too much while the stress level intensifies and relaxed family time disappears.

An Opportunity to Plan Family Fun: Planning activities for a family to share in isn't an easy task. If family members mutually plan their activities however, there's a better chance that everyone will willingly take part in them. The family meeting can be a forum for making decisions about recreation, vacations, etc. It provides an opportunity for individual interests to be considered when group activities are planned. Through the process of negotiation, compromises can be reached that are fair. One option might be a schedule of alternating activities. Each person is guaranteed an opportunity to do what he prefers during his designated week.

Development of a Sense of Unity and Mutual Goals: It's easy for ADD family members to become totally disconnected from one another. In a family meeting, family members can reconnect as a unified whole—*us* against the world. Struggling with issues of ADD can be difficult. The acceptance and support of a family unit go a long way toward bolstering the self-worth needed out there in the world.

How and Where to Get Started

When you consider the operation of your family, you may find yourself focusing on chores. Clearly, these are important issues, but they aren't the primary ones. If you jump into family meetings with a goal of solving the problems associated with these family responsibilities, your efforts will probably fail.

The first task must be to develop an awareness of the importance for boundaries. Professional help is generally required at the outset to facilitate this process of sifting through the complexity of family interrelationships. Family members are usually quite good at identifying their personal requirements for time and space. But they often need professional help to appreciate these needs in others. We know we're repeating ourselves. Understanding these family dynamics is difficult but essential if the family is to successfully work through other pertinent issues.

Next the family must develop a new set of rules that establish respect for the rights of individual members. As much as ADDers may rebel against them, rules are the prerequisites of family harmony. A chaotic, out of control ADD family often must rely on its therapist to calmly and objectively mediate the development of these rules.

As the family becomes stronger, it won't need the therapist's mediation any longer. Family members will be able to negotiate and renegotiate the rules in their weekly meeting. It is important that these rules have some built-in flexibility to handle the inevitable changes that occur in all families.

You will need to evaluate your family's ability to handle this on its own. You're ready to handle a family meeting without a professional if you're secure in your ability to let even the youngest child express himself and make suggestions about problems. You're ready if you can control your own *out of bounds'* behavior or at least can quickly recognize it, apologize and take action to correct it. You're ready if you can meet as a family to conduct business without getting into a shouting match or letting the biggest talkers take over. If things aren't going well, however, don't hesitate to ask for professional help.

General Principles and Rules of Conduct for Family Meetings

- Recognize the good things that are happening in the family, **not** just the "gripes".
- Schedule a regular time and planned duration of meetings.
- Share responsibility for chairing the meetings.
- Share responsibility for recording minutes of each meeting.
- Post a "sign-up" agenda for anyone to list concerns for next meeting.
- Review "old business" and evaluate previous decisions and unresolved issues.
- Institute a policy of Equal Opportunity Participation.
- Use positive communication and reflective listening.
- Focus on the group rather than on any one member.
- List necessary chores and their distribution per the agreement of parents **and** children.
- Use brainstorming techniques to identify possible solutions.
- Pinpoint real issues.
- Work for consensus.
- Clarify, summarize and acknowledge commitment at the close of the meeting.
- Acknowledge that all agreements are in effect until the next meeting.
- Follow through on all agreements.
- Plan fun activities at each meeting's end.

Using the General Principles to Design Family Meetings

Let's consider how these general principles work. The family meeting is regularly scheduled and attended by all family members. The purpose is to provide a forum for the discussion of ideas, values, complaints, family chores and mutual support. The meeting can also be used to coordinate the family's schedules for the coming week so that everyone knows about an upcoming school play or social event. Family members can rearrange their schedules and update their appointment books. This encourages family members to take responsibility for keeping track of their own schedules and to co-operate in planning the family's schedule.

Establish Rules During the Initial Meeting: These rules should include the procedures that will be followed in the family meeting. Together, the family will determine the format and agree on a meeting time and place. A decision should also be made about how long each meeting will last.

Try to agree to meet at a time that the family is most relaxed. Meeting as soon as Mom or Dad comes home from work or the children come home from school isn't generally a good idea because of stress factors.

The duration of the meetings should be at least twenty to thirty minutes with a maximum of an hour. An established ending time provides structure that keeps the meeting productive. During the first few meetings, the secretary should probably read the list of rules before the family conducts any business.

Enforce the Rule of Equal Opportunity Participation: This rule is essential for a productive family meeting. Everyone has an equal voice—no one is the boss who can silence the others. Everyone has a right to express feelings or opinions as long as there is no name calling or physical violence. Following the rules of positive communication prevents the meeting from becoming a gripe session. The chairperson may need to redirect non-productive complaining with a suggestion such as, "Do you want to solve the problem or just vent your frustration?" Established guidelines might include some of the following:

COMMUNICATION GROUND RULES

1. Stick to the topic.
2. Avoid interrupting the speaker who has X number of minutes to talk.
3. Focus on individual feelings. Lecturing, criticizing and blaming is not okay.
4. Avoid *You - messages* and inflammatory phrases such as, "You always" or "You never."
5. Discuss goals and expectations of the family unit.
6. NEGOTIATE AND COMPROMISE

Family members need to get their anger under control before trying to talk about what's bothering them. Yelling, screaming or *getting up in someone's face*, isn't an acceptable or helpful technique. Each person must be responsible for his own behavior.

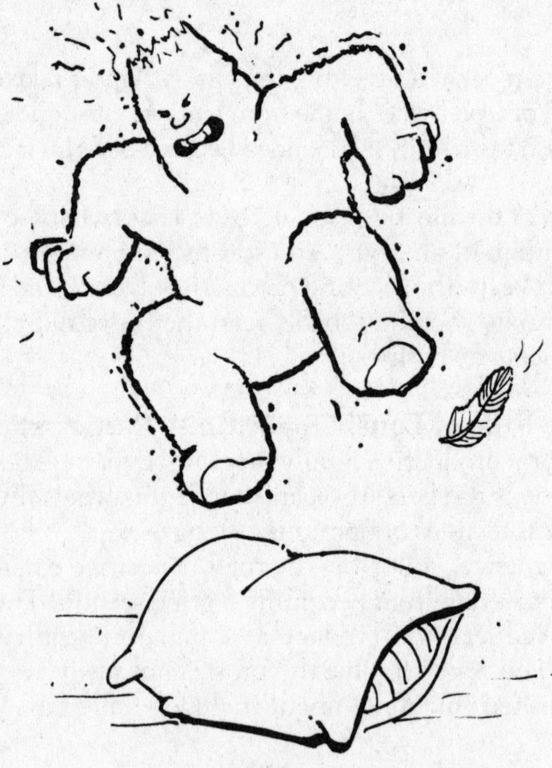

Your rules might include a plan for diffusing anger. The angry person might simmer down by going off alone, running around the block, writing an undelivered piece of hate mail or pounding an inanimate object. When he has calmed down, he is ready to talk out the problem using *I- messages*.

Plan the Meeting Protocol: Everyone should share the leadership role on a rotating basis. The chair is responsible for calling the meeting to order, identifying the agenda and making sure everyone has a chance to talk. At the beginning of the meeting, he should ask the secretary to read the minutes of the previous session. Family members should take turns talking about how family life has been going during the previous week. Complaints are okay if they are expressions of feelings without finger-pointing or escalating anger. It might help if everyone has a written list with examples of appropriate ways to say things.

Appropriate (I feel. . .)	Inappropriate (You. . .)
Dad isn't spending special time with me.	Dad is mean.
Zachary isn't putting his toys away.	Zachary is a slob.
Tom isn't paying attention to my concerns.	Tom is selfish.
Mom doesn't give me a chance to explain.	Mom is a bossy tyrant.

At a previous meeting, Dad might have agreed to spend twenty minutes of special time each day with your daughter. At the start of the current meeting, she might complain that he's mean because he hasn't done it. You should accept her comments. You can suggest, however, that she use more appropriate words: "Dad won't stick to his part of the bargain" or "Dad doesn't respect my special time—he doesn't let me choose what we're going to do together." You might express concern that your spouse hasn't been listening to you. Your son might complain that Mom is hurting his feelings by yelling at him too much. Everyone in the family might complain about noise and frequent interruptions.

Structure the Meeting for Effective Brainstorming and Problem-Solving: This sharing is beneficial in itself. More important, it provides the starting point for conflict resolution and problem-solving. We'll suggest several ways to structure the meeting for this purpose. In an ADD family, however, this can be quite tricky to *pull off* successfully. Use these ideas as a starting point but remember that you'll likely need guidance to fine-tune the structure for your family.

As a framework, let's consider the general steps of problem-solving. The goal of this process is co-operative negotiation of solutions to problems:

EFFECTIVE PROBLEM-SOLVING

1. Choose a problem to discuss.
2. Define the problem through statements of facts.
3. Generate solutions through brainstorming and record **all** suggestions.
4. Evaluate solutions as short and long term goals and offer additional ideas.
5. Plan implementation of the agreed solution(s) and discuss possible obstacles, benefits, etc.
6. Evaluate the effectiveness of the solution(s) and revise as necessary through brainstorming.

The process can be informal with each family member sharing concerns. It may be helpful for everyone to come to the meeting with a list of written concerns. This can help maintain focus and prevent one person from monopolizing the meeting. The secretary should record everything that is mentioned. This list will become the structure for later discussion and problem-solving.

Concerns and questions about family chores are often the focus of family meetings. The family can use everyone's input to generate a list of jobs. Since this is frequently a source of conflict, the leader must enforce the rule of Equal Opportunity Participation.

With the job list in hand, it's time to move on to the stage of problem-solving and negotiation. This will require a creative division of labor, particularly in your ADD family where members tend to be specialists rather than generalists.

Use Problem-Solving for Issues of Family Chores: In these liberated times, men and women are to expected to do everything and divide the work without consideration of traditional sex roles. Of course polls suggest that we're still far from this ideal. If the girls in the family you grew up in did the ironing and the boys took out the garbage, you might continue the tradition with your children. Don't do it! ADDers tend to march to the beat of a different drummer and don't fit very will into traditional molds. As the parent, you'll need to be vigilant about not taking on the role of *Task Master.* The goal is to use the group to make cooperative decisions about job assignments.

Every suggestion regardless of how useful it is, must be accepted and written down. Everyone must follow the rules of communication to establish an atmosphere of safety for sharing ideas. It's tempting to critique the suggestions but this shouldn't be permitted.

When the family runs out of suggestions, it's time to go to the next step and evaluate each one. The evaluation should appraise its merits without indicting the person who made it. Use the following questions to evaluate each idea. 1. Is it fair? 2. Does it include a consideration of everyone's feelings and individual abilities? 3. What are the benefits or disadvantages? 4. Will it improve the overall functioning of the family?

Family members should modify or eliminate the suggestions until they can reach a consensus. Decisions about specific jobs should be based on the best fit—who wants the job and who is most capable of performing it? This will improve family efficiency as it improves motivation and performance on tasks where there is a good fit.

Use Bargaining and Negotiation: Of course there will be difficult jobs that no one wants and easy ones that everybody wants! This is where bargaining and negotiation play particularly important roles. In exchange for the first choice at next week's meeting, one person may agree to do a particularly odious task this week. Or two people could agree to share a difficult job on alternating days.

Sometimes the family will be unable to reach a consensus. The chair of the meeting, or in some cases the parent, will have to intervene with a somewhat arbitrary decision. There are some ways to deal with an impasse. If the decision can wait, it can be tabled for discussion at the next meeting. If the impasse must be resolved, the parent may have to make a decision. He should acknowledge that it's unfortunate the family has reached this impasse. He might say, "I really hate to make this decision without a consensus. Since this can't wait, I will decide to. . .Let's try again next week to agree on a compromise about this."

Arbitrary decisions should be avoided but sometimes there may be no other choice. If no one wants to clean out the litter box, you might have to assign the job anyway! It's important that you distribute the unwanted chores fairly according to the age and abilities of each family member. Make it clear that you will assign the hated chore to someone else the following week. Remember to include yourself in these job assignments. In the spirit of fair play, you have to do these chores, too!

Brainstorming Can Be Structured: In most problem-solving sessions, participants generate ideas through a verbal exchange. The process can also work well in a more formal, structured system that uses written lists. A framework for this strategy is suggested in the book, *Sign Here: A Contracting Book for Children and Their Parents,* by Jill C. Dardig and William L. Heward.[26] The lists provide a focus on individual abilities and contributions and on the overall needs of the family as a cooperative unit.

This is how the system works. Each person fills out a *Personal List* divided into two columns: My *Contributions to the Family* and *Other Things I Could Do*. Then everyone makes a similar list for each of the other family members. For example, when Mom has completed her personal list, she uses her observations to make individual lists for Dad, Amy, Jennifer and Zachary. All the completed lists are passed to each person in turn around the table. Mom, Dad, Amy, Jennifer and Zachary add their own comments to each of the lists. When Mom gets her list back, it will include comments by each person in the family.

The lists help each person focus on his own responsibilities, the individual responsibilities of his siblings and parents and those of the family as a whole. They foster an awareness of the positive efforts that often go unrecognized and also on any imbalance of efforts.

Each person has a chance to read over the comments the others added and to compare them to his original list. If Mom has a question about something Zachary wrote, she can ask him for clarification. After this review and a group discussion, each family member is ready to choose his chore.

The family as a whole helps each person choose the most important task to undertake. Younger children should take on one or two tasks at most, while older children and parents should assume several. The decision-making should focus on considerations like the following:

Is this task something that the family member is capable of performing?

Is this a task that someone else is better suited for?

Is this a one-person task or should it be done cooperatively with someone else?

Would this task help the individual contribute more effectively to the family unit?

Would this task help the family function more cooperatively and productively?

Develop Contracts for Family Members: Systematic positive reinforcement can be a valuable part of your system. Similar to a paycheck, rewards can be given for successful completion of job assignments. To be most effective, rewards should be chosen by individual family members.

Each person can fill out a third list. This is a *Rewards' Preference* list that itemizes favorite activities. Everyone completes an individual list that can include anything from watching TV to eating chocolate ice cream to spending uninterrupted time with Mom.

Decisions about rewards should be made on the basis of both individual needs and interests and those of the family as a group. Factors should include the age and ability of the person, the fairness of the reward and the impact of the reward on other family members. Zachary may truly want the whole house to himself every Friday night but the value factor of that reward may be overblown for his task of taking his shoes to his room! His preferred reward may also be unfair to the rest of the family who doesn't relish spending every Friday night out in the garage!

With younger children, each task should have a specific, parallel reward.

A point system can be used with the older children and the parent(s) who choose several tasks and larger rewards. This *token economy system* uses points rather than specific rewards for performance of tasks. Points are accumulated to "purchase" a large reward *priced* according to its value. Points can be poker chips accumulated in a jar or deposits recorded in a checkbook.

When the family agrees on the tasks and rewards, each person signs an individual contract that includes the terms of the agreement. To be useful, a contract should include the following.

1. It must be **Specific:**

- in written form
- a statement of who will do the task and when and how often it is to be done
- a description of all the requirements of the task
- signatures of the family members as a statement of agreement to honestly and consistently fulfill all obligations

2. It must be **Attainable:**

- an appropriate match to the age and ability of the family member
- a statement of exceptions to the task performance: ie. extra garbage from spring cleaning will be shared with the parent, etc.
- an allowance for altering any part of the agreement if it isn't working

3. It must be **Positive:**

- a description of the reward: how much, when it will be given and by whom
- a statement of the consequences for non-performance: loss of the opportunity for the reward
- an agreement which must be fair and beneficial to the individual and the entire family

As the parent, you should not only be the administrator of your children's contracts but also an active participant in the contracts they design for you! Fair play is essential. The goal of contracting is to encourage and structure cooperation of the family as a unit. Even the parents have to agree to accept the consequences if they fail to perform their assigned chores.

This is only a brief survey of how contracts can be used. We will leave an in-depth discussion to your therapist or reference books you can read. We would also encourage you to explore a parenting class in your area. STEP programs, Systematic Training for Effective Parenting, are particularly helpful and are held periodically throughout the country. (See appendix)

Add Consequences to the Contracting System: The contract guidelines we've suggested use positive rewards and natural consequences to encourage compliance. This is always the best way to get started but negative consequences can be added to the system. As long as everyone agrees, your family might want to establish fines for nonperformance of chores or rules.

You can work out your own system but a lighthearted approach may work better than a punitive one. Your family might decide that offenders will be given "thumbs down" stickers on a chart. A predetermined number of stickers might *buy* the person an extra chore—perhaps the most hated one in the household! The rule-breaker might have to pay his fine in money, extra chores or the loss of a privilege. Perhaps the week's biggest offender will have to participate in a celebrity roast or appear on a *Most Wanted* poster that lists his offenses.

The whole family needs to be comfortable with the method for dealing with rule-breaking. Take care with the humorous approach—it's easy to go too far. No one's feelings should ever be hurt.

If fair play and positive communication are the rules of your family meetings, there is no magic formula or prescribed structure you must use. Individual families need to determine the best method—formal or informal problem-solving sessions, with or without accompanying contracts. Regardless of the structure, family meetings can be an excellent way for minimizing conflict, making mutual decisions and celebrating the positive aspects of family life.

Guard Against Expectations of Perfection!

The family setting makes particularly challenging demands on the fragile skills of someone with ADD. If you are the parent in your ADD family and are feeling overwhelmed by seemingly insurmountable problems, don't hesitate to get professional help.

Don't hesitate to take some time away from your family either. You need to regroup and reenergize your reserves of patience. You must guard against becoming preoccupied with the concerns and fears you have for your ADD children. Otherwise, you may fail to focus on your own needs. The people in your family need you but you can't help them if you sacrifice yourself to their needs.

Rethink your ideas of family and parenting. An ADD family may never be like the one on the happy television sitcom from the 1950's. As you work at accepting your own unique differences, you must also work at accepting those of your ADD family. Are you setting yourself up for failure through unrealistic expectations? Are you comparing your abilities as a parent to a friend whose family seems so well adjusted and happy?

It's easy to fall into the trap of comparing your family to a non-ADD one. Each of us gets caught up in these feelings from time to time. To meet the challenges, you have to reach inside yourself and grab hold of your reserves of creativity, perseverance, humor, compassion and love. You have to learn to compare your parenting skills to yourself, not to other parents. You may not be a perfect parent—whatever that means. But you may be the best parent you can be given your own disabilities and those of your individual family members.

The key is to focus on progress and to measure success in small steps. How is your family unit functioning *today* compared to *yesterday* or *last week* or *last year?* Congratulate yourself for your efforts and never give up.

Attend a support group for ADD families. Share your successes with the group. Use the support and suggestions of others who deal with similar issues. After attendance at their first ADD support group meeting, most parents express astonishment and joy at the discovery that many others share and understand their struggles. They usually come away with strengthened commitment and an appreciation for their own families.

With hard work and mutual respect, ADD families can learn to function successfully as a unit. Individual family members can provide a vitally important support structure for each other. Although some degree of conflict may be a constant in the ADD family, the homefront can become a safe retreat from the rest of the world that is often much less accepting.

We've spent several chapters discussing the dynamics of ADD and interfacing in a variety of settings. We could probably continue adding things as they pop into our brains but it's time to move on to some other issues.

Throughout the book we've made references to organization, memory and learning. Many adults with ADD manifest unique differences in these areas— differences that can compromise the quality of overall functioning. In the next two chapters we'll examine the interplay of attention, organization, memory, and learning. Our goal will be to help you identify the strengths you can use to compensate for any weaknesses in these areas.

CHAPTER 13

Dynamics of ADD in Organization: Mechanics and Methods

Before we get started on this discussion, we want to tell you what to expect for the remainder of the book because this chapter marks another shift in focus. Let's do a quick review to see where we've been and an overview to see where we're going in the next five chapters.

In the first part of the book, we focused on readiness—symptoms and causes, ages and stages, differences, defense mechanisms, grief, balance and the diagnostic process. Then we explored issues of communication and relating to people and to your job.

In this last section of the book, we'll talk about everything we haven't had a chance to say yet! We'll look at many *"How-To's"* for an ADDer—how to work around specific skill deficits, how to make medicine and therapy decisions and how to discover your ADDed Dimension. Now that we've properly prepared you for your reading, let's get busy talking about the bane of many an ADDer's life—disorganization.

Life is Difficult for the Organizationally Impaired

We recently saw this message on a greeting card and wondered if an ADDer had designed it! Disorganization seems a way of life for many of us. It makes us wonder if perhaps researchers have been missing an important diagnostic tool—a questionnaire that might go something like this:

1. When you go to a bookstore, do you head for the self-help aisle in search of books with titles such as: *Five Steps to a More Organized Life*, by Ima N. Disarray or *Systematizing Stuff*, by R.U.Tidy?

2. How many of these kinds of books do you own?

3. Do you decorate your rooms with post-it notes instead of wallpaper?

4. Do you try a new filing system several times per month?

5. How many reminders do you have written on your left hand? Your right hand?

6. How many times do you search for your missing car keys every day?

7. How many times do you arrive at the grocery store without your store list?

8. How many piles of unopened mail are there in your house?

9. How many items have you listed on your To Do list? Do you have a To Do list? Do you have a To Do list for your To Do list?

10. How many times were you late for an appointment in the past week?

11. Do you frequently say the words "I forgot"? How many times did you say them in the past twenty four hours?

12. How many times does your child go to a soccer game with wet socks because you forgot to put them in the dryer?

13. How many days after a business trip do you leave your suitcase unpacked in the corner?

14. How many times do you get to your hotel and remember that your suitcase is thousands of miles away on the floor of your bedroom?

15. How often do you have to call hotel room service for a toothbrush or shampoo because you forgot to pack yours?

16. Do you wear a water proof watch in the shower to keep track of time? Do you set the timer on your watch as a reminder to get out before you drain the hot water tank?

We haven't standardized the diagnostic criteria of our test, but we think we might be on to something here. If you passed this "test", consider yourself fortunate. If you failed, you are in good company with many other ADD adults.

Although we began this chapter with a reference to (dis)organization, it's impossible to separate it from the larger issues of learning, attention and memory. The jury is still out regarding the specific reasons for the ADDer's problems with time and space. Are they symptoms of the disorder? Are they specific learning disabilities that come packaged with the ADD? Or are they a result of a basic difficulty with selective focus?

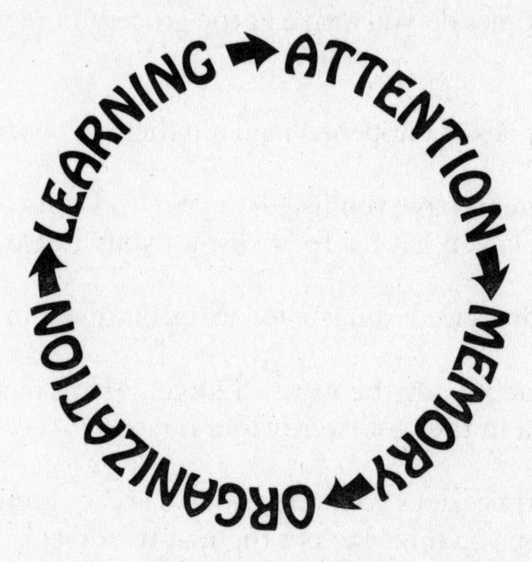

Creating Order—Where Do You Start?

Regardless of the specific causes of ADD adults' time and space problems, life is indeed difficult for the organizationally impaired! Feeling perpetually disorganized may be a daily reality. Many of us never seem to know how to manage the time and stuff of our world and often feel at the mercy of forces beyond our control.

Decide Whether the Disorder in Your Life Causes Stress: Your messy closets and desk aren't problems simply because your spouse thinks they're disorganized. If you can find what you need relatively easily and are comfortable with the seeming disarray, you don't have a problem.

If you decided when you compiled your balance sheet that a messy house was a satisfactory trade off for extra free time, you don't have a problem. Of course it's important that this tradeoff is acceptable to the rest of your family. Their needs should be a part of your balance sheet.

If disorganization isn't a problem for you, skip this part of the book and focus on the other areas of your life that require your attention. If you scanned the table of contents and immediately flipped open to this chapter, you know you have a problem with organization. If you're constantly putting out fires and your life is cluttered with missed deadlines and paperwork pileup, you need to make a conscious decision to work at developing a sense of order.

Remember That There is No Such Thing as a Perfect System: Although you may feel that organizing your life is an impossible task, it really isn't! With some creativity, hard work and planning, you can create order in your life. Don't worry, though, about coming up with the correct organizational system, because there is no right or wrong method.

Although you're an adult, you may still operate with parental admonitions ringing in your ears: "Put your soccer shoes in the closet as soon as you get home. . .Don't hang your jacket on the doorknob." Maybe hanging your jacket on the doorknob is a great system because it jogs your memory about the errand you still need to do. Perhaps leaving your shoes by the front door reminds you to polish them. The point is, you need to toss out the old "shoulds" and do what works for you.

Review your balance sheet. Think about your list and consider some of the following general time and space issues:

What are the spaces in your home and how do you use them?
Do you feel comfortable in the spaces you live and work in?
What objects fill your home and your life?
How often are these objects used—frequently, occasionally, never?
What things have remained unused for a long time?
How much time do you spend trying to figure out how to get started?
Do you have trouble controlling: Time? Stuff? Both?

To Get Organized, You Need to Approach Your Disorganization in an Organized Way: For starters, you need to divide the global idea of order in smaller pieces. When you characterize yourself as a disorganized person, what do you really mean? You need to identify the problem areas, prioritize them according to severity and then design a plan for dealing with a reasonable number of them. By establishing a limited number of goals, you're already on your way to becoming more organized.

Approach the reading and digesting of this chapter in the same fashion. We realize this section is chock full of suggestions, some of which may not apply to your individual situation. The volume of information may also be overwhelming. Break this chapter down into smaller chunks, tackling a piece at a time. If you find yourself becoming confused or overwhelmed, close the book for a while and come back to it later.

Organization Begins with a Pencil and Paper: To figure out your specific organizational problems, start with a pencil, a planning notebook and some quiet time. If you can find all three of these things, you may not be as disorganized as you thought you were!

Think about the things in your life that make you feel disorganized. If the first thing you write on your list is, "everything", tear off that sheet of paper and try again! Instead, you need to focus on isolated problems so you can systematically work out solutions.

In her book, *Getting Organized*, Stephanie Winston[27] suggests that emotions can be useful clues for identifying and isolating specific problems. Think about a typical day and run through it event by event in your mind. Stay tuned in to your emotional responses to various situations If you begin to feel anxious just thinking about the milk that's still on the grocery store shelf instead of in your refrigerator, you've hit on a problem! Continue the process by writing down each problem as you think about it.

Put Limits on the Numbers of Problem Areas: Don't give up if you end up with pages of identified problems. Pare down your list by initially setting aside everything but the first four to six items. You might try to analyze your list by ranking the problems in a general way and focusing only on the most problematic issues. Your ranking can be based on the level of personal aggravation: drives me crazy, sort of bothers me, and no sweat. Perhaps cleaning out the storage closet doesn't have to be done right now but if the mess constantly grates on you, rank it close to the top of your list.

Work with Your Prioritized List: If you get this far and file it somewhere in your unmanageable file cabinet, you will accomplish nothing except to have wasted some time. Although you may have precious little down time, schedule some extra to deal with your problem-solving list. If you simply wait to get around to it, it will never happen. Make a conscious decision to meet with yourself at prearranged times to attack your list and develop solutions. We've already talked about working out family organization issues, but this one is for you.

Winston and other organization experts focus on simplifying issues by breaking them down to smaller, more manageable parts. Consider the components of each problem area and individually list them on your paper. If your cluttered office is driving you crazy, think through the specifics of the problem. A cluttered office is a space problem with many sub-items. Is your desk messy? Are there too many papers tossed around carelessly? Are your garbage cans overflowing? Is your calendar still turned to the previous month?

This detailed list will help you get started with your personally designed organizational system. As you consider the discussion and ideas that follow, use your prioritized list as a framework. Think about your particular problems and individual style and try to match them to the ideas that appeal to you. Ignore the others and don't get distracted by things that aren't on your list. They may be important, but you can't fix everything at once.

General Mess Management

If you are like many ADD adults, your *What Drives Me the Craziest* list probably includes a variety of time and space problems. We'll save discussion of time management for later in this chapter and focus on space problems or *Mess Management*, now.

Mess management has two components: clearing out and storing. Keeping track of the stuff of your world requires the same effort and planning as many other areas of your life. It really is a shame that planning—the thing most of us hate more than anything else—is the singularly most important thing we can do for ourselves! It's probably more accurate to say we're planning impaired than organizationally impaired.

You'll have to make a careful plan if you're going to have control over the stuff of your life. A logical way to start developing this plan is with an analysis of the clutter in your world. Take a house tour and make an inventory that focuses specifically on stuff. By using this *Stuff Inventory* and the *What Drives Me the Craziest Inventory*, you'll have a framework for your action plan.

Compile Your Stuff Inventory: Do you live in a house with large storage closets? They are great places for dumping the stuff you clear out from other places but have a particularly troublesome drawback. They are deep, black holes into which stuff falls, never to be seen again! When it's time to get out your winter boots, you may not be able to remember where you put them. You're probably already late for the sledding party and in too much of a hurry to find them. You may arrive home hours later with wet gym shoes and frostbitten toes!

As you do your inventory, make a note of how often you use various items. Divide your paper in three columns and categorize everything: the things you routinely use, occasionally use and haven't used any time in recent memory. When your list is complete, schedule a time to come back and get to work clearing out the clutter in each room.

Arm Yourself with Three Big Boxes: Physically separate the objects in each room according to their frequency of use. For starters, put anything you access with great frequency in a *Use All the Time* box. Everything else should go in the garbage can or into one of two clearly labeled boxes: *Occasionally Use* and *Haven't Used in a Long Time*. If in doubt about what whether to keep something, don't waste time thinking about it. For now, just put it in your Haven't Used in a Long Time box.

Work with your first box, putting these routinely used items in readily accessible places. If you need to buy a book case or hanging shelves to maximize storage, jot a reminder in your notebook. Tape content's lists on your other two boxes, put them in a closet or out of the way somewhere, and schedule a time for their subsequent review. When you discover several months later that you still haven't used something, take the plunge and throw it away!

Make Liberal Use of a Trash Can: The trash can be an indispensable aid in the war on clutter! Each item you discard reduces the quantity of stuff you have to manage. Of course, some impulsive ADDers may use their trash cans to excess and end up rummaging through the debris to locate the tax refund check they hastily discarded by mistake!

Some of us, however, tend to keep everything. Perhaps we do this because we can't trust our memories or our organizational skills and are scared to death we'll discard something important. It seems easier to keep everything so we don't have to make any decisions. The more things you can clear out, however, the more comfortable you'll feel about managing the remaining stuff.

Schedule an Inventory Review: A recurring theme in Winston's book is the importance of scheduling review sessions to reassess organization decisions. During your inventory review, go through the contents of your stored boxes. Have you had to refer to your content's lists to find something you've needed? If so, leave it where it is or move it to a more accessible location.

If your boxes remain untouched, it's probably time to make liberal use of your trash can. After several periodic checks, you'll probably end up with boxes considerably emptier then when you started. If you still can't bring yourself to throw out some of the unused items, consider moving them to a fourth, *Almost Ready to Discard* box. Remove it from the main part of your house and store it in your garage or attic. Keep your list handy in the unlikely event you eventually need something in it. At least you'll remove these objects from your living space and perhaps convince yourself that you really won't ever use any of this stuff!

We'll leave it to the organization experts to help you with managing most of the stuff of your world. You can get ideas from a self-help book in your local bookstore. But let's look at just a few of sources of household clutter.

Newspapers and Magazines

We bet that when you do your household inventory, you'll find miscellaneous magazines and newspapers in many places other than your magazine racks. The clearing out part of mess management is the most important part of dealing with the clutter of these reading materials, so get out your trash can and use it!

If you find more than two unread back issues of a particular subscription, don't send in the renewal notice when it arrives. Save a few issues if you really think there's a chance you'll have the time to read them, throw out the old ones and resist the temptation to buy any more.

What about the newspaper? Do you typically put a week's worth of unread issues in your recycle bin on garbage day? If this happens regularly, cancel your subscription and buy a newspaper at the corner stand only when you know you'll have time to sit and read it. It's amazing how available space grows when the piles of newspapers and magazines are discarded.

If you want to keep some articles for future reference, don't just stack them in the corner. Tear out the pages you want to save and put them somewhere you have a chance of finding them again! A labelled file folder might work. If you prefer keeping the entire issue, note the article and page number on the cover as a prompt. Otherwise, you'll repeat the cleaning process when you come across the issue later and wonder why you kept it.

Miscellaneous Stuff

You've read our suggestions, referred to organization self-help books and organized some of the household clutter. Now what do you do with your car keys, sun glasses, bike lock key and miscellaneous puzzle pieces? Winston says that most of her otherwise organized clients are at a loss when it's time to deal with these items. Where can you put them so you'll be able to easily find them?

If you have an assortment of keys, try hanging a key rack with labelled hooks right by the door. A key rack in the line of traffic is readily accessible and prompts family members to use it. Dropping your keys in your purse or belt pack is fine, assuming you can remember where you've tossed them! Purses and belt packs can be moved but the key rack is always in the same place.

What about those puzzle pieces? Some children can manage to get the big toys put away but don't know how to handle the miscellaneous pieces. A labelled box in the corner of the bedroom or playroom can be a collection bin for these things. The child can drop them in her *Lost and Found* box for your help later in finding their rightful places. You can make a project out of painting the box or personalizing it in some way to encourage its use.

A box also works well for items that family members need to take with them. Your child's backpack or the dress that needs to go to the cleaner's can be dropped in this box. If people have to practically trip over the box to get out the door, there's a better chance they'll pick up the items in it.

General Office Management

If you take the time and effort to carefully design your *Clearing Out and Storing Mess Management System*, you'll begin to feel more in control over the disorganization in your world. Unfortunately, household stuff isn't the only source of organization problems.

We started with these general stuff issues because they're the easiest to manage. After you get some of these things under control, you need to think about some of the tougher issues of time and space management. These involve the daily handling, sorting and storing of a multitude of details—appointments, bills and To Do lists. Time and space issues are tough because they change frequently and require persistent, ongoing attention.

You can think of these details as home-based work that doesn't pay any salary! The payoff comes in peace of mind. Let's take a look at these management issues and some strategies that may help you realize your personal payoff.

Design a Personal Work Space: When you're on the job, you have a work space. It might be an office, a construction site or the back seat of your car if you travel as a salesperson. Regardless of the parameters of this work space, it provides the framework for the tasks you perform. When you're at home, your work space is usually less well defined. Without a plan, it's easy to become disorganized.

Do you have a specific place where you handle paperwork? Or do you handle it wherever you happen to be at the moment? When you note an error in your utility bill, do you have to go to several different places before you have the pen, stationery, postage stamp and bill you need to write your inquiry letter? To avoid this wasted time and energy, you need to set up an office where you will handle the organizational details of your life.

This space will become a structured place for your work. Ideally this space would be unused for anything else. If you don't have this luxury, set aside some space that will be exclusively yours at certain times. This must become the only place you do your "office work". And it has to be a place that makes you feel comfortable.

We were recently in a newly constructed business office that had virtually no exterior or interior walls. There were several large conference rooms with floor to ceiling windows and views of the rooms across the hall and the courtyard below. It was absolutely beautiful and totally useless for a distractible ADDer! Your office doesn't have to be big and beautiful. But it does have to be designed to match your style so you'll be more inclined to use it regularly and consistently.

So where will you set up your work area? Of course this depends on available space. Even if you don't have a house large enough to accommodate a separate room for your organizational chores, it's imperative that you find a space somewhere. Is there an unused corner in your attic? What about the garage? Don't forget one end of your living room, particularly if the family seldom uses it. With some ingenuity and an inexpensive free standing screen, you can create your office within a room.

Organization experts emphasize the need to assess individual needs in determining the best place to work. Do you prefer having a good supply of light in your work space? When is the best time for you to work?

Do you need to be able to look out a window or is this too distracting? Are some colors more comforting to you than others? Is the space in the line of incoming traffic? Do you work better away from family activity or right in the middle of it? If the space doesn't have a telephone, can you add a phone jack? What about storage space? Is there a place for a filing cabinet or drawers for your office supplies?

Think about these questions as you take a house tour with pencil and planning notebook in hand. Take a look at the spaces and note the pros and cons of each. If other family members use the space, how does the timing of their use correspond to your needs? The kitchen table may fit the bill for your work space. But if it's always in use during the early morning hours you prefer to work, the space may not be a good choice. You might not come up with a place that perfectly matches your needs, but you can find one that fits your greatest needs.

Consider the Ergonomics of General Office Organization: Ergonomics is a fancy word with a simple meaning—a design for easy and comfortable access. It's a key component in organization. If your telephone is within reach but the phone directory is in the closet across the room, you may opt to ignore making the call. It's just too much trouble to walk across the room to find the number you need.

You should do a personal office inventory in much the same way you inventoried the space and stuff in your house. Look around your space. Do you ever use the hole punch you keep in your pencil holder? If you use your stapler every day, do you keep it in the back of your drawer? Rearrange your space so the frequently used items are within easy reach. Store the hole punch in the closet and move the stapler to your desktop.

Note: If you're using shared space for your office, you'll need portable storage for your supplies. A rolling file cabinet or a box divided into sections may do the trick.

Practical Tools for Mess Management

As you design your work area, consider some of the tools and equipment you can use. Undoubtedly you'll equip your space with a desk or writing surface and some file folders, pens and pencils. But there are other, less obvious things you can use to make your life easier. You might want to add them to your supply basket.

Postage Scale: If you frequently mail more than just letters, consider buying a postage scale. Weighing your mail at home saves the time and trouble of driving to the post office. It also enables you to complete your task and get the extra paperwork immediately off your desk. Without a scale, your paperwork may end up on your desk a second time when the post office returns it for insufficient postage.

Assortment of Stamps: To avoid wasting money on excess postage, keep a variety of stamps on hand for your special mailings.

Return Address Stamp: Along with these mailing supplies, have a stamp made with your return address and several others for people you correspond with frequently. Although a rubber stamp is more expensive than paper mailing labels, it reduces the quantity of materials you need to handle. It also eliminates the problem of remembering to mail the reorder form before you run out of labels.

Letter Opener: This might seem like a rather silly item to list as an important tool. Your fingers probably work just fine for this job. But it really is a useful contribution to the order in your office. Torn envelopes are messy and don't lie flat in a pile. The postage date or return address you need for your records might also be unreadable. Neatness isn't essential to a sense of order, but it doesn't hurt!

Staples: Why would we bother including this in our list? Of course you have staples in your supply basket. We're not trying to insult your intelligence! We bet, though, that when your stapler is empty, you might reach for a paper clip instead. In a word–don't! Paperwork clipped together has a mysterious way of becoming unclipped! Then you have to take the extra time and trouble to find the missing page and reattach it in its proper place. Always keep your stapler loaded so you have to do a task only once.

Carbon Paper: With the arrival of quick copy centers, carbon paper has been relegated to something we give the kids to play with on a rainy day. But you should consider keeping a supply on hand to make instant copies of all important letters you write. Duplicating machines are great but they require a special trip and extra time. Until you can get to the copy center, you have the extra paperwork cluttering your space. If you get in the habit of using carbon paper, you can complete the job and get it out of your mind and off your desk.

Answering Machine: If you don't own an answering machine, we encourage you to buy one. It can become the secretary you don't have.

There are many models that time-stamp incoming calls so you'll know when a call comes in. They're useful not only for maintaining calls while you're out but also for screening calls while you work. If you routinely turn on your machine as you sit down to work, you can avoid many interruptions that tempt you to chat instead of pay your bills. If an important call comes in, you can intercept it. If a call comes in to sell you light bulbs, you can ignore it!

Answering machines can be real time-savers. Just make a rule to check your calls periodically so you don't miss the important ones. You might also want to investigate answering services offered by your telephone company. They have many time saving features that might work well with your life style.

A Computer and Printer: This is an invaluable aid for the organizationally impaired! You may treasure your annual ski trip but if forgoing it one year frees up money to buy a computer, you'll never regret it. We already talked about the value of using a computer to improve your ability to write but it can do many other things as well.

One advantage of a computer is the reduction of the sheer quantity of paperwork and files. Much of what typically has to be stored in files in a cabinet can be stored instead inside the magical electronics of the computer. The monthly chore of writing checks and reconciling your checkbook can be easily accomplished with accounting software.

A computer can also supplement calendars and appointment books. There are wonderful reminder and project planning programs that can sound alarms, organize the details of a long term job and compile prioritized To Do lists.

Fortunately, computers are within the financial reach of more people than ever before. As new models are introduced, the older ones are often sold at fairly reasonable prices. Keep an eye on the classified ads and you may find computer equipment at a price that you can afford.

As seasoned computer users we want to caution you about the limitations of computer magic! If your hard drive crashes and burns, you'll lose your data forever or at least until a data recovery expert charges a keen fee to retrieve it. Make sure you follow the suggestion of computer users everywhere: BACK UP YOUR DATA! Use a backup tape system or copy your important files on to three separate discs so you're protected against a crash and burn!

Paper Pile Management

As a child, do you remember longing for the mail carrier to deliver a letter with your name on it? We do. Were we nuts? Didn't we know that mail has the uncanny capability of multiplying when we're not looking? Well, at least that's how it feels.

Figuring out what to do with the paperwork is a source of aggravation and confusion. We can sort our belongings and cancel magazines and newspapers—but the paperwork keeps arriving in our mailboxes!

As soon as you order from one mail order catalog, you're quickly deluged with catalogs from other companies who have purchased your name and address. Mail order can be a great way for an ADDer to shop. Eliminating the distractions of other shoppers and rows of items to choose among can be a relief. The disadvantage is finding a place to put the four or five catalogs that find their way to your house every day.

Mail isn't the only source of paperwork. After a day of errands, you may arrive home with a large pile of bank slips, store invoices and credit card receipts. You also accumulate miscellaneous reminders that you've written for yourself. It doesn't take more than a a day or two for a mountain of papers to have grown on your counter. To deal with *Paper Pile Management*, you need a plan.

Use Your Planning Notebook Again: Every day when the mail arrives, jot down the things you receive. For a week or so, put all accumulated receipts and pieces of paper in a box. At the end of the week, go through your pile and add each item to your list. At the end of this process, you should have a reasonable idea of your paperwork inventory.

Categorize Your Paper Pileup: Your next job is to divide your general list into small, more manageable parts. For now, you might want to start out with two large, relatively easy to use categories: *Trash* and *Things to Keep*.

Divide a second sheet of paper in half and put everything from your master list in one of these categories. You might prefer to dump out your box and physically put everything in the proper pile. If you agonize over trashing vs. keeping, you might want to start a third pile for *Maybe's*.

Whether or not you realize it, you've just begun to create order out of paperwork disorder. You're working with a plan and that's what organization is.

The only category you need to be concerned about is your Things to

Keep. Things to trash should already be in your garbage can. If you can't do without your third category of Maybes, put that paperwork aside for now and don't use it during the next step of fine-tuning. Although your pile may not look much like a filing system yet, it will soon.

Sort your list in two smaller groups or make two piles on the floor: *Things To Do* and *Things to File*. Put anything that you need to act on, such as bills, in the To Do category. Put everything else in the File category.

As you continue this sorting process, keep in mind your needs and life style and those of your family's. The book club mailing may interest you, but be honest. Is there any way you'll have time to read any of the books you might order? If the book club uses a system of automatically sending selections, are you prepared to keep track of the deadlines and deal with the extra paperwork? As you make decisions to discard some of these things, you can significantly reduce the quantity of paperwork.

Set aside your entire To Do file for right now. To keep track of these current and pending items, you'll need to design a system for easy, automatic access. We'll talk later about managing these important "hot" folders. For now, you should focus only on your To File pile—the paperwork you seldom need to access. We'll start with this part of your filing system because it's more easily managed than your daily paperwork.

At this point, you should feel less anxious about the Paper Pile Management you've pared down in size. So, get out some file folders and sort the papers in your To File pile into sub-groups. We can't tell you specifically how to organize these because it will depend on the kind of paperwork you handle. But you might try using general categories of *House and Financial*, *Personal Files* and *Spouse Files*. The key is to keep your groups simple and broad. Although there will be some overlap, sorting according to these categories will be fairly straightforward.

Cardinal Rule #1: Use Your Filing System Regularly and Consistently

Should you set up your files alphabetically or by type? Again, we can't tell you how to arrange them because there isn't a right or wrong way to do it. But we can offer two guidelines. First, regardless of the system you design, you must use it regularly and consistently. We know we've already said this, but it warrants repeating.

Cardinal Rule #2:
Keep it Simple

Don't be tempted to be too organized. For example, you'll probably want to keep records of home improvements and related items in your Home/Financial file. You could keep separate folders for each item—carpeting, appliances, lawn care equipment, electronics, etc. If you fine-tune your divisions too much, though, your system will become too complicated. It would probably be better to group these related items in one or two folders. Since it's a good idea to keep records of home improvements for tax purposes when you sell your house, you might want to keep these separate. But keep other home-related records together in one folder.

Cardinal Rule #3:
Meet with Your Paperwork at Scheduled Times

After you finish sorting, labeling folders and filing every piece of paper, immediately make a decision about **when** you will file your incoming mail and paperwork. Check your schedule and pencil in an appointment to *meet with your paperwork* on an ongoing basis. If you don't make a specific plan to do this, you'll experience the perplexing phenomenon of the *Plague of Paperwork*—it spreads and multiplies with astonishing speed and disastrous results!

Cardinal Rule #4:
Always Handle Your Paperwork in the Same Place

Successful organization depends on thoughtful planning and a routine. You should make a habit of always handling your paperwork in your office space. Never open your mail on the kitchen counter, in the front hall or *on the run*. Always take incoming mail and miscellaneous paperwork to the place you've chosen to work. If you flip through your mail when it arrives or open several pieces on your way out the door, you will be greeted by a messy pile when you get home. You'll begin to feel out of control again.

To Do's and Paper Pile *Mis*management

Now that you've taken care of your permanent filing system, it's time to deal with the primary source of disorganization—your To Do pile. This is where problems of time management intersect and often collide with those of Mess Management.

To deal with the confusion of this paperwork, you need to assign an importance factor to every piece of paper. Use the degree of urgency to separate the paperwork in your To Do file: important —must act on now; important—must act on some time soon; important—pending a response; may be important; unimportant. If you've already made judicious use of your trash can, you shouldn't have many unimportant pieces of paper left.

As you do this sorting, use some kind of marking system to track how long and how many times you've been shuffling the same piece of paper. For example, you could date stamp each piece of paper every time you handle it. This serves two purposes. First, it will document the date of receipt of the paper. Second, it will prompt you to make some decisions.

If your piece of paper becomes wallpapered in date stamps, it's been handled too many times! Maybe it's time to schedule a special time to get the job finished and out of your To Do pile. Maybe it's time to question whether the job should be on your list at all. Weeding your flower garden may be something you really should do, but the weeds won't get any shorter as the days go by. Hire a neighborhood child to do the weeding for you so you can get the job off your list and on hers!

Make a Decision About Storage and Access: Now you have to figure out where to put this important paperwork so you can quickly access it. Many organization experts say that you should put it in a "hot" folder in the file cabinet. We're not so sure this is a great idea for an ADDer. Putting something away in a file can be akin to burying it in the yard under eight feet of dirt! Once it's out of sight, it's out of mind. You can't take action on it and you can't retrieve it.

If you need *to see it to do it*, you may need to come up with some alternatives to the file cabinet. Perhaps one of these suggestions will work for you.

Bulletin Board: Consider hanging a bulletin board. Divide it in four sections to match your *importance* categories. Instead of residing in the depths of your file cabinet or taking up residence over the expanse of your desktop, your pending notes and messages can be readily seen and accessed. Hang your bulletin board at eye level to act as a visual prompt.

In/Out Baskets: If you have sufficient space on your desktop, try using four baskets. Use three as *In Baskets* for your Important/Now, Important/Soon, and Maybe Important paperwork. The fourth, your *Pending Basket,* is for your Already Done/Waiting for Response paperwork. Put a label on each to remind you what the basket is for.

Desktop File: Without question, a file cabinet is useful. It efficiently stores a lot of paperwork and keeps office clutter to a minimum. It would be a great system if only it didn't *hide* everything! We can definitely see the advantages of a glass-fronted file cabinets and might consider investing in them if they ever become available.

Keeping papers sorted in piles might work—at least until a gust of wind sends them floating through the air. Since piles aren't particularly efficient, the next best thing is a desktop file. Although keeping files in plain view might not look neat, it can help you keep better track of your important and pending paperwork. It has the added advantage of being portable so you can move it off your desk to provide extra work space. If you don't have room on your desktop for a file box, buy one that hangs over the top of a drawer.

If your files are at your fingertips, you'll be more inclined to put your paperwork away before it accumulates. Having to walk across the room to a filing cabinet may be too much trouble!

Personal Yellow Pages: You might be using your permanent files for business cards or flyers of services or stores you'll need some time in the future. Although this kind of information shouldn't be with your To Do paperwork, it probably shouldn't be stored in your filing cabinet either.

A more useful system might be to set up a *Personal Yellow Pages' Directory*. It might be a good idea to list your entries alphabetically by service rather than by name. When you need to call John Alverstraton, the carpenter who fixed your porch steps, you may not be able to remember his name. It's a lot easier to find him under "C" for carpenters.

Cues, Prompts, Memory and Mess/Paper Pile Management

Mess and Paper Pile Management is largely dependent on the components of attention and memory. To be better organized, you have to work at your system and attend to the details of the task. Moreover, you have to REMEMBER what to do with the details. Do the following scenes look familiar?

You spend an entire afternoon clearing off, straightening up and filing away piles of paperwork. You look around your space and feel quite proud of yourself because you have efficiently filed everything in its proper place.

Fade to the same place, one week later

You confidently begin your scheduled chores of sorting and filing, secure in the knowledge that your great system will work again. You open the first letter and begin to feel uneasy. What should you do with this response to the inquiry you wrote last week? And just where did you put your copy of that inquiry? Did it go in the To Do file or pending file? With increasing anxiety, you scan your files trying to recapture the systematic process you designed last week. Much to your dismay, you realize that you don't have a clue how to begin. . .

Many ADDers find that this perplexing scenario repeating itself time and again. Our response to the dilemma is often to design yet **another** new system! We don't really need a better system—we need a better memory. Let's consider how Memory and Mess/Paper Pile Management can work together in our war on disorganization. In the following chapter, we'll look at other issues of *memory management*.

Regardless of the degree of your disorganization, when you want an ice cube, you go to the freezer and get one—assuming you remembered to refill the tray the last time you emptied it! When you want to put your hands on your car title, however, your search may be considerably more convoluted. Although you probably won't look in the freezer for it, you might look in many other places!

You know where the ice cubes are because you repeatedly access them from the same storage place. The car title is an entirely different matter because the possible storage places are innumerable. Did you file it alphabetically by name? Did you file it under your Personal File, Spouse File or in the Home File? Did you file it in your hot file because you knew you would need it soon?

Put Your Planning Notebook to Work Again: To prevent the panic of filing system blackouts, you may need to keep a running list of the contents of both your current and permanent files. Make a dated outline of your files, jotting down the contents of every folder. Be sure to update your list any time you make changes to your folders. If you need to see it to do it, your list will be the next best thing to having your files physically spread around you in plain view. If you'd rather take the time to sit and memorize the location of every paper, we suppose that would work! Somehow, we think you probably have more pressing things to do with your time.

Your planning notebook also comes in handy when you have to stop working in the middle of a task. Use it to jot down some notes about what you're working on and what still needs to be finished. While the process of the particular job is still clear in your mind, write a short description of how to restart the job tomorrow. Otherwise, when you get back to work next time, you may have forgotten that the job wasn't finished. You may also waste time reconstructing what you were trying to accomplish and how you were doing it.

Use a System of Color-Coding: Another prompt that might help you work more efficiently is color-coding. Your color-coded system can vary according to the categories of paperwork you handle. You might use green labels or green folders for banking and financial information—green for money items. If your house is yellow, you might want to put all house related items—mortgage papers, warranties and renovation expense documentation—in yellow files.

Using the color prompts of a traffic light works well for the hot files you keep on your desktop. The green folders can store your get going/must do now files. The yellow folders can store your slow down/should think about doing files. And the red ones can store your stop/already done and waiting for response folders.

You can probably dream up many other color-coding systems. The rationale for using colors or similar ideas you come up with is that they support the memory part of organization. They prompt you to remember.

Use Post-It Notes: We're not sure what people did before the arrival of these wonderful things. They can't replace a filing system but they're great as reminders of important To Do tasks. If you want to be really creative, you can use color-coded notes. Your *phone call reminders* could be on red notes, your *bills to pay reminders* on green and your *appointments* on yellow. If you want to make your own post-it notes, you can buy a special adhesive stick that works on any paper.

Removable color tags are another useful prompt. The colored end hangs off whatever you stick it on and is easily seen. If you're working on something and are interrupted, mark your spot with a color tag. When you come back to the task, it will be easier to know where to start.

Keep an Ongoing To Do List: You can use several of the ideas we've suggested to keep track of the pending "To Do's" in your life. Regardless of the method you use, it's essential that you don't rely on your memory. You must write things down in some fashion and keep your reminders where you can see them. If you've ever participated in a meeting without an agenda, you know the importance of a plan. Your To Do list is your personal agenda that keeps you focused and productive.

There are a variety of ways to organize your agenda. You can keep one running list or group things as timeline items—things to do today, tomorrow, by next week, etc. You might prefer to separate your agenda in categories of *Phone Calls To Make*, *Letters To Write*, *Appointments To Schedule*, etc.

You must keep your system up-to-date. It's a good idea to review your list every day, congratulate yourself on completed tasks and plan for the

next day. It would probably also be helpful if you date stamp your list as you did with your sorted paperwork.

One little trick that's great for the morale is to use the same To Do list for a couple of days. Seeing the crossed off tasks you've already completed is self-rewarding as you add new items to your list.

A final note is in order here. Don't get carried away with your daily To Do list! As an ADDer, you probably overestimate the number of tasks you can accomplish in a given time. You will be frustrated and discouraged by an impossibly long list and might abandon your entire organizational system. Don't become a slave to your list, losing sleep and leisure time as you pursue the impossible goal of crossing everything off the list. Remember this axiom and learn to be content with keeping up with your list just enough to make your life manageable.

You will never get to the bottom of your list!

Time Management

As a framework for our discussion of organization, we arbitrarily began with space and stuff management. In the real world, of course, it doesn't work this way. Regardless of what you set out to do, it is framed within the element of time.

Many people have little problem handling the time details of their lives. Sometime around the middle of December every year, they make a trip to their local store and buy calendars for the coming year. Armed with their purchases and their pens, they're prepared for their *Time Management* for the next twelve months.

Calendars and their close relation, appointment organizers, are things an ADDer loves to hate. Everybody uses them. They are the basic, number one tool for time management in this busy world of ours. It's virtually impossible to get along without them. We bet that many ADD adults with shelves of organization self-help books also have numerous unused or partially used calendars and appointment organizers!

If calendars are such great organizers, why don't they work? It seems so simple. If you need to remember an appointment, you just note it on your calendar, right? Well, for an ADDer, it's a bit more complicated.

First, you have to remember to add items to your calendar. This presupposes that you can find your calendar! You could hang it on the wall or on the kitchen cabinet as your mother did but then you'll be out of luck when you take a message in the TV room. During your trip to the kitchen, you're distracted by the doorbell or a crisis in the kids' room and completely forget to jot down the appointment with your boss.

Of course the problem isn't with the calendar, per se. It's a problem of poor planning or a faulty time sense. Noting an appointment on the calendar may help you remember an event but it doesn't help you plan what you'll need to do to get ready for it. Scheduling several activities in one day is fine as long as you have a realistic idea of how long each one will take.

If you've compiled the various inventories we've talked about, you've already started working on Time Management problems. At the heart of the discussion of balance were issues of simplifying the complexity of your life. The goal of the more practical inventories of the stuff in your life was to reduce the quantity of things you have to handle.

Many of us are too overwhelmed to manage all the details. Before you waste your time seeking out the perfect daily organizer, you need to take a studied look at your life style. Cut out everything you can to make your life more manageable. Then start thinking about some of the strategies that follow. We can't promise that these ideas will work but they may help you design up others that will.

Keep a Daily Time Log: We know that the inventories you've been making are adding to your paperwork pile. But, we're going to suggest that you do just one more. If your "One Rat Study" or moral inventory includes the details we'll mention, you can use them instead, adding anything that you haven't included.

For a day or two, keep a diary of how you use your time. Jot down everything you do, including eating lunch and taking a shower. Note starting and stopping times for anything that takes more than a minute or two. You should probably keep your diary in a small pocket-sized notebook you can carry throughout your day.

Your time log can provide information about productivity, wasted time and interruptions. You might spot time periods that seem to work better for you than others. You might be able to make some decisions about grouping certain jobs together in a time slot that affords you the most uninterrupted focus.

Determine the Best Time Management Tool: Calendars come in assorted shapes, sizes and colors. Many people browse the store's shelves searching for calendars with pretty pictures or appealing themes. In our opinion, most calendars make lovely wall decorations and do a fine job of cueing us about what day it is. But they're not particularly helpful for the details of Time Management, especially since they rarely offer enough space to write much of anything!

All-in-one appointment organizers also come in a variety of styles and have their own particular drawbacks. First, since they're preformatted, they can't be customized for individualized needs. Second, they can be too complicated. Third, a tendency to misplace things can cause an organizer to create enormous disorganization! If it's misplaced, the entire organization system of appointments, addresses, phone numbers and To Do lists is lost.

The point is, you should make a decision about the tools you use by analyzing your needs rather than the quality of the calendar's art work. Think about your living style and the details you need to manage. If you're seldom at your desk, a desktop calendar will be of little value. If you have problems planning, a calendar that displays one day at a time won't do you much good.

You might try using a combination of tools. Include a large, erasable master calendar of the entire year, a desktop "week at a glance" calendar with space for daily entries and a small pocket calendar. If you keep a steno pad in various places in your house, you can jot down important dates and then transfer them to your master calender(s). Make it a rule to cross check each of your calendars for updated reminders before leaving your office.

KK: "The key to my system is a simple week at a glance planner that I use to plan my weekly responsibilities. Of course there are tasks that require longer preparation. I handle this problem by breaking the job into smaller, weekly segments that I pencil in as weekly tasks.

I have trained myself to look at my planner several times a day but have also developed a system for reminding myself to look ahead to the next day. I pencil "see AM" in my planner the day before any important event. Without a cue for upcoming events or deadlines, I would fail to plan for them.

When I check my planner at the end of the day, my cue reminds me that my daughter has a field trip the next day. I avoid the inevitable morning scramble by organizing the night before. Before I go to bed, I pack her lunch, pull out the permission slip from the appropriate folder, sign it and put her money in an envelope. I leave everything on the kitchen counter so I'll see it, even in my early morning foggy state.

I use the same cueing system to keep track of birthdays and other important dates. Entering these reminders in your planner at the beginning of the year is a great idea but it doesn't solve the whole problem. Without an advance reminder, I would regularly read the current day's entries and discover that TODAY is the big day. Unfortunately, it's too late to send a card or gift!

A portable planner works best for me. I'm always on the go and need something I can take along on my travels. When I'm out shopping, I can remember to buy the cookies for the classroom party tomorrow."

Teacher Plan Books Are Useful Time Management Tools: The best are large, 8 1/2 x11-inch spiral bound books that open to display pages segmented by subject and days of the week. There is often a small section next to each row of boxes to jot down notes for the coming week. You can add your own dates and use the subject column for divisions of time.

Since they aren't formatted, you can design time frames that match your needs. They also have with sufficient space to write miscellaneous notes. There are often extra pages in the back for recording student attendance. You can use these pages for frequently called phone numbers, birthday reminders or anything else you want to keep with your weekly organizer.

Structure Your Planning with Daily Time Sheets: Time sheets are highly structured daily calendars that manage time by the hour rather than by the day and date. Many computer software programs offer preformatted daily calendars and time sheets. If you don't have access to these, you can make your own.

Although we suggest that you start with half-hour time segments, you'll need to decide how much structure you need. Your time sheet can help you compensate for a faulty internal timeclock.

Whenever you schedule something that involves preparation, get out your planning notebook and make a list of everything you'll need. Don't leave out anything! Will you need to wear a particular outfit? Add it to your list. Will you need to make provisions for the family while you're gone? What about calling a baby-sitter? And how about the emergency numbers the baby-sitter will need? If you frequently hop in your car only to discover that the gas tank is empty, add a note to your list to get gas.

Put your reminder list in a logical order, estimate how long each item will take and double your estimate. If you tend to grossly underestimate preparation times, triple your estimate! Write the time of the event on your time sheet and work backwards, entering each item on your list in an estimated block of time. When you've finished this process, you'll know precisely when you need to begin getting ready for your appointment.

An interesting experiment to evaluate your time sense is to jot down your "starting time" guess before you go through this process. After you make your list and complete your backward time entries, see how close you were to your guess. Our bet is that you'll discover you were pretty far off!

Compile Master Lists of Reminders: Consider making a master list for recurring appointments. Put the baby-sitter's emergency phone list in the kitchen cabinet so it will be there every time you need it. Keep a vacation checklist in your file, so you don't have to start from scratch each time.

A lack of planning usually causes overwhelming feelings of disorganization. Although this preplanning may initially take extra time, it will ultimately save you time, aggravation and the wrath of a boss who impatiently sits in the conference room waiting for your late arrival. When you think things through and make detailed lists, the readiness steps become more automatic. Over time, you'll probably discover that you can accomplish the planning steps more quickly as they become habits.

Compile "Everyday, Get out the Door" Master Lists: How many times do you spend your car trip across town trying to remember whether you turned off the iron and turned on the porch light? Rather than relying on your memory, make a list and post it at your door. Include the things you need to do whenever you go out: put the dog in the basement, turn on the answering machine, turn off the computer, turn on the porch light, leave a note for your son, etc.

Taking the time to think through your routine and write it down will save much time and aggravation in the long run. You won't have to remember these details every time you get ready to leave. You won't have to waste time racing back home to save your computer from getting zapped by the thunder storm and lightning that hits. A quick look at your list as you head out the door will shave precious minutes off your preparation time.

Prepare Duplicated "School" Master Lists: If you have school-age children, you undoubtedly write many notes for field trip permissions, absences, special after school bus changes, etc. Make some master forms for as many of these activities as you can. A generic "please excuse Zachary's absence" can be made with spaces for names, dates and reason. A quick fill-in-the-blank later, your note is finished more quickly than if you had to compose a new note for every occasion. Your forms may not be personal, but they will save you time.

Buy a (Waterproof) Watch with an Alarm: Alarm watches are wonderful. Depending on the style, you can set alarms to ring every hour or at the same time every day. You can use an alarm watch as a reminder for appointments or to keep yourself on track.

Set it to ring in a reasonable amount of time and then make a decision to work at least until the alarm rings. Plan a break at that point and reset the alarm. You can accomplish the same thing with an alarm clock but your watch is portable.

If your watch is waterproof, you won't have to take it off. It's one less thing you have to keep track of and it can prevent cold showers. You know what happens—you hop in for a quick five minute shower and emerge shivering thirty minutes later when your hot water tank is empty!

Use Stenographer Pads and Large Index Cards: Aren't index cards the awful things we were instructed to use when we had to write a research paper? They were supposed to help us organize our ideas but often ended up being used as paper airplanes! In spite of any negative experiences you may have had using them, index cards can help with organization of thoughts and daily details.

Even the best system in the world is put to the test by distractibility. Many of us get side-tracked because ideas keep popping into our brains. With some ingenuity, one ADDer we know uses steno pads, index cards and his distractibility to accomplish wonderful things.

He keeps a supply of steno pads at his work site and also by every telephone and chair where he may sit. He uses one exclusively for the phone calls he receives. Whenever he makes or takes a call, he jots down the name and phone number, the time and date of the call and any notes that apply. He checks off each call after he returns it. He starts a new dated list every day. This steno book is a permanent record he can refer to whenever he needs to remember the details of a particular call. More than once, he has been able to access a phone number he would otherwise have lost.

He also uses steno pads for jotting down ideas. His work is only briefly interrupted as he captures the essence of his ideas on paper. At the end of a work session, he transfers his random thoughts to index cards, categorizing them as he goes. He files his index cards alphabetically until his next work session when he adds new ideas to existing cards or creates new ones.

Our photographer friend's system may be helpful for you. The steno telephone record can act as a backup to your phone number directory and To Do list. And the index card system can enable you to use distracting thoughts to your advantage without interfering with the task at hand.

The key in using steno pads, a planning notebook or post-it notes is to use them to keep yourself on track and to regulate your impulsivity. In the middle of writing checks, don't stop to make the hair appointment you just remembered. Instead, jot yourself a note as a reminder and immediately get back to work.

Schedule Telephone Callback Times: Schedule specific times to make or return phone calls. Since you don't have a secretary to screen your calls, you will have to come up with your own screening script. Tell the caller that you're in a meeting and will call him back. Don't worry about lying. You are in a meeting—a meeting with yourself!

Discover "Found" Time: Take another look at your time diary. Are there periods of lost time? What about the waiting room in the doctor's office? How about the commercials during the TV program you were watching? See how much time you can find.

We aren't suggesting that you schedule your life to excess. That could be quite depressing. You don't want to carry your pending file around with you to work on while you wait for the red light to turn green!

But what about the time you spend in the waiting room? You've been wanting to write a letter to your friend who moved out of town. It's been on your To Do list for weeks. Rather than reading outdated magazines, why don't you write your letter while you wait? It's something you've been unable to find the time to do.

Structure Procrastination to Your Advantage: Procrastination is the number one enemy of Time Management. Although ADDers tend to procrastinate more than our non-ADD counterparts, no one is immune from the *Peril of Procrastination!* What if we make this enemy our friend? What if we make it an advantage rather than a disadvantage?

We really do need to preface this suggestion with a warning to use it at your own risk! It's possible to capitalize on procrastination but it involves **VERY** careful planning.

The unfortunate reality is that many people work best when deadlines loom. As the deadline gets closer, the adrenaline starts flowing, energy goes into overdrive and tasks are cranked out at astonishing speed. If you know your limits and are fairly good at estimating time, you can structure your task by purposely waiting until the last minute.

This is contrary to conventional wisdom. It's usually better to plan extra time rather than less time to get things done. So you probably ought to try using structured procrastination for a job that won't yield disastrous results if it doesn't get finished!

This is how it works. Figure out the absolute shortest time you can reasonably expect to be able to accomplish a particular job. Get out whatever time organizer you're using and write down the deadline for your job. Then add a second deadline—the absolute latest time you can possibly start working on your task. You absolutely must have everything else cleared off your daily time sheet for the starting deadline you've established. Then be prepared to do nothing else but use your pumped up energy to finish the job.

We've used many "absolutes" in this discussion of structured procrastination because this is a risky strategy. We would suggest that you try this as a last ditch effort. The safer strategies should be your first line of attack. But *Structured Procrastination* might be worth a shot.

We've considered time and space as distinct organizational processes. If you recall from the diagram at the beginning of the chapter, you know that organization is dependent on memory and attention. They're all interrelated—organization strategies depend on your remembering. And to remember, you must be able to attend in the first place. In the next chapter, we'll continue our discussion by examining the other two parts of this interrelationship.

CHAPTER 14

Dynamics of ADD in Memory: Mechanics and Methods

Two hundred years ago, the English author Samuel Johnson wrote, "*The art of memory is the art of attention.*" Does an impaired memory and its negative impact on organization skills result from an inability to focus?

Although debating this question would be interesting, we don't think we dare make this book any longer! Since we've already explored the organization piece of the puzzle, we'll focus on the interrelationships of attention, memory and learning now. In the first part of our discussion, we'll look at memory apart from associated learning problems. Later in the chapter, we'll consider the impact of specific learning disabilities.

Memory functions as the *starting pitcher* of a *learning team* that collectively processes language, organization, thinking, social interaction and *doing*. Models of anatomy and neurochemical brain metabolism have both been used to explain the process of memory. Since we can't control these aspects of memory, we won't examine them in this book. Instead, we'll consider memory as sensory information stored according to how well it is first acquired, or learned. Since we **can** control some aspects of learning, we can control some aspects of memory processes.

In Chapter 4, you learned that memory is a complex system of acquisition, registration, storage and consolidation, access and transfer. Since this isn't a textbook, let's put those terms into ordinary language.

Memory is the system for getting information in,
hanging on to it for a while
and getting it back out again when you need to use it.

In her book, *Don't Forget*, author Danielle Lapp[28] explores the concept of memory as a *conscious* and *subconscious* process with a potential for breaks in its chain. This is an important idea. It means that you don't have a *bad* memory. It means that you have a break somewhere in your memory chain. And it means that by understanding how the process works, you can strengthen or bypass the broken link. The following chart, adapted from Lapp's book, illustrates the memory chain.

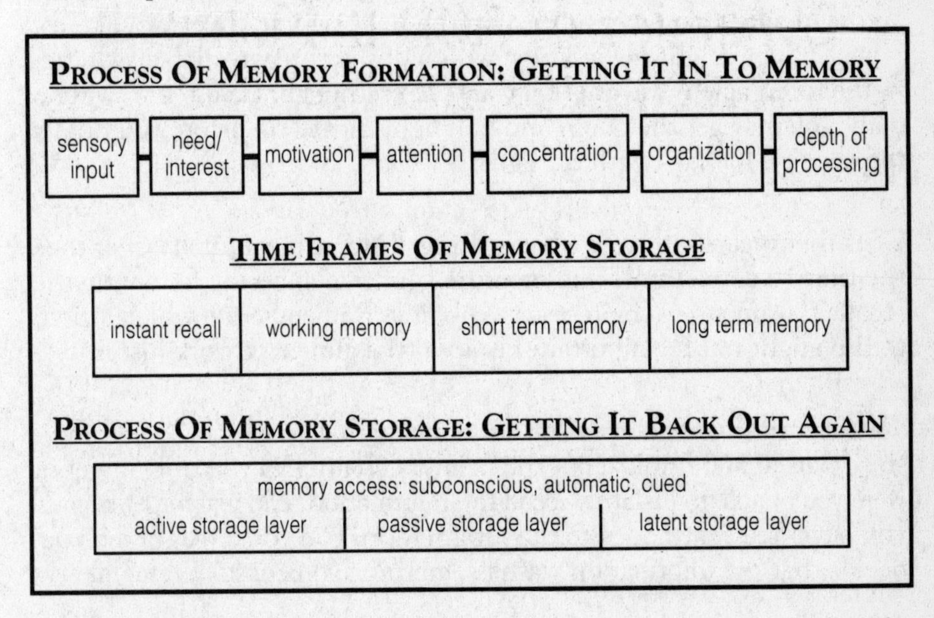

Let's think about how the process works. When you tie your shoes, take a test, repeat your phone number, tell humorous vacation stories or follow the clerk's directions to the boys' department, you're using your memory. You probably don't have any trouble remembering how to tie your shoes. You go through the steps on automatic pilot. Memory traces of the steps of shoe-tying are sharply and clearly etched in storage areas you can quickly access. The skill has become a subconscious memory because you worked hard to learn it years before.

You learned the skill as a young child *motivated* by the *need* for independence and being "grown-up". You *attended* to an adult tying his shoes and *concentrated* on repeating the steps he demonstrated. You *organized* the information in some fashion to learn the skill. You might have practiced the process by repeating the steps as you fumbled with your shoe strings. Maybe you learned a rhyme or visualized the steps as you repeated the skill again and again. All the links of the memory chain were in place. Over time, the skill was etched in your long-term memory so you didn't have to rely on cues any longer.

Many skills are stored below the level of consciousness. Similar to shoe-tying, you have practiced them so much that you can perform them without conscious effort. When you walk in to a darkened room, you automatically remember to turn on the light switch. If you are like us, however, you might never know which of the three available switches in the receptacle is the one you want! Even though you use the switches daily, you may get the porch and hall light turned on before you finally flip the one for the overhead light.

Does that mean you have a bad memory? No, it means you never took the time to concentrate and organize your remembering for automatic recall. Your memory chain has a weak link. Remembering which switch to flip might not be important because trial and error work just fine.

The next time you find yourself announcing that you forgot something, stop yourself and think about the memory chain. Did you truly forget or were you unable to instantly recall the information? Did you forget because you never really attended to the information? Did you forget or did you decide that the information wasn't something you chose to remember?

Memory lapses occur when one or more links in the chain are weak. The specific social, emotional, learning or living circumstances in which the information was originally presented affects the individual links. The use of memory techniques can also affect individual links and the quality of the memory chain as a whole.

Memory Storage and Access

For our readers with "poor memories", we'll do a quick review of memory in case you can't remember what you learned about memory earlier in this book! Memories aren't useful if you can't *recall* them. When you acquire information, you put it in one of several different safety deposit boxes, characterized by their time frames. When you talk of your great or terrible memory, you're talking about the *duration* of your remembering.

The shortest duration is that of **instant recall**. Closely related to instant recall storage is **immediate or working memory.** You use this storage capacity to hold in memory several different steps or combinations of data simultaneously as you work on something.

When you remember your license plate number long enough for your credit card purchase at the gas station, you're using **short term storage.** Short term memory has a maximum capacity of seven items and five seconds. Your so-called terrible memory is frequently a reference to this short-term memory.

Information that is remembered for a long time is stored in long term memory. Many people complain of their terrible memories, yet recount in precise detail, events that occurred ten years earlier.

Lapp, who has worked extensively with the memory problems of the elderly, uses another model of storage and access. She offers a visual representation of the brain as the layers of storage included in the memory chart. The upper one is the active, busy layer close to consciousness; Lapp visualizes this layer in a clear, bright blue color. This layer contains the memories of information used daily: frequently used names and telephone numbers, recurring appointments, etc. These memories are quickly and effortlessly recalled.

The middle layer contains the rusty, seldom used memories that are more difficult to retrieve. You remember these through cues that prompt recall. The layer is rust colored to represent the old, worn and passive quality of the stored memories.

Remote memories from long ago are stored deep in the brain in a large, gray colored zone. Although these memories are seldom accessed, there are literally millions of memory traces available for recall. Memories no longer needed are stored in this layer. Memories of emotional trauma are also stored here. When someone talks about repressed memories, he's referring to these memory traces of traumatic experiences.

Remote memory traces are recalled through involuntary memory. A mood or sensory perception typically prompts recall of the stored memories. The smell of perfume triggers a memory of playing dress-up with a childhood friend you haven't thought of in fifty years.

PR: "I'm sure that readers have had the experience of suddenly remembering something they had long ago forgotten. Several years ago, I accompanied my husband to the funeral of a family friend. I completely fell apart as soon as I walked in. I couldn't stop crying and felt emotionally beaten up. My intense reaction wasn't caused by my feelings about the person who had died. I had never even met him. Instead, it was an involuntary reaction to the smell of all the flowers. The scent triggered powerful, repressed memories of my brother's funeral that I had refused to think about for twenty-eight years."

Organization and Registration: The Key to Memory Access

Storage is just the first step of either organization or memory. The second step is accessing the data. The problem for many of us isn't that we can't remember the data but that we can't find where we put what we remember! In other words, we haven't lost the data *from* memory but *in* memory. It's floating around in there somewhere, but where?

Erratic storage results in slow and unpredictable retrieval. It's as if we head to our safe-deposit boxes with thousands of keys in our hands. Which box and which key should we use? By the time we finally figure it out, the teacher's question or the boss's comment has passed us by.

Although some memories find their way into storage with little effort, many require a conscious decision to remember. The key to storing and accessing the items in your home or the data in your memory is an efficient system of storage. This process involves coding and categorizing information similar to the organization systems we talked about. If you can't find the medical receipts after you've filed them, you won't be able submit a claim to your insurance company. If you've ever searched on every floor of a huge parking garage for your car, you understand the importance of memory registration!

Information Input

There is an aspect of memory we haven't mentioned yet. Although we've talked about the quality of memory, it's probably more useful to think about the quality of your *Memories*. We're not referring to pleasant or unpleasant memories but to your Auditory Memory, Visual

Memory, etc. How well do you remember things you've seen, heard, smelled, touched or tasted? Think about the quality of your memory for the varied kinds of sensory information listed below and rate yourself on a sliding scale from 1 (excellent) to 6 (terrible):

REMEMBERING

Auditory—Things You Hear:
oral multi-step instructions
oral one-step instructions
the names of people you meet
words–what you want to say in one-to-one situations
words–what you want to say in group situations

Visual—Things You See:
written one-step instructions
written multi-step instructions
how and where to get started after an interruption
the faces of people you meet
words–details of things you read

Kinesthetic—Things You Do:
episodic–personal experiences
how to get to various places
time details
space–where you put belongings

Overall Memory

(Adapted from a list in Lapp's book)

All human beings are born with unique memory differences. If we use the number of available memory training books as a measure, **many** people have problems with remembering! This list might help you better understand your own memory profile.

Memory problems aren't unique to ADDers but are compounded by the associated deficits. Systematic remembering requires concentrated effort, attention to detail, organized thinking and planning strategies. These tasks are difficult for many of us.

To remember, you need to figure out why you forgot! If you can determine where your memory chain breaks, you can work on the weak link. For instance, you can't change your attentional problems but you can take steps to minimize the distractions that interfere with focus. Further, if you know which of your *Memories* is the strongest, you can use it to develop memory tricks. Later in the chapter, we'll look at some ideas for doing this.

Memory and Learning–You Can't Have One Without the Other
If we enlarge the concept of memory to one of general learning, you can better understand how the interconnections play out in your daily life. If you've spent a lifetime with the label of underachiever, you may have a feeling of dread at the mere mention of the word "learning"! We hope you're using your new knowledge to understand the learning problems you may have had.

Knowledge and learning levels are typically assessed not by the storehouse of knowledge you carry inside your brain, but by your productivity—what you **do**, or **don't** do. When you were a child, your teachers often misinterpreted your failing test grades as a lack of learning. As an adult, your spouse and coworkers may attribute your inconsistent performance and slow reaction time to your lack of ability.

The difficulty for many of us is that we aren't always able to demonstrate what we know. Our problems are often not ones of learning, per se, but rather of performance. We can't process our knowledge fast enough, maintain our focus long enough or perform consistently enough.

Learning is often equated with listening. Many of us "learned" through one-way teaching—our instructors talked and we were expected to acquire knowledge by listening. Unfortunately, one-way teaching isn't particularly effective for many learners, including those without specific deficits. It's not that learning by listening is totally ineffective. Some people remember and learn best in this mode. But it's ineffective for those who learn best by seeing or doing. The key is to improve the effectiveness of the *learning team* by matching the mode of learning to the individual learning style.

Learning Styles
We want to expand our earlier discussion of learning styles to help you analyze your individual mode of learning. What is your particular learning style? What skills and information do you easily acquire?

How do you learn best and in what setting? Understanding your preferred mode of learning is important not only in school but in life. Learning is intertwined with memory and organization. The tips and tricks you use to tame your time and space monsters will be effective only if you match them to your preferred learning style.

Let's review what learning styles are. How do you figure out the one(s) that work best for you? We all learn through our five senses: by seeing (visual channel), hearing (auditory channel), touching (tactile/kinesthetic channel), tasting and smelling. Most learning takes place through visual, auditory and/or kinesthetic channels. The sense of smell and taste do provide important information but are less important in *higher order* thinking and processing—unless the other channels are impaired in some way.

Learning styles aren't mutually exclusive. You may learn best through one channel or a combination of two channels. Or you may be a multisensory learner who uses all three channels—many ADDers learn best this way. In their book, *Unlocking Potential*, Barbara Scheiber and Jeanne Talpers[29] explore the mechanisms of learning styles. The following chart adapted from their book for learning disabled adolescents and adults, offers some clues you can use to determine your preferred learning mode.

The Visual Learner . . .

has a strong color sense

follows written directions well

has difficulty following lectures

processes auditory input slowly

"translates" verbal input into pictures

needs to closely watch the speaker's facial expression and body language

is particularly distracted by noise or people talking in the background

uses visualization to remember things

takes notes with visual representations: pictures, diagrams, graphs, etc.

knows something by seeing it

The Auditory Learner . . .

effectively sorts out multiple word and sound input

follows verbal directions well

learns best in a lecture format

processes visual input slowly

has to vocalize written information to anchor it in memory

"translates" pictures into spoken words

is distracted by visual stimuli

ignores the speaker's body language to focus on the spoken words

knows something by hearing it

The Tactile/Kinesthetic Learner . . .

has an excellent sense of direction

is well-coordinated in sports and physical activities

uses his body sense and "hands-on" performance to anchor information in memory

has difficulty processing both visual and auditory input

"translates" pictures and words into movement

uses imprecise words: "talks" with his hands

follows directions best by watching and *doing*

learns best through physical activity

needs a lot of movement

knows something by doing it

You will undoubtedly identify with certain parts of this list. You probably notice similarities between this list and that of memory skills which was roughly divided into sensory modes. Since memory and learning are integrally connected, it isn't surprising that the quality of your memory is directly related to the mode of input. If your preferred learning style is auditory, you probably identified memory problems with visual tasks. In school, you may have had problems in reading and in subject areas like Geometry that require a visual orientation.

If you're primarily a visual learner, you probably identified memory problems with verbal input. You may be a good reader who picks up social cues well but who has difficulty responding to the verbal interactions in those settings. Unlike your auditory learner counterpart, you may have encountered particular difficulty when lectures became the teaching vehicle in junior and senior high school.

If you're a kinesthetic learner, you may be an excellent navigator, athlete and "fixer-upper" with your tactile, body sense memory. But you may have memory problems when input is visual or auditory without any action connected to it. School probably worked best for you when you were actively involved in learning groups or physically manipulating instructional tasks.

Of course learning and memory are more complex than this overly simplistic framework. Individual aptitudes for math, language and mechanical skills factor in to the equation. For example, you may learn best through auditory input of numerical data rather than language. Your unique ADD deficits are also part of the puzzle. You may be a visual learner who doesn't read well due to specific problems with cognitive fatigue or inattention to detail. Or you may be unable to clearly define your preferred learning style because you use them all. You may be a multi-sensory learner who needs to hear it, see it **and** do it to anchor information for learning.

Learning/memory styles are further defined by individualized systems of information processing. You may be a detailed, sequential learner who learns through step-by-step, logical, structured thinking. You may be a realistic, practical, concrete learner who prefers hands-on learning. Or you may be a perceptive, intuitive learner who begins with the big picture, learns through abstractions and loves fantasy and humor.

Tuning Up Memory Techniques

This framework doesn't provide clear-cut definitions and tidy boxes you can use to categorize your learning/memory modes. But it can help you customize the tips and tricks you use to bypass weak areas and maximize the strong ones. Consistently writing things down is helpful for many ADDers. But if you aren't a visual learner it may not work for you. You may do much better with tape recorded reminders. So, as you read some of the suggestions that follow, keep your learning style(s) in mind.

Analyze the Circumstances: Are you trying to remember something in a noisy, distraction-filled environment? Can you change the circumstances under which you're trying to remember? Can you find a time and place that enhances your memory power?

Relax: How are you feeling? Are you stressed or depressed? Mood and emotions impact on your ability to remember. If your thoughts are preoccupied by worry and various life stresses, you can't concentrate and remember.

Get in the habit of using various relaxation techniques. The techniques of progressive muscle relaxation, deep breathing or visualization can free your mind and body from preoccupation with thoughts that interfere with concentration.

Various kinds of relaxation training courses are offered in recreation and community learning centers and are outlined in a number of books and tapes on the subject. Try to find a system that works well for you and use it regularly. Make it a part of your daily schedule to improve your memory and also your general emotional well-being.

Minimize the Anxiety that Interferes with Memory: How many times have you started your sales presentation only to "blank out"? Your hands are shaking, your stomach is churning and your heart is pounding. As you begin getting the words out of your mouth, your brain is filling with words of its own: "You're going to blow it! You know you always forget what you're going to say."

Lots of people approach public speaking with a sense of dread. But an ADDer can experience a paralyzing degree of stage fright. He's terrified that his erratic memory won't work. He'll blank out at the wrong time and history will repeat itself. He'll fail miserably—again.

There isn't a simple solution to this problem but understanding that anxiety interferes with memory can provide a place to start. Use the anticipation to work for you instead of against you. In the comfort of your home, sit back and allow yourself to imagine all the details of the situation you dread.

Think about your physical reactions: your palms sweating and your heart racing. What does it feel like? Use the mirror as your audience and practice. Do you remember what to say? Is it firmly anchored in your memory? What questions might someone ask about your presentation? Are your prepared to answer them?

Consider a worst case scenario. What do you fear about the situation? Are your fears realistic or only remote possibilities? After you visualize the situation at its worst, visualize it at its best. Positive thinking puts you in control and gives you a useful frame of reference when you're talking to an audience instead of your mirror or spouse.

By thinking realistically about some of these things, you increase your focus on task performance. You have less time to focus on your fears and worries when your mind is constructively occupied. If you can decrease your anxiety, you can free up your energies for remembering instead of worrying.

When it's time to make your presentation, choose a neutral focal point such as a light fixture and gaze at it to ground yourself. Although you'll need to gauge audience reaction, you can use your focal point as your cue to relax. This can increase your attention to memory and distract you from focusing too much on the faces and reactions of individual audience participants.

You can also use an actor's trick to conquer stage fright. Imagine your audience sitting in underwear or in the nude. In your mind's eye, they will appear rather silly and much less threatening. Just don't indulge too much in this fantasy or you may burst out with uncontrollable giggling!

Make the Choice to Remember: To remember anything, you must be mentally present. Stimuli from the environment will make their way to your sensory organs whether or not you want them to. But you can't properly store anything until you make a conscious effort to file it somewhere.

When you were growing up you may have frequently heard the words, "I tell you what to do and it goes in one ear and right out the other".

Wasn't it great when you were punished for not listening and sent to your room? You had uninterrupted time to conjure up a wonderful mental picture of hundreds of tiny word rocket ships zooming into your right ear, travelling through the twists and turns of your brain and shooting out your left ear! Seriously, that visualization is an accurate representation of what happens when you don't work at remembering.

You need to slow down the velocity of those *data input rocket ships* to make use of the cargo they carry. It isn't easy but you have to make a conscious decision to remember or you will lose the information.

Train Yourself to Be a Better Observer: Simply seeing or hearing something doesn't provide an anchor to secure the data in memory. But careful observation does. When you meet someone new, say his name several times to yourself and make mental notes of clues that set him apart from someone else. Is there anything unique about his appearance? Does he wear a pocket watch that is his personal trademark? Does he continually readjust his belt?

Use planned practice sessions to improve your powers of observation. Years ago there was a TV game show that used visual memory as its format. Contestants examined a photograph and reported all the remembered details when the picture was removed. You can do the same kind of visual memory exercise by using a magazine photograph. Try allotting shorter periods of "study" time as your recall improves and keep track of the number of accurately remembered details.

Reduce Your Use of Rote Memorization: Simple repetition of information may be helpful for short term memory. It can help you remember which parking garage you parked in—at least long enough to write it down. But if you don't anchor that data in another way, you may end up calling a taxi to drive you home and a detective to find your missing car!

Understand What You're Trying to Memorize: If you try to remember information of a complex nature simply by regurgitating it, you won't be able to permanently store it in long term memory. Make sure that you clearly understand the meaning of what you're trying to memorize. Ask questions and anchor the new information to something you already know.

Put Information in a Larger Context: Struggling with, "It's right on the tip of my tongue," is extremely frustrating! The next time you find yourself hoping that you'll somehow miraculously remember where you left your raincoat last week, go in to your memory files and activate associations. What day did it rain? Wasn't it the day you got soaking wet running through a downpour with your briefcase and three bags of groceries? If you were carrying your briefcase, were you on your way to or from work during the rainstorm? If you were running, had you already lost your raincoat?

Through these side associations, you may be able to find both the memory and the raincoat you left on a shelf in the garage before you headed out to the grocery store. Finding the missing memory piece is easier if you can put the rest of the connected puzzle pieces together.

Use Your Senses–Visual Memory: The expression, "Do you see what I mean?" is an example of the use of imagery in thinking. Many people remember best through visual memory. Incoming information, feelings and experiences are rather effortlessly translated into concrete mental pictures.

An ability to design mental images and "play" with them in the mind is the basis for imagination and creativity and is a good anchor for remembering. You can use visualization and mental imagery to improve the initial registration of information and to prompt its recall when you need it. If you routinely misplace your car keys, try using the following technique the next time you start to put them down somewhere.

As you drop your keys on the bathroom sink where you've stopped to wash your hands, look at them and the faucet and create an imaginative mental image—visualize your keys tossing about as they are swept over Niagara Falls! Taking a moment to create the image may be enough to stop yourself from breezing out of the room without them. But even if you do leave them behind, chances are that an image of Niagara will pop up in your mind when you start searching for them later.

Mental imagery works well for remembering names. If you need to remember the name of your new client, Stuart Carpman, you might create a mental image of a giant fish *(carp)*. Your giant fish is covered with mounds of red hair because this is the real Mr. Carpman's most significant feature. Unlike ordinary fish, your carp is swimming in a huge bowl of *stew* which is, of course, your visualized connection to his first name. The more outrageous the connections and visualization, the more effective the image will be in prompting your memory.

Use Your Senses–Auditory Memory: Verbal learners can use their word, rhyme and sound sensitivity to prompt memory recall. Try putting your shopping list in a rhyme or inserting the things you need to remember in the lyrics of a well known song. Record your speech or list of errands on a tape recorder and repeat it as you play back your tape.

Use Your Senses–Kinesthetic Memory: If your preferred learning mode is kinesthetic, borrow from the actor's repertoire and use your body sense to memorize. Think about what you need to remember, visualize yourself doing it and then act it out. If you frequently leave the iron on, exaggerate the motion of turning it off and think about how wonderful it will feel not to wonder later whether you turned it off. The action can physically trace the memory in your mind.

Try sitting in your rocking chair and memorizing to the rhythm of the rocking. Use your restlessness as a memory aid. Instead of simply spinning in your desk chair or pacing around your office, practice remembering at the same time. On each spin or stroll across the room, repeat the names of your new clients or the things you need to do before you leave for vacation. Memorize to the rhythm of your movement.

Use Multi-Sensory Strategies–Don't Just "Try to Remember": We know we probably don't really need to say this again, but always write down your appointment if you want to arrive at the right place at the right time! You probably already have notes written and posted in a variety of places throughout your house. But don't stop at simply writing down your reminders. Notes are great prompts for short term memory but don't really help you store information for subsequent recall unless you actively use them as memory tools.

To do this, you need to write things down and practice them. Read your note, close your eyes, visualize it and say it aloud. Check the accuracy of your visual memory by looking at your note and then practice it again. By using your kinesthetic channel (writing it down), your visual channel (reading it and mentally seeing it) and your auditory channel (saying and hearing it), you'll have a more secure anchor for later recall.

Mental image associations are useful for folk with good visual memory and can be combined with other kinds of sensory awareness to improve the quality of remembering. Try memorizing your company's product specifications' list, for example, by seeing and speaking the words, writing them down and pointing to them in your catalog as a metronome beats. If you're trying to remember to turn on your security system before you leave your house, visualize the control box and the room sensors. Move around your house to each sensor and imagine yourself flipping a switch at each location. This will help you see and feel yourself proceeding through the activity and will help to fix the process in your conscious memory.

Use Visualization Combined with Associations: Much of what you learn is accomplished through various associations. One idea naturally flows in to another and creative thinking is born. Sometimes the associations occur logically and effortlessly—you associate the sound of the teapot whistling with the action of turning off the burner. The memory is called up automatically. When less obvious associations are required, your creativity gets a workout.

When you say, "That reminds me of. . .", you're using an association to prompt a memory. Your ability to accurately recall memories largely depends on how you initially organize the associations of input.

When you call your local animal pound to report the ferocious animal who just took a bite out of your leg, you quickly identify your assailant as a large brown dog. You don't have to describe the beast as a fur covered animal, with four legs, two ears and eyes, one tail and a snout resting over a powerful jaw of two rows of very large teeth! You know it's a dog because you have previously categorized the information in your memory bank. You rely on a mental outline.

Whether you're remembering dogs, history events or a current project at work, you need to put the multiple pieces of data into a mental outline. There are far too many details to remember if you attempt to do it piece by piece. Work at identifying common threads or logical ways of grouping the pieces under main headings so you have fewer things to remember. Your main headings become flags that guide you to the other items you need to remember.

When you use a comb on your hair or a glass for your drink, you're using the simplest kind of *paired* or *grouped* association. When you use *analogical thinking* to remember things, you associate them by similarity. You remember your friend's birthday because it is the same as your child's. The converse is *differential thinking* which uses comparison and differences to form associations. You remember that your doctor's office is on the east side of the street because his name is Dr. West.

Organizing your memory by using categories is particularly useful for lists. For instance, if you have to remember to go to the butcher shop and fill the gas tank for your grill, the two items are logically connected. With little more than a quick mental image of steaks on the grill, you will probably remember your two errands.

Sometimes, you have to be a bit more creative with your associations and mental images. If you have to remember to call the vet and go to the dentist, you can try visualizing your Great Dane lying back in a dental chair with cotton stuck in his jaws! By pairing the two items and visualizing them in a humorous way, you have a much better chance of committing them to memory.

It might seem that these techniques complicate things by adding extras to the memory burden. But they actually reduce the complexity by providing cues to remember things that would otherwise have no intrinsic reason to be remembered. Of course, if you're suffering from a terrible toothache and your dog has just broken its leg, you probably won't need any additional reminders!

Invent Your Own Mnemonic Tricks: Developing useful mnemonic tricks (memory techniques) is limited only by your imagination. Many tricks for remembering can be devised using letter codes. One well known one is using the word H O M E S to recall the five Great Lakes: **H**uron, **O**ntario, **M**ichigan, **E**rie and **S**uperior. The five letter code calls up the names more precisely and quickly than your trying to remember them without any cues.

How can you remember that the boss of the school is the princip<u>al</u> instead of the princip<u>le</u>? One trick might be to think of the ending—pal. A pal is a person so the correct spelling of the school's boss must be principal. Now it may be hard for some of us to think of our principals as our buddies, but we think you get the idea!

What about the spelling of the container we use to keep our drinks hot or cold? It sounds like it should be spelled therm<u>i</u>s, but it's not because a thermos has a circular opening. Thus, the correct spelling is therm<u>o</u>s.

Tricks are also effective for remembering a series of numbers which are random or which may not immediately suggest any mental image. One way to remember a series of numbers is to make the information familiar by designing a clever storage framework. The combination for your lock—14, 27, 30—might be difficult to remember without a memory trick. But if you remind yourself that the first digit in each number increases by one, and the second by three, you'll improve your chances of remembering them.

Chunking is another trick that many of us use. Remembering a seven digit telephone number becomes much easier when you break it in to smaller groups of two or three digits. If the smaller parts happen to contain your age or house number, it's even easier to remember.

A coding system combined with a visual association is another good way to remember numbers. Try setting up a list of numbers using either rhymes or visual cues: one=run, two=moo, three=bee, four=shore, five=hive, etc. If you prefer visual cues set up your list slightly differently: one=long stick, two=kids on a seesaw, three=a triangle, four=the tires on your car, five=fingers on one hand, etc.

When you need to remember that your car is parked in space 134, you can translate it to run–bee–shore and visualize yourself running from a bee that is dive bombing at you on your beach blanket at the shore.

At first glance this may seem complicated. With practice, you may discover that it can really work. Numbers don't have any intrinsic meaning—this trick assigns meaning to them.

Rehearse, Rehearse, Rehearse! Without planned rehearsal, the best memory techniques in the world won't work very well. When it's time to recall something, review the strategy you used to store it. And then practice, practice, practice the strategy—again, and again and again!

Cram sessions won't work! Your teachers were right about this one when they repeatedly warned you not to wait until the last minute to study. Information is retained best if it's practiced over time. This enables you to informally practice in between and build on the partially learned information from earlier sessions. Educators refer to this as *overlearning*.

General Learning Tips

Use Music or Background Noise: When you were a child doing your homework, were you continually amazed at the seemingly magical power of the radio or television set you turned on? Within *milliseconds* after you hit the power button, did your parents arrive at your door with dire threats of the consequences that would follow if you didn't turn it off? How did they get there so fast?

Although parents and teachers alike have preached for years that learning must take place in a quiet area with no distractions, their sermons may have missed the mark. In reality, quiet can be excruciatingly distracting for some of us! Quiet can foster wonderful mind trips and excursions to places much more exciting that the desks in our rooms.

Background noise, particularly music, can be an effective tool for blocking out the expanse of quiet that permits your mind to roam. It also helps to ground you on the task at hand by blocking out the extraneous noises in your environment. Although recent studies have suggested that Baroque music is a particularly effective backdrop for some kinds of learning[30], you'll need to figure out what music, if any, works well for you.

Television typically creates more distractions than it prevents because of the story line and the message created by accompanying music. But if you're careful about the specific program you watch, TV can be a useful learning aid. Reruns are probably best because you'll be less inclined to become distracted by the plot. Some ADDers report using the TV for the dual purposes of intermittent self-reward and a refocus of wandering attention. They report that periodic glances at the screen interrupts the wandering and grounds them on their work.

Schedule Learning Times: Try to become aware of the cycles of your internal clock. This isn't necessarily a simple task because ADDers typically have fairly unpredictable cycles of arousal and fatigue. But you may find that you are generally more efficient during one part of your day than another. You need to schedule intense learning during these peak times and leave the car washing for the other times.

Use Color to Maximize Learning: This is another tip primarily for the visual learner. Adding color to your workspace can make use of your strong visual channel. Use a large piece of brightly colored poster board under your paperwork. The color can *pull in* your focus. Placing a color transparency over a page in your policy handbook can improve the rate of your reading and the level of comprehension. The transparency makes the text appear sharper and clearer and therefore easier to read.

Walk, Ride an Exercise Bike or Juggle Fire Balls: Many of us can have extremely small mental fuel storage tanks. As we use up our meager resources of brain fuel, we become increasingly underaroused and just plain tired. Sitting down to read anything more complex than a comic book can be an instant sleeping pill! To keep our storage tanks filled, we need to continuously pump in additional fuel. We can often do this by moving.

We were kidding about improving learning by juggling fire balls. This might be a tad bit too distracting and hazardous to your physical health! But juggling during breaks might not be a bad idea.

What about reading while you pedal your exercise bike or taking a brisk walk with your upcoming meeting notes playing on your tape recorder? Can you watch a learning video while you do your floor exercises? Any physical activity paired with data input, can be helpful for visual, auditory and kinesthetic learners.

Get Comfortable! There is no right or wrong way to learn despite what you may have been told about sitting up straight and quiet at your desk. If you like to twirl in your desk chair, go ahead and do it. If you prefer standing up or leaning against the wall, go for it. If you need to chew on toothpicks while you work, that's okay too.

Go with your instincts and do whatever it takes to facilitate your learning. You know better than anyone else what works for you, so erase the teacher and parent *learning advice* tapes from your memory bank. Orchestrate your personal learning environment so it works for you.

A Final Word: Learning Disabilities and ADD

Estimates of the number of learning disabled individuals vary. The United States Office of Education estimated in 1978, that there were under two million learning disabled children. But most specialists disagree, some estimating that there are at least eight million learning disabled children.[31]

A specific learning disorder is described by the United States Department of Education as "a disorder in one or more of the basic psychological processes involved in understanding and using language, spoken or written, which may manifest itself in an imperfect ability to listen, think, speak, read, write, spell and do mathematical calculations".

All learning has four components: input, processing, memory and output. A learning disability is a disruption in the learning process within or between these components. The following chart from the book *The Misunderstood Child* by Larry Silver, M.D.[32] provides a summary of specific learning disabilities.

Input/Perceptual: A disability in the brain's interpretation of sensory impulses

visual perceptual disabilities
auditory perceptual disabilities
smell, taste and touch disabilities

Integration: An inability to understand the information registered by the brain

visual sequencing disability
auditory sequencing disability
visual abstraction disabilities
auditory abstraction disabilities

Memory:

visual short term memory disability
auditory short term memory disability
visual long term memory disability
auditory long term memory disability

Output: An inability to get information back out of the brain

spontaneous language disability
demand language disability
gross motor disability
fine motor disability

The following was written by a learning disabled nineteen year old and illustrates written expression/output disabilities:

> *"Dear Mother—Started the Store several weeks. I have growed considerably I don't liik much like a Boy now—Hows all the folk did you receive a Box of Books from Memphis that he promised to send them—languages. Your son Al."* [33]

Al was Thomas Alva Edison. He certainly went on to prove his teachers wrong about how *slow* he was!

Since this book is about ADD in adults, you may wonder why we're including this discussion. The primary reason is that some ADDers also have associated specific learning disabilites. In fact, some experts believe that the *majority* of ADDers have associated learning disabilities.

Probably the most common is a receptive or expressive language disability. In simple terms, this is an impaired ability to receive oral or written language and/or to process language for oral or written expression. A difficulty with written language may in fact result from an associated learning disability.

Attentional problems can mimic learning disabilities and learning disabilities can mimic ADD. It isn't easy to tease out the reasons for an individual's learning problems. Is it a specific learning disability, ADD or both? One could argue against the sometimes arbitrary divisions of ADD and learning disabilities because there are many overlapping symptoms. Despite the overlap, having a learning disability is different from having ADD.

Having ADD means having trouble initially getting information in to the brain due to attention problems. If you are present in body only, with your brain out on the golf course, you won't process incoming information very well.

Having a learning disability means having trouble processing information due to a specific impairment in the components of learning: input, integration, memory and output. A learning disabled brain flips letters and numbers around, puts data in the wrong order and confuses the meaning of incoming sounds, among other things. Medicine is useless for treating learning disabilities because it can't correct errors in the brain's interpretation and output of data.

The issue of ADD vs. learning disabilities comes down to definitions and descriptions. At this point in research and understanding, the two are considered separate entities. Although we don't want to get hung up on labels, we think it's important for you to consider the possibility that you are also learning disabled. It may be the missing puzzle piece in your recovery. If your medicine is working and you're making progress with your ADD issues but still have inexplicable problems, you may have an undiagnosed learning disability.

This possibility underscores the importance of having a complete psycho-educational evaluation. We encourage you to have additional testing if your diagnosis was based solely on history and observable symptoms. Unless you were in school after the 1975 passage of Public Law 94–142, the *Education for All Handicapped Children Act*, it is unlikely that your learning disabilities were diagnosed.

If your evaluation uncovers a learning disability, you should seek help for your LD as well as your ADD. Don't assume that educational remediation is just for children. There are tutors who work exclusively with adults. The Orton Dyslexia Society and the Association for Children with Learning Disabilities are two resources you can contact for a referral in your area. Both are national organizations with branches all over the United States. The Orton Dyslexia Society in Cincinnati, for example, has support groups specifically for adults with LD and uses local tutors who specialize in working with adults.

Paralleling the current interest in adulthood ADD, learning specialists are increasingly focusing on LD in adults. Special tutoring in the areas of specific learning disabilities can reap wonderful rewards. Whether you're 20 or 50, it's never too late to learn strategies for dealing with learning disabilities.

Many colleges and vocational schools are developing programs specifically for learning disabled students. In fact, these programs are often found in institutions for graduate education. The University of Cincinnati College of Medicine, for instance, has an excellent support service for LD medical students. Discovering an underlying learning disability can help you reevaluate educational goals you've been unable to attain. With your newfound knowledge of your ADD and LD, you may decide to try the higher education route again. Chances are, with some research and planning, you'll find a college that can meet your needs.

We have included some references for organizations that can help you accomplish this research. These organizations offer information about various universities and transitional programs with support services for older, learning disabled students.

We hope you don't feel overwhelmed at the prospect of another problem to deal with! But **not** dealing with it is the worst thing you can do. Accepting the reality of your ADD opens doors to understanding and gaining control. Dealing with the possibility of your LD can accomplish the same thing.

In Chapter 6, we talked about the importance of choosing your mental health professional and becoming an active participant in your treatment. We looked briefly at the categories of medical and mental health professionals who work with ADDers. We'll use this information as the basis for the next chapter as we begin to highlight the issue of strengthening self-help with outside help. Although a large piece of your recovery is the hard work of self-help, you can't do it totally alone. It isn't fair to yourself or to those around you.

To help you make decisions about specific treatment options, we'll examine the principles of a number of them. But first, we want to explore some general issues surrounding treatment and making decisions. Do you want to seek outside help? What separates mainstream therapies from alternative therapies? What issues should you consider in a decision to use medicine as a treatment? We'll consider all these questions in the next chapter.

CHAPTER 15

Crutches, Ladders and the Decision to Seek Professional Help

Although society has come a long way toward accepting mental health and emotional problems, there is still a stigma attached to those who seek psychiatric help. Before you consider various treatment options, you'll need to grapple with the issue of *whether you want to seek help at all.*

About Crutches, Ladders and Assumptions

An ADD adult who seeks help can be a paradox to mental health professionals. She doesn't fit into either of the two main categories of mental health care. In one category are professionals who deal with the chronic disabilities of the severely mentally ill. They assume that a *cure* won't be forthcoming. In the other category are those who work with the less severe mental and emotional health issues of patients who can be cured of their bothersome symptoms. It is expected that these patients will eventually *graduate* from therapy, prepared to function as whole and independent human beings.

By virtue of the chronic nature of her symptoms, the ADD woman fits in the first category. But she doesn't need treatment for a severe mental illness because she isn't severely mentally ill! By virtue of the degree of her disabilities, she fits in the second category. But she will frustrate her therapist's efforts to cure her because she can't be cured! She is a very confusing patient. She's obviously mentally healthy but doesn't seem to make sufficient progress toward graduation. The therapist may fall into the same trap as parents and teachers do, assuming that the ADDer is just difficult.

You might find that friends, colleagues and family are less than supportive about your need for continued medicine or therapy. Although it's

fairly well accepted that anyone can experience the need for short term psychiatric therapy, long term care is still viewed with suspicion. Many believe it's okay to take insulin for diabetes or blood pressure medicine for hypertension but that it's not okay to take an ongoing psychiatric medication.

Be prepared to face faulty assumptions about the nature of your disorder. Many people view mental or emotional problems as *diseases of the will*. In other words, they assume that the sufferer could, with sufficient effort, overcome the problems—but is choosing not to. We ADDers have our own faulty assumptions as well. If we can't go it alone, we erroneously perceive ourselves as lazy, stupid or crazy.

Given the stigma attached to chronic mental or emotional problems and the treatment dilemma, you may be tempted to stay "in the closet" as it were, ignoring your need for help. As many ADD adults do, you may regard your medication or psychotherapy as a last resort—a crutch to be used only for an emergency.

If you break your leg, you use a crutch for support. You know that within a few months, your leg will heal and you'll be able to toss your crutch aside. But a mental health problem or ADD lasts forever. Are you really going to use your crutch forever? And if a mental health problem or ADD is a defect of will or moral character, isn't your crutch just a cop-out?

It's unfortunate that the crutch of psychotherapy or medicine is often viewed as either short-term emergency medical intervention or regarded as a cop-out to avoid problems. In reality, there is little difference between needing to work in a quiet environment or taking medication, and using glasses to improve vision. Each is designed for improved functioning.

As you grapple with seeking help for your disorder, trust yourself to make the correct decisions about your needs. Ignore the advice and admonitions of other people who don't understand ADD. After all, you're the one with the disorder, not them. If you reject the crutch you need and try to cover up your struggles, you will suffer unnecessarily and sabotage your recovery.

It might help if you view your medication or therapy as a ladder —not as a crutch. Whether the treatment is therapy or medicine, it offers the rungs we can climb to better lives. Someday, non-believers may understand this. We look forward to the day that the faulty assumptions about ADD treatment give way to acceptance of the ladder(s) many of us need.

Decisions: Mainstream or Alternative Therapy?

We've already talked about the two broad categories of physicians and mental health professionals who treat ADD. We suggested ways to choose your mental health professional and you may already be using your support group's referral list to make your decision.

Your sister swears by her cognitive psychologist. Your physician suggests you consult with a particular psychiatrist and join a behavior therapy group. Your ADD friend highly recommends his massage therapist. But behavior therapy and massage therapy—these aren't on your referral list. Or perhaps there is a behavior therapist on your list but you don't know it because her specialty isn't indicated. The massage therapist isn't on your list at all because massage therapy is an alternative therapy, not a standard, mainstream treatment option.

In the following section, we'll provide an overview of mainstream and alternative therapies so you'll understand their basic differences. Then in Chapter 17, we'll examine the principles of several so you'll know what to expect if you choose to try one of them.

Mainstream therapies are generally well accepted by mental health professionals while **alternative therapies** aren't offered as standard treatments for mental health problems. In including alternative therapies in this discussion we run the risk of making some mental health professionals unhappy. Few support their tenets or suggest them as treatment options. Your physician might greet your request for a referral to a massage therapist with dismay and a lecture about the pitfalls of alternative therapy. So why have we included this discussion?

First, we believe that as adults, we all have the right to make choices for ourselves. Second, we believe that to make choices, each of us has to be informed about our options. We've included this discussion because we want you to be aware that there are other treatments that probably won't be listed on your referral list.

We also want to emphasize that we are neither proponents nor opponents of any particular alternative therapy. Nor are we encouraging you to forgo the well-established mainstream therapies. Having said that, let's consider the issues surrounding the two classifications of therapy.

The mainstream and alternative therapy labels imply a clear distinction between well researched, proven treatment options and *New Age*, unconventional experiments. This isn't necessarily true. Conventional, long-accepted mainstream therapies haven't in all cases been proven effective through research. They are based on theory and have become accepted through years of use. But in a sense, they are still experimental.

An example of this was the unproven, but widely held theory about Ritalin's paradoxical effect on children. For a long time, a prescription of Ritalin for an adolescent or adult was considered contrary to this accepted theory.

Paradoxical effects are drug induced changes opposite from an expected drug action. They typically occur in children or the elderly. It isn't unusual, for example, for children to become somewhat hyperactive when they take sedatives. Since researchers and physicians knew little about the attentional problems of ADD when Ritalin was first used, they focused on hyperactivity. They theorized that the decreased activity levels of children treated with Ritalin were the result of a paradoxical effect.

Paradoxical effects of drugs are uncommon between puberty and old age. So it followed that the medical community's professionals assumed that Ritalin wouldn't be effective for an adolescent. They also assumed it wasn't needed anymore because the teen had outgrown her disorder. This faulty reasoning resulted from the diminished hyperactivity in adolescent patients. At the time, that was the only symptom they were looking at.

The theory of the paradoxical effect of Ritalin was firmly entrenched until fairly recently. Although many ADD informed professionals have discarded this theory, it continues to be fairly well established in the minds of some professionals and consumers. The theory continues to die a slow death with many still holding it to be true.

Proponents of mainstream therapies have been criticized for categorically shunning the so-called alternative therapies. For example, many patients with various back, joint and muscle problems have been successfully treated by chiropractors. For years, however, the American Medical Association battled to discredit the claims chiropractors made about the benefits of their treatments. The result was unfortunate for consumers who chose chiropractic care. Medical insurance didn't consider this a legitimate expense under most policies. After many years and multiple legal fights, the scientific basis of chiropractic care was finally accepted and granted mainstream status.

This dividing line between mainstream and alternative therapy is sometimes somewhat arbitrary. A lack of research data doesn't make a treatment worthless. Sometimes research simply hasn't *caught up* with practice. For instance the idea of "faith healing" used to be ignored by the medical establishment who considered it a worthless alternative therapy. But lo and behold (!) pioneers like Norman Cousins[34] helped gather evidence that demonstrated the effectiveness of the intangibles of faith and hope in boosting the body's immune system.

In similar fashion modern science has discovered that many old, unproven folk remedies have a scientific basis. For centuries, physicians had used moldy bread poultices to treat festering wounds. With the discovery of penicillin, scientists realized that the use of poultices wasn't just an old wive's tale. Although these early health care providers didn't know it, they were prescribing penicillin which is in fact, a mold.

Documented anecdotal reports of the effectiveness of various folk therapies are having an impact on the somewhat arbitrary classifications of mainstream and alternative therapies. Many forms of therapy that began as alternative, *counterculture* treatments, such as Gestalt and self-help groups, have already become part of the mainstream.

Some mainstream mental health professionals are borrowing the alternative techniques of meditation and massage, to help their clients. A revolution of sorts is taking place within the mainstream establishment as a whole. A recent article in Newsweek[35] reported an interesting development. It reported that the medical establishment will begin to scientifically evaluate some therapies outside the realm of accepted scientific practices. Under the auspices of the Federal government, a new office has been formed within the National Institutes of Health. This *Office for the Study of Unconventional Medical Practices*, will use a two million dollar Congressional appropriation next year to study the most promising alternative therapies.

In part the basis for this examination is an emerging affirmation of individual patients and clients who experience beneficial effects from these therapies. There is, however, a more compelling reason for this move to reconsider the benefits of various alternative treatments: the ailing financial condition of medical care in the United States! Many of these alternatives are low-cost and in some cases, seemingly more effective than standard therapies.

As mental and medical health consumers, we welcome this movement. We believe it will encourage continued research and development of useful therapies for adults with ADD. We aren't suggesting that any of our readers ignore standard therapy in a quest for a magical cure in alternative treatment. That would be irresponsible on our part and counterproductive to your recovery. Our point is that treatment for ADD adults is somewhat experimental in that our issues are different from children. A scientific examination of alternative therapies might yield important information about treatments that can be used along with the standard options.

A Word About the Value and Limitations of Research Findings
As you review various treatment options, we encourage you to analyze scientific reports you read and the information you receive regarding their effectiveness. Your physician or mental health professional might not recommend options he considers alternative therapies and dissuade you from exploring them.

We want to hasten to add that this isn't a disparagement of the scientific establishment! There is an important rationale for caution in a treatment regimen. No one wants to be a guinea pig, placed in the hands of a professional who takes too many risks. On the other hand, research is only a tool, albeit an invaluable one, to increase knowledge. And it isn't a perfect tool, either. Design flaws and the complexity of human subjects both affect the outcome. Further, a lack of research or data supporting purported benefits doesn't mean that a particular therapy is worthless. It may be that the research simply hasn't been done yet.

Research has inherent limitations. Generally, it's based on objective measures that don't necessarily capture the essence of human behavior. Much funded research is designed to minimize bias or personal opinion. This tenet of objectivity is important to prevent researcher bias and opinion from distorting the findings. Following this approach too rigidly, however, can leave out the human element. The result can be incomplete and inaccurate information that creates confusion for us as consumers.

For example, the objective and structured questionnaires used to quantity information about ADD limit the responses a research subject can make. They force him to choose among answers prepared by the researcher. If his experiences don't match the prepared answers, they can't be factored in to the final research results.

The richness of individual experience can be better captured by an interview format in which the subject shares his experiences. This is useful for understanding the dynamics of ADD but is costly and time-consuming. This type of research is also funded less often than studies that use a questionnaire format because subjective information is difficult to quantify. Ideally, research should use both methods to balance objective information with individual experiences.

We don't want to leave you with the impression that we dismiss the value of research findings and the mainstream therapies they support. We do, however, feel a responsibility to inform you of as many options as space in this book allows. Our position is that as an adult, you should be able to try any unproven therapy. There are several important caeats of this statement, however. You should be able to try any unproven therapy, assuming, **1.** You use it as an addition to, not a substitute for your standard treatment; **2.** The treatment isn't harmful; **3.** You understand that it may not have been adequately researched.

Become Your Own Case Manager

The point of this survey of research methodology is to underscore the importance of being a careful mental health consumer. Although research offers clues, there is no singular method of treatment for all ADDers. In addition, significant differences exist in the knowledge and experience of individual medical and mental health care providers.

As you try to find your way among the bewildering array of available professional services, balance the research data with information from the experiences of other ADDers. Just one or two personal stories won't do—you need to rely on as many sources as possible. The effectiveness of treatments varies from individual to individual. Find out why your source feels the way she does about a particular treatment.

For instance, a friend might report that her medication didn't work or caused unpleasant side effects. Be a detective and find out why it didn't work—don't assume that you'll have the same bad experience. Was the dose too high or lower than that typically recommended? Was it monitored insufficiently or prescribed inappropriately? Search for as many clues as you can to evaluate your options. Some types of therapy will be helpful and some won't. Further, unless you're fortunate to live in an area with a good clinic that specializes in ADD, you'll be largely on your own when it comes to formulating a treatment plan. This can be a formidable task because health care services are specialized and fragmented. Without an ADD clinic, the next best thing would be a case manager who could help you find the services you need and coordinate your care with one or more professionals. Unfortunately, case managers typically work only with severely mentally ill people. These services are generally unavailable for those with less severe problems.

As an ADD adult you'll have to function as your own case manager. We recommend that you thoroughly educate yourself before you seek outside help and try to coordinate elements of your care. Being an informed consumer will help you avoid an unnecessary or even harmful treatment.

Watch Your Impulsivity

We have written these words of warning throughout this book. They warrant reemphasis as you make decisions about your treatment. Plunging simultaneously into several kinds of psychotherapy is counterproductive.

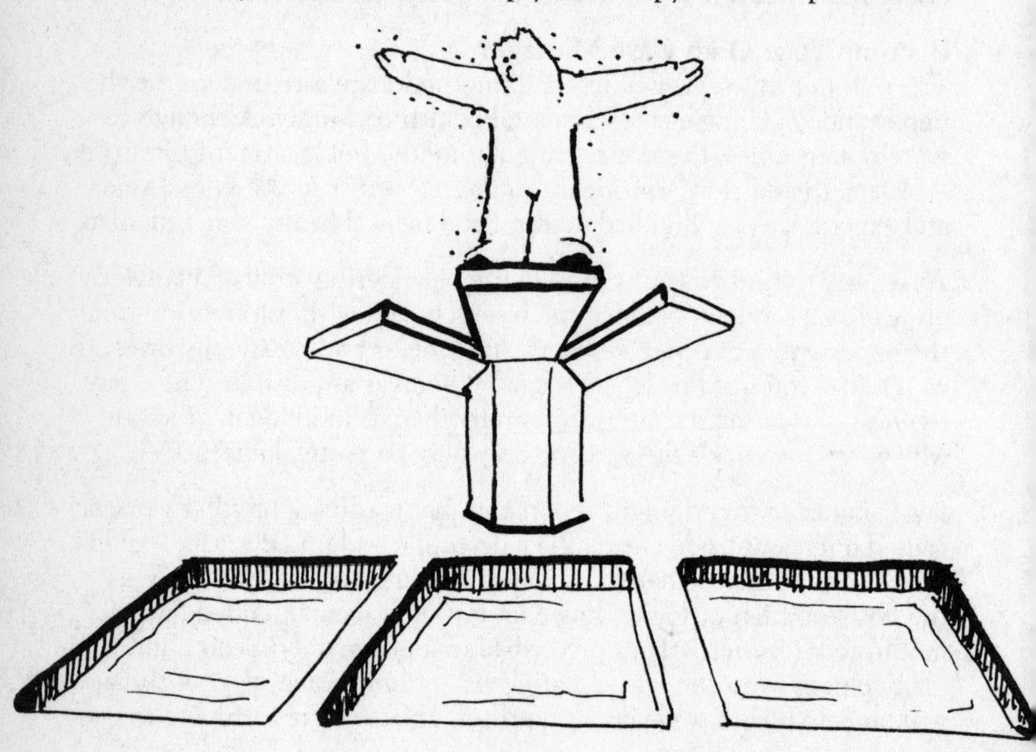

Trying one therapy at a time will give you a sense of what really works. Otherwise, you may become confused and deplete your energies as well as your bank account! The only exception to this advice is your treatment with medicine. If you choose it as a treatment option, you should use it along with a psychotherapy you decide to try.

Medication

This discussion of medicine isn't about specific drugs. It's about making the decision to use medicine at all. Although the decision is ultimately your's, we're going to tell you what we think. We believe that before you become a *therapy junkie* in search of the cure-all, you should at least consider standard drug treatment as an option. It has a proven track record of success in research and in the personal experiences of ADD adults. In our opinion, it's often difficult to take advantage of other therapies without the stabilizing benefits of medicine.

So, that's our position. Now we want to help you make your own decision. In this section, we'll consider the issues of active participation in decision-making, conflicting viewpoints regarding the inclusion of medicine in the treatment regimen and the concern about potential substance abuse.

"Take Your Medicine"

It's virtually impossible to read a magazine or watch a television program without getting medical advice about pills we should take to reduce fevers, maximize weight loss or free us from allergy suffering. The notion of a quick cure is pervasive.

At the first sign of illness, many people eagerly take medicine to relieve their uncomfortable symptoms. To encourage children to take their medicine, drug companies produce great tasting tablets and liquids in flavors of strawberry, grape and bubblegum.

The foul-tasting drugs of years ago spawned a less pleasant admonishment to "take your medicine". The administration of this *medicine* followed misbehavior and took the form of a spanking or lecture that wasn't intended to make anyone feel better!

In our experience, ADDers rarely feel ambivalent about the issue of medicine as a treatment for themselves or their children. They respond to the suggestion that they "take their medicine" in one of two ways. They either embrace it or totally reject it.

For ADDers who embrace it, taking their medicine has a positive connotation—they will finally experience relief of their troubling symptoms. But for those who reject it, taking their medicine has a negative connotation similar to the spanking we mentioned—it's something to be avoided.

To Be or Not to Be...Medicated and The Risk/Benefit Equation
It's fairly easy to understand the rationale of those who choose to take medicine. But what about ADDers who refuse this treatment option? Why wouldn't they choose to relieve their symptoms? If taking medicine were simply an effective, painless solution to troubling symptoms, most ADD adults probably would make the choice to be medicated. But it's neither a simple nor a perfect solution.

First, medicine in the treatment of ADD is effective—*sometimes* and for *some* individuals. Second, it is relatively painless but isn't without risks of potential known and unknown side effects. Third, it is a solution of sorts in managing symptoms but it's not a quick cure. Fourth, a choice to be medicated presupposes that the ADDer has accepted the reality of her disorder and is knowledgeable about the role of medicine in treatment. And finally, some ADDers equate the words *to be medicated* with mind control or loss of self-control.

Clearly the decision to be or not be...medicated, has to be thoughtfully made. Adults have a right to decide what they will or won't put into their bodies unless failing to take needed medication poses an immediate danger to themselves or others.

We encourage you take an active role in your medical management by sorting out the risk/benefit equation. Various sources of information have their particular biases with some individuals and groups polarized into rather extreme positions. Some believe that any new treatment or medication is a great breakthrough that should be embraced by consumers. In the opposite camp are those who believe that medicine is the root of all evil and shouldn't be taken for any reason.

In our opinions, both these positions are extreme. They ignore the gray areas and the risk/benefit equation. It's hard to argue the benefits of some medicines such as antibiotics for life-threatening infections. On the other hand, excess enthusiasm for newly developed medicines can be dangerous if caution is thrown to the wind. The bottom line is—do your homework! Educate yourself as thoroughly as you can to make an informed decision.

Whether the medicine in question is an over the counter medicine to relieve your cold symptoms or Ritalin to manage your ADD, you must cautiously approach its use. No medicine is without side effects, some of which can be potentially dangerous. Even aspirin isn't free of harmful effects. If it's taken by children following a bout with certain viruses, it can cause a rare but serious illness known as Reyes syndrome. It can also interfere with the blood's ability to clot and may cause bleeding problems in certain individuals.

If you're reluctant to use medicine as part of your treatment because you're uncomfortable with the thought of *drugging* or *sedating* yourself to prevent unwanted behaviors, you should probably reread the first chapter of this book. We're not promoting medicine as the answer for your ADD but are keenly aware of our responsibility to dispel myths about this disorder and its treatment.

To Be, or Not to Be...Medicated: The Issue of Substance Abuse
People have a variety of reasons for opposing medicine as a treatment option. Some are valid and some are without merit. The use of stimulant medications in particular has been the focus of heated debate with cheerleaders extolling its virtues and detractors predicting its dire consequences. An aura of sensationalism has developed with proponents trying to counteract the claims made by outspoken critics on the talk show circuit.

The publicity is framed in a variety of contexts but is largely based on concern about the potential for substance abuse. Although many medical and mental health professionals and their patients strongly object, drugs such as Ritalin are classified as controlled substances. They are strictly controlled by the FDA because they can produce feelings of euphoria and can be used as street drugs.

One of the first questions posed by a newly diagnosed ADDer is often, "Aren't stimulants addictive?" This question gives rise to a second question. "Are impulsive ADDers more likely to abuse stimulant medications than their non-ADD peers?"

Research comparing substance use and abuse in ADD adults with that of the general population hasn't found a statistically significant difference between the two groups. However, there was a slight but consistent trend for ADDers to have an increased use of drugs and possibly alcohol.[36]

There are several hypotheses about these findings. First, research in alcoholism and substance abuse is ongoing and focusing increasingly on a possible genetic predisposition. This suggests that there may be a genetic link between the disorder and substance abuse.

A second possibility is that the somewhat increased incidence of abuse in ADDers results from the disorder's symptoms of insatiability and impulsivity. The combination of a higher intensity of cravings and the tendency to take risks without considering consequences may put ADD adults at greater risk for substance abuse.

A third hypothesis is that the substance abuse is related to a lifelong pattern of failure. A psychologist who works with adolescents in a local hospital's psychiatric unit reports that some of his patients use drugs or alcohol as vehicles to gain acceptance with a peer group. Most of these patients hadn't been diagnosed prior to their admission to the unit and had endured years of failure in sports, academics and social skills. Drugs or alcohol enabled them gain acceptance and succeed in the foggy world of other substance abusers.

This psychologist offers yet a fourth theory about substance abuse in the ADD adolescent and adult population. It appears to be used by a number of his patients as self-medication to escape unpleasant symptoms they don't understand. Never diagnosed, they lack an understanding of their disorder and have no means of coping with it. Instead, they make their reality disappear by escaping into altered mental states.

Although the finding of increased substance abuse in ADDers wasn't statistically significant, it's important enough to discuss. Substance abuse in the general population is a major problem and even a slightly increased risk for ADD adults is worth noting. Further, the risk of substance abuse in ADDers over 30 years old is unknown due to insufficient research. It has been suggested that the risk may increase as the stresses of life accumulate.[37]

As we consider this, we want to emphasize that we aren't suggesting that there is no risk whatsoever that stimulant medication can contribute to substance abuse. Some ADDers whose impulsivity isn't well controlled even on medication, may indeed be at risk to abuse drugs.

Stimulants as Preventative Medicine: It's no revelation to our readers that the symptoms of ADD and the reactions of others to those symptoms can cause lifelong problems. If there is indeed a genetic predisposition to substance abuse, stimulants can't be realistically considered preventative medicine. On the other hand, they can be considered preventative in their affects on the symptoms of impulsivity and insatiability.

It's logical to assume that the positive impact of medications on the impulsivity of an ADD adult could help her control her impulses to abuse alcohol or drugs. The medications also control some of the cravings that can lead to abuse. Finally, the general improvements in the symptoms of attention, organization, social skills, etc., often stop the cycle of failure for an ADDer. She can find success without resorting to seeking the dubious acceptance of co-abusers.

Assuming that stimulants can, to a certain extent, be preventative medicine, can they be used by ADDers who are already substance abusers? If you are a recovering alcoholic or substance abuser, should you assume that stimulants out of the question? Don't substance abuse programs recommend total abstinence from all mind altering substances? The answers to these questions are, "Maybe", "Maybe not", and "Yes".

Some professionals who work with ADD alcoholics report that they don't deal with the alcoholism until *after* they work on the ADD issues. There is logic to this method. If the ADD issues are ignored, sobriety may be short-lived because the underlying neurological disorder continues to wreak havoc in the individual's life. Those who do manage to maintain sobriety may become the *Dry Drunks* described in the literature on alcoholism. The Dry Drunk is an alcoholic who stops drinking but remains irritable, hot-tempered and withdrawn from her family. We don't have any research data to support our assertion, but we think that the behaviors of the dry drunk resemble those of some ADD adults.

This brings us back to the question of whether stimulants are out of the question for an ADDer who is recovering from alcohol or substance abuse. The answer—maybe not, isn't given as an expert opinion. This isn't our field of expertise but we can tell you that some professionals with whom we've conferred sometimes *cautiously* use stimulants to treat the ADD symptoms before they deal with the issues of substance abuse.

This approach is generally used with an ADDer who hasn't recovered through standard substance abuse treatment. *It is, however,* ***imperative*** *that you don't take matters into your own hands through self-medication of illegal drugs!* You must work with someone who is not only an expert in the area of substance abuse but also in the field of ADD. Together you can explore your unique problems and determine the best way to deal with them. Your sobriety or recovery from other substance abuse is too important to compromise with careless decisions.

Your Job as a Partner in Treatment

Concern about medicine use in general and stimulants in particular has evolved from growing consumer awareness of careless medication management and the problems of substance abuse. Medicine has an unfortunate history of being carelessly prescribed. The medications have sometimes been given without a careful diagnosis or promoted to the exclusion of other interventions.

We don't believe that most physicians have indiscriminately prescribed medicine for ADD or have offered it with an implied promise of a cure.

But those who have done so have given the pharmacological treatment of ADD an undeserved, bad reputation.

If you're taking a passive approach to your health care by taking medicine without asking questions, **S**top, **T**hink, **A**ct and **R**eflect! A competent physician never carelessly prescribes any drug—she always weighs the risks and benefits. You must assume a similar approach and take responsibility for understanding and using the risk/benefit equation to make an informed decision.

If your physician doesn't inform you of the risk/benefit equation of your prescribed medicine, ask her about it. Even competent physicians who make sound medical decisions don't always effectively communicate the basis of their decisions to the patient. You have a right and an obligation to be part of the decision-making process. If your physician prescribes medicine with little forethought and without ongoing monitoring, find a new one.

Your job as a partner in treatment includes keeping your doctor informed of your progress and any side effects. If your medicine doesn't seem to

be effective, don't take matters into your own hands by using it in a way other than the way it's prescribed. It's irresponsible to increase, decrease or change the timing of your dose without consulting with your physician. This misuse of medicine can result in overmedication, undermedication or pronounced side effects. Arbitrarily adding a second over the counter or prescribed drug to your regimen can cause potentially dangerous side effects. Some medicines shouldn't be taken together.

Some Personal Experiences

ADD is a neurological disorder and medicine can temporarily correct the problems that cause it. Medicine can *dramatically* regulate the symptoms of ADD. If you let fear or misconceptions prevent you from exploring medicine as a possible option, you may do yourself a great injustice. We don't encourage you to blindly choose medicine as your treatment of choice but urge you to make an informed decision based on factual information.

KK: "My personal experiences with medication have been positive. I had to spend some time finding the proper dose and the combination of drugs that would work for me but am pleased with the results. My daily regimen is 20 milligrams of Prozac once a day and 10 milligrams of Ritalin, three times a day.

I take two medicines because they seem to relieve different symptoms. The Ritalin helps me concentrate, increases my mental stamina and improves my organization skills, among other things. The Prozac doesn't help me think or perform better but it does help my moodiness and impulsivity. It makes me calmer and keeps me on an even keel.

Although Ritalin is beneficial, its effects are uneven. It doesn't last long and leaves me with several periods of the day when I'm irritable or short-tempered. The Prozac, a long lasting drug, provides a calming effect that lasts throughout the day. The combination of the two is the best symptom relief my doctor and I have discovered.

These medicines do have some side effects. When I first took Ritalin, I was bothered by a dry mouth but the side effect disappeared after a few weeks. A more serious side effect developed when my blood pressure began to elevate. The Prozac hasn't caused any side effects except one that I find beneficial—I've lost my tendency to overeat! I haven't lost my appetite, I just eat like a "normal" person.

I had found that taking Ritalin four times a day was best for my mental functioning but it increased my blood pressure too much. By eliminating the fourth dose, my blood pressure returned to normal and I learned to adjust to the foggy period.

I'm functioning better and am happier on medicine than I am without it. Once in a while I take a day off just to see what it's like and am always amazed at the difference. Without medicine I can still function but less well and with twice as much effort. For me, living life without the benefit of medication is like trying to run a race with leg irons on. It's a tremendous handicap."

PR: "I was diagnosed with ADD before Kate and remember telling her, somewhat apologetically, that I was taking Ritalin. It was early in my recovery and I wasn't as comfortable with the reality of my ADD as I am now. I told her that the fog I had lived in for thirty-nine years had finally lifted. I shared my relief at discovering a world painted in clarity instead of confusion.

I arrived at my decision to take Ritalin about two seconds after my diagnosis. It wasn't a careless, impulsive decision. I had already gotten my Ph.D.—**P**arent **h**andling the **D**isorder—through my research to understand my son's ADD problems. I had already gone through a year long process of initial refusal, skepticism and final acceptance of using Ritalin for Jeremy. There was no hesitation about trying Ritalin myself.

My experience with medication has been positive. My physician told me to expect a subtle rather than a dramatic change. The first day I took the Ritalin, I discovered that my baby's car seat had been stolen from my van. It wasn't until I had taken care of buying a new one and doing a number of other errands that I thought about the subtle changes my doctor had mentioned.

I had greeted the missing car seat with annoyance but little yelling and screaming! I accomplished everything I needed to do that day in an organized fashion, remembering an assortment of details that would otherwise have eluded me. The benefits of my medicine may not have been dramatic but they were undeniably significant!

Ritalin has been particularly effective for my organizational problems. I haven't tamed my *Time and Space Monster*, but I have managed to get it on a fairly secure leash. I can handle interruptions better and still maintain my focus on tasks. My short term memory also seems to have benefitted, probably because I can focus long enough to register incoming information.

I have had some minor side effects of headaches and mild stomach discomfort but none that have been particularly troublesome. The only change my doctor and I have made since my initial prescription was to add one dose. Now I take four doses of 10 milligram tablets. I briefly tried taking 15 milligrams but experienced dizziness and headaches that were definitely not worth the negligible benefits of the higher dose.

I do experience some degree of unpleasant unevenness from the Ritalin. I have to take care of myself during these periods when I become more irritable. If the up and down cycles ever become too bothersome, I will undoubtedly consider a different medication or combination of medications.

My experiences with the higher dose emphasize the need to start with a low dose and gradually increase it, carefully monitoring positive and negative effects. Medicines often have a therapeutic window, a narrow range of effectiveness that disappears at high doses. If your optimum dose is 5 milligrams but you start a Ritalin trial on 10, you might never know that the medicine could be effective. The negative effects of the higher dose might lead you to conclude that you can't tolerate Ritalin.

On the other hand, my Ritalin dose may be too low for you. Concern about the abuse potential of stimulant medication sometimes causes an overly conservative approach. My trial with a higher dose was warranted by the positive effects I had experienced. In the experience of my psychiatrist, some patients never realize optimum symptom relief because their physicians are reluctant to prescribe higher doses. The goal of your drug trial should be to find the optimum dose level that offers the most effective symptom control with the fewest side effects."

We have made several references to the importance of a drug trial in determining optimum dose levels of medicine. In the following chapter, we'll consider this in greater depth and examine the how's and why's of a variety of medicines—their individual mechanisms of action, characteristics, side effects and benefits.

Chapter 16

Medicine and Medicine Management

We are fortunate to have many well-informed mental health professionals in our community. Several work specifically with ADD adolescents and adults. Not long ago, one group asked that we spend some time with the staff sharing our personal and professional experiences. This growing interest in and commitment to the needs of adults with ADD is very encouraging!

Regrettably, many communities have limited resources. It's disheartening that there are physicians who still tell their ADD patients that Ritalin is never used in adults. It's disheartening that some mental health professionals continue to be skeptical about the existence of ADD in adults.

These comments aren't made to discourage you but to reemphasize the important role you play in your recovery. You must take control of your own situation to make things happen, including teaching sometimes resistant physicians about the value of medicine in the treatment of your disorder.

The good news is that knowledge is spreading. It's becoming easier to access needed resources. But it can still be a struggle. It can be especially difficult to find a physician experienced in using the newer, less commonly prescribed drugs or combinations of drugs such as Ritalin and Prozac.

Before we all jump on the medicine band-wagon, let's remember there are excellent reasons for a conservative approach to drug treatment: **drugs aren't harmless and they can't cure ADD!** They can be, however, an important piece of the treatment puzzle. With careful monitoring, unwanted side effects can be minimized and desired benefits maximized.

Medicine Management: A Process of Trial and Error

Even though John and Kim both have symptoms of impulsivity, John's may be caused by an insufficient amount of one neurotransmitter and Kim's by an excess of another. When their respective physicians prescribe Ritalin which often helps to manage impulsivity, John's symptoms are relieved but Kim's remain unchanged. The reason John and Kim respond differently to the drug is the diversity of symptoms and causes of the disorder we call ADD. This diversity strongly supports the notion that there are probably a number of ADD subtypes, each with its own particular cause and "cure".

The drugs used to treat ADD appear to have individual mechanisms of action—increasing or decreasing one chemical but not another. Does John need more of one neurotransmitter or does he need less of another? Medical science isn't advanced enough to identify the specific brain alteration(s) that cause John's impulsivity and the one that causes Kim's. With all these unknowns, matching the medicine to the symptom is a process of trial and error. Let's look at how a drug trial will work for you when you decide to use medicine.

As we look at the process of your drug trial, we'll use Ritalin as an example. Although other drugs are used in ADD treatment, Ritalin is often the drug of choice. Even if your physician prescribes something else, much of the framework of a drug trial of Ritalin will apply to the drug you take.

Your physician should monitor your drug trial as carefully as a scientist watches over an experiment. He should start with a detailed medical history and information about your particular symptoms and patterns of daily living. He should inform you of the expected desirable and undesirable side effects of various drugs. Together, you and he will consider various options and make a decision about the drug you'll use.

After a decision is made to use a particular drug, the next step will be to determine how large your dose should be and how often you will take it. For many drugs, extensive testing establishes their safety and dosage ranges. With Ritalin, the ranges are less clear because the accepted ranges are largely based on experience with children.

In fact, it wasn't until fairly recently that researchers began to systematically explore the risks and benefits of Ritalin doses higher than the recommended maximum of 80 mg./day. A growing number of experts are questioning current dose recommendations, particularly for adults. Intriguing reports of clinical experience with much higher doses warrant at least a closer look. For example, professionals within one large health care system report successful outcomes for hundreds of ADD adults treated with higher doses (.3-.8 mg./kg./dose) of Ritalin. Closely followed over a period of 5-6 years, the vast majority of these patients experienced significant improvement of attention with minimal or no side effects. Further, these adults experienced improved general health, an outcome not surprising in light of growing knowledge about the mind/body connection. (See Liden, C.B. in reading list).

Generally, the initial prescription is a low dose taken three times a day. Unlike other classes of medicines, research hasn't found anything resembling a therapeutic blood level to indicate Ritalin's effectiveness. Instead, your physician has to use your subjective experiences of positive and unwanted side effects to determine your proper dose. Your spouse may also be involved in this process. Her "objective" observations can add valuable information to your personal experiences of the medicine's beneficial effects.

Your physician will make dosage adjustments, gradually increasing the dose level until side effects indicate the level is too high. At that point, you will have discovered the optimum balance between maximum benefits and unwanted side effects. Keep in mind that even at a maximum dose, Ritalin may not be helpful. In that case, it will be time to think about another medication. Some ADDers don't improve on Ritalin but have good results with other medications.

Undoubtedly, new medicines will be added to those currently used in ADD treatment. Research is ongoing and will yield additional information about the neuropsychology of the brain and the mechanism of action for various drugs. We hope this research will provide clues to make the medicine/symptom match easier to determine.

The How and Why of Medicine as an ADD Treatment

In the first chapter, we briefly considered the hypotheses of the neurological cause(s) of ADD. Now, we want to examine how these relate to the effectiveness of various medicines.

The attention control system in the brain has two primary parts, the cerebral hemisphere and the brainstem. In overly simplistic terms, the cerebral hemisphere receives input via the primary sensory organs, associates and translates the input into symbolic functions and prepares the brain for a response. The brain stem includes groups of nerve cells that regulate automatic functions, ie. blood pressure and wakefulness.

Chemical messengers such as dopamine, noradrenaline and serotonin travel across synapses, the gaps between nerve cells, and make connections between the nerve cells in various parts of the central nervous system. The different parts of the brain are intricately connected with the brain stem and cerebral hemisphere and continually send and receive messages.

It has been suggested that changes in normal attention, concentration, motor activity, restlessness and impulsivity are caused by particular *settings* of the systems within the attention control center.[39] This control center functions as a high-tech post office with a department for Receiving and Processing, and one for Delivery. Both departments have their own particular responsibilities.

For the post office to operate efficiently, however, the employees in the two departments have to work together. Their jobs are closely interrelated. The job of the regulatory neurons' employees is to accurately receive and process incoming information. When they finish their task, they pass the processed data to the messengers who have to quickly transport all of it to the proper locations.

If the postal employees make errors in their individual departments, the system breaks down. If data aren't properly shared between departments, the system also fails to operate efficiently. This is analogous to dysfunction in the CNS. If you recall from an earlier discussion, some experts hypothesize that dysfunction anywhere throughout the central nervous system pathways causes symptoms of ADD. Due to the complexity of CNS interrelationships, symptoms have great variability depending upon the specific area of dysfunction in the individual.

Medicine is used with ADDers to alter the neurochemicals that impair functioning. The drugs accomplish this by either increasing production of neurotransmitters or slowing down their breakdown so more remains available for use.

Some researchers, for example, theorize that stimulant drugs improve alertness and concentration in an ADDer whose particular dysfunction is an insufficient production of the neurotransmitter dopamine. The associated regulation of activity levels in this individual is believed to be a secondary effect. With focused attention, she is less distracted and less likely to randomly run around in circles. Other experts suggest that some stimulants directly reduce hyperactivity by decreasing the release of norepinephrine (noradrenaline).

We have referred several times to the classes of drugs. Drugs are classified according to their action on various chemicals in the brain. The drugs in each class have unique side effects that must be monitored differently.The two classes used most often in ADD treatment are the stimulants and the tricyclic antidepressants. Other classes of drugs are also used with varying degrees of success.

Before we begin our discussion of available drugs, it would probably be wise for us to state a disclaimer of sorts:

We are not physicians although Kate has had a lot of experience with psychiatric pharmacological management. We are offering readily available information, gathered both from colleagues and available literature. Some of the sources we think you'll find particularly helpful are included in the reading and reference lists in the appendix. You may want to refer to some of them to expand your personal knowledge.

The inclusion of various available drugs should not be construed as our endorsement of their use. It isn't our intent to encourage you to try any particular medicine or disregard the advice of your physician. Our goal is to educate and provide information you can use to become an active partner with your physician in your medical management.

Stimulant Medications

Methylphenidate (Ritalin®)
This widely prescribed drug is available in 5, 10 and 20 milligram pills. Ritalin 20 SR, a long-acting form of methylphenidate, is roughly equivalent to a 10 milligram dose of the regular pill. The dosage range for ADD adults is approximately 20-80 milligrams per day.

With only a general dosage range for guidance, physicians rely on a drug trial to determine individual dosage levels. Since the drug is regulated as a controlled substance, your physician can only write one prescription each month and can't call it in to the pharmacy. The ADDer who repeatedly forgets to call his physician when he needs a new prescription might consider this a serious side effect!

The benefits of Ritalin include increased alertness, improved concentration, and reduced distractibility and disorganization. It has a short half-life so the body breaks it down and uses it quickly. The beneficial effects wear off within two to seven hours, with an average duration of three to four hours.

The short duration of Ritalin has two advantages. It starts working immediately and doesn't linger very long in the body. An ADDer who is concerned about the effects of medication on the body might find the fast in and out action of Ritalin appealing.

This advantage can also be a disadvantage. If you think of stimulant medication as replacement therapy similar to insulin for diabetes or iron for anemia, the prospect of several daily periods without symptom relief is disappointing. Since Ritalin isn't usually prescribed at intervals less than every four hours, many ADDers have several essentially unmedicated hours each day.

The short half-life also creates fluctuations and uneven management of symptoms. Some adults metabolize Ritalin so quickly that it doesn't last long enough to be of much help. These ADDers might consider medications such as dextroamphetamine, pemoline or one of the anti-depressants that have longer half lives.

In the PDR, Physicians Desk Reference[40], you'll find a long list of Ritalin's reported side effects. Don't be frightened by the long list! If you flip to the entry for aspirin you'll discover another long list of side effects.

Keep in mind that the PDR includes *every* reported side effect—the majority are rare and peculiar to the individual about whom they were reported. Information about the incidence of various side effects isn't provided so it's difficult to know which are common and which are rare.

If you develop an unusual symptom and wonder if it's related to the drug, use a reference such as the PDR as a starting point for a discussion with your physician. Also keep in mind that adults have a fairly short history of treatment with these medicines. Reported side effects for most of the drugs used to treat ADD are found in children and may or may not be applicable to adults.

Despite some negative publicity, Ritalin has a decent track record in terms of side effects. In fact, no long term harmful effects have been found in two decades of wide use. The most commonly reported side effects are irregular appetite and sleep patterns. The effects are variable and seem less problematic for adults than children. In some ADDers, Ritalin actually improves the regulation of these cycles.

If you're bothered by these side effects, you can work around them with careful regulation of the timing of the doses. High protein shakes and vitamin supplements can compensate for a decreased appetite. These troublesome side effects are often—but not always!—temporary and disappear after a few weeks.

Stomach aches and headaches are also associated with the drug, particularly in the first weeks of the drug trial. Though more common in children, some adults also experience these side effects. Considerably more common and troubling for ADD children and adults alike is the behavioral *rebound effect*. Rebound effects occur when the medication wears off. What seems to happen is that the medicine temporarily changes the body's biology. The body responds by returning to its usual state—with slightly more intensified symptoms—when the medicine has left the body. It's like love on the rebound, intense but short-lived!

Some ADD adults experience no rebound while others find it so severe that they can't tolerate the medication. The symptoms that were managed effectively during the interval of Ritalin treatment come back with a vengeance as the medicine leaves their bodies.

Temporary, intense confusion or irritability are characteristic during rebound. Most ADDers can tolerate these effects by making some minor adjustments. Taking a break from a task or getting away from other people during these periods can ease temporarily heightened symptoms.

While rebound effects are annoying for ADDers, elevated blood pressure levels are considerably more serious. Since Ritalin tends to stimulate the cardiovascular system, rapid pulse or high blood pressure sometimes results. This is rarely a concern in children although research hasn't studied the relationship between Ritalin usage and later coronary disease.

You might not have any trouble with elevated blood pressure levels. Many adults don't. High blood pressure can be life threatening, however, so it isn't something to ignore or take lightly. Monitoring this potentially dangerous side effect is simple—you should have your blood pressure taken at least once a week during your initial drug trial. After your doctor determines that you aren't having any blood pressure problems, he will periodically monitor it, usually a few times a year.

If you monitor your blood pressure yourself, you should call your physician if the top number, (systolic) goes higher than 140 or the bottom number (diastolic) goes higher than 90. Even if your pressure isn't elevated that much but is higher than usual, you should report it to your physician.

If you have benefitted from Ritalin but develop blood pressure problems, don't despair. Your physician may try a decrease in dosage to bring your pressure back to normal. Even if you have to discontinue the drug, there are other medications you can use.

Another extremely rare, but potentially dangerous side effect is bone marrow suppression that causes a lowered white blood cell count. The body's ability to fight disease is impaired if the white cell count drops.

Most physicians don't routinely monitor white blood cell counts because this side effect is so rare. If it worries you, ask your doctor to order a blood test before and after you begin taking Ritalin. In this way, he can monitor any changes in your white blood cell levels.

You may have read reports about Ritalin causing the tics of Tourette Syndrome. Tourette Syndrome (TS) is a genetic, neurological disorder that causes involuntary movements and behaviors. The symptoms can be mild, severe, simple or complex and include one or more facial and motor tics, and compulsive, repetitive behavior and speech. The age of onset is between 2 and 15 years of age. If you don't have TS, you won't develop it as an adult. But the possible connection between its onset and Ritalin usage is important to mention.

Reports of the development of tics shortly after children had started taking Ritalin were frequent enough to be considered a serious side effect of the medication. The concern was further magnified when the tics, unlike other side effects, didn't disappear after Ritalin was discontinued.

These observations formed the basis for the hypothesis that Ritalin *caused* tics. Although Ritalin does appear in **rare** cases to cause tics, the original hypothesis has changed as a result of ongoing research into both TS and ADD.

Statistics suggest that 50% of Tourette's individuals also have ADD.[41] In children with both disorders, the ADD is typically diagnosed first. The incidence of overlapping ADD and TS suggests that the development of tics is the result of an undiagnosed Tourette Syndrome. There is fairly widespread consensus that the emerging tics would eventually have manifested themselves as part of the normal course of TS.

The current theory is that Ritalin might cause an earlier onset of the underlying TS and in some cases might worsen the tics. It's important, therefore, that your physician is aware of a family history of tics. Although Ritalin is generally avoided as a treatment for ADD/TS children, it is prescribed for those with severe attentional problems. Some physicians also prescribe it in combination with medication for the tics.

We want to include a final comment before we move on. Most prescribed drugs are available under their trade name or as a generic drug. Many insurance companies require clients to purchase the less expensive generic brand. In our experience, generic methylphenidate isn't necessarily a bargain. Sometimes it doesn't seem to work very well.

PR: "My pharmacy often runs out of CIBA Ritalin—maybe there are lots of ADDers in my neighborhood! For several months I used methylphenidate instead. Although I didn't instantly make a connection, I began experiencing increased irritability and fluctuations in my symptom control.

During my periodic visit with my physician, I informed him that my medicine hadn't been working very well and wondered whether we should consider a medication change. One of the first questions he asked was regarding the brand of medicine I had been using.

It soon became obvious that my problem was the methylphenidate. I had never experienced these effects with CIBA Ritalin. Interestingly, my doctor told me that several of his patients had recently reported that their medication problems disappeared when they switched back to Ritalin."

Contrary to what insurance companies say, there are discernable differences between generic and trademark drugs. There are logical reasons for the anecdotal reports of poor symptom relief with methylphenidate. Federal regulations permit a *fudge* factor for generic drugs. Our local pharmacist reports that in general, generics vary from about ten to twenty percent of a trade drug's dose. Medical texts state that the variability can be as high as twenty-five percent. Thus, a 20 milligram dose of methylphenidate can be as high as 24 milligrams or as low as 16 milligrams. With the small therapeutic windows of effectiveness for ADD drug treatment, this variability can be significant.

In fairness to the drug companies, many probably don't push the regulatory limits to the limit. The problem for consumers is that pharmacies use a number of different suppliers. Some have better quality control than others. The methylphenidate from the ABC Company can contain a significantly different quantity of medicine than pills from the XYZ Company.

One solution is to ask your pharmacist for the supplier's name each time you have your prescription filled. Then you'll need to carefully monitor your symptoms to discover the company that seems to have the best quality control. When you have your next prescription filled, request a specific company's medicine.

A simpler solution is to use only CIBA Ritalin. If your doctor specifically prescribes it and indicates the medical necessity for the trade brand, most insurance companies will either cover the added expense in full or charge you for the difference.

You may not experience any problems with the generic drug. But if you do, before you switch to another medicine you may want to consider the issues we've raised. We want to emphasize that these experiences aren't documented in any research we've read and may be unique to a small group of ADDers.

Dextroamphetamine (Dexedrine®)

Dextroamphetamine is another stimulant medication that appears to have a slightly different pharmacological action than Ritalin. Both work to boost the amount of available dopamine. Dextroamphetamine, however, blocks the reuptake of the neurotransmitter while Ritalin increases its production.

Dextroamphetamine *dams up* the precious amounts of dopamine to make it available for continued use and Ritalin searches for more of it to add to the reservoir. The result is the same for both medications—an increase in available dopamine—but the differences in action can be important in treatment. ADDers may respond differently to each of these stimulants because of the particular dysfunctions in their attention control systems.

Dexedrine is available as a 5 milligram/teaspoon strength elixir or a 5 milligram tablet. The duration of both is about four to six hours. Long-acting spansules in 5, 10 or 15 milligram strengths, with a duration of eight to twelve hours, are also available. The typical dose for ADD adults ranges from 10 to 40 milligrams per day, approximately half that of Ritalin. As a matter of financial practicality, Dexedrine is less expensive than Ritalin.

The side effects of this stronger stimulant are similar to those of Ritalin with one exception—it has a slightly greater abuse potential when used in very high doses. Dexedrine's side effects seem to have some relationship to the age of the ADDer. Children appear to experience more pronounced side effects than adolescents or adults do. This may be related to this stimulant's strength.

Physicians are often reluctant to prescribe Dexedrine for ADD adults because of its abuse potential. This is unfortunate for Ritalin non-responders who might be helped by the different mechanism of Dexedrine. The longer duration of this drug might also be beneficial for those who rapidly metabolize Ritalin or experience severe rebound effects.

Pemoline (Cylert®)

The stimulant Cylert was used for many years in Europe before it was introduced in the United States. It has no other medical use except in the treatment of ADD.

Unlike Ritalin and Dexedrine, Cylert may need to be taken for two to four weeks before you notice symptom relief. You might, however, experience beneficial effects in the first week. With an eighteen to twenty-four hour duration of action, Cylert is taken only once a day. It comes in either 37.5 or 75 milligrams tablets and has an accepted dosage range of 18.75 to 112.5 milligrams per day. Your physician can write only one non-refillable prescription each month but he can call it in to the pharmacy.

After this stimulant gradually builds up in the body over several weeks, it provides a steady effect on symptom management without any rebound. Rebound becomes an issue only if you suddenly stop taking the drug.

The long duration of action has an advantage/disadvantage equation similar to that of Ritalin's short duration. The continued symptom relief is beneficial but it means that the drug is always in your body in varying degrees. Unlike Ritalin which you can take as needed, you have to take Cylert every day. If you decide to stop taking the drug, you have to do it gradually.

Cylert isn't classified as a controlled substance because it's non-addictive and doesn't produce any feelings of *being up* or *euphoric*. An advantage of this drug is that it isn't water soluble and can't be converted to an IV form for abuse. Since serious drug abuse frequently involves intravenous drug use, Cylert might be the treatment of choice for recovering substance abusers. If you have a history of substance abuse, you might want to consult with your physician about Cylert as a treatment option.

Side effects associated with Cylert are similar to those of the other stimulants with one exception. A rare but potentially serious side effect is damage of liver function. If you take Cylert, your doctor will do periodic blood tests to monitor the level of liver enzymes. If he finds elevated blood levels of these enzymes, he will immediately stop the medication. This elevation indicates that damage has occurred. If you've already sustained some liver damage as a result of substance abuse or other causes, Cylert would be contraindicated.

Antidepressants

Tricyclic Antidepressants

The drugs in this class are prescribed primarily for mood disorders (depression) but also for sleep and anxiety disorders, bedwetting and ADD. For ADD treatment, Imipramine (Tofranil®) and desipramine (Norpramin®) are the most commonly prescribed drugs in this class.

Most tricyclics are in tablet form and range in strength from 10 to 100 milligrams. They are taken once a day, usually between dinner and bedtime. Children seem to metabolize the tricyclics more rapidly than adults and might need to take two doses per day. Your physician can write a six month prescription with a one month refill and can phone it in to the pharmacy.

When a tricyclic is used for depression, the patient needs to take it daily for one to five weeks before improvements occur. Interestingly, beneficial effects in ADD children can be apparent within days of starting tricyclic antidepressants.

The usual dosages of these drugs vary. For example, the usual range of Desipramine in the treatment of adult depression is 25 to 300 milligrams per day. Unlike stimulants, blood tests can be used to indicate rates of metabolism and determine proper dose levels. If the therapeutic range of a particular drug is 150 to 300 milligrams, a higher or lower blood level would indicate a need to adjust the dose.

Blood tests are less valuable in determining the therapeutic doses of tricyclics in the treatment of ADD. Dose levels aren't well defined due to a lack of research. Therefore, if your physician prescribes an antidepressant, he will use a process of trial and error to determine your optimal dose.

The action of tricyclic antidepressants is related to an increase in available amounts of the neurotransmitters norepinephrine and serotonin. The drugs in this class aren't *uppers* or *downers*. They aren't habit-forming and don't have any mood-changing effect on people without chemical depression.

Tricyclics have a steady effect on the body because they have long half-lives. ADDers whose symptoms fluctuate excessively with Ritalin treatment might prefer the even symptom control of an antidepressant.

Side effects vary slightly with various tricyclic antidepressants and seem to be more common in adults than children. A dry mouth, excessive sleepiness, constipation and occasional dizziness are the most common.

The problem of decreased saliva production often disappears over time. If this is a problem, you can alleviate it by chewing gum or sucking on hard candy. You can manage constipation by drinking more fluids or increasing fiber in your diet. If you develop dizziness, you can minimize it by slowly getting up from a lying or sitting position.

You might experience a problem with the sedative effect of the drug you're using. Each of the tricyclics causes varying degrees of sedation. Some of the drugs in the following chart aren't typically used with ADD but you can see that all tricyclics aren't created equal. If after a few weeks you haven't adjusted to your medicine, you might need to try another one that causes less sedation. You might also find that none of the tricyclics work for you. A change to a different class of drugs might be in order. Of course, as with any medication you take, you need to report any side effects to your physician.

RELATIVE SEDATIVE SIDE EFFECTS OF VARIOUS TRICYCLICS[42]

Drug	Sedative Activity*
Amitriptyline	+ + +
Desipramine	+
Doxepin	+ + +
Imipramine	+ +
Nortriptyline	+
Protriptyline	+/0
Trimipramine	+ + +
*Number of + indicates relative activity	*+/0 indicates no activity

The tricyclics decrease the ADD symptoms of mood swings, impulsivity and hot temper but haven't been particularly helpful for attentional problems. Some ADD experts report, however, that very low, 10-25 milligram doses are effective. Likely, this results from a "therapeutic window effect." It is common for psychiatric medications to lose effectiveness at doses that are too high or too low.

The positive effect of these new low doses is documented only in physician anecdotal reports; it hasn't yet been widely researched. With no standardized dose schedule to guide a psychiatrist, he would need to use a trial and error approach, starting with a very small dose.

MAO Inhibitors

MAO Inhibitors are a second class of antidepressant drugs. Isocarboxazid (Marplan®), Phenelzine (Nardil®) and Tranylcypromine (Parnate®) are three drugs in this group. Similar to the tricyclic antidepressants, MAO inhibitors increase available norepinephrine and serotonin. But the mechanism of action is different.

Monoamine oxidase (MAO) is an enzyme that breaks down norepinephrine and serotonin. MAO inhibitors decrease the action of the MAO enzyme so the brain has more neurotransmitters available for use. The final effect on the norepinephine and serotonin neurotransmitters is the same for the tricylics and MAO inhibitors but symptom relief is different with these two categories of drugs.

Scientific research has documented the action of the antidepressants on norepinephrine and serotonin. It isn't known, however, whether this action is directly responsible for the beneficial effects of the drugs. Drugs intervene in a complex chain of events involving combinations of various neurotransmitters and chemicals that create new enzymes or neurotransmitters. It's probably far too simplistic to assume that any single chemical is entirely responsible for a particular change in brain function.

The MAO inhibitors appear to do a better job of treating ADD than the tricyclic antidepressants.[43] Their effects are similar to those of stimulant medications with the added benefit of twenty-four hour symptom relief. The beneficial effects combined with the long duration of action would seem to make MAO inhibitors an excellent choice for ADDers. So why don't physicians prescribe them very often?

If you take an MAO inhibitor in combination with certain foods or medicines, you can experience a blood pressure crisis. Your blood pressure can shoot up high enough to create a medical emergency. An interaction between other medications, food containing tyramine and the MAO inhibitor can cause this sharp rise in blood pressure. To avoid this dangerous side effect, you must avoid substances containing tyramine. Foods high in tyramine include, among others, bananas, all cheese except cottage cheese, liver, raisins, sausage, yogurt, wine, beer and chocolate. A number of drugs must also be avoided, including stimulant drugs and many over the counter cough and cold medicines.

Your physician will give you a detailed list of foods and medicines to avoid. We would also recommend that you ask your pharmacist to teach you about the over-the-counter medicines you shouldn't use. Although nurses and physicians are knowledgeable about drugs, your pharmacist will have more detailed information about the specific compounds used in common non-prescription drugs. Pharmacists are generally the best source of information about dosage, side effects and drug interactions.

Other side effects of the MAO inhibitors are similar to those of tricyclic antidepressants. They include dry mouth, constipation, difficulty urinating, rapid heartbeat and low blood pressure. The high blood pressure crisis occurs only in conjunction with excess tyramine.

Patients with depression usually don't experience symptom relief for several weeks after taking an MAO inhibitor. ADDers, however, seem to have a different response. Some report improved symptoms in a matter of days. It is probable that these drugs work differently to correct the biochemical imbalances in ADD.

The MAO inhibitors might be a good choice for ADD adults who can live with the dietary restrictions. Physicians don't prescribe them for children partly because the diet is difficult to regulate and the consequences for cheating are serious. Adults, however, should be able to decide if they are capable of abiding by the restrictions.

Newer Antidepressants

Two recently introduced antidepressant drugs that merit mention are fluoxetine hydrochloride (Prozac®) and bupropion (Wellbutrin®). You have undoubtedly heard of Prozac. It has received much recent publicity. It has been heralded as the new wonder drug and denounced as a destructive drug that causes violence or suicide. The publicity has confused the public, leaving some people unnecessarily fearful of the drug.

Fluoxetine Hydrochloride

Prozac is similar to other antidepressants in its positive effects on irritability and regulation of general mood dysfunction. It doesn't appear to have any positive effects on the cognitive symptoms of ADD. It might, however, be particularly helpful in decreasing impulsivity. Some of the more intriguing reports about Prozac indicate its usefulness in treating assorted problems of impulse control, including kleptomania and bulimia.

Unlike other antidepressants, Prozac is more specific in its effects. It increases the neurotransmitter serotonin but doesn't affect norepinephrine. The effect of this is akin to going after a brain problem with a dart rather than a sledgehammer. In the best of all possible worlds, medication would act specifically on only those parts of the body that cause trouble. Many drugs act on multiple body systems and thus create unwanted side effects.

Prozac doesn't cause drowsiness and has fewer side effects than other antidepressants. Nausea, diarrhea and weight loss are the most common. Although it has a calming effect in most people, it sometimes causes insomnia, anxiety or *jitteryness*. It seems to *jazz up* the central nervous system in these people, causing symptoms not unlike those experienced by an ADDer is his natural state.

This surprising reaction to Prozac might result from the diversity of brain alterations we've talked about. People with similar symptoms don't necessarily have the same thing going on in their brains. It might be that Prozac's action on the CNS corrects a particular deficiency in an individual ADDer's brain. If there is an inadequate supply of a certain chemical, perhaps serotonin, the drug acts to increase available quantities and causes the expected calming effect. Much like vitamin supplements, it replaces something vital that's in short supply.

On the other hand, if Prozac increases the quantity of the chemical in people who already have an adequate supply, it may create a kind of overdose with the resultant jitteryness. The effect is similar to taking a supplemental vitamin when the body already has enough—the overdose can sometimes cause unwanted side effects.

Determining the proper dosage of Prozac is relatively simple. It comes in 20 milligram capsules and has a standard dose of one or two capsules per day. Most people take it in the morning to reduce the insomnia it sometimes causes. Although there is little research on Prozac as a treatment for ADD, anecdotal reports suggest that ADDers seem to experience beneficial effects more quickly than individuals with depression do.

Prozac initially received extravagant praise because it truly is a new type of drug. The development of this drug represented a giant step forward to more specific drug treatment for the chemically imbalanced brain. Unfortunately in the excitement over this breakthrough, many people got carried away.

Much of the publicity surrounding this new drug was excessively positive, seeming to promise a cure for a variety of problems with virtually no side effects. Many had such high expectations about this wonder drug that they were understandably angry when reports of some serious side effects began to emerge. People who blindly took Prozac with high hopes for a cure felt deceived when it didn't work or caused troublesome side effects.

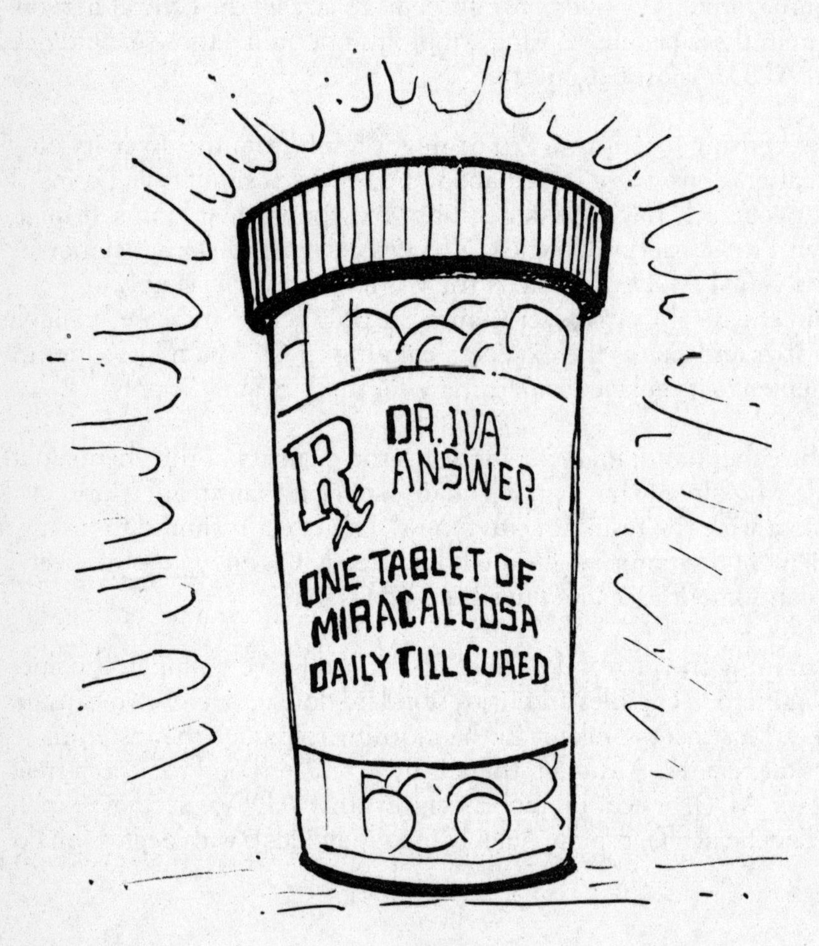

A reported serious side effect that became apparent after Prozac was on the market was its potential for precipitating violence or suicide in certain people. Although this side effect is rare and may be associated with more serious mental illness or combinations of disorders, it has received notable media attention.

Support groups for Prozac survivors have sprung up. Some are legitimate. Others have been orchestrated by the same group that opposes Ritalin and all other forms of drug management of psychiatric disorders.

In the midst of all the hoopla over the new miracle drug, people forgot an important caveat—*no drug is harmless*. All drugs have side effects and the potential to create serious problems for some people.

The intensity of the negative reaction to this drug resulted in part from the realization that its miracles didn't pan out for everybody. This comment isn't intended to minimize the pain of those who have had bad experiences with Prozac. Violence towards oneself or others is a serious problem, indeed. Unrealistic expectations, however, have played a part in the confusion surrounding Prozac.

If you consider the risk/benefit equation of Penicillin, for instance, you can understand the inherent danger in assuming the safety of a drug. Penicillin is a widely used drug that fights the infections that used to kill people. It's a valuable drug that has saved many lives, but some people are *allergic* to it and have life-threatening reactions if they take it. There is no way to predict in advance a person's reaction to this wonder drug. The only safeguard is for the physician and patient to closely monitor the drug's effects.

The situation with Prozac is similar. It can be helpful for many people, but a few have a serious *allergy* to it. They become violent or suicidal and must immediately stop taking it. Although this reaction is quite rare, side effects must be closely monitored.

Prozac might be a viable choice for ADDers as symptom relief of moodiness and impulsivity. In combination with Ritalin, Prozac can provide even better symptom management. A decision to use this drug should be made according to your unique needs and in consultation with your physician.

Bupropion (Wellbutrin®)
The anti-depressant Wellbutrin, used with adolescents and adults, is a relative newcomer as a treatment for ADD. It has particular promise because it appears to increase the levels of norepinephrine and serotonin and also those of dopamine. This means that Wellbutrin is useful not only for mood regulation but also for improved cognitive functioning. In effect, it is a combination of an antidepressant and a stimulant that is less powerful than Ritalin but longer acting.

The safety and effectiveness of Wellbutrin hasn't been established yet by the extensive clinical trials required for FDA approval. Therefore, it hasn't been approved as a drug for treating ADD. Although clinical reports support its effectiveness in some people,[44] it's still considered somewhat experimental.

Wellbutrin is used primarily in individuals who haven't responded to stimulants or tricyclics. As more is learned about this drug, it might join the mainstream medicines. If you don't mind trying an experimental drug, you can talk with your physician about Wellbutrin. You might experience the dual benefits reported by other ADD adults.

Other Drugs

Caramazepine, (Tegretol®), is an anticonvulsant drug prescribed for seizure disorders. It has also been used in the treatment of manic depressive illness. Physicians rarely prescribe Tegretol as a primary treatment for ADD. It has been reported, however, that some ADD children who took Tegretol for their seizures, experienced relief of their ADD symptoms. If you have a history of seizures, you might want to talk with your physician about the possibility of using this drug.

Catepres, (Clonidine®) is an antihypertensive medication (one used for high blood pressure). Recently it has been used increasingly as a treatment for ADD. Clonidine is also used to reduce the tics of Tourette Syndrome. It might be particularly helpful for ADD/TS individuals whose tics increase when they take stimulant medications.

It appears that Clonidine's mechanism of action is similar to a stimulant medication's. It seems to treat the attentional problems of ADD better than antidepressants do. It's also a good alternative for ADDers who can't take stimulants. Clonidine hasn't been studied as thoroughly as Ritalin, however. Generally, it isn't the first drug of choice for treatment of ADD alone.

Although the side effects aren't well documented because of its relatively recent arrival on the scene, Clonidine might have two particular disadvantages for ADDers. It causes fatigue and worsens a tendency toward depression. These side effects outweigh the benefits of the drug for some people. It does, however, have several advantages over other medicines.

Clonidine stimulates the appetite and lowers blood pressure. Of course, a stimulated appetite isn't necessarily a benefit if you have spent your life trying to lose weight! An additional advantage is its longer duration of action that provides steady symptom management.

The standard dosage is a daily treatment of 5 micrograms per kilogram of weight. Clonidine is available as a skin patch that slowly releases the drug. Reports suggest that the skin patch provides symptom relief that can last up to five days. The patch can cause a skin rash that can sometimes be minimized by changing the application site.

Less is known about Clonidine's effectiveness in adults but in children it works for about 60% of those who take it. It might be a good alternative if you haven't responded well to other drugs. It might also be an option if you are a recovering substance abuser because it doesn't have any abuse potential.

Clomipramine, Anafranil® is a relatively new medication used to treat obsessive-compulsive disorders. Previously available only in Canada, Anafranil is sometimes prescribed for ADDers with obsessive-compulsive symptoms. We have received anecdotal reports from physicians and ADDers that it has relieved ADD symptoms by decreasing the *brain clutter* caused by obsessions. If you have associated obsessive-compulsive symptoms, you might find this drug helpful.

Lithium is a simple salt used in the treatment of manic-depressive disorders. The FDA approved it in the '70's but restricted its use to adolescents and adults because it had been insufficiently researched in children.

Lithium comes in varying strengths in capsule, elixir, and short and slow release tablet forms. Its effectiveness is related to the salt and water balance in the body. Individuals who take lithium need to maintain adequate salt and water intake in their diets. They also have to monitor drug interactions because other medications can cause adverse reactions by interfering with the metabolism of the lithium.

Side effects include drowsiness, muscle weakness and lack of coordination at high doses. Increased thirst and urination, nausea and diarrhea, weight gain and worsening of acne in adolescents are all reported side effects. In rare instances it can cause abnormal kidney or thyroid function. Periodic blood tests are needed to monitor these functions.

Although lithium isn't a standard treatment for ADD, it provides benefits for certain people. It has been suggested that the overactivity of some ADDers overlaps manic symptoms. Lithium might help to regulate these symptoms. Data from some studies suggest it can be effective in managing the ADD symptoms of impulsivity, temper outbursts and stress intolerance. It might be an option if you have a family history of manic depression.

Antipsychotics

Thioridazine (Mellaril®), chlorpromazine (Thorazine®) and haloperidol (Haldol®) are drugs used primarily to control psychotic symptoms. Physicians also prescribe Haldol for the severe tics of Tourette Syndrome that Clonidine can't control.

These drugs are also sometimes used to treat the severe impulsivity, hyperactivity and self-destructive behaviors of a subgroup of ADDers. Although antipsychotics are rarely prescribed for ADD treatment, they do seem to help a few individuals with extreme, self-destructive behaviors.

The antipsychotics have side effects that make them undesirable for the treatment of most ADDers. Side effects include stiffness, excessive sedation and slower cognitive processing. For these reasons they will be useful only in rare cases. Besides the previously noted side effects, antipsychotic medications can also cause a potentially disabling movement disorder known as Tardive dyskinesia.

Tardive dyskinesia causes involuntary movements of the face and body. This severe side effect usually appears only after long-term use of antipsychotics but it doesn't disappear when the drugs are stopped. Because of this serious side effect, clinicians rarely prescribe antipsychotic medication for non-psychotic disorders.

Newer Possibilities
A few physicians report that Buspirone (Buspar®) and Nadolol (Corgard®) may be helpful in treating ADD symptoms. Buspar was developed as a non-addictive, anti-anxiety drug. A few case studies indicate that Buspar appears to minimize the aggressive behavior sometimes associated with ADD.

The antihypertensive drug, Corgard, may help ADDers with symptoms of irritability, short tempers and physical restlessness. The best news about Corgard is that it acts only on the body, not on the brain. Unlike Clonidine, it doesn't cause the unwelcome side effects of fatigue and depression.

Neither Corgard nor Buspar help with attentional problems so they would be most effective in combination with stimulant medications. We want to emphasize that the use of these drugs in ADD treatment is very new and thus highly experimental. Stay alert for further information from the medical profession.

Miscellaneous

Nicotine: Are you a smoker? Perhaps many hard-core smokers who have great difficulty quitting are ADDers. This is nothing more than an educated guess based on personal experience and anecdotal reports of other ADD adults. But it's an interesting theory.

Nicotine is a stimulant so it isn't surprising that it might relieve symptoms of ADD. Some smokers who tried to quit smoking report that they had little success until they started treatment for their ADD.

KK: "I was a pack and a half per day smoker for many years and had unsuccessfully tried to quit several times. I knew that it would take several weeks or months to get past the urge to smoke. But my need to

smoke to maintain my concentration never stopped. I was unable to update my resume when my grant dependent job ended and I procrastinated about doing anything that required sitting down for a long time.

This behavior was out of character. I had trained myself in my early '20's to tackle the hardest jobs first. I became panicky about the tendency of my mind to wander and feared that I wouldn't be able to cope with adult responsibilities. I also had serious problems with my temper that I had managed to control for at least fifteen years. Interestingly, the only time I didn't have these troubling symptoms was during the month I chewed nicotine gum to withdraw from cigarettes. During that time, quitting seemed easy.

With great effort, I did manage to stop smoking. The residual concentration problems didn't get better, however, until I started taking Ritalin a year and a half after I had stopped smoking. I believe that I used smoking all those years to treat my undiagnosed ADD."

We certainly don't advocate smoking as a treatment for ADD but it's an interesting consideration. Maybe nicotine patches or gum might have some effectiveness. You won't find nicotine in a list of options for treatment of ADD, but who knows? Even if it doesn't have any treatment potential, perhaps it has research potential.

Caffeine is a stimulant ADD adults frequently use for self-medication. Many adults we've talked to drink pots of coffee and numerous cans of caffeinated drinks every day. They say these habits help them calm down and concentrate. They also report that they consume fewer of these drinks after they begin taking medicine for their ADD symptoms.

The problem with caffeine is that it's too mild to be effective. It can also cause excessive jitteryness and the cardiovascular problem of a rapid heartbeat. It makes much better sense to get medical help for attentional problems than to use caffeine as self-medication.

Finding a drug to manage some of your symptoms can be extremely helpful in your recovery. But you should regard it only as a starting place in your journey, not as the final destination. Remember the earlier discussion about the grief process and the stage of "It can all be fixed"? If you operate under the erroneous assumption that you are cured after you start taking your medicine, you will sabotage your recovery. You still have a lot of work to do.

Part of this work will include the self-help strategies we've discussed. You might, however, need the guidance of a therapist to help you use these strategies to their best advantage. If you're dealing with unresolved issues around your ADD, you may need professional help to deal with them.

Have you ever visited a brain massage therapist? Have you ever tried computerized Virtual Reality? In the next chapter we'll talk about these *next generation* therapies as well as other less exotic alternative therapies that are finding their way into the mainstream establishment. And of course we'll also devote a large part of our discussion to the well-accepted mainstream therapies that have been used for years.

CHAPTER 17

Therapy and More Therapy

There is a bewildering array of available mainstream and alternative therapies. Some are geared toward helping people with severe mental or emotional problems. Others cater to those who are sufficiently well adjusted to cope with adult responsibilities but who may have symptoms that interfere with everyday life. Still others, especially those developed in the self-enhancement oriented '60's and '70's, are designed to increase the potential of normal individuals.

The Therapy Dilemma for ADDers

Since the concept of adult ADD is relatively new, it can be difficult to find a therapist who understands your special needs. Most mental health professionals have a particular orientation. They assume the tenets of a school of thought that provides direction in the *how to* of psychotherapy and theories regarding the *cause* of psychological problems.

For example, Freudian therapists believe that traumas of childhood result in neuroses, the less severe emotional problems. These traumas include lack of *good enough* parenting. The Freudians believe that the resultant psychological symptoms relate to the child's stage of psychosexual development at the time the trauma occurs.

If the child is in the Oedipal stage around age five, the primary issue for her in adulthood will be competition. If the trauma occurs during infancy, the issues in later life will be oral, or dependency needs. On the other hand, behaviorists view psychological problems as learned behaviors. They focus their efforts on helping the client substitute positive behaviors for negative ones.

There are as many theories about the cause of psychological problems as there are therapies to help them. The problem for ADDers is that many psychotherapists don't receive training in recognizing and treating ADD. They may attribute your symptoms to other causes. The Freudians label you neurotic and the Behaviorists assume you had bad role models when you were growing up.

A particular therapeutic technique based on a theory of causation can be helpful for some who seek professional help. For example, identifying sexual abuse as the cause of an individual's emotional problems can lead to an appropriate decision about therapy. But in the treatment of ADD, connecting a cause to a specific therapy is often counterproductive, especially since the process often starts with a faulty assumption.

An acquaintance of ours spent thousands of dollars with three different therapists who focused primarily on the emotional climate of her home. She had been seriously ill when her son was an infant and had been unable to spend time with him. "Poor Bonding" was the diagnosis she received when she sought help for her son's severe behavior problems. She wasted two years in expensive, ineffective psychotherapy for him until a fourth mental health professional finally diagnosed his ADD.

Clearly, a diagnosis of "Poor Parenting" isn't a useful explanation for an ADDer's problems. Her parents may have received failing grades in *Parenting 101* but the poor parenting diagnosis is faulty and incomplete.

We aren't suggesting that the techniques used in Behavioral or Freudian therapy are useless for an ADDer. The Behaviorists can teach her how to control her symptoms and the Freudians can help her modify defense mechanisms that aren't working.

The important thing for you is to become actively involved in the choices you make regarding psychotherapy. If you remain unconvinced that your therapist understands the impact of ADD in your life, you must find someone else who does.

How do you know where to start? You already know that both physicians and psychologists treat ADD. You already know that the listing in your local telephone book isn't the way to find an ADD informed professional. So you do your homework and get a referral from a member of your support group. You make an appointment with Dr. Great, walk into her office and lie down on the couch she directs you to. There seems to be some kind of terrible mistake! This isn't at all what you had in mind! Welcome to the confusing world of therapy.

As you begin seeking professional help, you may find yourself baffled by the variety of available therapies. Or you may have been in a particular kind of therapy that was helpful and wonder why it isn't included on your referral list.

In the sections that follow, we'll look at a number of different therapies and briefly outline the tenets of each. They are roughly divided into categories of individual therapies and group therapies. Within each category, the most commonly used therapies for ADD are discussed first. Also included are several options that aren't psychotherapies but which can be an important part of ADD treatment.

A number of other therapies that we'll mention aren't standard treatments but we'll examine them so you'll know what they are. They don't offer help specifically for ADD issues. Rather they focus on the emotional baggage of failures people carry with them throughout their lives. We've also included comments about their possible value for certain problems associated with growing up with ADD. You can decide if you think any of them have value for you.

Cognitive Psychotherapy

The basic tenet of Cognitive Psychotherapy is that thoughts profoundly influence one's emotional state and behavior. This psychotherapy is emerging as a powerful way to help people with a variety of problems and is particularly helpful for those who suffer from depression.

An ADDer often receives much negative feedback during her childhood. She adds to it by comparing herself to other people. Although she has deficits unique to her disorder, she often exaggerates her difficulties. She may create a tape in her mind that continually replays a negative script. The distorted thinking may go something like this:

> **Rachel:** *"Nobody knows this, but I flunked out of college the first time I tried it. I finally have my degree, but I still feel dumb because I flunked.*

I'm not as qualified as the other people at work—I know they look down at me."

A cognitive therapist would help Rachel examine her script for illogical thinking. She would help her separate the facts from the feelings. Rachel did flunk out of college: that is a fact based on reality. Because of this fact, she feels dumb.

She makes an illogical leap in reasoning and assumes that if she feels dumb, it's a fact—she is indeed stupid. Her assumptions are faulty. In reality, she has compensated for her deficits and performs well on the job. Her coworkers respect and admire her.

The therapist would help Rachel use the facts to rewrite her negative tape. Her new tape would include affirmations of her successes. She would learn to replace, "Because I flunked out of college, I am stupid," with:

"I am very smart. When I went to college the first time I didn't know about my ADD and how to handle it. I was overwhelmed by the work. I'm proud of myself for getting my degree. It wasn't easy but I even managed to make the Dean's List most of the time."

The principles of Cognitive Psychotherapy can also be used to influence behaviors. You can learn to control your actions by *talking to yourself* in the privacy of your own thoughts. If you are impulsive, you can learn to say, "Stop, look and listen," before taking action. This strategy can limit the number of times you interrupt or blurt out inappropriate comments.

Cognitive Psychotherapy has recently become popular. Although some professionals question its effectiveness, others believe it can be helpful for a variety of problems. A recent study suggested that even computerized Cognitive Therapy *without* a therapist, could alleviate depression.[45]

Self-talk can correct the ADDer's illogical thinking that interferes with a positive sense of self. This can free up energy to focus on other issues.

Behavioral Therapy

Behavioral Therapy is a pragmatic approach that deals with the symptoms and behaviors that cause problems. The innermost secrets of the mind aren't issues for Behaviorists. Some people are uncomfortable

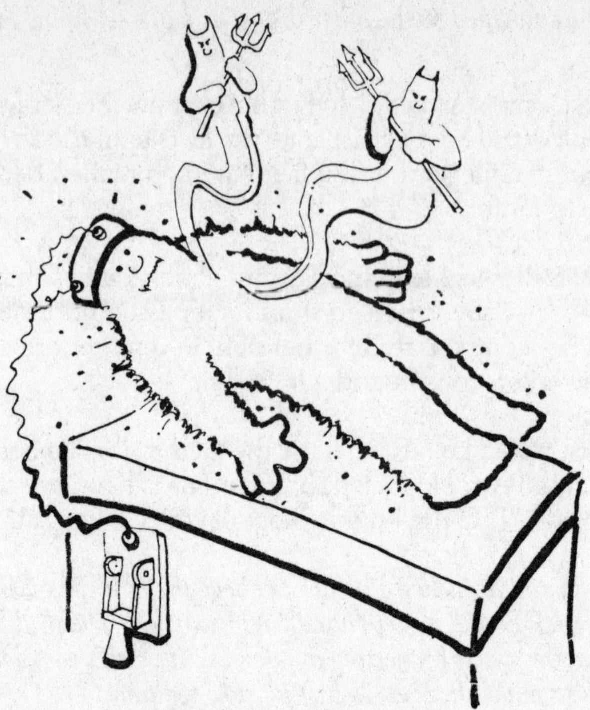

"Behavioral Exorcism"

with the idea of Behavioral Therapy because they conjure up images of researchers, rats and electric shocks! The thought of being controlled and manipulated by a Behavioral therapist isn't a welcome one.

Current behavioral treatment is not about manipulation, however. It's about acquiring the tools you need to control your own behavior. Each person is expected to be ultimately responsible for her individual treatment.

In a behavioral approach, actions are viewed as responses to stimuli from the environment. Many successful self-help programs use behavioral principles. Programs to control weight and stop smoking are two examples. The overeating or smoking is considered as a learned response to stressful events. The task in self-help groups is to unlearn the unhealthy responses by substituting new, more positive behaviors.

Early in the program, a participant begins a diary and makes an entry each time the problem behavior occurs. She notes the events that immediately preceeded the behavior and how she was feeling at the time.

These feelings and events are *triggers* that set off the unwanted action.

After she has identified her individual triggers, the participant learns ways to avoid them or substitute an alternative response. For instance, if she's trying to lose weight, she might avoid walking past the refrigerator or learn to reward herself with things other than food. If her typical response to a stressful day at work is to binge on food, she might try renting a movie she's been dying to see or taking a long, relaxing walk. Rewards are an integral part of behavior therapy—personal treats reinforce positive behavior.

Good Behavioral Therapy puts control in the hands of the individual. The client makes the decision to change a particular behavior. The therapist or trainer helps her learn how to control it through a personalized plan of actions and rewards.

An ADDer can have a variety of behaviors that get her into trouble. If she learns to use behavioral techniques, she is less likely to experience the effects of others trying to control her. After a while the changed behavior rewards itself through the positive responses from other people.

You can apply behavioral principles to many situations in your life. When it's time to face the drudgery of balancing your checkbook, plan a specified period of time for the chore and a reward at its conclusion. The prospect of a treat can smooth the way through hated activities. If you've had a particularly difficult day, use the idea of the trigger and avoid the shopping mall and crowd of people that will set off increased irritability.

The techniques of Behavioral Therapy work best in a group setting that provides mutual support. Groups designed for ADDers, however, are scarce. Until you can find one, you can work individually with a behavioral therapist.

Speech and Language Therapy

Speech Therapy focuses on a variety of speech and language issues. It isn't just for children. Many adults have communication problems related to their ADD symptoms. Others may have distinct speech disabilities that might require the help of a speech therapist. The therapist uses the results of a language evaluation to pinpoint specific problems areas and to design an appropriate therapy program.

Educational Remediation
Although not a therapy per se, educational remediation can also be an important part of your treatment. In an earlier chapter, we briefly examined the overlap of ADD and LD and emphasized the importance of identifying learning disabilities.

Learning disabilities aren't the only cause of learning problems. Some result from gaps in knowledge because ADD interfered with the ability to focus. Even if you aren't in school anymore, learning problems can continue to compromise the quality of your performance.

As awareness and knowledge of the unique learning issues of adults have grown, resources to meet these needs have also evolved. You might want to access these resources through an educational psychologist, local university, vocational school or support group. One of these sources can refer you to tutors who work with adults.

Psychodynamic Psychotherapy
This is a catchall term used to describe psychotherapy derived from Freudian theories. Psychodynamic Psychotherapy can help an ADDer come to terms with past hurts and failures. She can learn to accept her imperfections and drop old defenses that create barriers between herself and others. She will still have the same neurological problems she had as a child. She might, however, be able to shed some of the emotional problems caused by her repeated failures.

Psychodynamic psychotherapy is definitely more an art than a science. A major criticism of psychodynamic therapy is that its effectiveness hasn't been supported by outcome research. This doesn't mean it's worthless. The lack of research is in part due to the difficulty of studying the complex process of personality development. The limited available research suggests that a good working relationship between therapist and client is more important than the type of therapy.

Analysis is classically Freudian. In Analysis the client spends four or five days a week for several years, lying on the therapist's couch and free-associating about the past. The goal is to work through old traumas and restructure one's personality, substituting healthy defense mechanisms for unhealthy ones.

The analyst sits out of view and speaks little. She purposely becomes a shadowy figure the client uses as if she were the parent(s) or various other figures from the past. By using the analyst to *play out* past experiences, the client relives the traumas of growing up and robs them of their power.

Analytic Psychotherapy is similar to Analysis except that it is less intense. The client sits up in a chair and interacts more directly with the therapist. This type of therapy involves fewer weekly sessions of one to three per week. Because the personality restructuring in this therapy is less drastic than in analysis, there is usually less anxiety or regression (temporarily going back to an earlier stage of development).

Both therapies may have usefulness for an adult with ADD. A choice of one over the other probably has most to do with your comfort level. Do you prefer sitting up and interacting more directly with your therapist or lying down and interacting less?

There are other types of Freudian based therapy. Each is slightly different but all share the goal of restructuring defenses.

Jungian Therapy is based on the concept of the collective unconscious that consists of memories and themes shared by the entire human race and common to us all. Mythology, fantasy and dreams are the clues to help unlock the secrets of the soul. This therapy can be appealing to an ADDer with a bent for creativity. She may be comfortable with the language of myths and dreams.

Interpersonal issues are the focus of therapists who follow the teachings of **Harry Stack Sullivan.** The nurturing relationship between therapist and client encourages the client to understand herself better. This approach may be helpful for ADD issues because so many problems occur within the context of relationships.

Self-Psychology is another psychodynamic therapy. Therapists with this orientation believe that psychological wounds result from a failure of empathy. Self-psychologists who are from various mental health professions, put an emphasis on understanding the client and *putting themselves in her shoes*. This empathic approach might offer a comfortable sense of safety and security for an adult who has always felt misunderstood.

Time-limited, short term **Dynamic Therapy** operates with the same theories and techniques as other Freudian based therapies. It focuses on a single symptom or conflict over a shorter time period. At the outset of this short-term therapy, the therapist and patient choose specific goals and plan the number of sessions, typically between six and thirty. It has the advantage of not requiring a long term commitment.

Miscellaneous Schools of Therapy

It's impossible to list all available therapies because there are so many. Forgive us if we fail to mention a therapy that has been particularly helpful to you. Because of space constraints, we will include some of the better known therapies and leave the research of additional ones to you.

Reality Therapy operates on the principle that people are responsible for their behavior. Therapists don't apply diagnostic labels to their clients. At the beginning of therapy, the client and therapist negotiate a contract that outlines short and long term goals.

The primary goal is to help the client learn ways to satisfy her needs without violating the rights of others. The therapist is confrontive about irresponsible behavior but accepts the person as a whole. Emphasis is on the present—past experiences are discounted as factors in irresponsible behavior.

Reality Therapy could offer some benefits for individual ADD adults. This no-nonsense approach could help her understand the boundary issues of her needs and others'. In this therapy that uses confrontation to change behavior, it's vitally important that the therapist is knowledgeable about ADD. Some of an ADDer's behaviors are an integral part of her disorder—she has limited control over them.

Transactional Analysis (TA) borrows some of the principles of Dynamic Psychotherapy, describing different *ego states* in terms the client can understand. The rigid, moralistic part of the self that sets standards of behavior is labelled **The Parent. The Child** is the immature *I want it right now* part of the personality and **The Adult,** the mature, reality oriented part. A basic tenet of TA is that problems occur when a person inappropriately uses these parts of the personality—acting in the Parent mode with peers or giving the Child free reign.

TA also helps the individual examine patterns of communication by teaching the maladaptive patterns or *games* people play. The therapy generally has a group format. An advantage of TA is that the abstract workings of the mind are defined concretely with games and labels. This approach uses liberal amounts of humor to foster self-understanding and may appeal to your creativity and sense of humor.

Gestalt Therapy

A major goal of Gestalt Therapy is to increase self-understanding by focusing awareness on the present moment—the Here and Now. Issues from the past are explored by reliving them in the present as if they were occurring now. For example, the Gestalt therapist might have you pretend to discuss a past conflict with your parent who *sits* in the empty chair next to you.

Gestalt Therapy also emphasizes the creative and expressive aspects of the self. Group therapy is the preferred format but it can be done on an individual basis. For an ADDer, the emphasis on creativity is an advantage as is the focus on the present. This focus can help you learn to control the insatiability that drives you to miss the positives in your life while you long for things in the future.

Psychodrama

As the name implies, Psychodrama uses dramatic techniques to foster an understanding of problems. This therapy is done in a group and uses role playing, role reversal and soliloquies to portray conflicts within one's self and between people. The dramatic format encourages the expression of pent up feelings. The therapist, known as the *director,* helps the group to brainstorm and then act out better ways to deal with various problems. If you have a flair for the dramatic, you might find Psychodrama useful.

We hope we haven't overwhelmed you with the variety of available options. With the exceptions of Behavioral and Cognitive Psychotherapy,

Speech/Language Therapy and Educational Remediation, none of the therapies we've discussed are routinely offered as treatment options for ADD. Each does, however, offer an approach that can be helpful with different pieces of your problems. There is nothing magical about any of them.

Freudian Analysis will probably not work very well if you are a practical, concrete thinker. If you are uncomfortable *on the stage*, Psychodrama probably isn't the best choice unless your goal is to increase your comfort level in this kind of arena. Rather than trying to figure out the *best* therapy, you should probably try to figure out the *best match* between a therapy and your individual problems and style.

We don't want to leave you with the wrong impression. Seeking a particular "school of psychological thought" may be unnecessary for effective treatment. The psychologist or psychiatrist with whom you are already working is trained to provide specific guidance and counseling for a variety of emotional and behavioral issues. As an ADD-informed professional, she may have important insights that can be very helpful for you. Remember that exploring too many kinds of help at one time can be counterproductive.

Our focus thus far has been on the specific approach and psychology of various therapies, some of which use a group format. We will move on to a discussion of the benefits of therapies whose focus is on group interaction rather than a specific psychological school of thought.

Group Psychotherapy

There are a variety of psychotherapies that use the group as the vehicle for skill building and fostering understanding of behavior. The rationale of group therapy is that struggling individuals need a connection to other people and can benefit from a feeling of unity. Most people who seek therapy feel alone with unique experiences unlike anybody else's. One of the best things about being part of a therapy group is feeling you're all in the same boat. It can be an enormous relief to discover that others share your fears and fantasies.

Group Therapy provides role models. In most groups, members are at different stages of recovery. Those who are coping well offer hope to those who are struggling. Participants can provide support to each other

and learn coping skills from one another. Helping others in the group is a powerful therapeutic experience that can boost individual self-esteem.

A group setting provides a safe place to learn social and interpersonal skills. There is an opportunity to observe the process of social interactions and how it affects the group as a whole. For many of us with ADD, this is invaluable information. Group Therapy is ideally suited to our needs and may be one of the best methods of treatment.

Research hasn't compared the benefits of individual and group therapy for ADD adults. Few groups are designed specifically for us. But anecdotal reports suggest that the group setting can be very helpful. Without a designated boss, everyone in the group is on equal footing. Within the framework of shared ADD experiences, we don't have to work so hard at raising our defensive shields.

Even if you can't find a group specifically for ADDers, you may still benefit from psychotherapy in a mixed group. Although the ingredient of shared ADD experiences will be absent, the shared experiences of other struggling people will still be available.

Before you commit yourself to any Group Psychotherapy, ask questions about the group's goals. Find out how long you are expected to be in therapy and what kinds of problems other group members have. Groups have personalities. Check out the personality of the group you're thinking about joining. How does it feel to you? Trust your instincts and gauge your comfort level. No group will be helpful if you don't feel comfortable.

Family Therapy

The primary goal of Family Therapy is to help the family become a healthier unit. To accomplish this, family members need to learn to communicate more clearly, unlearn rigid or inappropriate roles and restructure the family system so it functions better.

Since we discussed the role of family therapy when we met the Bakers, we won't review it now. Instead, we want to offer some general information about family therapy as a framework to help you choose an individual professional.

Family therapists come from different schools of thought and learn slightly different techniques to achieve their goals in the group setting. When you shop for your therapist, ask other ADDers for recommendations. If you know a trusted mental health professional, ask her who she would use if her family needed therapy.

A professional's therapeutic orientation is probably less important than her ability to work effectively with a family. Do you *like* her? Is she going to *fix* your family or does she seem to have genuine respect for your family's ability to help itself? Is she knowledgeable about ADD? This is really critical!

Most family therapists are not physicians. They are social workers, counselors, psychiatric nurse specialists and psychologists. A family therapist typically goes through intensive family therapy training beyond his basic education. When you research the credentials of a prospective therapist, check for this additional training.

Family Therapy is usually a short term affair. Many family problems can be dealt with in a few sessions. If your now fourth grader was a baby when you started therapy, you should start asking some questions! Your family might need to check in periodically with the therapist but the therapy won't go on for years.

The therapist will expect every family member to be present for each session because absent members block progress. It's important to get a commitment from everyone in your family before beginning therapy. This might not be an easy feat but family therapy doesn't work very well without the family!

Social Skills Training

Social Skills Groups are organized to provide a setting for practicing skills and learning from observing the social errors and successes of others. Group members learn to take turns, read non-verbal cues and initiate conversations. Although all groups indirectly provide opportunities to polish these skills, social skills groups teach them directly. Group members role-play social situations and study them to acquire new, more appropriate behaviors.

These groups have traditionally been used to treat people with schizophrenia and other severe mental or emotional problems. The goals for an individual with severe mental illness are usually quite modest, such as learning to make eye contact and introduce herself. The goals for ADDers may be different, but the vehicle is the same—specific practice in a group setting.

This group therapy has been available for ADD children and adolescents but rarely for adults. Perhaps this is a throwback to the hypothesis that adults don't have ADD. In any case, Social Skills Groups can be a useful piece of the treatment puzzle.

If you don't have an available group in your area, you might be able to connect with other ADD adults to organize one. Unlike a support group, a social skills group requires the services of an experienced therapist. The therapist should have experience in facilitating a social skills group and also be well-versed in ADD.

Psychoeducation

Psychoeducation teaches a person about her illness or disorder. Specific information is provided as a tool to manage individual problems. The underlying principle is that an adult can learn to care for herself. Although psychoeducation for ADD is more of a wish than a reality, it has great potential. Even severely disabled people can learn to take better care of themselves if they're treated as intelligent adults.

Psychoeducation is a relatively new addition to the resources available for people with mental or emotional problems. Although professionals from various fields lead psychoeducational groups, the concept has evolved from the growing consumer movement in mental health. Consumers have become increasingly aware that an important piece had been missing from their mental health care—the individuals themselves as active decision-makers.

The old medical model was of a paternalistic, benevolent mental health professional who made decisions for her client. She was the professional with the answers or at least the best guesses. This prompted the move toward a health care system in which the consumer is more knowledgeable about her health care and assumes more responsibility for it.

We have used the present tense but in reality there is little organized psychoeducation for ADD at this time. Some ADD support groups incorporate a variation of it by scheduling speakers to share information. Conferences use a similar format but they are a one-shot situation. Follow-up isn't possible because the speaker is on a plane heading back home at the end of the day.

This book is yet another variation. Our goal in writing it has been to provide information that readers can use to educate themselves. Of course, the disadvantage of this medium for exchanging information is that we can't interact with our readers. Effective psychoeducation should take place in an interactive forum.

As we envision it, a psychoeducational program for ADDers would provide information about medications and side effects, what to expect at different stages of life and coping strategies. Education for the entire family would be the focus of specific sessions. Some programs might be structured with ongoing support groups for "graduates" of the program.

Psychoeducation shouldn't be just a series of lectures. ADDers are often *different* learners who become quickly bored with traditional teaching methods. A good leader would use a variety of educational techniques to teach the material and hold the interest of the participants. Group discussion, films, poetry and role playing could all be used to enhance learning.

Although this section appears at the end of a long list of psychotherapies, it should probably be the place to start. Until you understand the nature of your problems, you may be unable to determine the kind of professional help you need. Education should always be the first step.

It might seem unfair to discuss the rationale and benefits of psycho-educational groups that don't yet exist! We are strong advocates, however, of these groups and have facilitated similar educational forums. The curriculum we outlined is the one we plan to use as soon as we find the time to organize a psychoeducational group. We hope some readers can use it as a framework to develop a similar group in their areas.

If you become aware of a psychoeducational program for ADDers, take advantage of it. For some, it might be the only therapy needed beyond medication. With luck, we'll have a program like this in place before too long. Perhaps if you can't find a group in your area, you can join us in Cincinnati!

Self-help or Support Groups

The rationale of Self-help, or Support Groups is that individual group members can offer invaluable help to each other. The focus is generally on *caring* and *sharing*. These groups are free of charge or operate with donations. In most cases consumers of mental health services organize and lead these groups. In Twelve-Step groups such as AA, there is no permanent leader. Instead, the members take turns organizing and facilitating the meetings.

Support groups have in part sprung up as a response to a "we know best" mental health system. Angry with the professional establishment, many have embraced the self-help movement. Consequently groups are often leery of professional involvement. There is often a requirement that if a professional facilitates the group, she donates her services and shares

the experience of suffering from the same problems as other group members.

These groups are empowering for members who can actively assume responsibility for their problems. This is an integral part of recovery and is often missing in traditional therapy. Unless the psychotherapist has ADD, the important experiential piece is missing from the therapy. Within the structure of the Self-help Group, members can share the hard-earned knowledge of coping strategies sometimes unknown by a therapist who doesn't live with the disorder.

Although we are enthusiastic proponents of these groups, we must add a word of caution. Not all self-help groups are helpful! Because they are organized and run by people with different backgrounds, there is great variability in the quality of individual groups.

The main qualifications for a support group leader are that she has good people skills and a commitment to the goals of self-help. Regrettably, some people assume leadership roles for the wrong reasons—a need for power. A group led by a controller won't be effective.

Another potential problem is a lack of structure. The benefits of a self-help group are lost if the group is too chaotic. There must be rules to ensure equal opportunity participation. A totally free-form group can become boring if the discussion wanders without a focus. Without clear rules about how to treat one another, members can be hurt psychologically.

In an ADD support group, structure is imperative so that members will take turns and stick to a topic. This doesn't mean that the group should have a rigid organization complete with an agenda set by the facilitator. It does mean though, that the group should establish rules about starting and ending times and rules of common courtesy. A group facilitator should be prepared to step in to provide added structure as needed.

For example, an unstructured discussion about coping with ADD is fine if members maintain interest and everyone is free to contribute. If someone begins to dominate the discussion, however, it's time for the leader to intervene. She needs to use techniques such as asking for input from silent members or encouraging each member in turn, to share her thoughts. These techniques often stimulate a discussion that seems to be going nowhere or that a few individuals are monopolizing.

Although the leaders of support groups aren't professionals, they should have some training. The training should include issues of confidentiality and how to deal with a suicidal group member or one who admits to child abuse. It should also teach the basics of group dynamics and strategies for dealing with verbal aggression.

The training can be a weekend workshop followed by periodic mini-sessions. Leaders can also gain experience on the job. In an Alcoholics Anonymous group, for example, members assume the leadership role after spending time as participants. They work the program and serve apprenticeships before taking the lead.

The services of a professional consultant can improve the quality of a group. Whether she provides her expertise gratis or for a fee, she doesn't make decisions about the group's programs or policies. The group remains the responsibility of its members.The ADD Council of Greater Cincinnati, for example, has a support group coordinator who monitors and trains support group leaders. A social worker with a mental health background, she works with volunteer and paid consultants to provide support and training to the leaders.

Don't suspend your good judgment when you approach a self-help group. Be a wise consumer and ask questions. Find out if the leader has had training and observe how she facilitates the group. If you attend a group and feel uncomfortable with what's going on, look for another one or consider forming your own.

You might be part of an organization that is thinking about starting a support group. Be sure to lobby for a training program for the leaders and some mechanism for quality control, such as periodic surveys of group members. Non-professional does not and should not mean poorly run—consumers can learn the required skills.

Assertiveness Training

Assertiveness Training teaches the participant to communicate clearly with assertive messages rather than aggressive or passive ones. We highly recommend assertiveness training for an ADD adult. She often has difficulty with effective communication, either bowling over her *opponent* with aggressive commands or cowering with passive vagueness.

In Assertiveness Training sessions, an ADDer can practice the *I messages* we mentioned in an earlier chapter. These messages are assertive, clear statements of needs and feelings that don't communicate blame. Aggressive *You messages* are statements of accusation that turn conversations into battlegrounds complete with an attacker and a defender. Passive communication may not be confrontational but it's equally ineffective. It doesn't provide any information. Whether you fail to say something you should or say something so vague that your point is lost, your message won't be communicated.

The goal of Assertiveness Training is to help participants learn to recognize passive or aggressive modes of communication and avoid using them. Although many books attempt to teach these skills, they are difficult to learn by just reading about them. Assertiveness Training groups provide the practice arena for trying them out on people who are learning together.

It should be fairly easy to locate a group in your community. They are available through community groups and universities. Many companies offer training to their employees to enhance their communication skills. They are willing to pay for it, knowing that effective communication improves productivity.

Sensory Integration

Sensory integration (SI) is a form of therapy developed and practiced by Occupational Therapists. The theory behind SI is rather complex and a detailed explanation is beyond the scope of this book.

Breifly, Sensory Integration is the organization of sensory input for use. The well-functioning brain organizes sensory data in an efficient manner and makes an adaptive response. SI therapists believe that sensory integration dysfunction is the core problem in many individuals with ADD and/or LD.

Dr. A. Jean Ayres is an expert who has done extensive writing and research in the area of SI. She submits that the ability of the brain to react to complex auditory and visual input depends on the development of the brainstem's organizational capacity early in life[46]. Mastery of sensory input, therefore, generally becomes automatic by the time a child reaches school age. This becomes the foundation for more complicated processes such as reading, that develop later.

The basic senses integrated in the brainstem include the *tactile*, *vestibular* and *proprioceptive* senses. The tactile sense involves touch and the vestibular sense, balance. Proprioception is somewhat more complicated, involving the ability to sense the movement and position of individual body parts and the body as a whole.

With normal development, early integration of these three senses leads to well-organized eye movements, posture, physical balance, muscle tone and a secure relationship with gravity. SI theorizes that if an individual doesn't master these basic senses, she will experience several problems. These include sensitivity to touch, difficulty with balance and hand-eye coordination and awkward posture and body movement.

According to Dr. Ayres these problems also lead to dysfunction of more advanced skills, such as planned motor activity, attention span, activity level and emotional stability. In turn, gaps in these more advanced skills interfere with the purposeful activity of writing, using eating utensils or constructing something.

Sensory Integration Therapy is designed to strengthen the brainstem's ability to organize the basic sensations of touch, balance and body position and movement. Rubbing, vigorous brushing or applied pressure to the client's skin provides tactile stimulation. The therapist works gently and slowly with a client who doesn't like to be touched. SI therapy uses swings to stimulate the sense of balance and ramps and scooter boards to help the client master the sense of her body in motion.

To the casual observer, SI therapy can appear to be little more than a supervised play session. In reality, the therapist carefully plans the sessions to gradually increase the stimulation as the client learns to tolerate and master lower levels of stimulation.

The ADD literature doesn't usually mention Sensory Integration Therapy as a treatment option. Lacking sufficient research to support its claims of benefits, SI is frequently described as a questionable alternative therapy. The flip side is that SI is practiced by occupational therapists who are valued and respected members of the established mental health system. After wrestling with this, we decided for several reasons to include SI as a mainstream therapy.

The first reason for this decision is related to the lack of supportive research data on SI. It's true that limited data supports SI's claims of its benefits. But it's also true that limited research disproves it. The discipline of Occupational Therapy has generally taken a pragmatic hands-on approach to problems. Perhaps this is why the theoretical and research aspects of the practice haven't been well developed yet. In other words, SI therapists place more emphasis on *doing* therapy than studying it.

Dr. Ayres' research suggests that SI helps improve physical coordination, balance and difficulties with touch. The unproven aspects of SI relate to therapists' claims of improved sensory integration at higher levels, such as improved concentration and attention. Even if extensive future research fails to support these claims, SI might still be a valuable method of treatment for some adults with ADD.

Poor coordination and balance can certainly interfere with an individual's ability to function. It also seems logical that improved functioning in certain systems would reduce the strain on an overloaded brain. Conceivably, this would free up mental energy to perform other tasks.

Available SI research has focused on the treatment of children. Some experts have suggested that the adult brain would be less responsive since it has already developed and matured. There is growing evidence, however, that the brain and nervous system are more repairable than previously believed.

For example, stroke victims often learn to regain their skills through practice. New pathways are created in the brain as constant practice forges connections between neurons to bypass the injury. There are also promising anecdotal accounts of SI therapy's value. Montesssori education, particularly in Europe, has incorporated SI principles into its curriculum for a long time.

KK: "For many years, my daughter's teacher worked in a Montessori classroom in Europe. She reports that the use of swings and scooter boards is common in these settings. She is enthusiastic about the results. She has observed that using this equipment enhances the children's abilities to concentrate and learn."

As an ADD adult, you might want to consider SI therapy as an option. It might help with coordination and balance and might even improve your attention. Although many unanswered questions remain, SI therapy appears harmless and might be beneficial for you.

Alternative Therapy

Holistic healing centers or New Age philosophy healers offer a variety of alternative therapies. We have included some that don't seem harmful in any way and might offer benefits for individual ADD adults.

You will read about some that are probably familiar to you. You will also read about some that are as far removed from the mainstream as they can be! Throughout this book, we have included some words of caution. We're going to add a few more now. You should regard these alternatives as experimental treatments that may or may not be helpful. If you decide to try any of them, don't use them to replace conventional treatment options.

Yoga

Yoga is an ancient Indian discipline that uses meditation, breathing and physical exercises to gain mastery over the body. The goal is to heighten consciousness by learning to shut off stimuli from the outside world.

The mind and body are disciplined to enable the Yogi, *one who lives by the discipline*, to focus her mind on a single, simple thought. Accomplished Yogis are able to perform astounding feats such as stopping their hearts from beating or walking over live coals. Scientists have recorded and validated these feats.

Yoga has enormous potential for general health care but is alien to our Western society. As a result, it isn't widely practiced in this country. It could be beneficial for an ADD adult because it promotes relaxation and concentration, among other things. To be effective, however, Yoga requires a great deal of discipline and practice that could be a drawback for a restless ADDer.

Massage Therapy

Massage Therapy uses manipulation of the body to achieve muscular and mental relaxation. If you decide to try it, be sure to look for a licensed therapist who has trained in the safe practice of massage. An untrained person who uses vigorous massage, can cause bodily injury.

Many people benefit from massage and treat themselves to this form of relaxation. It can reduce tension, replacing it with feelings of peace and renewed strength. This can be quite helpful for those of us who often experience muscle tension as we strain to cope with tasks that stress fragile skills.

Massage therapy isn't for everyone, however. If you dislike being touched, you may experience massage more as torture than therapy. If this is the case, you might find massage helpful in reducing this reaction.

For example, an acquaintance of ours is currently working with several sexually abused clients whose psychiatrists have referred them to her. Her therapy is designed to gradually desensitize the aversion to touch. Her anecdotal reports suggest that therapeutic massage might be useful for anyone with tactile defensiveness.

If sessions with a licensed therapist are beyond your budget, trading massages can be an alternative. An amateur can perform massage on a friend or spouse, assuming the techniques are gentle and comfortable.

Brain Massage

Here's the therapy that sounds as if it's straight out of the twilight zone! Brain Massage[47] is a technique popular on the west coast but it certainly hasn't hit the medical establishment!

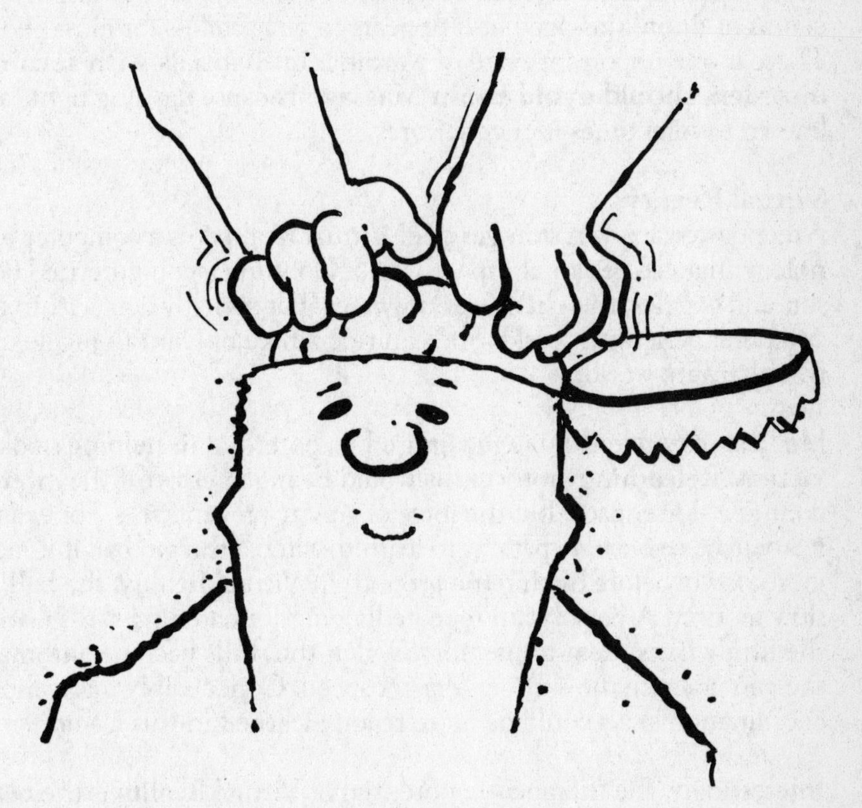

Clients go to centers called mind gyms or spas where they are hooked up to headphones and goggles. Patterns of flashing lights and monotonous sounds, such as the patter of rain, induce a dreamlike state. The treatment is supposed to increase relaxation and creativity and improve concentration.

The cost of brain massage is about $20 per session. Home brain machines named Dreamachine and Relaxman are available for costs ranging between about $300–$1000. If family members are looking for something different to give you for your birthday, maybe they can order one of these machines for you!

This intriguing therapy appeals to our imaginations but we certainly don't recommend that you replace your medicine with goggles and headphones! There isn't any research to either support or dispute the claims of Brain Massage but it appears to be harmless for most people. There is one important word of warning: **individuals with seizure disorders should avoid Brain Massage** because flashing lights are known to sometimes induce seizures.

Virtual Reality

And now for an even stranger one! Virtual Reality[48] is a computer technology that creates an alternate world. Donning a computerized body suit and goggles, the client not only sees, but actually acts within a computer generated world. She can ride a bike or learn to juggle in this alternate world.

Medical researchers have recognized its potential in helping stroke victims. Relearning motor skills would be much easier if they were done at a slower pace. But the force of gravity prevents this. For example, it would be easier for a patient to learn to catch a thrown ball if it moved more slowly before hitting the ground. In Virtual Reality, the ball is in slow motion. A person can repeatedly practice catching skills until she firmly fixes them in memory. When the skills become automatic, she can practice the skills at a faster speed. Conceivably many motor coordination skills could be more readily learned in this fashion.

Interestingly, the therapeutic potential of Virtual Reality is the result of a glitch in the technology. Since the computer isn't fast enough to simulate reality accurately, Virtual Reality time is slower than actual time. One of the developers of this technology taught himself to juggle in Virtual Reality and then gradually increased the speed so he could do it in the real world.

We haven't included this discussion of Virtual Reality because we think it can replace traditional ADD treatments. But we do think it could have some limited use for problems with fine or gross motor control skills. In Virtual Reality, an ADD adult might be able to learn motor skills such as bike riding or handwriting. At *$200,000 per suit* (!), it's an expensive new technology still in an early research stage. Keep your eyes and ears open for new developments related to this therapy that appeals to our imagination.

Progressive Muscle Relaxation

This therapy has really made its way into the mainstream but we've included it here because it's similar to many of the alternatives that promote relaxation. The client learns relaxation techniques by herself or in a group setting and then practices them daily. After she learns the techniques, she can use them as needed, although it's best that she does the exercises regularly.

Deep muscle relaxation is achieved by individually tensing and relaxing the various muscle groups in the body until all the muscles are relaxed. This is usually enhanced through deep breathing and visualization of pleasant images. Along with learning these techniques with a therapist or trainer, relaxation tapes can guide the client through the exercises.

A variety of problems associated with anxiety or tension are treated with Progressive Muscle Relaxation. The techniques are easy to learn, virtually cost-free and available anywhere the individual happens to be. It can be useful as a stress reducer for an adult with ADD, helping her calm down and improve his focus.

Visualization

Visualization has begun making its way into the mainstream because research indicates it can help people with a variety of medical problems. In his book *Head First, The Biology of Hope*[49], Norman Cousins presents evidence that Visualization can enhance the immune system. These techniques can increase the number of T-cells, an important component of the immune system.

Currently, Visualization is being used extensively in cancer wellness programs and as an adjunct treatment for AIDS. Relaxation is an important component and benefit of this therapy.

Visualization is fairly easy to master, especially for strong visual learners. The client learns to create a mental picture of the results she desires. A cancer patient might visualize her body's immune system as an army of soldiers fighting cancer cells. An anxious person might picture her brain sending out the calming neurotransmitters, endorphins. The client works with a therapist to learn the techniques she will eventually use at home. She sometimes uses a specially designed audio tape that includes the imagery she has found helpful.

The effectiveness of Visualization Therapy in treating ADD hasn't been documented by research. Its usefulness in treating a number of other problems, however, suggests that it might have value. An ADDer might try visualizing the neurotransmitters as tiny maids, cleaning out and sorting things in the brain. If nothing else, visualization could be a great diversion for a creative and inventive brain!

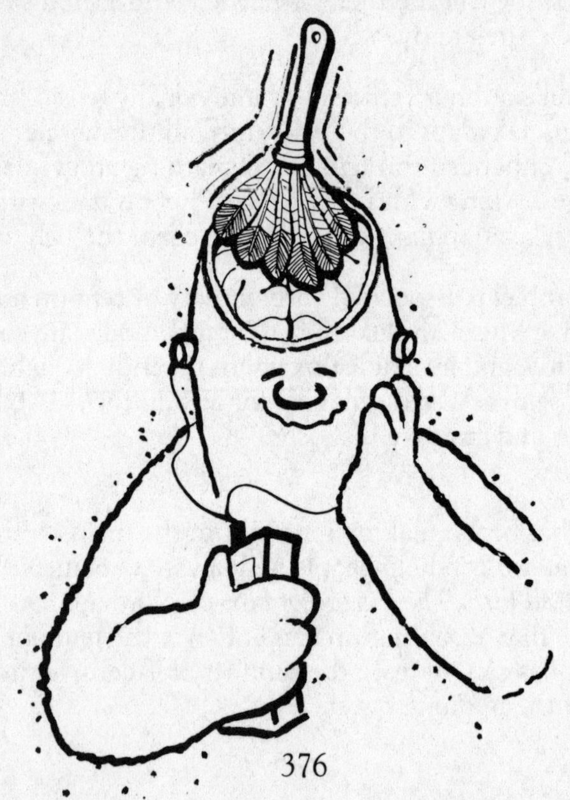

Transcendental Meditation (TM)

TM is a simple mental technique that produces deep body relaxation and mental clarity. The meditation technique is usually taught in a period of approximately two weekend sessions and then practiced at home twenty minutes, twice a day.

The instructor selects a special *mantra* for each participant to use during her meditations. The mantra is a secret sound unique to each person and matched to her personality. During meditation the participant closes her eyes as she silently repeats her mantra. The meditator permits thoughts to flow freely with no attempt to focus concentration.

TM has recently gone high tech with the use of computers to measure brainwave activity. A client is hooked up to the computer while she meditates and follows her progress towards reaching a deeper state of relaxation.

Research has demonstrated that TM produces relaxation as measured by the physiological effects of decreased blood pressure and lactate concentrations in the blood. Proponents of TM also claim that it increases energy and creativity but research supporting these claims is incomplete. Nonetheless, we can recommend Transcendental Meditation as a relaxation technique that might help in other ways, as well.

Natural Childbirth Techniques

The most common use of these techniques is, of course, in the management of pain and anxiety during childbirth. The well-known Lamaze technique uses different kinds of breathing exercises and borrows some meditation techniques—using a picture or object as a focal point to divert the laboring mother from her pain.

These techniques might have wider applicability. Perhaps an ADDer could use them to block out excess stimulation from the environment. The exercises are safe and simple to use. It certainly wouldn't hurt to try them.

EEG Biofeedback

In EEG Biofeedback, the client receives continuous feedback from machines that measure brainwaves. She gradually learns to exert control over the activity of his brain through practice and self-monitoring.

In the *Woman's Day* magazine of September 9, 1991, an article entitled, "My Child Couldn't Pay Attention"[50], described the dramatic benefits of Biofeedback as an ADD treatment. Author Alducci reported that her son's symptoms hadn't responded to traditional treatment options but improved significantly with Biofeedback treatments.

The article was greeted with outrage by some in the mainstream mental health community who emphasized the experimental nature of EEG Biofeedback and the lack of scientific substantiation of its claims. The concern was that parents might latch on to this *miracle breakthrough* to the exclusion of better researched treatment options.

Although we advocate a cautious approach to any new treatment, we feel that EEG Biofeedback offers some interesting possibilities. Reports that this treatment has normalized mixed handedness (lack of a strong preference for one hand over another) and eliminated bedwetting in ADD children suggests that something powerful may be going on in the brains of those receiving the treatment. It has also been reported that attention and other important mental processes improve with EEG Biofeedback training. There is even evidence that the changes may be permanent, persisting after treatment is stopped.

This is all very heady stuff! Critics of EEG Biofeedback are correct in asserting that large numbers of controlled scientific studies haven't been conducted yet to support these therapeutic claims. Proponents of Biofeedback counter by pointing out that these studies haven't been conducted yet to dispute their claims, either. They also express their frustration with a mental health community they perceive as self-serving. They argue that this conservative establishment has vested interests that slow down the acceptance of information that threatens the status quo. And we want to add a comment to those of Biofeedback's proponents and opponents. Keep in mind the discussion about the value and limitations of scientific research—unproven doesn't mean worthless.

New, experimental approaches such as this may not pan out and will likely not become **the** treatment of ADD. But while various positions are argued in the professional community, ADD adults continue to ask, "But why" and "What if. . ." We regard EEG Biofeedback as a treatment with intriguing possibilities. We encourage you to approach this new treatment with your best judgment intact. Its possible benefits seem to warrant at least a cursory, and maybe a second, look. As far as we can tell, the only unwanted side effect if the treatment doesn't work is an emptier wallet!

Diet Therapy

As you may recall from an earlier discussion, a number of people have made claims that dietary factors cause ADD or make it worse. You have probably heard that sugar causes hyperactivity and that the Feingold Diet can treat ADD. Dr. Doris Rapp[51] has written several books that focus on allergic reactions as the cause of various symptoms of ADD. The supporting evidence of both these claims is shaky at best.

Scientists have been unable to repeat the high percentage of success that Feingold[52] reported with his diet and there is no research to support the notion that sugar causes hyperactivity. Many ADD children do have allergies. When these children receive treatment for their allergies, their ADD symptoms do frequently improve.

Although Dr. Rapp would disagree, it appears in most cases that the symptoms improve as the children experience less discomfort from their allergies. Nonetheless, some parents report that an "allergy-free" diet dramatically reduces their child's troubling symptoms. Others swear by the restrictive Fiengold diet.

Despite the lack of supportive research, these diets undoubtedly help a small percentage of ADD children. Although dietary changes probably shouldn't be used as a primary treatment, a subgroup of ADDers might respond favorably to them. There isn't anything lost in trying dietary changes to see if they help. If you don't find the diets unbearably restrictive and they seem to work, that's great!

As you design your individual treatment program, you might consider including medication, some kind of group therapy and perhaps an alternative therapy such as Transcendental Meditation to promote relaxation. Just don't overload your circuits with too many kinds of outside help at once. Don't become a Therapy Dilettante, briefly sampling everything without investing sufficient time and energy in anything. We don't have to tell you that ADDers tend to operate in that fashion.

We've shared a great deal of information and examined many strategies for managing your ADD. We hope you know a lot more now than you did when you started your reading. But we're not quite finished. In fact, we've saved the best for last. So turn to Chapter 18 to see where we've been heading throughout this book!

From Obstacle to Opportunity

This is it. We're joyfully writing the final chapter of our book. This is an exciting process in part because we can finally retire our computers and reacquaint ourselves with our families! More than that, it is a joyful, exciting process because this chapter is about hope and possibilities.

We've tried to weave a thread of optimism and hope throughout this book even as we described the difficulties we face as ADD adults. We hold a firm conviction that we are much more than people with disabilities. We also have unique and valuable abilities that give us advantages over non-ADDers! Consider this recent posting that appeared on a computer bulletin board:

> "Of course there are good aspects to ADD! Sleep for instance, is just not an issue and you can amaze your friends and confound your doctor by swallowing a couple of Ritalin just to GET to sleep. You can (and don't, cause I did and it's horrible) write a senior thesis in under 36 hours. You're quick enough to catch the jokes in movies. You're probably well-read.
>
> I just moved to Tucson with the intention of building an adobe house. Today someone very negative gave me the 'But it's a big project' routine. The joke, I guess, would be—
>
> > *How many hyperactives does it take to build an adobe house? One: Okay, and maybe someone to steer him back when he gets distracted!*
>
> In all seriousness, someone asked me this a while back and I didn't

know what to say: 'If you could push a button and not have ADD anymore—to be, I don't know, normal I guess—would you push it?'

I don't know if I would.

I CAN'T BELIEVE IT, BUT I HONESTLY DON'T KNOW THAT I WOULD."

This ADDer captures the heart and soul of this book. When you understand your disabilities, you can begin the process of discovering your abilities and unleashing your potential.

This isn't an easy task. Our talents are often buried beneath layers of defenses and hurts and our history of failure makes us afraid to try things. Don't forget, however, the caveat of this book: *You are worth all the effort it takes to recover.* Get help, muster up a support system and take courage! There truly is a Jewel buried beneath your rough exterior.

About Joy, Hope and Possibilities

We're going to do one of our favorite things now. We're going to let our imaginations and creativity roam as we possibilitize. We'll explore the exciting opportunities available to ADDers who learn to take control of their own complicated selves, maximizing their gifts and minimizing their difficulties. We'll look at our so-called disabilities from a different perspective and identify the abilities within them. In the sections that follow, you'll read about current and future trends that suggest that our abilities will be in great demand in the decades to come.

We feel compelled to add an additional comment before we move on. We take our responsibility seriously to provide honest, accurate information. We know that our readers are at many different stages in their recoveries. If you're dealing with extremely serious consequences of the symptoms of your disorder, you may greet this discussion of possibilities with suspicion, disbelief and sadness. Struggling with your deficits, you might feel that these possibilities are improbabilities for you.

Please don't be discouraged! Your life is already changing through a better understanding of your ADD. Don't decide when you compare yourself to the successful ADDers we'll meet later in this chapter that you don't measure up. Don't compare yourself to anyone but yourself. Progress comes in small steps and the measure of your success must be different from the measure of anyone else's.

Our goal in writing this chapter isn't to minimize the difficulties inherent in ADD but to change the way we look at them. Our basis is the oft-repeated empty glass metaphor: *Is your glass half-empty...or half-full?* Your attitude about your "glass" has a great deal to do with your ability to be successful.

ADD and the Specialized Brain

We ADDers are a diverse group. It's impossible to generalize about either our disabilities or our abilities. But each of us seems to have a specialized brain that contains pockets of great ability as well as disability.

When knowledge is more complete, we may discover that many of the world's more gifted individuals have had subtle neurological problems or specialized brains. Many of the great creative thinkers and artists in history struggled with mental health problems or learning difficulties. Picasso and Mozart were troubled, Einstein and Edison had severe learning disabilities, and Hemingway committed suicide after lifetime bouts with severe mood swings. Experts have endlessly debated an observed link between creativity and madness. There is so little known about the human brain that it will take years for science to understand this apparent relationship.

We're not suggesting that madness is an ingredient in ADD or that all ADD adults are gifted! The point is that we ADDers often have enormous gaps in abilities and disabilities. Many of us have great gifts mixed in with and often hidden by our deficits. We share the dimension of a specialized brain with some incredibly gifted people.

Much of the work you've been doing has been identifying your individual gaps in abilities and disabilities. Many of the strategies we've suggested have focused on bypassing your weaknesses by capitalizing on your strengths. Now, we're going to suggest that you focus on your disabilities—not as deficits but as assets.

Throughout this book we've given examples of how the symptoms and differences of ADD adults can be both advantages and disadvantages. In the following section, we want to summarize some of things we've talked about and remind you about something we said in the introduction.

If you take the "dis" out of disabilities, you will find abilities.

So let's take a new look at the disabilities many of us with ADD have. And let's discover the abilities inside them.

The Advantage of Inattention and Distractibility

Distractibility/inattention is one of the primary symptoms of ADD. We've mentioned in a number of contexts that being distractible has advantages and disadvantages. Without question, an inability to shift focus can be problematic in various places in your life. Frequently it's misinterpreted as oppositional behavior, particularly in childhood.

As you know, this inability to shift focus can also become an ability to lock in to a task. This can become a powerful coping tool in adulthood. The stubborn child often becomes a determined adult, capable of blocking out distractions to concentrate on a chosen task. An ability to lock in operates most effectively when tasks are matched to individual interests and talents.

As a child you weren't able to use this to your advantage because children are expected to be generalists who are good at everything. But as an adult, you can be a specialist. In fact the adult world not only permits specialization, it demands it.

If you review your school report cards, you might find poor grades in conduct and effort and comments such as "Doesn't stay on task. . .daydreams." The poor conduct grades and comments were in large part a reflection of your distractibility. The teacher didn't mention, however, that you were a human encyclopedia of trivia!

Being distracted by so many things might not have helped your grades but did enable you to notice and store lots of miscellaneous information in your memory bank! You ended up with an interesting and eclectic body of knowledge. When you can design your life to maximize your abilities, you can make invaluable use of your knowledge.

Creativity: We mentioned creativity in our discussion of an ADDer's specialized brain. It's impossible to determine exactly what's responsible for creativity. Distractibility doesn't cause creativity but it does play a part in the vast array of disjointed thoughts and ideas that come together in imaginative thinking. Although each of us has an individual profile of abilities and disabilities, many of us share the gift of creativity.

Some writers have suggested that this creativity results from our overcoming so many problems—that we exercise our creative "muscles" to bypass our weaknesses. This may be true, in part. Creativity can be enhanced if it is nurtured. We submit, however, that this gift is part of our specialized brains.

It is a fact that as a group, ADDers tend to be more creative than the "average" person. Studies of ADD children have repeatedly noted this. How does the hardwiring of the ADD brain contribute to creativity?

Although this question remains unanswered, the hardwiring seems to provide some of us with a distinctive advantage in this and other areas.

Many adults with ADD are talented artists, musicians or actors. There is, however, another form of creativity: thinking. Many of us have an innate talent for creative thinking. As we happily go off on our mental journeys, we discover fascinating connections between seemingly irrelevant and divergent thoughts. Our thinking style enables us to come up with wonderfully imaginative ideas.

In a brainstorming session, for example, whether the forum is a family meeting or a corporate marketing meeting, participants dream up possible solutions to a proposed problem. Many of us find this process enormously rewarding and entertaining! Our free flowing trains of thought are invaluable assets to the creative process. Best of all, there are no wrong answers.

We often live our lives in a constant brainstorming session in our own minds! Unfortunately, this powerful resource sometimes remains untapped because other difficulties interfere. We might have great ideas but be unable to express them clearly and concisely. Or, we might not be taken seriously because impulsivity interferes as we excitedly blurt out embarrassing statements.

The Advantage of Hyperactivity

For starters, let's consider your property tax bill that's due in the courthouse by 5:00 p.m. today. Would you send it by regular mail and pay the penalty when it arrives two days late? Or would you call a one hour rapid messenger service whose representative delivers the bill to the clerk's office exactly forty-five minutes after you phoned?

Hyperactivity can be a rapid messenger service that gets things done fast! Similar to the delivery person who starts out without referring to his map, however, the ADDer's actions are inefficient and purposeless if they are unplanned.

The good news is that by the time we become adults, most of us have learned to purposefully channel our hyperactivity. We can use the extra energy to accomplish more than others do. If we guard against sliding into workaholism, we can have rewarding and productive lives. A fast-talking ADDer can fill a variety of adult roles. He can become a super salesman, public relations expert or talk-show host, to mention a few possibilities.

An ADDer's drive toward activity may also help him stay slim and physically fit, giving him an edge over the couch potatoes. Hyperactivity may be an asset in middle age. The authors figure that we've always been about six to eight years behind our peers. The score has evened out, however, since we've hit mid-life. We seem to have the energy and enthusiasm of much younger folk. It's great hearing people exclaim, "Oh, you can't be over 40!"

The Advantage of Impulsivity

We're going to contradict ourselves now. We know that we've tossed out several warnings throughout this book about keeping your impulses reined. But loosening those reins sometimes isn't bad because impulsive people can be exciting!

If you think about some of the heroes in recent action adventure films you know that they were risk-taking, dynamic, overcome-all-odds people. Our eyes remain riveted on the screen as we watch our impulsive hero plunge into one exciting adventure after another—and escape unscathed! Now we don't recommend that you head off for the nearest jungle in search of treasure but we think you get the picture.

In similar fashion, the excitable, moody ADD child frequently becomes an adult with an extra measure of sparkle that draws people to him. People with calm temperaments may be easier to live with but may not be nearly as interesting as those with more excitable natures! Opposites do attract and many calm people are drawn to mates with more dramatic temperaments. A marriage between two people with opposite temperaments can often work out well. The excitable spouse makes life interesting while his calm wife works to keep things on an even keel.

As we pointed out in our discussion of the work world, impulsivity can become ambition and a drive to succeed. The insatiable ADD child who wants everything right now can become a decisive adult with a strong need for closure—getting things done. If the impulsive ADD adult learns to take calculated risks, he can orchestrate success by jumping in where others fear to tread.

Verbal disinhibition also has an up side. If you learn to inhibit hurtful words, your natural ability to say anything and everything can become an asset. A forthright style can be an admirable trait. Not everyone can readily admit their weaknesses without embarrassment or apology. Your honesty can be a refreshing quality that others appreciate. Finally, without your disinhibition, you wouldn't be able to charm others with your wonderful and outrageous sense of humor!

Now let's look at some character sketches that illustrate the ways these ADD characteristics can translate into success stories. Read them, recognize your own qualities and allow yourself at least a moment of pride as you consider all the wonderful things you are!

The Inventor

Many authors have referred to Thomas Edison as learning disabled. His teachers couldn't handle him, criticized his handwriting and distractibility, and predicted that he would be a failure in life. His mother took him out of school in the fifth grade and taught him at home. Since learning disabilities were unknown in those days, accounts of Edison's childhood don't mention specific learning problems. It's a good bet, however, that he might have had ADD. His disruptive behavior in school certainly fits with the diagnosis.

Thomas Edison's childhood is typical of an ADDer. He was a square peg in a round hole—disruptive, misunderstood and unappreciated. Under his mother's tutelage he flourished, becoming an extraordinary adult. The rest as they say, is history. As we sit in front of our computers at 3:00 a.m., we do so with gratitude to Tom who made it all possible! His fertile mind created an astonishing number of inventions when it was freed from the burden of memorizing facts, performing endless recitations and listening to the drone of his teachers.

Not all ADD adults are cut out to be inventors nor are we all as brilliant as Mr. Edison. But many of us do have qualities that make us uniquely qualified for his profession. An inventor needs a restless, curious mind

that he can never satisfy. A freewheeling thinking style is a necessity because a more structured mind censors wild ideas before they can be modified and developed into something useful. The ADD tendency to notice things and relationships that other people miss often leads to an "Aha!" experience—the flash of insight about the answer to a problem. These streaks of inspiration, coupled with the persistence to keep trying when a solution doesn't work, are the building blocks of the inventor. The ADDer who is highly distractible while he works on something mundane can exhibit superhuman persistence in an area of interest.

KK: "I once worked as an *Au Pair* for a wealthy family who had made its money with the patent on a single invention. The father was a spacey man with no head for details and little idea of the practical necessities of life. In retrospect, I'm sure he had ADD.

At the time I knew him, he had no need to work any longer because his invention had made him independently wealthy. He spent his time generating fantastic ideas. Many of them were silly and some incredibly worthwhile.

He was a man lacking many skills for daily life. Fortunately, he had enough money to hire housekeepers, accountants, lawyers and gardeners to handle the daily details. Then he had time to do what he did best—generate ideas. . .Not such a bad life!"

The Writer

The writing process can activate an ADDer's natural creativity. We believe that many ADD qualities are great assets in the process. We know from experience that writing is a good niche for us.

Our thoughts can flow into our computers without the need to censor them. Later, when the manuscript has sufficiently cooled, the editing process shapes and fine-tunes the barrage of ideas. Metaphors, jokes, outrageous and novel thoughts pop effortlessly into our ADD minds.

One of the most satisfying things about writing is that we can finally talk as much as we please. We don't know about our readers but nothing makes us happier than having a chance to talk without interruption! In most situations, we don't have the luxury of unlimited, uninterrupted time to express ourselves. Our need to talk doesn't usually match the attention spans and interests of listeners who may feel they are facing a firing squad of words! Eyes start to glaze over as our companions begin edging away from the verbal onslaught.

Writing quenches a thirst for self-expression and provides an outlet for verbal excesses that can drive people away. After pouring our thoughts into the computer, we are more content to take turns in conversations and listen. The ability to listen not only enhances popularity but also feeds the writing process with the valuable insights and information others share.

You may hate to write. This is often a problem of written expression more than a lack of ideas. If you don't like writing, you may find that talking into a tape recorder serves the same purpose. It can be therapeutic because the tape recorder won't talk back! The following is the story of a late-blooming ADD woman who has learned to use a gift for writing to enhance her life.

Carrie is 50 years old and is envied and admired by her friends. She seems to have it all: money, critical and popular success as a writer, a family, close friends and a rich variety of interests. She's an energetic athlete who looks at least ten years younger than she is.

Many who envy Carrie are unaware of the rocky road she traveled to get to this point in her life. A difficult and unhappy child, she was shunned by other children because she was a braggart, always trying to grab the center of attention. In school, her peers ridiculed her absent-mindedness and the odd outfits she wore.

After many years of rejection, Carrie became a recluse. She avoided her peers, becoming preoccupied with books and fantasies. She snarled at anyone who intruded on her world. Eventually, her only companions were her make-believe characters.

Her school performance disappointed her teachers and parents. She was intelligent but received only mediocre grades and rarely turned in projects or homework. Her favorite subject was reading but she avoided writing. Her messy handwriting and jumbled, disorganized thoughts resulted in little but criticism and poor grades.

As an adolescent and young adult, Carrie seemed to have great difficulty finding herself. She was briefly enthusiastic about various careers or interests but quickly dropped them as she became bored or unable to focus long enough to learn the needed skills. After dropping out of several colleges and drifting from one boring minimum wage job to another, Carrie decided to make some goals for herself.

She went to night school to get a degree in psychology, eventually landing an interesting job as a research assistant. Her interviewing skills were an unexpected gift. She discovered that she enjoyed delving into the lives of the research subjects. The only problem with this job was that Carrie had her own ideas about the direction of the research. Unfortunately, she didn't have the proper credentials to be in charge.

She managed to swallow her frustration and to realistically assess her options. Her long history of failure created doubts about her ability to be successful in work that required an advanced degree. She had found a measure of peace and decided to accept the niche she had found.

At this point in her life, Carrie had a serious romance with a psychologist she had met through her work. On her thirtieth birthday, they married and began to plan for a family. This was a happy time for Carrie because she had always wanted children.

She enjoyed the next several years as a wife and then the mother of two children. She liked being her own boss, choosing activities she and the children enjoyed. She used her fertile imagination and creativity to solve child-rearing problems. A part time job provided the respite she needed from her responsibilities at home.

When the children started school, Carrie began to get restless. Her job was no longer satisfying and her success as a parent gave her the confidence and courage to enroll in a graduate program in psychology.

Writing papers was the scariest part of her new endeavor. Carrie knew she was good at taking tests but had avoided writing since the days of messy grade school papers covered in red ink. In preparation for graduate school, she decided to buy a computer and learned how to use it.

She bit her nails and held her breath as she waited for the professor to return her first offering. Miraculously it was an "A" paper, the first of many. Carrie's love of reading had taught her to organize her thoughts. Unencumbered by a concern about handwriting, her words began to flow with ease onto the paper.

She never finished her graduate program. After she discovered her writing talent, she dropped her courses to have time to write articles, short stories and a novel. She hit the jackpot when her book broke records on the best seller list.

During this process of self-discovery, Carrie began attracting friends and acquaintances. Freed from negative self-perceptions, her potential could finally shine. Others came to appreciate her unique talents. As she moved through her forties, her confidence continued to grow until she reached a point of deep peace and self-acceptance.

Carrie is now celebrating her fiftieth birthday with joyful visions of traveling, writing and grandchildren. The years have taught her to laugh at herself and roll with the punches of her life. Discovering her buried gift made all the difference.

The Entrepreneur

According to Peter F. Drucker[53], America's foremost management authority and author of *Innovation and Entrepreneurship*, the entrepreneur is someone who "always searches for change, responds to it, and exploits it as an opportunity." The restless, insatiable ADDer can be a natural as an entrepreneur, his nature yearning to seek out new and improved ways to do things. Here is the story of Jim, a successful entrepreneur.

Jim is friendly and optimistic. As a child he received mostly D's and F's on his school work but his teachers weren't too rough on him. They never stayed angry with him very long because he had such an engaging manner.

Overlooking his academic problems, many of the adults in his life admired his personality and enterprise. His energy was boundless and he required little sleep. He had the biggest paper route in town because he delivered the papers earlier than anyone else. As a young child, he went in to the banking business, lending money to his brothers and sisters at somewhat excessive interest rates! His older siblings were happy with the arrangement because they needed the money for their adolescent activities.

When he was 14 years old, he started a housekeeping and lawn care business. He hired and trained local teenagers to work in teams. His business was successful because many of his clients were working parents with limited time to do these chores.

High school was a positive experience for Jim. Although he didn't do well in academics, his teachers and peers alike praised his ability to organize and raise funds for big events like the prom. His idea for a faculty slave auction raised a lot of money every year for the sports'

program. When he graduated, he eagerly left his books behind to devote his attention to his budding enterprises.

Over the years, he started numerous businesses, some that failed and many that prospered. He has always used the failures as learning experiences, figuring out what went wrong and eagerly moving on to the next project.

Jim is now a wealthy man who sells franchises for his nationally known cleaning service and his chain of sick child day care centers. He is currently developing a vacation service that caters to families with young children and is studying the feasibility of opening a chain of geriatric day care centers. He also does a brisk business selling videos of himself sharing the secrets of his business successes.

He doesn't need to work anymore, but retirement is unthinkable. Without his projects to absorb and channel his energy, he would feel like a caged animal. For Jim, it isn't the money—the primary motivator is the chance to play with his own ideas.

The Scientist

You might wonder how an adult with ADD would fit in the rigorous world of science. Science demands precision that isn't typically an ADDer's strong suit. It can be, however, a highly creative endeavor. A lab technician's job, full of repetitive tasks and endless exacting detail might not be a good position. The scientist who designs these experiments, however, needs to be an imaginative dreamer.

Generating hypotheses and analyzing surprising test results can be fun for the idea people of this world. Scientists do need to acquire a storehouse of facts, skills and technical know-how along the way. But the dreamy would-be scientist can use vision to get through the difficult years of apprenticeship. Let's meet Robert, an ADDer who has found his niche in the world of science.

Robert is an MD with a specialty in biological research. He doesn't see any patients except as his research subjects. He is free to use his talents as the creative director of the enterprise. He has sufficient knowledge of statistics to find out anything he needs to know and to talk intelligently with statistical experts.

He works with a large medical center where he spends his time teaching students, designing research projects, writing papers and grants, and giving presentations all over the world. His efficient assistant handles the management and endless details of the research projects.

Robert has organized his research team to function at peak efficiency. People on the team love their jobs and have fun at work. Research meetings are stimulating sessions that encourage everyone's participation. Some of the best ideas for interpreting data and designing future research projects come from the group.

Robert has many strengths and has won numerous awards for teaching. He uses his sense of humor, enthusiasm and acting ability to create presentations that mesmerize his audiences. His passion and optimism are assets in fundraising. He practically charms the money out of potential donors' pockets!

He has developed a rich network of support and interests that counterbalance his tendencies to workaholism. He sings in his church choir, occasionally performs in community theater productions and participates with his family in a number of sports. Since both his sons are hyperactive, Robert has learned that physically demanding activities suit them best. In his marriage, Robert is the visionary who generates the ideas to solve problems and his wife Susan is the implementor. They make a good team.

Robert seems to have a perfect life. There were, however, many obstacles along the way. He was a bright child and a mixed blessing to his teachers and friends. He was curious, noisy, hyperactive, and disruptive, continually interrupting lessons to ask, "Why?" Although he never became a serious behavior problem, he spent many afternoons in detention. His friendships were always short-lived. His charm attracted friends as his bossiness quickly drove them away.

His dream of becoming a scientist motivated him during his long years of school but he ran into serious problems during his post-doctoral year. He had trouble accepting authority and argued constantly with the senior researcher on the project. He also made several serious mistakes related to his difficulty with detail work.

During this time, his wife of a year filed for divorce. He had become distant from her and from many of his friends with his over-involvement in his work. Lonely, frightened and facing the prospect of a failed marriage and career, he acknowledged his need for help.

The marriage counseling he began with his estranged wife had an unexpected benefit. It helped him understand the problems he had always experienced at work and in his relationships. His life began to run more smoothly but problems periodically resurfaced whenever he forgot his hard earned lessons. At one point, he lost a series of grants and a good research team because he neglected to take care of the relationships and the details. His health and marriage also suffered whenever he failed to maintain the balance in his life.

Now in mid-life, Robert has finally developed the coping skills he needs to make all the areas of his life successful. He still has ADD—it's obvious if you carefully observe his behavior. He writes everything down, asks others to jog his memory when he loses a train of thought and has a watch with an alarm to remind him of meetings. He also occasionally puts his foot in his mouth but these days he's quick to apologize or poke fun at himself.

The Salesperson

Have you ever met someone who could sell anything to anybody—you know, the enterprising soul who could sell sand in the desert or sh-- at a circus! This fast-talking, charming individual may be an adult with ADD. Sales jobs are often good niches for many of us.

In sales, interactions tend to be rather brief and well-suited to a restless person with a limited attention span. The enthusiastic and energetic ADDer can generate a contagious excitement about the product or service he promotes. The salesperson can also discharge excess energy by passionately pitching the product or physically moving around. The extensive travel required in many sales jobs is a bonus for the individual who craves stimulation and change. Anne is a woman with ADD who has found success in her work in sales.

Anne is a 29 year old registered nurse who worked for several years in an intensive care unit. The exciting nature of this environment suited her personality but the constant, technical details were not her forté.

She began to read the newspaper want ads and read a job description that seemed perfect for her. A large medical supply and equipment firm needed a critical care nurse to sell their products. The job offered a good salary with benefits and the chance to earn more in commissions. The sales territory included locations throughout the country. Anne was intrigued by this opportunity to travel.

She was hired for the position and has thrived as a medical salesperson. Her friendly manner and gift of gab have helped her earn large commissions. She has used the quality of the products and her enthusiastic manner to make a lot of money as the top salesperson in her division.

Financial success is only part of the picture. Anne loves meeting new people and exploring different cities. Acquaintances sometimes ask if she gets lonely being on the road so much. This isn't a problem for her, however, because she continually makes new friends everywhere she travels.

Anne is energetic and loves to spend her free time downhill skiing, surfing, backpacking and roller blading. Her travels offer the opportunity to pursue many interests year-round. Her family and friends ask about her plans to settle down. She isn't sure how to answer their questions. At this point in her life, she doesn't have any urge to marry and doesn't envision children as a part of her future. She wonders, "Is there a rule that says you have to be settled in one place by a certain age?"

We hope that Anne doesn't give in to societal pressure to fit into the mold. She is happy as a rootless butterfly and may well become a senior citizen who happily goes off on safari when she's 85 years old!

The Plumber

Not all ADDers have the gift of gab. Some have a gift for constructing or repairing things. In her book, *The Conative Connection*[54], author Kathy Kolbe calls this person an implementor. The implementor has his own brand of intelligence. He understands the world and expresses himself through action.

An implementor intuitively understands how a machine works or how something should be designed or constructed. He seems capable of simply looking at something and immediately knowing how to fix it. If your spouse is an implementor, he is more likely to express affection by making or fixing something for you than showering you with loving words. Here is the story of Margaret, a successful ADD implementor.

Margaret hated every minute of school. Her peers teased her when she read aloud in her painfully slow, halting fashion. Many of her teachers punished her when they caught her daydreaming. One of her art teachers gave her F's in effort because he was so angry about the erratic quality of her projects. He couldn't understand why Margaret turned in well designed sculptures but refused to work equally hard on her pencil sketches.

At home things were different. Margaret's dad was a machine tool designer and her mother a homemaker who sewed, built furniture and tended a large garden. The family expressed their affection for one another with hugs, smiles and shared participation in projects.

Margaret was happy at home doing what she did best—fixing things. She loved to repair the family car, fix malfunctioning appliances and perform as the resident handyperson. She also liked to construct things. With minimal help from her father, she made an elaborate tree house when she was 10 years old.

Margaret was lucky to come of age at a time when there were growing opportunities for women. After high school, she enrolled in a vocational program to become a plumber. Later, she became a member of the plumber's union through a combination of her abilities and society's push to employ women in non-traditional fields. She is now a master plumber married to a graphic designer who is also more comfortable with deeds than words. Their three children are bright, talented and gifted in art and mechanics. Margaret and her husband have enjoyed designing and building their own house with some help from friends and relatives.

Margaret remembers her tortured school days only too well and has taken steps to ensure that her children will have better experiences. They attend a Montessori school that emphasizes hands-on learning. The school also respects the unique learning styles and talents of each child.

The Comic

Think of the funniest person you know. Webster defines the word humor as "that quality that appeals to a sense of the ludicrous or absurdly incongruous". The expression, *Doc in a Box* is an example of absurdity as the foundation of humor. It's used to describe urgent care centers that provide drop-in health care during the hours when most doctors' offices are closed.

The phrase resembles the name of a fast food restaurant and conjures up mental pictures of rapid, smiling, impersonal and uniform servicing of your sore throat or urinary tract infection. This image runs counter to our ideal of physicians as professionals who should know each patient as an individual. We all know that reality often falls short of the ideal. So we laugh at the exaggerated mental picture of impersonal medical care stimulated by the phrase Doc in a Box.

Humor is nourished by irrelevant thinking and enhanced by noting the contradictions. Many ADD children and adults have a gift for noticing things others routinely miss. Unhampered by inhibitions, their wild, wandering monologues can be quite funny.

Most classrooms have at least one resident comedian. Although some born comics are shy, the ones best remembered are usually those who had well-developed capacities for disrupting the class with their clowning. Of course, not everyone in the audience always appreciated the disruptions. For some reason, the comic's teacher never seemed to have a very good sense of humor. He never appeared amused at jokes that pointed out the inconsistencies of his rules and regulations!

The secret of success for an ADD professional or amateur comic is learning when, where and how to share the humorous associations of his thoughts so others laugh with him, not at him. When Dennis finally learned to do this he was able to take advantage of his talent.

"Humor Impairment–The New Disorder"

Dennis was called "Dennis the Menace" as a child. The nickname fit so perfectly that his parents wondered if some kind of ESP had guided them when they named their infant son. The baby grew into a red-haired, freckled-faced toddler who talked early and nonstop and was always into everything. Cute and funny, Dennis managed to escape criticism when he was little. When he entered school, however, his teachers didn't think he was cute at all.

He constantly interrupted the class and told too many jokes. His peers initially thought he was hilarious but they became irritated after a while because he never turned it off. He was *on* all the time, hogging center stage and never letting anyone else share the limelight. Dennis was particularly hard to take when his classmates were tired or in serious moods.

By the time he entered middle school, Dennis had become a social outcast. He still had some humorous material but it never got any laughs because everybody had tuned him out. His peers preferred laughing at him for being such a jerk rather than laughing at his jokes.

In junior high school, Dennis went to a school guidance counselor for help with his problem. The counselor Tony, was a sensitive man who had experienced rejection as a kid and knew how to help. Tony and Dennis made a deal that they would regularly get together to do things they both enjoyed, like walking or shooting pool. Tony agreed to point out when Dennis's behavior got out of hand and to help him modify it. The sessions made a big difference.

Dennis entered high school armed with important self-knowledge. He was no longer the class pariah and had begun to gain some popularity. His sense of humor could finally be appreciated as he had learned to turn the jokes on and off at the appropriate times. A number of high school activities provided showcases for his comic talent. He was the *Master of Ceremonies* for many school events, did a comedy routine each morning over the PA system and was sought out by various organizations for his ability to develop humorous and novel ideas.

Dennis is now in his early '20's and has launched a promising career as a standup comic. He has close friends and a strong sense of identity. He is particularly proud of his social successes because he had to work so hard at them.

The Professional Dilettante

Who made the rule that we have to choose a few activities in our lives, master them and stick with them until death or disability? There's no reason that we can't sample many different interests, provided we can support ourselves.

The Professional Dilettante works at a job for money, not for fulfillment. He doesn't link his identity to the way he makes a living. He isn't an aimless wanderer, however. He is a self-supporting individual who has chosen for a variety of reasons, to redefine success for himself.

One reason may be that he is absorbed by his interests and chooses not to be consumed by a job. By refusing to invest excessive emotional energy in his work, he frees it up for use in other areas. In this free time, he can study ballet, read philosophy for hours or take up long-distance cycling. He dabbles in a little of everything because it makes him happy and doesn't hurt anyone else. He may also have decided not to pursue his heart's desire in his work because the daily grind ruins the fun. Cranking out commercial art on a weekly basis may be a hated proposition for the creative artist whose spirit motivates him.

Finally, he may realize that his love of singing doesn't match his ability level. He knows he lacks sufficient talent to make a living doing the thing he loves most. Rather than being mature and accepting that his dreams are unrealistic, he decides to plan his life so he can still sing in neighborhood theatre productions. He just doesn't plan to earn money doing it.

The Professional Dilettante figures out a number of ways to keep the investment in a paying job to a minimum. He may work part-time or schedule his work hours in double shifts to allow blocks of time for pursuing his real interests. Or he may choose to learn a skill he can perform with little effort. He uses these approaches to detach himself from his paying job.

Connie is a Professional Dilettante who is happily and successfully living her life as an ADD adult. She has decided not to focus her energies on developing a corporate career. Her interests have always been too broad to limit herself to one activity.

Connie makes a living as a house painter, a choice she made as a young adult because it fit her lifestyle. In high school she felt sorry for Mrs. Miller, the guidance counselor who failed miserably at counseling and guiding her! Despite great effort, Mrs. Miller remained unsuccessful at persuading Connie to make decisions about college and a career.

Connie couldn't bear the thought of narrowing her life to a single choice. She acknowledged her preference for skimming along in life, sampling everything but not stopping to delve deeply into anything. She couldn't imagine giving up a minimum of four years of her life to go to college.

Her parents, teachers and counselors worried about her seeming aimlessness. They couldn't imagine anyone as bright as Connie choosing to waste her potential by not making specific plans for her life. They couldn't imagine how she would ever be happy.

Connie, however, couldn't imagine being happy any other way. She decided to ignore their advice and keep her options open. She has never regretted her decision. She believes that other people's lives are dull in comparison to her own.

The work she has chosen is perfect for her. She can do things she enjoys while she works. She daydreams and listens to books on tape. She periodically chats with her partner and sings as she works. Because she is an experienced painter, she can work on autopilot while her mind is largely elsewhere. When she finishes her job for the day, Connie throws her abundant mental energy into whatever happens to catch her fancy at the moment.

In the past year she has studied among other things, clogging, voice, photography and Eastern philosophy. Her list of current and former interests is extensive. Her varied interests have helped her form bonds with many interesting people.

For many years, Connie has done volunteer work with inner city teenagers. Her assorted interests and experiences are assets in working with these adolescents who are busy trying out new ideas in their search for their identities.

Many people criticize Connie's lifestyle: "What's the use of flitting from one thing to the next? She never excels at anything." Although it's true that Connie isn't an expert at any one thing, she has a wealth of experiences and knowledge many others never have the opportunity to acquire. And, she is an expert in one very important area. She is tops at connecting with other people.

We don't want to imply that Connie's life has no structure or substance or that she's careless about her work. She has worked hard to learn her skills and always gives every client a quality job. She carefully plans her schedule to include adequate time for her work, her volunteer activities at the teen center and her leisure time with friends. She has a marriage her friends envy. She and her husband are still best friends after five years together and are looking forward to having children one day soon. Connie can't wait to introduce them to all the wonders life offers.

What Is Success?

These composite sketches are just a few examples of the successful lives ADD adults can fashion. Although we believe all these individuals are undeniably successful, some would argue that they aren't. It depends on the definition of success and its standard of measurement.

The traditional yardstick measures success as an orderly climb up the career ladder with accompanying raises and promotions. Measured against this yardstick, some of the people we met might fall short. In fact, many ADDers might fall short. Success, however, can be measured in more important ways.

An ADDer doesn't always follow the prescribed route to success. He tends to take an alternative one with surprising twists and turns that might not lead to fame and fortune, at all. The underlying definition of success embodied in the composite sketches is the following:

Success is achieved when you figure out what you were born to do and fashion a lifestyle that enables you to do it.

If your gifts and talents are in demand, you might indeed become rich and famous. You can be successful, however, without substantial money or position. Connie is an example of a successful ADDer who has a modest income. She lives life on her own terms but manages to give back to others through her volunteer work. Jim is also successful. He has earned not only the respect of his colleagues but also pots of money! For Jim, these are secondary rewards. The primary reward is the excitement of his work. Similar to an artist or a parent, he nurtures each creation until it's fully developed.

Finding Your Niche–Better Late Than Never

An ADDer is often a late bloomer who experiences a number of false starts before he finds his unique niche. His natural developmental time table appears to be somewhat slower than his peers'. For one thing, his progress may be slowed by the time and energy required to learn bypass strategies. While he's learning to use memory devices and organizational strategies, his age mates may be moving ahead. The good news is that an an individual with ADD often progresses quickly after he has mastered the basics.

For many of us, school remains a difficult obstacle course, more to be endured than enjoyed. We do, however, encourage you to consider pursuing more education. It's becoming more difficult to survive in today's world without advanced skills. Unskilled or entry level jobs that place a premium on speed and organization are difficult for ADDers and should be avoided. In general, the jobs that allow for a greater level of flexibility and creativity require more education. If you gave up on school because of unpleasant high school experiences, consider trying it again with your newfound commitment to yourself.

You might discover that school is more pleasant and meaningful as you advance to higher levels. In college, you have freedom in course selection and can set your own pace. You can choose an area of study that matches your interests and talents. In graduate school, you have additional flexibility to select an area of interest and design your studies with guidance from the faculty. Look for accredited universities that encourage self-directed learning and allow you to design your own curriculum.The *Union Institute*, for example, is an excellent choice. Based in Cincinnati, it uses the whole country as its campus.

If you decide that additional education is simply not a choice for you, that's okay too. Connie, for instance, is doing just fine in her chosen work without the benefit of additional education.

The Bright Outlook for ADDers

At the beginning of this chapter, we promised to tell you why we think current and future trends bode well for adults with ADD. Although we are a diverse group, a few generalizations can be made. We ADDers tend to be better with gestalts, or the big pictures than we are with details. We also tend to be more creative than organized. Finally, we are often mavericks who are generally happier doing things in our own unique ways. We are delighted to tell you that these characteristics fit beautifully in the world of the 1990's and beyond!

When we finished reading some books and articles by experts who analyze current trends and project their analyses into the future, we became unbearably excited! Right there on the page was the picture of a friendlier world for ADDers. Here are a few examples of what we are hinting at.

"Job Skills for the '90's"[55]

- Evaluation and Analysis
- Critical Thinking
- Problem Solving (Including math)
- Organization and Referencing
- Synthesis
- Application to New Ideas
- Creativity
- Decision-Making with Incomplete Information
- Communication in Many Modes

When we saw this list, we were stunned. All the skills, with the exception of organization and referencing, relate to creative problem-solving. It seems to us that the work world is making room for those who are more innovative. The computer age may have helped to usher in the change.

Before the arrival of computers in the office, human workers spent most of their time on routine tasks. It was desirable to have employees who could organize a large volume of routine work and perform it in a speedy manner.

Now computers can manage much of the organizing for us. They can often run the assembly lines and take care of routine office work better than humans can. They don't get bored or burned out—except when they crash!

But computers aren't yet capable of creativity. The development of computers that can think is still the domain of science fiction. The work world of the computer age needs workers who can solve problems and think creatively.

We think our ADD qualities fit the profile of the new worker. Many of us are talented at creating ideas, synthesizing information from different sources and noting relationships. Of course, we do need to work on some of our weak areas before we can expect to breeze into this new workplace.

Communication is an area that could be problematic. Developing the self-discipline essential for the critical thinking and analysis skills of the 1990's might be another difficult task. These skills require disciplined application of logic to the problem at hand. Logic, however, can be learned and communication can be improved. The wonderful part about this shift in the workplace is that most of the new job requirements will tap an ADDer's strengths rather than his weaknesses. We think the balance has tipped in our favor.

There's more good news from the crystal ball of John Naisbitt, the world's leading trends' forecaster. His book, *Megatrends*[56] published in 1982, accurately predicted many of the great changes that shaped the 1980's. Naisbitt and Aburdene in *Megatrends 2000*[57], predicted that the 1990's would dawn as a new era in which the individual would triumph. We're already seeing this trend in a surge of entrepreneurship. Over the past several years, small businesses have been started at record rates.

The most profound change of the '80's and '90's has been the shift from an industrial to an information society. Technology has created a world that values workers for their unique ideas and talents rather than their physical strength, speed or endurance. This change will undoubtedly continue to evolve rapidly in the next century.

The information-based economy is transforming the workplace and new technology is bringing new freedom to the corporate employee. Naisbitt and Aburdene contend that this technology will ultimately free us from the oppression of working within large bureaucratic systems. Growing numbers of people are enjoying the flexibility of working at home. The ability to link quickly with others through computer, fax machine or federal express has made this telecommuting possible.

ADDers will no longer have to endure being chained to desks in cubicles within organizations that are bureaucratic nightmares. More of us will be able to work in the privacy of our own homes. We will be free to fidget, hum, play loud music or otherwise indulge ourselves in harmless but annoying habits. Working at home will enable us to exert greater control over noise or interruptions and schedule our days to fit our individual styles. If we're brain dead in the morning, we'll be able to perform our mindless tasks first and save the rest for when we're fully awake!

The dramatic shift to the information age will tax some of your fragile skills. Your problems with rapid information processing will make you more susceptible to overload than your coworkers. We believe, though, that the technological age will offer more opportunities than obstacles.

The emerging era of the individual described in *Megatrends 2000* will offer exciting opportunities. Naisbitt and Aburdene state that we've already begun to enter a "new golden era where humankind earns its daily bread through the creativity of the individual instead of as a beast of burden"[58]. You will be increasingly free to shape and define your own job, tailoring it to fit your individual strengths and weaknesses. With creativity emerging as the most sought after quality for workers of the 1990's and beyond, the ADDer who has learned to effectively manage his temperament, will be in demand.

We're not naively suggesting that the future will be easy for an adult with ADD. He'll always struggle with his invisible handicap and wrestle with his unpredictable nervous system. We believe, however, that the work world just might be a friendlier place for many of us. It might offer a better match for ADD talents. It might offer an easier way to deal with ADD deficits.

We have lived our lives as ADDers. We awaken every morning and go to sleep every night with ADD as our constant companion. We know that you do too. We feel a kinship to our unknown readers and hope that you feel a kinship to us. We share your struggles—we are all in this ADD world together and can help each other in many ways.

We truly hope that you've found both help and encouragement in this book. We hope we haven't offended anyone with the sometimes quirky sense of humor we share. We hope that no one feels we have in any way minimized the struggles you face as an adult with ADD. As women with ADD we personally understand those struggles and face them daily in our own lives.

We challenge you to work hard at your recovery. We challenge you to put aside your defenses and squarely face the reality of your ADD. We challenge you to use your self-knowledge to work on the weaknesses that have a negative impact on your recovery. Most of all, we challenge you to celebrate your unique gifts and talents.

Never, ever lose sight of the many gifts you possess! We truly believe that ADD is more than just a disability. . .

It is also an ADDed Dimension!

Epilogue

Imagine a world without ADD.

We invite you to glimpse such a futuristic world created by the imaginative mind of our colleague, Darlene Contadino of Cincinnati, Ohio.

Thank you for your insights, Darlene, and for you permission to include your essay in our work.

We think it is a compelling conclusion for this book . . .

Galaxy 298 Planet Press May 10, 2390

Scientists Debating Wisdom of TNT Gene Removal

Dr. Smarty is credited with the original discovery in 2275 of the illusive TNT gene that caused impulsivity, distractibility and poor reinforceability. The discovery of this gene and the subsequent development of a surgical procedure to remove it from patients constituted a major scientific breakthrough.

With this discovery scientists made great strides in eliminating most madadaptive behaviors. But in a recent Gene Removal Conference, scientists from around the galaxy gathered to debate the wisdom of the decades old TNT gene removal project.

The original discovery was welcomed by people everywhere. Society did not know what to do with people who were born with this gene. Many of these people failed to contribute to the goals of the community, refusing to attend the Intergalactic Training Academy and never fulfilling their responsibilities in society. Half the people in our prisons exhibited these maladaptive behaviors as did some who were addicted to illegal drugs and alcohol.

Therefore it was reasoned that if the gene that caused these dysfunctional behaviors could be eliminated, these people would be relieved of their suffering and society as a whole would greatly benefit. So the Gene Removal Project was undertaken in 2290 to eliminate this troublesome gene from the Galaxy's populations.

Initially this appeared to be a wise decision. Fewer school children displayed behavior and learning problems. No longer inattentive, they readily acquired great knowledge. Eliminating the insatiability of these children caused a significant reduction in the rates of juvenile delinquency because these individuals were no longer driven to seek out adventures.

But as a fourth generation of children whose TNT genes were surgically removed reach maturity, some rather disturbing facts can no longer be ignored. Largely unnoticed in the early stages of the gene removal project, scientific research and discovery have gradually slowed and come to a virtual standstill. Without the insatiable curiosity to drive the scientific process, increasing numbers of scientists have become content with the status quo. Only now are people in our society becoming aware of the glaring absence of new scientific and medical discoveries since the project began.

There has been a parallel decrease in the numbers of new developments in business and industry. It is now hypothesized that when impulsivity was erased, people were no longer capable of taking risks. Virtually no new management systems have been introduced since the project began. The technology used today has evolved little from that used many years ago.

There appears to be yet another troubling byproduct of the TNT Gene Removal Project. Many members of our society at large report a general discontent with their lives and the communities in which they live. Paralleling the elimination of impulsivity, spontaneity seems to have disappeared from their lives. There is no more adventure. The lives of many people in our society are well-planned but mundane–it has been many years since anyone has climbed a mountain or explored a cave.

The world of literature, art and music also appear to have suffered. Since the elimination of distractibility, people have not been compelled to write imaginative poetry, paint the colors of a sunset or compose beautiful songs.

It is impossible to ignore the benefits enjoyed by our society in the years since the removal of the TNT gene. Without the troubling maladaptive behaviors caused by this gene, life has become significantly more orderly. But the behavior of many of our citizens is beginning to resemble that of computer robots.

The recently held meeting was to study the data compiled in the years since the project began. The questions raised at the Gene Removal Conference can be summarized as follows:

"Has Science created efficient machines, lacking in creativity and initiative? Has Society killed personality in the name of order?"

The scientists in attendance were in unaminous agreement that the answer to these questions is, "Yes". It was noted in the records of the proceedings that the Gene Removal Project may have had some unexpected negative results and that future scientists might at some point choose to revisit the decision.

This journalist is concerned that a third more important issue was not raised:

"How can we put the gene back?"

Unfortunately even the brightest of our scientists appear satisfied to inquire no further than to simply review and comment on existing data, so things are unlikely to change in the forseeable future.

After all, there is no one with the passion and imagination to ask the questions. . .

References

[1] Stills, G.F. (1902). Some abnormal psychological conditions in children, Lancet. i, 1008-1012, 1077-1082, 1163-1168.

[2] Goldstein, S. and Goldstein, M. (1990). Managing Attention Disorders in Children. New York: John Wiley and Sons.

[3] American Psychiatric Association. (1968). Diagnostic and statistical manual of mental disorders (2nd ed.). Washington, DC: Author.

[4] American Psychiatric Association. (1980).Diagnostic and statistical manual of mental disorders (3rd ed.). Washington, DC: Author.

[5] American Psychiatric Association. (1987).Diagnostic and statistical manual of mental disorders (4th ed.). Washington, DC: Author.

[6] Zametkin, A.J., Nordahl, T.E., Gross, M., King, A.K., Semple, W.E., Rumsey, J., Hamburger, S. & Cohen, R.M. (1990). Cerebral glucose metabolism in adults with hyperactivity of childhood onset. The New England Journal of Medicine, 323 (30), 1361-1366.

[7] Zametkin, A.J., & Rapoport, J. (1987). Neurobiology of attention deficit disorder with hyperactivity: where have we come in 50 years? Journal of the American Academy of Child and Adolescent Psychiatry, 26, 676-686.

[8] Levine, M. (1987). Developmental Variation and Learning Disorders Cambridge, Massachusetts: Educators Publishing Service Inc.

[9] Ingersoll, B. (1988). Your Hyperactive Child: A Parents Guide to Coping with Attention Deficit Disorder. New York: Doubleday.

[10] Tellegen, A., Lykken, D.T., Rich, S., Bouchard, T.J., Wilcox, K.J. & Segal, N.L. (1988). Personality similarity in twins reared apart and together. Journal of Personality and Social Psychology, 54 (6), 1031-1039.

[11] Chess, S., & Thomas. (1984). Origin and Evolution of Behavior Disorders: From Infancy to Early Adult Life. New York: Brunner/Mazel.

[12] Ingersoll, B. Your Hyperactive Child.

[13] Feingold, B. (1975). Why Your Child is Hyperactive. New York: Random House.

[14] Smith, L. (1975). Your Child's Behavior Chemistry. New York: Random House.

[15] Toffler, A. (1970). Future Shock. New York: Random House.

[16] Comings, D.E. (1990). Tourette Syndrome and Human Behavior. Duarte, California: Hope Press.

[17] Erikson, E.H. (1950). Childhood and Society. New York: W.W. Norton & Co.

[18] Weiss, G. & Hechtman, L.T. (1986). Hyperactive Children Grown Up. New York: The Guilford Press.

References

[19] Weiss, G. & Hechtman, L.T. Hyperactive Children Grown Up.

[20] Weiss, G. & Hechtman, L.T. Hyperactive Children Grown Up.

[21] Levine, M. Developmental Variation and Learning Disorders.

[22] Goleman, D. (1992, January/February). Wounds that never heal: how trauma changes your brain. Psychology Today, pp. 62-66, 88.

[23] Kiley, D. (1983). The Peter Pan Syndrome. New York: Avon.

[24] Alchoholics Anonymous. A.A. World Services: New York, New York.

[25] Longacre, D.J. (1980). Living More with Less. Scottdale, Pennsylvania: Herald Press.

[26] Dardig, J.C. & Heward, W.L. (1981). (2nd ed.). Sign Here: a contracting book for children and their parents. Ann Arbor, Michigan: Edward Brothers.

[27] Winston, S. (1978). Getting Organized. New York: Warner Books.

[28] Lapp, D. (1987). Don't Forget: Easy Exercises for a Better Memory at Any Age. New York: McGraw-Hill.

[29] Scheiber, B. and Talpers, J. (1987) Unlocking Potential. Maryland: Adler and Adler.

[30] Scheiber, B. and Talpers, J. Unlocking Potential.

[31] Smith, S. (1986). No Easy Answers, The Learning Disabled Child at Home and at School. New York: Bantam Books.

[32] Silver, L. (1984) The Misunderstood Child. New York: McGraw-Hill.

[33] Scheiber, B. and Talpers, J. Unlocking Potential.

[34] Cousins, N. (1989). Head First, The Biology of Hope. New York: Dutton.

[35] Glick, D. (1992, July 13). New age meets hippocrates. Newsweek, p. 58.

[36] Weiss, G. & Hechtman, L.T. Hyperactive Children Grown Up.

[37] Weiss, G. & Hechtman, L.T. Hyperactive Children Grown Up.

[38] Weiss, G. & Hechtman, L.T. Hyperactive Children Grown Up

[39] Goldstein, S. & Goldstein, M. (1990). Managing Attention Disorders in Children: A Guide for Practitioners. New York: Wiley.

[40] Medical Economics Company. (1991). Physicians Desk Reference. (45th ed.). Author.

[41] Comings, D.E. Tourette Syndrome and Human Behavior.

[42] Clark, B. Queener, S. & Burke-Karb, V. (1990). Pharmacological Basis of Nursing Practice. St.Louis: C.V. Mosby Company.

[43] Ingersoll, B. Your Hyperactive Child.

[44] Wender, P.H., & Reimherr, F.W. (1990). Bupropion treatment of attnention-deficit hyperactivity disorder in adults. American Journal of Psychiatry, 147 (8), 1018-1020.

[45] Selmi, P. M., Klein, M.H., Greist, J.H., Sorrell, S.P. & Erdman, H.P. (1991). Computer-administered therapy for depression, M.D. Computing, 8 (2), 98-102.

[46] Ayres, A. J. (1981). Sensory Integration and the Child. Los Angeles, California: Western Psychological Services.

[47] Little, P. (1990, October 12-14). Mind game for the 90's. USA Weekend, p.16.

[48] Williams, G. (1990, June). Experiencing eternity. Longevity, pp. 52-58.

[49] Cousins, N. Head First, The Biology of Hope.

[50] Adduci, L. (1991, September 3). My child couldn't pay attention. Womens Day. p. 102, 106.

[51] Rapp, D.J. (1979). Allergies and the Hyperactive Child. New York: Simon & Schuster.

[52] Feingold, B. Your Child's Behavior Chemistry.

[53] Drucker, P.F. (1985). Innovation and Entrepeneurship: Practice and Principles. : New York: Harper & Row.

[54] Kolbe, K. (1990). The Conative Connection: Uncovering the Link Between Who You Are and How You Perform. New York: Addison Wesley.

[55] Noel/Levitz Conference. (1989, October). Visual of job skills for the nineties, presentation at Thomas More College.

[56] Naisbitt, J. (1984). (2nd ed.). Megatrends. New York:Warner Books.

[57] Naisbitt, J. & Aburdene, P. (1990). Megatrends 2000: Ten New Directions for the 1990's. New York: Morrow.

[58] Naisbitt, J. & Aburdene, P. Megatrends 2000: Ten New Directions for the 1990's.

Suggested Reading List

Bain, L. (1991). *A Parents Guide to Attention Deficit Disorders*. New York: Dell.

Comings, D.E. (1990). *Tourette Syndrome and Human Behavior*. California: Hope Press.

Cowart, V.S. (1988). "The ritalin controversy: what's made this drug's opponents hyperactive?" Journal of the American Medical Association, 259, 2521-2523.

Dardig, J.C. and Heward, W.L. (1981). *Sign Here: A Contracting Book for Children and Their Parents*. Bridgewater, New Jersey: F. Fournies & Associates.

Gauthier, M. (1984). "Stimulant medications in adults with attention deficit disorder". Canadian Journal of Psychiatry, 439 (29), 435-440.

Golin, M., Bricklin, M., Diamond, D. and the Rodale Center for Executive Development. (1991). *Secrets of Executive Success*. Emmaus, Pennsylvania: Rodale Press.

Goldstein, S. and Goldstein, M. (1990). *Managing Attention Disorders in Children*. New York: John Wiley and Sons.

Ingersoll, B. (1988). *Your Hyperactive Child: A Parent's Guide to Coping with Attention Deficit Disorder*. New York: Doubleday.

Lapp, D. (1987). *Don't Forget: Easy Exercises for a Better Memory at*

Any Age. New York: McGraw-Hill.

Levine, M.D. (1987). *Developmental Variation and Learning Disorders*. Cambridge, Massachusetts: Educators Publishing Service, Inc.

Levine, M.D. (1990). *Keeping Ahead in School*. Cambridge, Massachusetts: Educators Publishing Service, Inc.

Liden, C.B., Zalenski, J.R. and Freytag, L. (1992). Attention deficit disorder: Toward establishing a standard of care for adults. *Transaction Monograph Series, (No.2)*. Transact Health Care Systems, 2566 Haymaker, Monroeville, PA 15146.

Lorayne H. and Lucas, J. (1974). *The Memory Book*. New York: Dorset Press.

Mattes, J.A. and Boswell, L. (1984). "Methylphenidate effects on symptoms of ADD in adults". Achives of General Psychiatry, 41, 105-106.

Satir, V. (1976). *Making Contact*. Berkeley, California: Celestial Arts.

Scheiber, B. and Talpers, J.(1987). *Unlocking Potential: College and Other Choices for Learning Disabled People–A Step by Step Guide*. Maryland: Adler and Adler.

Silver, L. B. (1991). *Attention-Deficit Hyperactivity Disorder: A Clinical Guide to Diagnosis and Treatment*. Washington, DC: American Psychiatric Press, Inc.

Tannen, D. (1990). *You Just Don't Understand*. New York: William Morrow and Company.

Turecki, S. (1985). *The Difficult Child*. New York: Bantum.

Weiss, G. and Hechtman, L.T. (1986). *Hyperactive Children Grown Up*. New York: Oxford University Press

Weiss, L. (1992). *Attention Deficit Disorder in Adults: Practical Help for Sufferers and Their Spouses*. Dallas, Texas: Taylor Publishing.

Wender, P.H., & Reimherr, F.W. (1990). "Bupropion treatment of attention-deficit hyperactivity disorder in adults". American Journal of Psychiatry, 147(8), 1018-1020.

Wender, P.H. (1987). *The Hyperactive Child, Adolescent, and Adult: Attention Deficit Disorder Through the Lifespan*. New York: Oxford University Press.

Winston, S. (1978). *Getting Organized*. New York: Warner Books.

Wolkenberg, F. (1987, October 11). "Out of a darkness". New York Times Magazine, pp. 62, 66, 70, 82-83.

Woods, D. (1986). "The diagnosis and treatment of attention deficit disorder, residual type". Psychiatric Annals, 16, 23-28.

Yellin, A.M., Hopwood, J.H. and Greenberg, L.M. (1982). "Adults and adolescents with ADD: clinical and behavioral responses to psychostimulants". Journal of Clinical Psychophamacology, 2, 133-136.

Zametkin, A.J. et al. (1990). "Cerebral glucose metabolism in adults with hyperactivity of childhood onset". The New England Journal of Medicine. 323 (20). 1361-1366.

Resource List

Organizations: Support, Education and Advocacy

ADDult Support Network

Mary Jane Johnson, 2620 Ivy Place, Toledo, OH 43613

This organization is really a one-woman operation, but Mary Jane Johnson has done a superb job of developing a nationwide network for ADD adults.The network publishes a quarterly newsletter (ADDult News), has a pen pal program and compiles informational packets for ADD adults. Ms. Johnson is also collecting data on adult ADDers through a questionnaire she has designed. If you are interested in participating in her research, write to Mary Jane and request a questionnaire. She has also informed us that she is organizing a national ADD adult conference scheduled some time in 1993. The conference will most likely be held in the Midwest and will probably be just the first of many to follow.

Attention Deficit Resource Center

Lawrence L. Melear, Ph.D., Director, 1344 Johnson Ferry Road, Suite 14, Marietta, GA 30068 1–800–537–3784 (voice mail)

The center is a non-profit clearinghouse for information on Attention Deficit Disorder with a special focus on ADD in adults. It publishes a bimonthly newsletter, The *ADDVISOR*, that offers a wealth of practical information on coping with ADD as an adult. Books and cassette tapes on the topic of adult ADD are available through the Center's resource services. There are also periodic conferences, workshops, and home-study programs for ADD adults. Write for free information.

Attention-Deficit Disorders Association (ADDA)
P.O. Box 972, Mentor, OH 44061 1-800-487-2282

Children with Attention Deficit Disorders (CHADD)
499 Northwest 70th Avenue, Suite 308 Plantation, FL 33317
(305) 587-3700
Both these organizations serve as national clearinghouses for information, support and advocacy for ADD individuals. CHADD has numerous satellite support groups throughout the country.

Challenge, Inc.
P.O. Box 488, W. Newbury, MA 01985 (508) 462-0495,
(800) 233-2322
Challenge, Inc. is a national, nonprofit, parent-based organization founded in 1986. The organization's primary focus is its bimonthly newsletter, *Challenge,* which was the first national newsletter on Attention Deficit Disorder, and which features articles on children as well as adults. Challenge, Inc. offers members many other benefits, such as prescription medication at wholesale prices.

Individual Membership—$25/year
Professionals Membership—$45/year (for professionals in the field who wish to be listed on Challenge's Professional Referral List)

Disabled USA
President's Committee on Employment of the Handicapped 1111 20th Street NW, 6th Floor, Washington, DC 20036
This publication includes reports about the continuing progress for disabled individuals and new opportunities for rehabilitation employment.

Learning Disabilities Association (LDA) (formerly the Association for Children and Adults with Learning Disabilities)
4156 Library Road, Pittsburgh, PA 15234 (412) 341-1515
This international organization of parents of learning disabled children, adults with learning disabilities and professionals has approximately 800 state and local affiliates whose activities include education, legislation and research. The *Newsbriefs* newsletter is published six times a year and includes information about new developments in the field. Free informational packets and numerous publications,

including a list of post-secondary programs, are also available from the LDA.

National Network of Learning Disabled Adults (NNLDA)
808 West 82nd Street, F—-2, Scottsdale, AR 85257
Formed in 1980, the NNLDA provides a support network for learning disabled adults, self-help groups, and national organizations. It also advocates for accommodations for the learning disabled adult in institutions and the work place. National activities include a newsletter and annual workshop.

National Rehabilitation Information Center (NARIC)
8455 Colesville Road, Suite 935 Silver Spring, MD, 20910-3319
(301) 588-9284; (800) 34-NARIC
For a nominal fee, this organization can search its database for information regarding the rehabilitation or employment of individuals with disabilities.

Orton Dyslexia Society
8600 LaSalle Road, Chester Bldg., Suite 382 Baltimore, MD 21204
(800) ABC-D123
Numerous state and local chapters of the international Orton Society provide education and promote research in dyslexia. A variety of materials, a newsletter and information about post-secondary education options are available. The Orton Society also holds national and state conferences.

OSERS News in Print
Office of Special Education and Rehabilitative Services 330 C Street, SW, 3018 Switzer Bldg., Washington, DC 20202
This newsletter contains ongoing reports about federal activities related to individuals with disabilities.

STEP Systematic Training For Effective Parenting
STEP AGS Publishers' Building, Circle Pines, MN 55014
STEP groups are offered by various community organizations, local schools, community centers, churches, synagogues, adult education programs and mental health providers. For additional information, contact the national STEP coordinator.

Vocational and Postsecondary School Organizations

Association of Independent Colleges and Schools
One Dupont Circle, NW, Washington, DC 20036
A free directory is available that includes a list of 630 accredited private business schools and colleges in the United States.

National Center for Research in Vocational Education
1960 Kenny Road, Columbus, OH 43210 (800) 848-4815;
(614) 486-3655 in Ohio
The center offers a variety of materials on technical education, career planning and employment preparation.

National Association for Trade and Technical Schools
2252 Wisconsin Avenue, NW, Washington, DC 20007
This association distributes a handbook with lists of accredited trade and technical schools throughout the United States.

National Association of Vocational Education Special Needs Personnel (NAVESNP)
2020 14th Street, Arlington, VA 22201 (703) 522-6121
This national organization of professionals in vocational education, focuses on the educational needs of handicapped, disadvantaged, and other special needs' individuals.

Learning Materials

A.D.D. Warehouse
300 Northwest 70th Avenue, Suite 102, Plantation, FLA 33317
(800) 233-9273
This catalog offers a variety of books and tapes available for purchase. Although other sources may be less expensive, this is an excellent compilation of available materials.

Recording for the Blind, Inc.
(RFB) 20 Roszel Road, Princeton, NJ 08540 (800) 221-4492 or (609) 452-0606 in New Jersey

Approximately 60,000 free-of-charge recordings are available by mail. Tapes can be borrowed for one year. All requests must be accompanied by an application form and detailed diagnostic information regarding the individual's need for these recordings. Eligible individuals include those who are visually, physically and perceptually handicapped.

Talking Books
National Library Service for the Blind and Physically Handicapped The Library of Congress (NLS) 1291 Taylor Street, NW Washington, DC 20542 (202) 882-5500
Popular novels, classical literature, magazines, etc. are available free of charge to individuals with specific reading disabilities. The collection is available through local and regional libraries.

Please note that the tapes available from each of these sources must be played on special tape players that are available for loan.

Variable Speed Tape Recorders
Available at Radio Shack, other electronics' retail stores and mail order catalogs, these tape recorders permit changing playback speed without loss of voice quality.

Newsletters for ADD Adults

ADDendum,
Paul Jaffe, editor c/o CPS, 5041-A BackLick Road, Annandale, VA 22003

ADDult NEWS, Mary Jane Johnson, editor
2620 Ivy Place, Toledo, OH 43613

These are excellent newsletters, each with its own particular specialty. *ADDendum* highlights the latest research while the *ADDult* NEWS focuses largely on the personal experiences of ADD adults. We highly recommend both these quarterly newsletters.

The ADDVISOR
See the Attention Deficit Resource Center in the section on organizations, for information on this newsletter that includes valuable information for ADD adults.

Computer Resources and Software

ABLEDATA National Rehabilitation Information Center
The Catholic University of America, 4407 Eighth Street, NE
Washington, DC 20017 (202) 635-5822 This center distributes a detailed list of commercial products for use by individuals with a variety of handicaps.

Electronic Bulletin Boards

(Accessed via Modems and Personal Computers)
A variety of on-line support groups are available through several computer services. For example, America On-Line© has a Disabilities Forum that includes a folder related to ADD in adults. Prodigy© and CompuServe© also have ADD bulletin boards. Look for files labeled Attention Deficits, Learning Disabilities, etc. You can network with other ADDers across the country through these files.

Macintosh Editing Software and Letter Templates

Letterworks ©
Round Lake Publishing

American Handbook of Business Letters©
Nova Development Corporation

Quickletter©
Working Software, Inc.

Correct Grammar©
Writing Tools' Group

Macintosh Organization Software

First Things First©
Visionary Software

Miscellaneous Macintosh Software

Last Resort©
Working Software Inc.
This is for impulsive ADDers who fail to back up their work or use surge protectors! This software maintains a copy of every keystroke and enables you to recreate the document you lost when you forgot to save your work or when the power went out.

Mindset©
Visionary Software
This is a wonderful positive self-talk product that displays personal affirmations. Phrases such as, "I accept myself here and now" and "I trust the intelligence within me" flash across the top of your screen at periodic intervals.

IBM Letter Templates

Key Correspondence©
SoftKey

IBM Organization Software

About Time©
SoftSystems Inc.

Messages©
Software Grove

Commence©
Jensen-James, Inc.

Index

About the Authors

Kate Kelly
Ms. Kelly is a master's prepared clinical specialist in psychiatric nursing. Her professional background includes experience as as a therapist, assistant professor and clinical coordinator for psychobiological research. Her graduate education focused on chronic mental illness and this orientation eventually led her to an interest in the mental health self-help movement. She became a champion for individuals with severe mental illnesses, such as schizophrenia, believing that even those with severe impairments could learn to manage their own illnesses.

Ms. Kelly's prior publishing credits include an article entitled *Fostering Self-Help on an Inpatient Unit*, published in the Archives of Psychiatric Nursing. This article chronicled the results of her work in developing a model for an inpatient group that helped chronically mentally ill patients learn and share effective coping strategies.

Following her diagnosis with ADHD in 1989, Ms. Kelly's work moved in a new direction. Combining her personal and professional interests in adult ADD, she began to focus on this emerging area of mental health. Responding to the need to provide services for ADD adults, she founded the adult support group of the Attention Deficit Disorder Council of Greater Cincinnati in February of 1990. Although she no longer facilitates this group, she continues to consult with the Council on adult ADD and support group issues.

The information Ms. Kelly gathered from available literature and the personal stories of ADD adults in Cincinnati and nationwide lead to her work in writing *I'm Not Lazy, Stupid or Crazy!?* Currently she is using her personal and professional experiences and knowledge to give presentations on adult ADD for lay and professional groups. She also works in private practice leading psychoeducational therapy groups for ADD adults.

Peggy Ramundo

Recognized as an outstanding teacher, Ms. Ramundo completed post-graduate work in learning disabilities, behavior disorders and Montessori education. Working with culturally disadvantaged children most of her career, she became an advocate for the right of every child to learn. She designed and implemented a non-graded primary curriculum, taught summer enrichment reading programs and served as a demonstration teacher. A committed and innovative parent, Ms. Ramundo has served as president of the boards of the Clifton Child Study Parent Group and Center Rooms West Montessori. When the parent corporation closed the West site, she spear-headed a movement to create a new school. Under her direction, the new non-profit Clifton Montessori Center was formed to continue the tradition of providing tuition-free scholarships to many children from low-income families.

After her son's ADD diagnosis in 1987, Ms. Ramundo began extensively researching the disorder. Drawing on her experience as a dedicated teacher and parent, she co-founded the Attention Deficit Disorder Council of Greater Cincinnati and continues to serve as a board member.

Ms. Ramundo works professionally as an educational consultant. In 1990, she founded NIADD, The National Institute for Attention Deficit Disorder. As Executive Director, she conducts workshops and in-service training sessions throughout the country for parents, educators and mental health professionals, and lectures extensively on ADD.

After Ms. Ramundo's diagnosis, she began to focus on ADD issues in adolescents and adults. Currently, she is helping college students and young adults access available services, manage their learning at the post-secondary level, and make decisions about course selection and careers.

You Mean I'm Not Lazy, Stupid or Crazy!? has evolved from Ms. Ramundo's research, personal and professional experiences and the experiences of the countless numbers of ADD children, adolescents and adults with whom she has worked. Her other publishing credits include handbooks for parents and teachers entitled, *Tips, Tools and Techniques for Managing Attention Deficit Disorder* and *Understanding and Managing Attention Deficit Disorder in the Classroom*.